ACROSS CONTINENTS
AND OCEANS

**РАБОЧАЯ КАРТА ИЗ ПЛАНШЕТА
ПОЛКОВНИКА М.Н. ЧИБИСОВА
С МАРШРУТАМИ ПЕРЕГОНКИ
ГИДРОСАМОЛЕТОВ ИЗ США В СССР
В 1944-1945 гг.**

ACROSS CONTINENTS AND OCEANS

The Life and Military Career of Major
General of Naval Aviation Maxim Chibisov

E. M. Rubina and E. M. Telyatnikova

Library of Congress Control Number:		2021913879
ISBN:	Hardcover	978-1-6641-8406-0
	Softcover	978-1-6641-8405-3
	eBook	978-1-6641-8404-6

Print information available on the last page.

Rev. date: 07/23/2021

To order additional copies of this book, contact:
Xlibris
844-714-8691
www.Xlibris.com
Orders@Xlibris.com
828174

Remember!
Through the centuries, through the years—remember!
The ones who shall never return—remember!
Tell your children about them so that they remember!
Tell your children's children about them so that they remember!
—Robert Rozhdestvensky, *Requiem*

CONTENTS

PREFACE

The Story behind the Book

We, Emilia Telyatnikova and Elena Rubina, the daughters of Major General of Aviation Maxim Nikolayevich Chibisov, have written this book in an effort to preserve the memory of our father for his descendants—his grandchildren and great-grandchildren—as well as for anyone who is interested in our country's recent past and the dramatic, tragic, and heroic pages of its contemporary history.

Our father was a distinguished aviator, a brave soldier, and a commander during the years of the Great Patriotic War (World War II). He led a special group who ferried aircraft from the United States to the Soviet Union as part of the Lend-Lease Program. Following the war, he took charge of polar aviation operations as one of the leaders of high-latitude aerial expeditions that made major discoveries in the central polar region. Possessing a remarkable gift for teaching, he also educated several generations of military pilots over the different periods of his service.

We could list many of his services to the Fatherland, his exploits during the war and in peaceful times, and his professional talents and personal qualities, but for us, his daughters, he was above all a dear and beloved person.

We decided several years ago to write a book about our father based on his diaries, in which he recorded memories about the years of his childhood and youth, the chronicles of his studies and service in naval aviation, and other episodes in his life. These diaries depict many of the monumental events for our country in which Maxim Chibisov was either a participant or a witness at different times in his life. The diary materials are seamlessly complemented by a manuscript in which our father described the experience of his final flight home from the United States in October 1945. Unfortunately, he was not allowed to publish this story in the 1980s due to secrecy concerns.

In addition, we have many different items associated with the life and service of Major General Chibisov that have been carefully preserved by his youngest daughter, Elena Rubina, including Chibisov's pilot logbook recording all the flights he made over his life; a map of the routes he flew from the United States to the Soviet Union, contained in his flight chart, during his time in North America; and numerous group photos of Russian and American pilots. There are also many other personal items: an American leather flight jacket, headsets, gloves, overalls, and colorful postcards and slides with scenes from America. In a box belonging to our mother, we found a small cigarette case presented to him by his American counterparts. This cigarette case was destined to play an important role in the writing of this book about Maxim Chibisov.

All the things that once belonged to our father arouse great interest among our family members.

In the mid-1990s, Maxim's eldest granddaughter, Ksenia, and her husband, Nikita Mishin, suggested publishing the manuscript materials left behind by Maxim.

Implementing this plan, however, proved to be no simple task and required serious preparatory work. Our father recorded his diary entries in scribbles while on the go ("on his lap," as the saying goes): in planes, cars, and places where he would have a short rest or sleep. The diary manuscripts, which in some places are sun-bleached and faded, contain a lot of special terminology, unfamiliar geographic names, and Russian and foreign names. They required thorough deciphering.

This difficult job was undertaken by our friends Viktor and Viktoria Akhobadze, who knew our father personally and had great respect for him. It took them almost a year and a half to decipher the diaries, organize them (to the extent that was possible), and reprint them.

Even after their efforts, however, a number of puzzling circumstances and obscure events remained in the biography of Maxim Chibisov that took shape from the diaries. To shed light on these matters, we needed additional information, which would be difficult to obtain, considering our father's official activities almost always involved areas shrouded under the veil of state secrecy.

In 1997, Major General Chibisov's eldest daughter, Emilia, was on a business trip to the United States, where she met and befriended Vera Sheynina while they were both working on a project to sponsor gifted children. During one of their conversations, Emilia told Vera about her interest in the history of Lend-Lease supplies during World War II, specifically the activities of a special group led by her father who ferried seaplanes from the United States to the Soviet Union in 1944–1945.

In 2005, Vera Sheynina recalled their conversation and informed Emilia about several events being held to mark the 60th anniversary of victory in World War II and about a private museum called Allies and Lend-Lease that had opened in Moscow (on Zhitnaya Street, Building No. 6).

This information turned out to be significant. Emilia took part in a Moscow–Washington teleconference (a televised question-and-answer session), during which she met Igor Lebedev, a retired Lieutenant General who had worked in Washington in 1943–1945. It turned out that he had known Maxim Chibisov well at that time and had also met with him after the war, when our father was chief of polar aviation. We learned many interesting facts from him that we then used when working on this book.

A meeting with the founders of the Allies and Lend-Lease Museum, Nikolai Borodin and Alexander Nesterov, turned out to be a watershed moment for us. These two wonderful, enthusiastic, and creative individuals—worthy heirs of their valiant fathers, who were World War II veterans—built this unique museum virtually from the ground up without any government support, solely for the sake of preserving historical memory.

They suggested we set up a display dedicated to our father at the museum. Taking advantage of this offer, we brought our exhibits: copies of documents, photos of awards, a printed version of the diaries, the flight logbook, photos of our father with American pilots, copies of US maps with flight routes drawn by our father, and more. In addition, we donated his American-made flight gear and general's uniform to the museum.

While collecting exhibits for the museum, Elena Rubina remembered the cigarette case given to our father by his American colleagues as a memento of their work together, which had been lying around the house for sixty years untouched. When Elena got the cigarette case out, she accidentally dropped it on the floor, and a hard paper insert fell out of it. On the back, she found the autographs of American pilots and specialists with whom Maxim Chibisov had worked in 1944–1945. This accidental discovery led to a chain of events that would prove highly important to our cause.

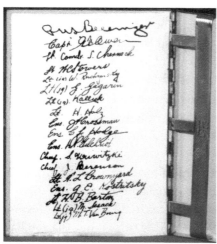

A paper insert dated 1945 found in Maxim Chibisov's cigarette case displayed the autographs of: Admiral P.N.A. Bellinger, Captain G.T. Owen, Lt. Com. S. Chernack, Lt. W. Stauers, Lt. S. Kallick, Lt. V. Rushinsky, Lt. G. Gagarin, Lt. H. Holtz, Second Lt-s J. Crossman, K. Hodge, O. Gilchrist, T. Brownyard, G. Kostritsky, Lt. H. Barton, Second Lt. M. Sesak, M. van Burgh, Sergeant S. Krivitsky and the photographer J. Berenson.

In April 2005, the Pushkin Museum hosted a theme night called "Meeting on the Elbe: 60 Years Later," which we attended thanks to information provided by Vera Sheynina. At the event, we met many World War II veterans and activists of the movement to preserve the memory of the fathers and grandfathers who achieved victory over fascism with their own hands. The daughters of prominent military leaders were there: Natalya Koneva, Natalya Batova, Tamara Kazakova, Natalya Malinovskaya, Olga Biryuzova, and other members of the Foundation for the Memory of the Victorious Commanders. The event was also attended by American veterans, in particular participants in the meeting on the Elbe: Frank Cohen and Igor Belousovich.

At our invitation, the American guests visited the Allies and Lend-Lease Museum. Examining the exhibits, they were amazed that the memory of Allied relations during World War II had been so carefully preserved in Russia. They were also interested in the display dedicated to Maxim Chibisov. The autographs on our father's cigarette case caught Frank Cohen's attention. He took a picture of them and said he personally knew half the people who had signed their names on the paper, but he had not spoken to them for ages. Upon returning home, he promised to post a note and the picture in the veterans' newspaper. Perhaps someone would reply.

The noble and considerate American veteran Frank Cohen fulfilled his promise. A few months after the remarkable meeting at the museum, Emilia received a letter from Washington. The letter had been sent by Gregory Gagarin, an American citizen of Russian descent and a World War II veteran who had been personally acquainted with Maxim Chibisov and worked together with him as part of the Lend-Lease Program, serving as an interpreter and consultant on electrical equipment. The letter contained a photo of a Russian American crew and the short text "If you are related to Colonel Chibisov and recognize him in this photo, that's me sitting next to him. Gregory Gagarin."

From that time on, we began active correspondence with Gregory Gagarin. He then came to visit us, along with his lovely wife, Ann.

The visitors spent a week with us. Possessing an excellent memory, Gregory shared many interesting facts with us and clarified numerous circumstances concerning the activities of Chibisov's special group that had previously been unclear to us.

After talking with Gregory, we developed a clear, coherent, and logically connected picture of one of the most important episodes in our father's life. Work on the book picked up steam. Thanks to the declassification of previously sealed archives, we managed to obtain the personal file of Major General Maxim Chibisov, which, combined with his diaries, helped to create a general chronological pattern for our story. The time had come to begin shaping the text of the book. Without any previous experience in writing a book, we received a major boost in this work from the full support of our closest relatives: our adult children and members of their families. They all helped as much as they could. Elena's son-in-law, Nikita Mishin, provided invaluable assistance in resolving financial issues associated with the creation and publishing of the book.

Thanks to our family, we always felt we were working for a greater purpose and believed our book would have thoughtful and interested readers. One seemingly insignificant episode particularly inspired us.

In August 2006, the whole family gathered together to celebrate what would have been Maxim's 100th birthday at the Allies and Lend-Lease Museum, where we once again met with Nikolai Borodin and Alexander Nesterov.

They spoke about naval aviation and its importance for the navy during the war years. They showed us some models of ships and aircraft and also talked about the delivery of Lend-Lease equipment to the Soviet Union.

They pointed out all of Chibisov's flight routes on the map from his flight chart.

Not only did Maxim's adult grandchildren – Ksenia, Kirill, and Maxim – —listening intently to them, but his six year-old great-grandson, Mitya Mishin, was also highly engrossed. The young boy's eyes burned with genuine interest at everything going on as well as the words of the narrator and the museum exhibits. In Maxim's family photos, he immediately noticed a resemblance to his mother, Ksenia; his grandmother Lena; and uncles Maxim and Kirill. After the tour ended, Mitya long continued inspecting the motorcycles from America and those captured in Germany, touching the jeep that had belonged to former marshal of the Soviet Union Konstantin Rokossovsky as well as the headset and flight gloves of his great-grandfather; counting the medals on his uniform; and asking his daddy, Nikita, a ton of questions.

Following that memorable event, we gained a firm belief that our book would be popular among the current peers of Mitya Mishin as well.

CHAPTER 1

The Call of the Sky

1.1 The Son of a Peasant

Maxim Nikolayevich Chibisov was born August 15, 1906 (August 28 under the Gregorian calendar), to a large, close-knit family in the village of Pushchino in the Serpukhov District of Moscow Province. This village still partially exists today and retains the same name. The scientific city Pushchino-on-Oka, however, has sprouted up right next to it—all the way up to the village homes and gardens—having inherited the village's name and taken over a large part of the old rural community.

Nikolai Chibisov (1862–1918) and his wife, Darya (1865–1935), experienced several tragedies in their early lives; both of them had to endure the deaths of their parents, orphan life, and an upbringing with strangers.

They fell in love and got married when they were very young. The started out with nothing; they initially lived in poverty and some days did not even have a full meal. Yet they always managed to maintain their most important treasures: a strong mutual affection and great diligence. They gradually established their household and built a spacious wooden house with their own hands. People began to regard Nikolai as a "good, sensible fellow." At one point, he even served as a village elder (which was more of a hassle than a benefit).

Their children were their greatest joy. Starting with their first child,

Mikhail (in 1886), little Chibisovs began to appear every two to three years. Mikhail was followed by Pyotr (1889), Vasily (1891), Ivan (1893), Aksinya (1895), Evdokia (1901), and Alexei (1903). In 1906, the youngest child in the family, Maxim, was born and quickly became everyone's darling.

He was baptized in the village Church of the Savior. According to family legend, when the priest announced the newborn's name, his mother began to cry since nobody in their village had ever been given the name Maxim before. In giving the child an uncommon name, however, the priest foretold an extraordinary fate for him and pronounced words that would become prophetic: "Repine not in vain! Your son shall be most fortunate!" Perhaps the priest had in mind the meaning of the name Maxim, which he knew well from Latin seminary class: "the greatest."

Maxim Chibisov's character and moral values were shaped within a strong, tight-knit family who lived in accordance with the laws of God and humanity. They worked productively and happily with one another, overcame difficulties together, and shared joy. Everything was done properly in their family: Easter cakes for Easter, pancakes for Maslenitsa, weddings at Pokrov and Krasnaya Gorka, and farming concerns year-round.

The farm owned by the Chibisovs was neither rich nor poor: it included roughly 13.5 acres of land, a horse, a cow, sheep, and chickens. They were typical middle-class peasants by the standards of the early twentieth century.

The eldest Chibisov son, Mikhail, from a young age, was a reliable helper to his parents in all toils and troubles. He looked after his younger brothers and sisters. When barely an adult, he would go to Serpukhov in the winters and work at a textile factory, bringing all the money he earned home to his family. The other children followed his path, taking part in farming affairs as they grew up and then going off to the city for additional work. The family managed to achieve a certain degree of prosperity.

This period in the Chibisov family history was highlighted by Mikhail's marriage to Praskovya, a girl from the neighboring village of Dubavino. They were married at Krasnaya Gorka on the first Sunday after Easter, and virtually the entire village then celebrated for three straight days.

When the young couple began having children of their own, the Chibisov family home became a bit crowded. In addition, the modest land plot was clearly insufficient for the burgeoning Chibisov family. In 1910, Mikhail moved to Serpukhov permanently with his wife and daughter.

From this time on, the Chibisovs began to fly away one by one from their native nest. Following the example of Mikhail, his brother Pyotr and then his sisters, Ksenia and Evdokia, settled in Serpukhov. Ivan, Vasily, and Alexei moved to Moscow.

At this time, Maxim (or Simushka, as he was called at home) remained with his parents in Pushchino due to his young age. According to an

ancient Russian custom, the youngest son in a peasant family usually inherited the farm from his parents in order to continue their toils on the land. It seemed destiny itself had prepared such a fate for Maxim Chibisov.

He later told the story of how his dreams of the sky were born. On one nice summer day, Maxim and his mother were returning home from working in the fields. Groups of clouds were gliding peacefully and pleasantly through the bright blue sky, when the young boy saw a barely noticeable dot on one of them. He then heard the rumbling sound of an engine. The dot rapidly increased in size—initially to the size of a may bug, and then it began to look like a dragonfly.

Daria Chibivosa

Finally, it turned into a two-winged airplane that looked like a set of shelves. Whizzing over their heads with a deep roar, it smoothly made an arc toward the horizon and vanished off into the blue sky. Frozen and riveted to the ground, the peasant child gazed after it. It was fantastic, unreal, and unlike anything the boy had ever seen. From that memorable day onward, he dreamed—both while awake and while asleep—of flying in the sky.

He realized if he wanted to fly, he had a great deal to learn.

The first step toward fulfilling his dream was a three-year parochial school, which Maxim entered in autumn 1914. He continued his studies at a school in the village of Shepilovo, which was six kilometers from home. He walked there every day, rain or shine. In the winter, he would take a stick to fend off wolves. He studied diligently and consistently received good grades.

Meanwhile, the country in which the young peasant boy lived had entered an era of great upheaval. World War I began; then came the October Revolution, followed by the outbreak of the fratricidal Civil War.

The bloody front lines did not pass through the village of Pushchino, but the quiet area surrounding the Oka River was also engulfed by the devastation that had spread throughout Russia. The lives of the Chibisovs became extremely difficult and meager as the family was on the verge of poverty. In 1918, Nikolai, the head of the Chibisov household, passed away. For the widowed Darya, her youngest son became the main source of support in the daily struggle for survival.

Maxim had to work so much that in the evenings, fatigue literally knocked him off his feet, and his head would plunge into a pillow on its own. Looking back on that time later, he too was surprised at himself; after all, he had managed to study for six whole years while maintaining this rigorous work schedule.

In 1920, however, he was forced to put an end to his studies. He was fourteen, practically an adult by peasant family standards during those harsh times. He had to take charge of the farm. By 1926, Maxim was already mimicking the fate of his older brothers and sisters, combining his work on the farm plot with seasonal jobs in Serpukhov. In the winter of 1926–1927, he was hired as a general laborer at the Krasny Tekstilshchik factory, based on a recommendation from his brother Mikhail. During the next winter season, he was already working on his own initiative at the construction site of the Zanarskaya factory.

1.2 The People Gave Us Steel Arms—Wings

In 1928, Maxim Chibisov was drafted into the army. He ended up in the first radio regiment of the Moscow Military District, which was located in Vladimir, an ancient Russian city with old churches and villages covered with cherry orchards.

Active compulsory service snatched the peasant lad away from the cycle of the hopeless struggle for existence. After the monotonous and difficult farming work, army life, which involves strict routine and discipline, did not seem cumbersome to him. In some ways, it was more comfortable. At home, during the busy season, leisurely reading was not an option—sometimes there was not even time to lift his head up from the scythe, harrow, or plow. In the army, though, special time was set aside for collective newspaper reading.

Chibisov did not shy away from political activities, viewing them as part of his overall educational discipline. Like millions of his contemporaries, he believed in the bright future of the country, was prepared to serve a just cause without hesitation, and delved with unfailing interest into the latest news from the field and top-priority projects. In short, he was a normal Soviet citizen like most of the people in his generation.

Maxim excelled in combat and political training in his very first year of service. He graduated with honors from the regimental school for junior commanders with a degree as a radio telegraph operator and remained at the school as an assistant to the platoon leader.

Following his compulsory service, it would have been easy for him to find a good job in the civilian world with such experience. Platoon leader assistant Chibisov, however, firmly believed he should remain in the army and become a military pilot. The twenty-four-year-old's desire was so strong that in the summer of 1930, he persuaded his command unit to grant him leave so he could take the exams at the Ivanovo Flight School.

The prospective student was anxious during the entire trip from Vladimir to Ivanovo. He understood that he had been unable to obtain in-depth knowledge from his rural six-year education. The last thing on his mind was his health; he was the right flank man in formations, and everyone in his platoon followed his lead. Then something happened that nobody expected: he failed the medical exam. His vision was the culprit. Maxim's left eye was normal, but his right eye was a little below the requirements. He returned to the unit with the verdict "Not fit for flight service."

He didn't attempt to conceal his failure from his fellow soldiers, but he didn't elaborate on the details. He reported the news to his commanders. He briefly explained to his comrades that his vision was to blame. He did not show his feelings outwardly, but he never gave up his dream of the skies. As he always said, "The important thing is to remain calm. Endure! And then we'll see."

After completing his compulsory service in the fall of 1930, Maxim decided not to return to the village. He went to Moscow to see his older brothers. Ivan was working at the Serp i Molot factory at the time, while Alexei was a locomotive driver.

Maxim's radio technology knowledge acquired in the army enabled the demobilized Red Army junior commander to become a highly skilled worker. Moscow factories welcomed such experts with open arms. At the Profradio factory, Maxim mastered the profession of radio equipment assembler in only five months. He worked so hard that he was quickly awarded the honorary title of Shock Worker.

At the recommendation of the leaders of the factory's party organization, Maxim Chibisov became a candidate for membership in the All-Union Communist Party (of Bolsheviks). At that time, it was rare to be accepted into the party. Exclusion was much more common for people who, for one reason or another, were suspected of insufficient loyalty or deviations from the general line pursued by Lenin's Central Committee led by Comrade Stalin. A wave of purges was sweeping over all branches of the Communist Party (as the ground was being prepared for future mass repressions, although nobody could have imagined it at the time).

Maxim Chibisov with his sister Aksinya pictured prior to his departure to serve in the army. Village Pushchino, 1928

Under such circumstances, the awarding of a candidacy card was a sign of special trust for this top performer. Such trust opened up enticing opportunities for career advancement through political or administrative chains, particularly since the young Communist Chibisov had a flawless background: he was a proletariat of working peasant origin from a machine factory who had undergone military conditioning.

Maxim, however, did not have any propensity for speaking or administrative activities. He had inherited a negative predisposition to gibberish from his father, who used to suppress idle talk with his saying "Don't speak more than you have to." Maxim followed this rule, which was born from the peasant wisdom of Nikolai Chibisov, throughout his entire life. In addition, his dream of becoming a pilot had not dissipated and only intensified with time.

Such dreams, which captivated the hearts and minds of many Soviet people, were strengthened by the general mood of the people, the backbreaking efforts to overcome the chaos in the country, and the belief in a bright socialist future.

"We were born to make fairy tales a reality!" was a popular refrain in the Land of the Soviets, which was in dire need of aviation. A fascination with the romanticism of steel wings and flaming motors became widespread, especially among young people. The Communist Party and the Soviet government cleverly exploited and guided this enthusiasm, turning it into an organized movement and using its energy to help compensate for the lack of material resources as well as to overcome the Soviet Union's technological gap with the leading aviation powers.

Cadets of the school of junior commanders (left to right): A.A. Korovkin, M.N. Chibisov, G.S. Zynoviyev, city of Valdimir, 7 May 1929

In 1927, aviation enthusiasts from the general public united to form Osoaviakhim.[1] In January 1931, the IX Congress of the Lenin Komsomol adopted a pledge to support the country's air fleet. Aero clubs and groups of glider pilots, sky divers, model airplane builders, and amateur radio operators sprouted up all over the country.

In March 1931, Maxim came across a leading article in the *Moskovskaya Pravda* newspaper about the training of aviation personnel for the Soviet Union. The Communist Party had set the goal of training 100,000 to 150,000 pilots over the next two years.

The preliminary selection of candidates for flight schools was to be held by the district organizations of the Communist Party and the Young Communist League. In his mind, Maxim immediately began weighing his odds. He was already a candidate for party membership—that was a major

---

[1]   Osoaviakhim: the Society for the Advancement of Defense, Aviation, and Chemical Construction. It was established on January 23, 1927, and given its present name of the Voluntary Association for Assistance to the Army, Air Force, and Navy in 1951.

plus. He was highly regarded in radio matters. He was a social activist. In the army, he had received the highest marks in combat and political training, as confirmed by his attributes. All signs indicated it could be realistic for him to obtain a referral from the party committee. In terms of his health, nature had endowed him well; vision was the only problem—a few measly fractions of a percentage point in one eye were lacking to meet the strict flight standards.

He decided he could not squander the opportunity fate had granted him. He appealed to the party committee secretary, Shibayev, for a recommendation to enter flight school.

The party organizer, who was responsible for the factory's performance, was sorry to part with one of his best young workers, especially during the period when increasingly strained production plans were supposed to be fulfilled and exceeded. But it was impossible not to respect the patriotic passion of the young man, who had decided to contribute to the consolidation of the Soviet Air Force. Maxim received a recommendation from the party committee without any problems.

1.3 Running Down a Dream

A modest person by nature, Maxim did not like to flaunt his achievements, but when it came time for him to take to the skies, it was as if he were preparing to march in a parade: the brave reserve commander adorned his military uniform with all its decorations.

At the district committee, everything proceeded like clockwork. Following the interview, he received the sheet of paper with the coveted signature opening the door to the acceptance commission. The conversation with Turkov, the acceptance commission chairman, went just as smoothly. Upon reading the decision, which stated, "Permit Comrade M. N. Chibisov to take entrance exams for aviation school," Maxim felt as if he were in seventh heaven. Then he heard the words that brought him tumbling back to earth: "Proceed to the medical commission in room No. 34!"

This time, however, the medical commission declared Maxim "conditionally fit to fly." The doctors felt the slight vision deficiency in his right eye (0.9% below the requirement for 100% normal vision) would be more than offset by the left eye. "Here you have 1.25 vision. It would seem that only eagles can see that well. And thank God you see with both your eyes," the old eye doctor told him.

Maxim successfully passed his entrance exams on general subjects and the political primer and was enrolled in the Myasnikov First Aviation Pilot School. The prospective cadets were informed of the school's address: the village of Kacha, outside of Sevastopol, in the Crimea.

Classes began in the second half of April. The district committee had promised to send out a notice in advance to specify the departure date and assembly place. In the meantime, all the cadets were told to return to their jobs to tender their resignation and to say goodbye to colleagues and relatives.

When Maxim told his brothers and their families about his impending departure, they were more concerned than happy since, at that time, the common view of a pilot was akin to our current notions about manned space flight. Ivan and Alexei tried to persuade their younger—and favorite— brother to find another less dangerous occupation. Maxim, however, never considered the idea of giving up on the goal he had deliberately worked toward since childhood.

The hardest part was leaving Pushchino, which the youngest Chibisov visited for a few days in order to see his mother and talk with his brothers and sisters who had settled in Serpukhov.

Darya was already 66 years old. She lived alone in the empty house, worked on the farm, and dreamed that Maxim – her last child, her pride and joy would return home after the army. After meeting his mother and holding her frail body in his arms, he decided that as soon as he got everything arranged after flight school, he would invite her to come live with him. But when he tried to share this idea with her in order to calm her, he realized there was no way she would ever leave her familiar nest. Later, having traveled around the country and lived in the backcountry and garrisons, Maxim came to understand that a restless life spent living out of suitcases would not be appropriate for an elderly woman accustomed to her regular village ways.

For several years, Darya's only consolation consisted of the long letters her son regularly sent in addition to monthly remittances. His duties prevented him from returning to his native village, which he came to bitterly regret in 1935, when his mother passed away.

On April 9, 1931, Maxim bade farewell to the Profradio factory. At the end of his shift, a festive send-off was held for the future flight school student, at which everyone—from his colleagues to the head of the workshop, Smirnov, and the party organizer, Shibayev—congratulated him, showered him with kind words, and wished him well. Everything else was simply a formality: a brief talk with the personnel department, a statement of resignation, and goodbyes all the way to the door, beyond which an unknown yet glorious—he firmly believed—future awaited him.

The date of departure to flight school, April 16, 1931, and even the exact departure time of the train, 12:45 p.m., remained forever etched in Maxim's memory. In his handwritten notes, he wrote,

> Having bade a warm farewell to my relatives, my brothers and I took a taxi and went to the assembly point. A crowd of mostly young people had gathered at the district committee in the courtyard and inside the building. I didn't see anyone familiar. After finding the person in charge of our team's departure, I reported my arrival … and received food for the road.
>
> Soon the command was given: "Get in the cars!"
>
> The convoy stopped at Kalanchevka, at the square of the three train stations. We dismounted and in a single file proceeded to the trains. There was a brass band playing on the platform. Accompanied by the music of famous upbeat marches, the young men said goodbye to their loved ones and it seemed like the sendoff along with the hugs and the tears would never end. But then the command came: "Onto the train!"
>
> Outside the windows, Moscow drifted by for a while, but soon its outskirts finally faded away into the distance. Ahead of us was a meeting with the Black Sea and the city of Russian naval glory—Sevastopol.

CHAPTER 2

Flight School

2.1 Learning to Fly

In the early morning, the train brought the future flight school students to a small train station not far from Bakhchysarai, where they were met with a ceremonial greeting.

Maxim recorded the events of the day in great detail in his diaries:

> We were met by nearly all the commanders of the Myasnikov First Aviation Pilot School led by Commanding Officer R. K. Rataush. A brass band was playing … on the platform. Upon hearing the command "Form two rows!" we lined up and stood at attention for the approaching chief instructor. He was met by the senior officer who had accompanied us: "Comrade Commander! The group of students of the first party and young communist league recruitment from Moscow has arrived in full! No incidents occurred while en route!" The commander greeted us and congratulated us on our arrival. In reply, we shouted "Hurrah!" three times. Next came the command "Into the cars!" And the convoy of trucks … left for the garrison located in the village of Kacha.

The students were first sent to the decontamination facility. A simple but nourishing meal followed. The next day, Maxim went back to the medical commission and once again heard the familiar words "Conditionally fit." From that point on, Maxim began a regular student life, in which his priorities were determined well in advance for the next 24 months: studies, an army routine accounting for virtually every minute of the day, and the orders of senior officers.

The Myasnikov First School of Military Pilots—the famous Kacha school[2]—was established in 1910, when it was called the Sevastopol Aviation Officer School. It was one of the two first aviation educational institutions in Russia (the other was the Gatchina Aviation School, which was also founded in 1910). Among those who learned to fly at Kacha were Alexander Pokryshkin, Boris Safonov, Polina Osipenko, Yakov Smushkevich, and numerous other heroes of the Soviet Union and Russia, as well as a wide range of brilliant military commanders, astronauts, renowned aircraft designers, and test pilots. Joseph Stalin even entrusted this eagle's nest with the education of his son Vasily.

In 1931–1934, the head of the Kacha Aviation School was Brigade Commander Robert Rataush, an elderly, stern-looking Latvian. A man of few words who was virtually inaccessible to the students, he was a true celestial. People trembled before him as they would have before a supreme authority. This remarkable aviator, however, subsequently experienced a tragic fate. In 1939, Rataush was convicted based on false accusations, and he died in prison in 1943.

Commander P.F. Zhigarev, 1939

Pavel Zhigarev held the position of chief of staff at the school. He began his career as a cavalryman and then studied to become an observer pilot, the name

[2] Kacha Aviation School existed under different names from 1910 to 1998. It was disbanded by the decision of the authorities of independent Ukraine. The successor of the Kacha school is the 783rd Order of Lenin Red Banner Aviation Training Center in Armavir, where the colors of the Kacha Higher Military Aviation Pilot School are housed.

given to flight navigators during the dawn of aviation. He studied to become a pilot on his own while continuing in the navigator service. At the Kacha school, Zhigarev was highly regarded as a brilliant specialist who had a perfect understanding of all the intricacies of flying. He went on to a highly successful career. In 1937–1938, Zhigarev achieved fame for leading a group of Soviet volunteer pilots who were fighting with China against the Japanese. At the beginning of World War II and also from 1949 to 1957, he served as the commander of the Soviet Air Force. He was granted the title of Marshal of Aviation.

The students were split into groups of seven or eight people. Each group was trained and looked after by one instructor. Four groups made up a squad. Two squads made up a detachment. Two detachments made up a squadron. The entire school was comprised of two squadrons in a manner reminiscent of the structure of a combat flight unit.

Among the students, junior commanders and sergeants were designated in the groups, squads, detachments, and squadrons. Maxim, who already had military experience with the rank of a junior commander, was entrusted with the position of squadron sergeant.

Maxim had to master a wide range of general and specialized disciplines in the shortest possible time. This was no simple task: all the knowledge he had acquired over six years of studying at the village school and supplemented with what he had managed to learn on his own without neglecting his job left much to be desired. He was saved, however, by the extraordinary qualities of his mind and will, which had been bestowed upon him by nature and sharpened by his life experiences. He studied in the same way he had grown accustomed to working and quickly gained a profound understanding of ideas and concepts of which he had previously been unaware.

Throughout the rest of his life, Maxim would cherish the memory of the people who helped him master the profession of flying. Later, he listed all of them by name in his diaries—teachers, commanders, and colleagues. Maxim made his first flight on a Y-1 trainer airplane with Instructor Nikolai Trunov. According to Maxim's memoirs,

> this instructor was of fairly short stature (approximately 168 cm (5 feet 6 inches)). But there was something about this smiling blonde guy with his rosy face, blue eyes and level, gentle voice that made all the students perform their

jobs as best they could. The results spoke for themselves. In the performance program, our training team placed first in the squadron. It fully completed the training ahead of schedule. All the students—as one—were given high marks. There wasn't a single violation or incident in the group, while such incidents did occur in other groups.

After 38 flights, Instructor Trunov noted in his official report that Cadet Chibisov "had never given any reason to speak about any serious deviations over the entire flying season."

For his 39th flight, Detachment Commander A. Savotkov decided to inspect Maxim in action. "After taking his place in the instructor's seat, he never once touched the controls from takeoff through landing … As he was getting out of the cockpit, he dryly remarked, 'No observations! The assignment was performed excellently!'"

The next test proved to be even more challenging. Maxim not only had to demonstrate his ability to fly a plane but also had to make decisions during emergencies. For his 40th flight, sitting in the instructor's seat was none other than the director of the school, Rataush, who generally did not fly with students. This news spread instantly throughout the airfield. Everyone who was free at that moment came running to observe the flight.

In his diaries, Maxim wrote:

> There was nothing special about the assignment— circling at 400 meters (1,312 feet). The nervousness I felt from the honor being shown to me passed as soon as I took hold of the wheel. I started the engine. As usual, I looked forward, back and side to side. I checked once again—there was nothing in front of me. After taxiing to the runway, I raised my hand as a sign I was ready … I took off as I was taught: picking up speed, smoothly lifting off from the runway, and beginning to ascend. But we had not even reached 150 meters (492 feet) when the director began to cut the throttle from his instructor's seat. Naturally, the motor began to fail. What was I supposed to do? I was in charge of the controls, so it was up to me to make a decision. And there was no time to think. Remember, there is virtually no vertical clearance.

I immediately switched the plane into a gliding descent. In front of me were houses and the hangar. There was nowhere to land the machine. I made a sharp turn to the left, thinking I could land the plane on the tall rye crops. I descended to an elevation of 30 meters (100 feet). Then the director opened up the throttle and the motor started running at full strength again. And I immediately began to ascend. In accordance with the assignment, I climbed to 400 meters (1,312 feet) and began circling: a first turn, second, third. The director gestured to me: "Come on! Finish it up!" I considered how I was going to land. On the fourth turn, I began the descent ... I reduced the speed over the runway as usual, and the three wheels smoothly touched down. All I had to do from there was continue the landing run until the speed was fully reduced, taxi to the parking area, and switch off the motor.

The director jumped out of the cockpit in a good mood and interrupted Maxim's report with a commander's wave of the hand: "So, Comrade Cadet, I certify that you performed the entire flight on your own without my intervention. When I simulated engine failure, your decisions were intelligent and correct. I thank you for the excellent performance of the assignment!" Adhering to the chain of command, Instructor Trunov reported to Squad Commander N. Ossovsky that Cadet Chibisov was prepared for solo flight. Ossovsky also conducted a test flight and gave Maxim another "excellent" grade.

For his 42nd flight, Maxim flew solo in an exemplary and flawless manner. With no instructor in the cockpit, he felt entirely confident, although he was aware that from then on, he was responsible not only for himself but also for the machine with which he had been entrusted.

The Y-1 planes on which the cadets learned to fly had a substantial amount of wear and tear, particularly the 120-hp M-2 engines installed in the aircraft. The service life of these engines between overhauls was only 25-30 hours. Due to the unreliable equipment, unpleasant situations frequently occurred during flights.

Maxim remembered two incidents (described in his diary) in particular from his first solo flights. Each of them could have ended in disaster. On one occasion, "the aircraft motor shut down while performing aerobatic maneuvers and the propeller stopped rotating." The plane was in a wing slide at the time. Cadet Chibisov did not lose his bearings: he turned the plane into a nosedive, and the motor switched back on. Another time,

> one of the cylinders fell out of the motor during a sharp turn. With the momentum of centrifugal force, the cylinder flew upwards and then began to fall, barely missing the wing. The propeller continued to rotate, but the plane was shaking violently due to the symmetrical imbalance as the center of gravity in the spinning engine shifted away from the axis. It was shaking so badly that the pilot[3] could hardly distinguish the topographical features of the ground below—and everything flashed before his eyes. It was only by sheer luck that the engine did not catch fire. If the plane had crashed, the pilot would have certainly died since cadets at that time did not fly with parachutes. Maxim managed to keep his cool even in this potentially fatal situation.
>
> Since the piloting zone was close to the airfield, he managed to descend for landing and routinely landed the plane near the "T" sign without damaging any part of the aircraft.

2.2 When the Country Commands One to Be a Hero

Maxim described the situation with aviation equipment at the Myasnikov school with a couple of terse lines: "Major difficulties have been encountered with the planes and particularly with the engines. No new engines have arrived from the factories. The wear on the old ones is at the limit."

Domestic aircraft construction and other related industries were still in their early stages of development and could not keep up with the rapidly increasing needs of civil aviation and, especially, military aviation. The country lacked planes, aircraft engines, spare parts, aluminum, tire rubber, electronic equipment—anything and everything.

---

[3] Here and in a number of other places in his diary, M. N. Chibisov refers to himself in the third person.

But flying was necessary. Without aviation, it was impossible to address many of the biggest challenges in the development of the national economy. Without aviation, it was impossible to provide secure protection to the borders of the enormous Soviet Union, which was surrounded by nations that were not particularly friendly (and sometimes were openly hostile).

Cadets preparing for a training flight, 1932

It was also necessary to train those who would be responsible in the future for flying the outstanding Soviet-produced aircraft. The future aces were forced to master the fundamentals of airmanship using old equipment that was completely run down.

"When the country commands one to be a hero, any one of us could become the hero" were the words of a song that millions of young people enthusiastically sang during these years. There might not have been enough aircraft engines, but there was no shortage of heroes. A fervent desire to fly and serve the country was welcomed and encouraged despite the circumstances and deficient equipment.

Like all the students, Maxim accepted the risky flights as part of his duty. Later, when he was much older, Maxim recalled the following episode:

> One day, the weather was bad. There was a gusty wind with force of up to 17 meters per second (38 miles per hour). Only instructors could fly at that wind level—students weren't allowed. The director of the school was present for the flights. Noticing that almost none of the instructors were able to land without committing an error, he turned to Detachment Commander Savotkov and remarked:
> "Wow! Even your instructors are unable to fly without errors in this weather!"
> This clearly struck a nerve with Savotkov, who replied, "Negative, Comrade Commander! Even the students in

the detachment are capable of flying in such weather. Would you allow me to release one?"

"That's your business," the commander replied. Savotkov took aside the squad commanders and instructors in order to answer one question: who could be allowed to make such a flight on his own. My instructor (A. Shcherbakov) immediately called on me.

Despite his youth, Maxim had already learned a lot about flying and was able to appreciate the complexity of the impending flight, not to mention doing it under the watchful eyes of two dozen commanders! Half a century later, he wrote in his diaries,

> I still get a shiver up my spine today when I think back on that assignment. And at that time I approached the plane with the same shivers. The gusting wind was tearing at me, roaring and blowing dust up everywhere from the airfield. In order to somehow make the light machine heavier, we fastened a sand bag to the back seat. I got in the cockpit. I warmed up the engine. With the starter motor kicking on, the plane smoothly began to move forward. I gave it some gas and proceeded to take off. A strong headwind caught the plane at the right time because it easily lifted off the ground almost without any yaw. I began to climb. Then a strong gust of wind began hurling the machine in different directions like a leaf. Nevertheless, I made my first turn at an elevation of 200 meters (660 feet) followed by a second and a third. After the third turn, I switched into glide mode, eased off the gas, and went to make the fourth and final turn. When gliding with such a strong wind, it feels like the plane isn't flying but, rather, rapidly sinking or almost falling. And the ground is right there! It seems like the landing gear is going to crack from impact at any second.
>
> I nevertheless managed to level it out. And, despite the shaking, I kept it above the ground. The landing and the subsequent run were also a success. Meanwhile, the wind continued to blow with the same force. As I taxied

to the parking area, the attendants had difficulty holding on to the plane's stabilizer and wings.

When describing this incident, Maxim proudly pointed out that he was the only one among all the cadets who was trusted to fly in such difficult conditions. He then casually mentioned that the director of the school ordered him to repeat the flight, so he fulfilled the assignment for a second time.

For his impressive results in the first stage of training, Maxim was awarded a theater ticket and a trip to Sevastopol. While there, he was first photographed in the military uniform that would go on to serve as his work clothes for the next quarter of a century: a flight suit, a headset, and goggles.

The natural selection had been completed within the group by the start of the second year of training at the Kacha school. Those who had no chance of succeeding as pilots had been dismissed during the stage of instructor-guided flights. Later, the "non-heroes" flunked out. Perhaps they would have gotten the hang of it had they been using more reliable planes equipped with top-notch engines and the necessary navigational devices, but such aircraft did not yet exist, so the commanders parted with the "non-heroes" without regret. As a result, the only cadets left at the flight school were the ones who were fanatically in love with the sky, fearless and assertive, strong-willed and resourceful—pilots by the grace of God.

Soon Maxim would be entrusted with a more complex machine: the R-1. This Soviet-produced aircraft, which was built based on the image and likeness of the far-from-new English plane Airco DH.9A (with the use of structural elements from wood and other materials), was put into mass production under the guidance of famous aircraft designer Nikolai Polikarpov.

Later, Maxim spent a lot of time flying on the plywood-and-percale (percale is high quality weave cotton fabric)

Cadets of Myasnikov First Aviation Pilot School (left to right): foreman of an echelon V. Kozhevnikov, foreman of a squadron M. Chibisov, foreman of a flight group V. Korolev, 1932.

machine built by Dmitry Grigorovich. In summarizing his experience, he noted,

> It is worth describing the features of the R-1 fighter in greater detail. It was a very rugged plane that was difficult to manage. It did not forgive mistakes such as skids and deceleration during turns. When such mistakes were made, the plane went into a tailspin, and in most cases this led to disaster. The number of such incidents decreased dramatically following a study of the causes for why the plane entered into a tailspin and theoretical explanations were provided on the proper actions for a pilot to take to pull the plane out of the tailspin.

Yet this machine was much more sophisticated than the Y-1 training "stack" plane on which Maxim and his classmates had begun their flight practice.

In addition to a study of the hardware and motor, navigational equipment, and weapons of the R-1, year two of the training program included such subjects as the theory of flight, tactics for using aviation in combat, and several special practical exercises: flying routes with landing at other airfields, firing at ground targets, and others.

The program ended in October 1932. After taking tests and exams in the disciplines they had studied, the cadets received a document on graduation from the Myasnikov Aviation School.

Following exams, an order was to be ceremoniously read out to the cadets, conferring their ranks and appointments. On the eve of the ceremony, each cadet received a commander's uniform: low-top box-calf boots, dark blue breeches, and a jacket of the same color with the two highly coveted rhombus-shaped pins on the buttonholes, plus a snow-white shirt and equally blinding white gloves.

On August 11, 1932, Maxim Chibisov set off for the ceremony, along with his comrades.

However, upon hearing his name and the site of his future service, he experienced a feeling akin to shock: he had been assigned to remain at the school as an instructor. Meanwhile, his comrades all rejoiced, as they had been assigned to combat units.

2.3 From Student to Teacher

The professional fliers who had best demonstrated their abilities were appointed as flight school instructors. Only a select few of the graduates had ever been awarded such an honor. But Maxim Chibisov dreamed of becoming a military pilot, envisioning himself in the army ranks and in the cockpit of a formidable fighting machine! The position of instructor seemed uninteresting to him. It was distressing and thankless work. In addition, the teaching staff climbed the career ladder more slowly than combat personnel and had fewer opportunities to distinguish themselves. But an order was an order.

Following a brief leave, Maxim took an instructor training class and received the flight personnel booklet of the Workers-Peasants Red Army Air Force—a document that accompanied an active pilot for his entire life. From that point on, a record was kept of each flight he took, including each minute spent in the air, the route, the plane type, and the number of landings. The section detailing disasters, accidents, minor damage, and forced landings was completed with particular care. The booklet, without fail, specified the year, month, engine type, and circumstances of the disaster, as well as the probable and established cause of the accident. It was also mandatory to indicate the degree of material damage to the plane or crew.

Maxim flew approximately 300 hours over a year. The equipment occasionally failed, but he did not have a single accident or incident resulting in serious consequences.

Instructor M.N. Chibisov (second from the left) with the cadets of Kacha Aviation School, 1933.

Even though the flight lessons with the cadets were conducted every other day, it was an exhausting conveyer belt. The flights began at 3:00-4:00 a.m. because they had to shut down before lunch. At temperatures of 27 to 35°Celsius (81 to 95° F.) at the dusty Crimean airfields, visibility on the runway was close to zero. Thus, by midday, an instructor had to complete three circle flights with each cadet assigned to him and spend roughly just as much time in the piloting area. At

5:00-6:00 p.m., post-flight debriefing began (i.e., a thorough analysis of the cadets' behavior in the air). Each cadet had to give a detailed and clear explanation of where, when, and how he'd committed an error, as well as what consequences had been inherent in the error.

Instructor Chibisov began to enjoy this laborious work and demonstrated outstanding teaching abilities. Feeling a sense of responsibility for his pupils, he did not rush to expel even the most hopeless cadets from the school and took them under his wing without worrying about the time or effort this involved. The pupils saw how much heart he put into teaching them—not because of fear but for the sake of his conscience—and tried to perform what was required of them.

With his busy schedule, time flew by unnoticed. The young instructor already enjoyed working with the even younger students. Moreover, what previously had seemed like a routine process to him now gave him the opportunity to polish his own flying skills.

His piloting skills became masterful, and he perfected his control of the aircraft to the point that it became automatic. During flight, it was as if he himself became part of the machine he was wielding. Using the language of professionals, all of this is defined in one word: *school*. The emergencies arising in the air due to unreliable equipment or the errors of the trainees taught Instructor Chibisov to never give up under any circumstances and to act particularly clearly under extreme circumstances so that in a fraction of a second, he could make the only correct decision. Because of his experience as an instructor, in later years, he managed to avoid certain death in disastrous situations while saving those who flew with him.

He had the occasion to demonstrate his flying skills not only for the cadets but also for experienced aviators during the inspections held regularly for the entire instructor staff. Maxim described one such instance in his diary:

> I particularly remember a check flight with piloting equipment inspector K. Loginov sitting behind me. The assignment was a circle flight. We took off and reached an altitude of 400 meters. The flight was precise in terms of its box pattern, turns and accurate calculations. At the end—gliding, leveling out and holding the plane at an elevation of three-quarters of a meter above the

ground. Three-point landing. After landing, I maintained direction during the landing run. That was it. I pulled into the parking area. I turned around and the inspector motioned to me expressively as if to say: let's go a second time. I mentally shrugged my shoulders. But an order is an order. I turned around, took off, repeated everything, and returned to the parking area. This time the inspector got out of the plane. I followed him. In the proper manner, I asked if he had any observations. The inspector stood there, thought about it, and then said, "No observations! The flights were performed excellently!"

But he hadn't dismissed me. Then he told the flight monitor, "Suspend the flights! All instructors assemble in the neutral zone!"

We all gathered, looking around at one another and wondering what he would say. The inspector spoke:

"Well then, comrades! I flew check flights with several instructors today. I have bad news! None of the flights were performed without error. The one exception was Chibisov. He performed two check flights, both without a single deviation, and with excellent marks. I believe that such work should be the standard for the instructors planning to train cadets. Therefore, Comrade Chibisov will now perform two circle check flights. Everyone else remain on the neutral zone and watch closely how he operates. I ask that you pay particular attention to how he takes off, gives the plane gas, the run, how he holds the plane above the ground after takeoff, begins to climb, and the flight path. Another thing—which everyone needs to learn from him—is the precise calculation of the elevation for leveling out during landing. Watch how he holds the plane over the ground. How he accurately puts it down on three points and maintains direction during the landing run."

"Go!" he said to me. I performed the assignment and landed the plane. During my report, once again I naturally asked if there were any observations.

The inspector looked at everyone else and asked, "So what do you think?"

Nothing else was added except "excellent."

"That's it!" the inspector concluded. "Consider that the standard. Strive for a similar performance so that you can then teach your cadets the same thing."

Time continued to fly by. During the second year of training, the cadets from Instructor Chibisov's group successfully mastered the difficult-

to-manage R-1, just as he had. Meanwhile, in spring 1934, the entire Soviet Union was anxiously following the news that polar aviation pilots were fighting for the lives of the crew on the *Chelyuskin* steamship, which had become ice-bound in the Chukchi Sea. Maxim monitored these events as a professional. Almost every political class at

Aircraft R-1 was used throughout 1920s and 1930s as a reconnaissance and a Short-Range Bomber

the Kacha aviation school began with a discussion of the latest news from the Arctic.

All of the pilots and cadets at the school would have been thrilled to take part in this great feat, but their assistance was not requested. All they could do was envy and admire their comrades from polar aviation.

When the *Chelyuskin* rescue operation was completed, Anatoly Lyapidevsky, Sigizmund Levanevsky, Vasily Molokov, Nikolai Kamanin, Mikhail Vodopyanov, Mavriky Slepnev, and Ivan Doronin were awarded with the title of Hero of the Soviet Union, which had just been instituted by the USSR Central Executive Committee.

In Moscow, a ceremonial welcome was held for the *Chelyuskin* rescuers. This triumph of the Soviet Air Force demonstrated the power and reliability of its wings to the whole world. It was also a triumph for the Soviet Union, which found true heroes worthy of this title.

In August 1934, the flight training program for the latest class of Kacha cadets came to an end. The group trained by Instructor Chibisov was recognized as the best in the 1st Squadron.

A government Air Force commission arrived from Moscow and spent an entire week drilling Maxim's students on theory, piloting technique and shooting at ground targets. All the cadets (22 students) received good or excellent grades. They all went on to serve in combat units, and when the war began, they courageously defended the nation at the front. Two of them were awarded the title of Hero of the Soviet Union.

Instructor Chibisov's results left a very good impression on the distinguished guests from Moscow, and this led to important changes in his career.

At that time, the leaders of the Soviet Air Force had decided to establish new branches of naval aviation. Promising pilots of the highest quality were in high demand, and soon the director of the Kacha school found an order lying on his desk from the USSR Revolutionary Military Council appointing Maxim Chibisov the flight commander of the 10th Aviation Squadron of the 10th Naval Air Brigade in the city of Yeysk.

His departure was scheduled for August 18, or the official Day of the Air Force. A parade was held at Kacha to mark the occasion. The orchestra played the anthem of the Soviet Air Force: "Higher and higher and higher." Maxim was sent off to his new post by most of the school's employees and cadets. Everyone said something and wished him well in the high skies.

He left Kacha with a young wife to whom he had just tied his destiny.

2.4 Military Romance

It all began when one of Maxim's colleagues, pilot Dmitry Leshko, married a nurse by the name of Maria (called Marochka by her family). The wife of the young but already respected commander was then paid a visit by her older sister, Rosalia (or Rosochka), whose beauty had the entire male population of the Kacha military town in a flutter.

The sisters were born and raised in the large family of Boris Alterman and Anna Tarakanova in the city of Dzhankoy. Their family were well off: their father worked in tailoring, going from house to house to serve customers. However, he died at an early age, and Anna remained the sole provider for seven children. Taking her late husband's place, she began performing his tailoring work. Sometimes she would leave the house for an entire day, putting 11-year-old Rosaly in charge of everything. The young girl learned at a young age how to cook and sew, wash and clean up, set the table, and feed her brothers and sisters what she had prepared.

Rosochka had a great ear for music, an amazing natural voice, and a remarkable memory. She could memorize songs as well as arias from operas and operettas at lightning speed. She sewed herself a long dress from cheesecloth and would spin around in front of the mirror, singing the entire radio repertoire of the time. On Sundays, she would organize actual concerts at home.

Left to right: Isaak, Rosalia, Maria and her husband Dmitry Leshko, June 1935

After graduating from secondary school, Rosaly enrolled in accounting courses and then tried to find work in Simferopol but was unsuccessful. Her younger sister Maria had already married and was living at Kacha. She invited Rosaly to the military town to visit and earn some additional money (Dmitry Leshko had already found a job for his sister-in-law at a bank).

Rosaly gladly accepted the offer and showed up one day in the village, where the overwhelming majority of the population consisted of young unmarried pilots, cadets, and instructors, who could not help but notice the slender new beauty. Many of them attempted to win her affection, but to no avail.

She tried not to give rise to gossip and talk and consistently rejected all overtures for acquaintance. It was not easy for her to do: she was a pretty and flirtatious young lady. Sociable, smiling, and cheerful, she was always the center of attention.

Maxim saw her for the first time in the commander's mess hall, and his heart began thumping anxiously. Meanwhile, his colleagues all told him about their fruitless attempts to find an approach to this new "target." Seated close by, Rosaly intuitively felt she was the subject of their conversation. Then the handsome young pilot approached her table, broadly extended his hand, and introduced himself: "Maxim Chibisov."

The unapproachable young lady cut him short, saying, "Gentlemen do not extend their hands first to a lady."

He realized his tactical mistake and began developing a strategy to win over the beautiful girl's heart. He thought in advance about where he could

meet her, politely say hello, or catch her on the way from work. Finally, he managed to talk to her during a lunch break, on the way from the mess hall, and invited her to a movie. Succumbing to the charm of the persistent suitor, or perhaps trying to dodge his attempt to accompany her all the way back to work, the straight-laced girl agreed to come to a club at 7:00 p.m., and then ran off to her bank.

Upon returning to work, she changed her mind about going to the movie and sent her sister and her husband to the club in her place. She stayed at home, cleaning up and washing the floors.

Sisters Rosaly (on the right) and Marochka, 1931.

After not meeting her at the club, Maxim set out for the Leshkos' home to find out why the young lady had failed to show up for the movie. He approached the house, knocked on the door, and opened it without waiting for a reply. He had arrived at the worst time possible: Rosaly had just finished washing the room and, having tucked up her skirt, was moving backward toward the front door to wring out the rag and put it in the hallway by the entrance. Later, she would say that this position, as well as the narrow space in which they found themselves alone, left her utterly embarrassed. The unexpected guest took advantage of this circumstance; he decisively stepped on the rag she had just wrung out and, while wiping his feet, said, "I'm sorry. Am I disturbing you?" He stepped inside and took a seat at the table. Both of them were embarrassed, their conversation was strained, and Rosaly left her guest alone and rushed off to the kitchen to make tea.

Soon the movie ended, and the Leshkos returned home. Dmitry, a well-known jokester, had a long laugh over the idea that his mother-in-law, as he jokingly referred to his wife's eldest sister, had sent them to a movie in order to arrange a date. The sisters then quickly set the table, and Maxim's courtship was made official over a cup of tea and amid jokes and laughter. He received the go-ahead from his senior comrade, as well as an invitation to stop by for a visit.

Rosalia Borisovna and Maxim Nikolaevitch Chibisov, 1934.

When Maxim decided to propose to Rosaly, he came to Dmitry and Maria Leshko's home to seek her hand in marriage, as was customary in his village of Pushchino. Rosochka was no longer considering a return to Simferopol. She realized she had fallen in love— for the rest of her life, as it would turn out.

Even though the newlyweds were happy in Kacha, they left the military town with no regrets. They were both young, overwhelmed by the force of mutual love, and beckoned away by the suspense of ambitious plans. In short, they were focused on the future. They had no doubt it would be challenging yet happy.

Pilot instructor M.N. Chibisov, 1933.

That's the girl whom Maxim
Chibisov married in 1933.

Commander of an echelon,
Senior Lieutenant Maxim
Nikolaevitch Chibisov.

Rosalia Borisovna, 1931.

CHAPTER 3

Introduction to the Sea

3.1 Politics, Strategy, Tactics, and Family Practice

The transfer of military pilot Chibisov from outside Sevastopol to Yeysk was preceded by important events of a geopolitical and geostrategic nature.

In 1931–1932, Japan occupied Manchuria, which belonged to China, and established the Manchukuo puppet state in the occupied lands. The Soviet Union's most important territories in the Far East—the Primorye and Khabarovsk territories—ended up being sandwiched within the strategic grip of Japan's Kwantung Army, which had taken up position on the Amur and Ussuri rivers, and the Imperial Japanese Navy, which controlled the northwestern part of the Pacific Ocean.

The Soviet government was forced to take urgent measures to strengthen its Far Eastern borders. Numerous combat units were deployed to the Far East, and fortifications were set up in the border areas. Thanks to these measures, the USSR land border was closed rather tightly. But the sea border, which ran for thousands of kilometers along the sparsely populated and uninhabited coastline, remained vulnerable in many places to a strike by the enemy naval forces, which were vastly superior to the Soviet Union's Pacific Fleet in terms of the number of ships and firepower.

Given these conditions, the commanders of the USSR Armed Forces turned to aviation. The deployment of powerful aviation formations in the

Far East was supposed to nullify the strategic advantages held by Japan, which dominated the sea. One of these formations was to be the 10th Naval Aviation Brigade. The brigade included the 10th Squadron, in which Maxim Chibisov was a squad leader.

The units of the 10th Brigade assembled in Yeysk, on the Sea of Azov, where the necessary conditions were present for pretraining as well as flight and combat practice. Not only aircraft and pilots but also formidable combat units – squads and squadrons already prepared for battle – were to be sent to the Far East.

Departing for Yeysk, Maxim sent his wife to Simferopol to stay for a while with her mother, Anna, while he made arrangements and got settled in the new location.

He arrived in Yeysk on August 20, 1934. He contacted the commandant's office to find out the address of the Military School for Naval Pilots and Observer Pilots, at which the 10th Squadron was assembling, and quickly reported to Chief of Staff M. Selivanovsky.

Following a detailed study of the documents, Selivanovsky offered him a seat. He wanted to know where Junior Commander Chibisov had arrived from, what kind of aircraft he had flown, and about his marital status. For his part, Maxim inquired about the composition and structure of the unit as well as the situation with allowances, accommodations, and food.

Flight commander M.N. Chibisov, Yeysk, 1934.

Selivanovsky explained everything clearly: the squadron included three detachments, each of which contained two squads, with three crews in each squad. They would be flying on the R-5, which was slightly more advanced than the R-1. "But"—the chief of staff pointedly lowered his voice—"there is talk that new ones will be sent soon." He also informed Maxim of the expected departure time to the Far East, where two squadrons that were part of the 10th Brigade were already located. As for living conditions, he offered little assistance. The squadron did not have its own housing facilities, and officers with families usually found their own private apartments. This unfortunate circumstance was consistent with the rational logic of the top military and administrative authorities: "Why provide housing to migratory birds who are here in Yeysk today and God only knows where tomorrow, thousands of kilometers away?"

But even a pilot who loves his work cannot live in the skies for 24 hours, particularly one who is married. Solving the housing problem on his own (a major priority for every Soviet citizen), Maxim ran around to almost half the city for two straight days. Finally, on the third day, he found something suitable in building 47 on the small street of Pervomayskaya. Even then, he had to resort to trickery and pretend to be a bachelor. People were reluctant to billet families. From his talk with the landlords, it became clear they wanted not only money for the room but also part of his flight rations. Picturing the looks they would have on their faces when they saw his dear Rosochka, he almost burst out laughing. *Sure!* he thought. *They will like the rations—they will like the wife too!*

The small town on the shore of the Sea of Azov, buried in verdure, appeared cozy, but the empty store shelves vividly attested to the fact that life in this little corner of paradise was actually far from paradise. Fruit and vegetables could be purchased at the markets, but everything else was issued based on ration cards or sold at astronomical prices, also at the markets. A similar picture could be seen in every corner of the country that had triumphed over socialism, with the exception of a few large cities.

Civilian life was much harsher than life in the army. This was not a revelation for Maxim, who had already experienced a great deal in his twenty-eight years. What was said during political classes was correct: the people gave all their best things to their defender, the Red Army.

Two months later, when the pretty wife of the gallant pilot who had settled on Pervomayskaya Street arrived, the homeowners were disappointed and angry and almost refused to rent the room to the young family. However, the diplomatic behavior of the tenant, who promised to pay more, and his wife's charm took their toll, and the landlords' anger was replaced with kindness.

Following his wife's arrival, having finally arranged everything with their rented room, Squad Commander Chibisov no longer worried about domestic problems. The assembly of the squadron was in full swing. Here he could handle any task.

3.2 A Cheerful Song Goes Easy on the Heart

Working with pilots on advanced classroom training as well as training in the air did not differ much from Maxim's job as an instructor at Kacha. Numerous training flights were performed—338 hours in the first half of 1934 alone. Working with seasoned pilots was much simpler than teaching beginners. Squad Commander Chibisov could now allow himself to swim in the sky. He did, however, frequently encounter specific problems caused by the unique features of naval aviation.

From July 1934 until February 1935, the 10th Naval Squadron flew over the sea in the land-based R-1 and R-5 without losing sight of the shore and being guided by landmarks. Several years later, after flying over plenty of seas and oceans, Maxim wrote in his memoirs,

> Flying aircraft over water makes it impossible to use landmarks as orientation. Therefore, a flight is performed using compass and time calculations. When visibility is poor (for instance, in a dense cloud cover), the pilot uses the flight indicator, compass and other instruments. Such piloting requires special training.

Aircraft R-5 of Naval Pilot School, 1934.

There were often thunderstorms along the shoreline during the warmer months. The interaction of two wayward elements—water and air—would create unpredictable movement in the air mass, both horizontally and vertically. When the plane entered a powerful updraft, it would either be tossed upward like a twig or just as suddenly be pushed down into the air pockets. It was not a pleasant feeling. As an experienced pilot, however, Chibisov quickly adapted; his time as an instructor helped him in this cause.

Maxim also had to work with his subordinates quite a bit. Sparing neither time nor effort, he worked them into a sweat. The squad was slightly lacking in discipline, especially when it came to drinking. The commander had to tighten up his subordinates. His manner was tough and low-key. Initially, his subordinates grumbled, but Chibisov knew how to command respect for himself and his demands. They were more inclined to emulate Maxim than oppose him; therefore, the problem with alcohol in the squad was quickly solved.

An entry was made in Maxim's personal file by Detachment Commander G. Poplavsky:

> He developed good aircrew cooperation in his squad for the performance of training and combat assignments. He is disciplined himself, has never been observed drinking alcoholic beverages, and flies with confidence. His personal marksmanship training was good ... He does not have a single flight accident in the unit. He has expressed a certain desire to serve in fighter aircraft. The position of squad commander fits.

Everything was perfect in the personal life of the newlyweds. Their relationship was based on the classic formula of harmony and love. Material prosperity came from Maxim's army salary and flight rations, which were quite sufficient despite their having to share some of it with the apartment owners. What else is required for happiness by beautiful young people for whom "a cheerful song goes easy on the heart"?

They brought the song that starts off with this line into their home after watching *Jolly Fellows*, the most popular Soviet film of that time. The upbeat characters in the film and, above all, the famous duet of Lyubov Orlova and Leonid Utesov radiated cheerful optimism and imbued viewers with unrestrained joy. The enthusiastic spirit of the picture, with its straightforward plot and boisterous buffoonery in an effervescent musical design, was in tune with the spirit of the era that had triumphed over socialism and the worldview of the Soviet people, who believed they were living in a proper, wonderful, and free country.

3.3 Concerns and Joy at Home and Work

In March 1935, two important events occurred in the life of Maxim Chibisov. The first—the most memorable and joyful—was the birth of a daughter, Alisa, affectionately known as Alenka. The second event involved Maxim's official duties: the 10th Squadron received new MBR-2 flying boats. From that time on, the squadron soldiers could consider themselves real naval aviators—prior, they had only been conditionally listed as such.

By the early 1930s, seaplanes were in demand for both military and civil aviation. The development of enormous, sparsely populated areas of Siberia and the Far East was in full swing. The aerial reconnaissance required for this task was made all the more convenient by the use of flying boats, which could use any river, lake, or bay as a landing site. Permanent land-based airfields would later be built in places where specific plans were required for the development of settlements and production facilities. In the event of any military conflicts, the seaplanes were to be used as reconnaissance and to strike at the enemy on sea or land.

During the early stages of the development of Soviet aviation, seaplanes were purchased abroad. Among them were the floating machines of the German aircraft manufacturer Junkers (J-20, J-13, and J-1), the He-5su and Dornier-Wal hydroplanes produced by the German firms Heinkel and Dornier, and the Italian aircraft Savoia-16 and Savoia-62.

Seaplanes were also built domestically at the time, under the guidance of famous aircraft designers such as Andrei Tupolev, Igor Chetverikov, and Dmitry Grigorovich. But the best aircraft for naval aviation—a plane that met all the requirements of the Navy and was easy to build and operate—was created by a young engineer named Georgy Beriev. He was able to bring his design ideas to life at an aviation factory in Taganrog, a city not far from Yeysk. It was here that the MBR-2 naval short-range reconnaissance aircraft, which the airmen soon nicknamed Chetvertak and Ambarchik, were created and put into production. Starting in early 1934, the MBR-2 planes were put into service, after which they were used in the Navy and civil aviation for a good two decades. The manufacturing of this these planes enabled the Soviet Union to minimize the number of hydroplanes purchased abroad.

In March 1935, the first Chetvertaks appeared in the 10th Squadron and were almost immediately handed over to Chibisov's squad for a flight test. Being familiar with different types of aircraft, he appreciated the well-chosen design of the monoplane right away, including its closed cockpit, which the squad commander particularly enjoyed. In his mind, he was already picturing how the machine would handle in the conditions of the Far East, where he would have to fly in all kinds of weather at any time of the year. His review of the design data confirmed the impressive features of the new seaplane.

Maxim could not wait to test out the new plane, as well as his ability to fly it. Moreover, the most important factors during takeoff and landing now were ones that were generally more significant for seamen: wind speed, wave height, groundswell, and more. For instance, he had to be prepared for the plane to dangerously porpoise amid strong winds and waves that were several stories high (i.e., make risky jumps, or porpoises, when hydroplaning and sliding across the water surface). There is a reason seaplanes are not permitted to take off or land when waves are at extreme heights.

On the eve of Maxim's first flight on the MBR-2, Squadron Commander Poplavsky was informed by the weather service that the waves were reaching heights of 0.7 meters (2.3 feet) and gave orders to postpone the flight after deciding it was not worth the risk. The flight chief, however, either decided against passing this order on to the rest of the team or failed to do so in time.

Maxim recalled the experience in his diary:

> The waves were a little high, but not overly large. I "porpoised" some during takeoff, but once it became clear that I had separated from the water smoothly I realized that I had handled the first challenge. I climbed and performed some maneuvers without any problems. The machine was behaving well. The only issue was during turbulence when the plane was tossed up and down in the same way as the land-based R-1. There were a few difficulties during the landing. But the wind quieted down and the surface of the sea took on an almost mirror-like appearance.

Experts know that it is not easy in such a situation to determine a plane's break-off altitude.

Nevertheless, Maxim managed to land the flying boat perfectly. A crowd was already waiting for him on the pier. His colleagues expressed their delight with approving gestures.

Seaplane MBR-2 was designed for short-range reconnaissance and as a light weight Bomber. Crew of 3 – 4 people. MBR-2 manufacturing was stopped in 1940. Total production amounted to 1365 units.

Poplavsky, who was also present, did not conceal his satisfaction either. Later, he would firmly scold the flight chief in front of everyone for his disobedience, which, fortunately, did not result in any negative consequences. While the flight chief was explaining himself, the hero of the day was mentally assessing the quality of the new machine, as reflected in his diary: "Wow, a 0.7-meter (2.3 feet) wave! The MBR-2 has excellent seaworthiness." Maxim Chibisov had been initiated into naval aviation.

Chibisov brothers (left to right): Alexei, Ivan and Maxim, 1935.

He adapted to the peculiarities of flying over water more quickly than his other squadron members did and acquired the skills needed to take off and land on water. He managed to deal with the turbulence and the lack of visible landmarks. He enjoyed training the crews of his squad. Later, he recalled,

I quickly got used to the sea and felt a kind of remarkable kinship with the navy. Having mastered the piloting of the seaplanes, I began training my subordinates. In those days, there were no restrictions on fuel. We flew a lot. We were only restricted by bad flying weather and the days on which the aircraft equipment was inspected. The flight mission generally included: flying a particular route for up to 5 hours; the bombing of stationary and moving targets; aerial shooting at cones; photography; and communication with ground control and among aircraft.

The training quickly produced the desired results, and the squad crew attained the required level of flying skills on the MBR-2. For his performance in combat and political training, Maxim was granted leave and rewarded with a trip to the prestigious Marfino health resort. Prior to their trip, the Chibisovs, including their young daughter, visited Rosaly's relatives in Simferopol and Maxim's brothers in Serpukhov. Everyone noted what an incredible resemblance Alenka had to Vasily, her uncle on her father's side, with her curly red hair and cheerful, bright blue eyes.

3.4 Our Journey Is a Long One

Shortly after Maxim returned to the unit, an order was issued on the completion of training and the relocation of the 10th Squadron to its permanent post.

The squadron members excitedly and anxiously awaited their departure date. Before entering flight school, Maxim had already managed to travel a considerable journey from north to south, from Moscow to the shores of the Black Sea. Now he was about to travel from west to east and see his country, which stretched over several thousand kilometers to the banks of the Pacific Ocean. Later in life, he recalled this memorable event:

> The first train with aircraft and flight officers departed from Yeysk on May 25, the second on May 28 and the third on May 30. Of course, we were all very eager to know where they were taking us. But this was a military secret. We only knew where we were "registered": Far East, Pacific Fleet. The Far East, however, is a loose concept. And we tried to guess which direction we were traveling by checking the map with the names of the stations we passed along the way … At the stations, we saw cargo trains. They were carrying ore, coal, machinery … The heated train cars were transporting cattle, and the troops were deployed in basically the same cars. The Ural mountains with their abundant forests flashed by outside the windows. Endless fields of wheat and rye stretched across the plains of Siberia. On the tenth day of the trip, we passed Novosibirsk. On the twentieth day, we reached the banks of Angara River. When Lake Baikal appeared, everyone rushed to the windows and began spontaneously singing, "Glorious sea, sacred Baikal." Then mountains, taiga and the plains again began passing by outside the windows.

Not a single complaint can be found in Maxim's diaries about the general discomfort of traveling in a train car ill-adapted to transport people. Due to the conditions of the highly drafty train car, however, he fell ill along the way. His temperature rose to almost 40 °C. (104 °F.). At one of the Siberian stations, he was taken off the train and hospitalized with a middle ear infection.

Maxim decided not to tell his wife about what had happened, thinking he would still make it to the garrison before her and manage to get things arranged for his family.

Rosaly, however, was in a hurry to reunite with her husband. As soon as she learned where to go (i.e., the military unit number and route to take), she immediately got on a regular passenger train with Alenka and set off for the long journey.

The train car was poorly ventilated and stuffy. At all stations and during random stops along the way, Rosaly trekked outside to get some fresh air, along with all the other passengers. During one such stop, the train suddenly set off and began picking up speed without giving any signals for departure. The young mother, who had been walking near the side of the tracks with Alenka, kept her bearings. Clutching her daughter against her chest, she ran after the train and tried to jump onto the footboard. According to her later recollections, everything after that seemed like a dream or an adventure movie. Jumping onto a moving train car with a child in one's hands required the skill of a well-trained athlete. Rosaly Chibisova was no athlete, but a maternal instinct can sometimes help one perform true miracles. At the very moment when her strength was running out, someone's strong arms firmly grabbed her and pulled her onto the train. After this episode, she no longer got off the train and tried not to think about what could have happened if she had been unable to catch the train.

Chibisov spouses with daughter Alenka, Krasnaya Rechka garrison, 1935.

New adventures, however, awaited her ahead. At Krasnaya Rechka, the name given to the terminus station and the military town located outside Khabarovsk, nobody was there to meet the commander's wife. She was told coldly and without any details, "Maxim Chibisov has not reached his destination. The reasons are unclear." Only after several weeks did her husband make it to Krasnaya Rechka and meet up with his family.

In order to accommodate the pilots of the 10th Squadron and their families, the Krasnaya Rechka garrison command ordered the longtime residents to make room for them. True to form, neither the veterans nor the newcomers complained.

Maxim wrote,

> The crew personnel understood this decision and patiently endured the challenges ... We were used to difficult living conditions in the private apartments in Yeysk. We also understood the complex situation on the Far East borders, where the Japanese were making intensive preparations to attack the Soviet Union and had already engaged in acts of provocation.

The garrison command allotted two days for the newcomers to get settled. Families with children were given top priority for the vacated rooms, followed by couples with no children. The bachelors were temporarily housed in tents along with the rank-and-file troops. Someone had to live for a little while in a bathhouse next to the sewer. It wasn't pretty, but after 48 hours, everyone was packed in. There was no more time for personal affairs.

3.5 The Inhospitable Banks of the Amur

The crew's airfield was located only 25 kilometers (15.5 miles) from the border with Japan. They began assembling the aircraft delivered on the rail cargo platforms right on the spot. Then they immediately took to the air in order to thoroughly wrap up the training that had begun in Yeysk and, at the same time, explore the new flight area.

The crews began their usual work, assimilating to their new machines, polishing their piloting techniques, perfecting their bombing and aerial shooting at cones, and learning how to carry out reconnaissance by photographing different objects. An inspection conducted in September 1935 confirmed the 10th Squadron's high level of combat readiness.

Despite their preoccupation and distance from centers of urban civilization, the garrison personnel and all the residents of the military town were conscious of their involvement in what was happening in the country and around the world. The radio worked, and newspapers were delivered regularly. A portable film projector was often brought to Krasnaya Rechka, and on a screen stretched between two tall pine trees, the residents were able to see what important things were going on in the great country.

At the First All-Union Stakhanovite Conference, Stalin uttered his famous phrase, which immediately turned into a popular aphorism: "Life has become better, life has become merrier." As confirmation of the leader's words, the screen showed a continuous series of parades, sports competitions, national art, banquets in the Kremlin, and awards ceremonies for heroes of labor and defense. The wonderful melodies of Dunayevsky played, and the incomparable Lyubov Orlova, the main Soviet movie star, captivated everyone with her charm.

In early 1936, the country finally declared an end to the rationing system, so life had, in fact, improved.

The Soviet Union was building socialism and surrounded by enemies. The proximity of the dangerous enemy was felt with particular acuteness in the Far East, right next door to the territories of northern China and Korea, which had been captured by the aggressive Japanese.

M.N. Chibisov - commander of the Stankhovite echelon of 10th Naval Long-Range Brigade.

Starting from fall 1935, scramble aircraft that could be in the air in ten minutes were on alert round the clock at the Krasnaya Rechka airfield. Since Maxim's crew was considered the leading squad within the squadron and bore the honorary title of Stakhanovite, it was always the first one to take to the skies when there was a combat alert. It was also the first one tasked with flying complex routes for reconnaissance.

Their brigade was called the 10th Marine Long-Range Reconnaissance Squadron until late 1936, but in reality, it was unable to perform any strategic reconnaissance or even operational function, due to the performance of the MBR-2 seaplanes, primarily their insufficient range. The most they were capable of were short-range flights aimed at solving tactical objectives.

Squadron Commander Poplavsky felt there was no need to hide the deficiencies of the MBR-2 from his superiors. Somewhere, he had read a description of a real marine reconnaissance aircraft designed in the United States with amazing capabilities compared to the Soviet Chetvertak. The American twin-engine reconnaissance boat plane could reach speeds of 300 - 320 kilometers per hour (186 – 199 miles per hour) and had a flight range of approximately 4,000 kilometers (2,486 miles).

The pilots of the 10th Squadron couldn't even dream of such a machine. But they squeezed out everything they could from their beloved MBR-2 and even a little bit more.

The warm season eventually came to an end, and the squadron carefully prepared the equipment for use in winter conditions. This involved insulating the aircraft engines, applying a special lubricant to the control modules, and putting skis on the planes so they would be able to take off from the snow at the airfield or from the icy surface of a river until spring returned.

They prepared the residential facilities for the cold as best as they could. For families with small children, the relentless Far East winter was a particularly severe test. Things were also difficult for the patriarchs of the families—experienced young men. They were outside every day for long periods, even during the most severe frosts, when neither thermal coveralls nor fur boots could provide protection from the pervasive cold.

With each passing day, Stakhanovite Squad Commander Chibisov filled his flight book with more entries about the missions he had completed, which included introductory flights, control flights, and combat flights. There were also frequent so-called passenger flights in remote regions of the Far East, when military aviation would come to the aid of the public and assist civil airfields in conducting emergency operations. Some of his flight book entries are virtually indecipherable or unexplainable today. For instance, there was one long flight "for a special assignment" when Maxim spent nearly nine hours in the air.

There was a steady increase in the number of training flights in which the squad commander coached young people. He had to be ready to fly at any time, day and night. The specific skills needed to fly a plane with zero visibility were perfected in flights under the hood. In such a flight, the first pilot had his sight blocked by a hood made of fabric and flew the aircraft using only the instruments, while the second pilot pointed out his mistakes and was able to take the controls in emergency situations.

The days flew by as the aircraft practiced detachment formations for weeks and squadron formations for months. The weather changed outside the windows of the military town. The seasons passed by like a parade, and the battle formation came together in 1936.

Squad Commander Chibisov had spent a total of 207.5 hours in the air over the preceding year and, along with his fellow crew members, navigator T. Belikov and radio gunner V. Stefanov, managed to do so without a single accident.

While there were no accidents, there were a few close calls. Sometimes it seemed disaster was virtually inevitable, and the crew were saved only by their courage, resolve, and expertise.

Later in life, Maxim recalled one such episode:

> This all took place in the warm days of spring when our squadron of 19 aircraft took off from the water near the garrison's airfield at Krasnaya Rechka and began making our way to the summer camp. It seemed like a short distance to fly—approximately 100 kilometers (62 miles). After takeoff, the squadron assembled in the general combat formation and at an altitude of 1,000 meters (3,281 feet) headed in the direction of Yelabuga. We made it past the nearby area where the Amur and Ussuri rivers converge. And suddenly, after we had flown a considerable distance from this area, the motor in our MBR-2 abruptly stopped working. Not only that—the propeller became jammed. In this condition, a plane quickly loses altitude. The situation was exacerbated by the fact this occurred over terrain on which you couldn't land a flying boat. And we were already quite far from the Amur and Ussuri. There was no time to think. The radio gunner tried to contact the airfield. Nothing! ... The crew remained calm, but neither navigator Belikov nor radio gunner Stefanov could do anything to help. They were relying solely on me, the commander. I began to act. The first thing I did was switch the plane into gliding mode. I took a close look at the ground surface. No chance! Even

flat land promised to be a rough landing for us, and here the thick pointy treetops of the taiga forest that stretched all the way to the horizon were rolling by right under the belly of the fuselage. I estimated how far we had traveled from the water: it might be a little closer to the Amur than to the Ussuri, but it's basically the same distance. The altimeter wasn't working. I was calculating the clearance by eye and the angle of the plane's inclination. We'll try to make it, I thought. But making it wasn't all. We had to make our approach in such a way so as not to slam into the water, bury the nose of the plane and sink straight deep down to the bottom, but, rather, smoothly put the Chetvertak down on the surface. I remembered that the water surface in the Ussuri channel is better protected from wind. The channel, however, ran somewhat crosswise to our course, which could entail additional loss of altitude upon approach, but ... wait! I decided to heads towards the channel. From this moment on and throughout the entire descent, all my attention was focused on two things—the flight speed and the speed of descent. My crew was excellent, just a fantastic group of guys! Maximum stress, but no fussing or panic. And it was even more difficult for them than for me: at least I was occupied with something, while they were simply waiting for my actions and orders. Don't worry, we'll make it, I said! Only the ground was getting closer and closer. O Lord! Where did the channel vanish? Finally!

At the helm of MBR-2 seaplane.

Ahead a blue strip of water twinkled like silver against the backdrop of the green taiga carpet. This was the most difficult moment, requiring a clear head and nerves of steel. Suddenly I noticed that the channel, which was literally squeezed into the taiga, was moving further away. Instead, the sharp tops of the pine trees were approaching rapidly. I realized that this was an optical illusion: visibility became reduced as we descended and one got the impression that the loss of altitude was occurring more quickly than in actuality—at least 11 meters per second (36 feet per second). The thought flashed through my head: "How much gas is in the tank?" But then I immediately chased it away, "The plane has an almost full tank." I estimated the altitude—roughly 25 meters (82 feet). "Did I make an error in calculation?" I chased this thought away just as quickly. The ground was spreading out literally under our noses. But the plane was still in the air. It was only a matter of seconds now. At some point, I realized that our altitude had run out. Even though we were still over land, I had to try to get the plane into landing position. Just ahead I saw a clearing—that would be easier! No trees, not even a shrub. We were at a very low speed. But we were headed right towards the edge of the river bank. It was time! I pulled the diving rudder towards me. I made a smooth turn to the right. At some almost imperceptible moment, the plane lost speed and began to drop, skipping within only a few centimeters of the river bank edge, and we splashed down immediately. We started to brake. There could be no delay: there was a real threat of colliding with the opposite shore. I made a sharp turn to the right to avoid this. The machine was reluctant, but it obeyed. After noticeably losing speed, the plane began gliding along the channel. It seemed like we had made it! But what was that?! The plane continued to speed along, then got caught on something and turned around. Leaning out of the cockpit, I could see that there was a strong current in the channel. The plane wasn't able to withstand it and, with its wings getting caught on bushes on the banks, continued to move with the current. We eventually managed to firmly secure it with an anchor. That was it! We had arrived! We climbed out to where our feet could touch the ground! We rushed to each other on the shore and embraced. Belikov and Stefanov shouted, "Hurrah, our master of the wheel!" But … I was already thinking ahead, "How are we going to get out of here and drag out the Chetvertak?" That was all I could think about. And then suddenly, a miracle took place! A boat appeared in the channel as if out of a fairytale. It turned out the other planes had reported that we had fallen out of the formation, and people at the Krasnaya Rechka airfield had even been watching the final part of our emergency landing, at least until we were close to the ground and out of view beyond the trees. By this time, the command post had figured out that we weren't going to make it back and at best would only make it to the channel. Preparing for the worst, but hoping for the best, they sent out a boat to meet us. A few minutes later, the boat pulled away our plane on a cable and towed it to the airfield dock unscathed—not even the glider was damaged.

Upon returning to the airfield, they were met by Acting Brigade Commander P. Sanchuk. After listening to a brief report of the incident, he embraced the commander of the crew.

The next morning, an order from the commander of the Amur Flotilla, which at that time included the 10th Brigade of Naval Pilots, was read out to all the military personnel. In particular, the order stated, "For saving the plane and the crew as well as for the courage and skill he demonstrated under the extremely difficult circumstances of a forced landing, we express our gratitude to the squad commander of the 10th Squadron of the 10th Air Brigade of the Special Red Banner Far Eastern Army, M. N. Chibisov, and award him with a bicycle."

A present of this sort was highly valuable in those times, particularly since Maxim was fond of cycling and served as the 10th Squadron's representative during races held within the brigade.

Maxim calmly accepted the award and gratitude from the command. It was all pleasant, but it could not compare to the experience of learning what it was like to fall from the sky.

In August 1936, Maxim turned thirty. He still loved flying, but he realized he was needed more on the ground for his colleagues, subordinates, and students. At home, he had a wife and daughter waiting for him; he could not, nor did he have the right to, leave them without a husband and a father.

The commission assembled in the wake of the incident, which was mandatory in such situations, and quickly found the cause of the engine failure: damage to the crankshaft pin of the fourth cylinder. They concluded that all of the pilot's actions had been absolutely correct. That the pilot had managed to instantly find the only proper place to land seemed almost like a miracle. If the seaplane had made contact with the ground surface a fraction of a second earlier, it would have been a landing instead of a splashdown. Filled with fuel, the machine would have burst into flames, and there would have been no trace of the crew. Likewise, an extra second of delay after the splashdown would have caused the plane to slam into the bank on the opposite side of the channel. The result would have been the same: the destruction of the plane and death for the crew. Only one course of action had given them a chance to survive—precisely calculated actions made with lightning speed and pinpoint accuracy.

Squadron Commander Poplavsky continued to ask Maxim questions in the presence of the squadron commissar:

"How did you act when the engine stalled, Comrade Chibisov? Why did you decide to land on the channel?"

"I switched the plane to gliding mode almost immediately. Making a rough estimate based on the angle of its inclination, I determined how much longer we could remain in the air. It turned out that, while we may have been short on altitude, we had enough to make it to the channel. At approximately the same time, I decided that I would land the plane at a low speed with a turn to the right, which in general turned out well," Maxim replied.

"But why on the channel and not the Amur? Wasn't it closer?" he asked.

"If it was closer, it was only by a few meters. I remembered the weather conditions. The wind was rather strong that day—about fifteen meters per second. The water on the Amur is rough under such conditions, plus we would have been going against the current. What would it have been like to land in those conditions? Without any of the airfield equipment for landing? Also, given the need for technical assistance following the landing, the conditions would not have been any better there than in the channel," Maxim said.

"And you had time to think about all of this?" Poplavsky asked in bewilderment.

"I had to think about a lot of things all at once, Comrade Squadron Commander," he replied.

"Okay, okay! Let's suppose! And how did you manage to land the plane in an almost perpendicular manner in the channel? The width is no more than 30 meters."

"That was just it—it wasn't completely perpendicular. I already explained: with a turn to the right ..."

The conversation continued for a long time and ended with the meticulous squadron commander saying with particular warmth, "Good job, Chibisov! You are a true, well-seasoned pilot. I wish you good health and continued flying skills."

Belikov and Stefanov later told Maxim they had been summoned on that same day to the squadron commander, who

First Marshals of Soviet Union (left to right): M. N. Tukhachevsky, S.M. Budenny, K.E. Voroshilov, V. K. Blyukher and A.I. Yegorov, 1935.

simply told them without any ceremony, "You see here, boys! Keep close to your commander! During that ill-fated flight, he not only managed to keep the plane intact with his proper actions but saved your lives as well!"

The experience of an emergency landing of a seaplane in the Ussuri channel was then repeatedly reviewed during lessons conducted by Poplavsky with the squadron's flight and technical personnel. This experience was intended to help other pilots stay alive and safeguard aircraft in similar situations.

Meanwhile, a new engine was installed in Maxim's plane. After the machine was tested in the air, the squad commander flew to the summer camp, along with his navigator and radio gunner. The other crews had arrived earlier and were already actively engaged in combat training. Summer passed by unnoticed amid all the strenuous work.

At some point in late August, Poplavsky was unexpectedly replaced by A. Kravtsov. Perhaps this was connected to the inspection of the social structure of the troops, which had begun back in early 1935 "to prevent foreign elements from penetrating the Red Army." The new commander headed the squadron until the first half of October, when the squadron returned to its permanent place of deployment.

Following their flight navigation in 1936, the 10th Squadron received a score of "good." The detachment that included Maxim's squad received the same mark, while the squad itself not only received an "excellent" result but also confirmed its title of Stankhovite.

An order was issued toward the end of the year to change the number of their military unit. The new title was the 110th Aviation Brigade of the Far East Army, which soon became known as a short-range instead of a long-range brigade, a title more fitting for the true capabilities of the MBR-2 seaplanes.

In December 1936, Maxim Chibisov was appointed commander of the 2nd Squadron Detachment when his predecessor was promoted.

A detachment had much more equipment than a squad: six MBR-2 aircraft, which meant six crews, as well as a detachment engineer, mechanics for components and aircraft, and armorers. Everything—on the ground and in the air—had to work precisely and cohesively as a single mechanism. Maxim was given only three days for the new adjustment. This was more than enough time for the new commander to gain a thorough understanding of all the details of his division, all the way down to the condition of the uniforms of the pilots and military technicians.

People were important to Maxim. They weren't cogs in a machine; they were individuals. Having studied the individual features, strengths, and weaknesses of his subordinates, Maxim managed his detachment just as skillfully as he managed a combat vehicle in flight. He got to know his younger comrades and found a special approach for each of them. He was able to say the right things at the right time, whether to encourage, praise, correct, or even strongly scold his subordinates.

The detachment respected their commander and were proud of him. In informal settings, they called him by his first name and patronymic, and when he was not around, they affectionately referred to him as "our Max."

The year 1936 ended on a positive note for the Soviet Union and the USSR Armed Forces, as well as for Maxim Chibisov personally.

On December 5, 1936, the VIII All-Union Congress of Soviets adopted a new Constitution that was to guarantee Soviet citizens the most democratic governance, rights, and freedoms. Three weeks later, the residents of Krasnaya Rechka cheerfully rang in the New Year. They raised toasts to Comrade Stalin, to the Red Air Force, and to the new officer ranks (their restoration had begun in September 1935 with the presentation of marshal's stars to military commanders Kliment Voroshilov, Mikhail Tukhachevsky, Alexander Yegorov, Vasily Blyukher, and Semyon Budenny).

Another entry appeared in Maxim Chibisov's service record: "Assigned the rank 'Senior Lieutenant of Naval Aviation.'"

A new year, 1937, began, and everyone was confident it would be even better and happier than the previous year.

CHAPTER 4

Through Hardships to the Stars

4.1 Family Ttragedy

In early 1937, a severe illness took the life of two-year-old Alenka Chibisova. She came down with a cold in nursery school, where the negligent nannies decided to air out the room and took the children out for a walk but failed to notice that one little girl was still sleeping. They left her in the room with an open window. She woke up red-hot, threw off her blanket, and stood in the bed for a long time in nothing but a shirt. By the evening, Alenka was running a fever of 40^0 C. (104^0 F.).

There were no pediatricians in the local area. The young doctor in the military unit had only encountered the names of childhood diseases in textbooks. He was unable to provide a proper diagnosis (it turned out she was suffering from double pneumonia made even more complicated by a case of the measles, which had infected several other children from the nursery school at the time). Figuring the young girl was suffering from the common cold, the doctor suggested she would reach the crisis soon, after which her temperature would go down, and the illness would pass on its own. Her temperature never subsided, however, and ten days later, Alenka passed away just two weeks shy of her second birthday.

The relatives and friends of the Chibisov family maintained fond memories of the little girl. From all appearances, she was a gifted child, and she began speaking, singing, and dancing at an early age. When guests came over, she would stand on a stool and recite poetry without the slightest bit of shyness.

Overtaken with grief, Rosaly fell ill. She refused to eat and was categorically opposed to taking any medical advice. At night, she imagined her little daughter was standing in her bed and calling her mother's name, even though Maxim had given away the bed and all the child's things to neighbors so Rosaly would not have to see them.

She grew thin, and it became difficult to recognize the formerly cheerful and beautiful woman. After Maxim finally persuaded her to undergo a medical exam and x-ray, it turned out she had open tuberculosis.

Many are familiar with the healing properties of the Crimea. It's no coincidence that famous people, from members of the royal family to Anton Chekhov, have traveled there for treatment since ancient times. Wasting no time, Maxim obtained a ticket and sent his wife to a health resort in the Crimea.

She did not resist, for she knew firsthand about the dangers of tuberculosis: two of her older brothers, Vladimir and Boris, had died from the disease. Maxim felt that some time in her native home and with her mother, whom she had not seen in several years, would help the health resort doctors deal with her severe illness.

He was right. She returned to him in stronger shape and more cheerful spirits. The cavities in her lungs had cicatrized, but her emotional wounds would not heal for a long time.

Maxim tried as best as he could to provide his wife with care and attention. It was largely thanks to his efforts, patience, tact, and sensitivity that Rosaly managed to cope with her depression and find the desire to go on living. As usual, he did not show his feelings to anyone else. Only his wife knew the price he paid for his calm outward appearance.

Concealing his grief from strangers, Maxim suppressed it with endless work and dove headfirst into his official duties. He supervised flights, regularly inspected the readiness of his subordinates to fly in difficult conditions as part of his habits as an instructor, and also flew missions on his own both day and night.

4.2 Hardships and People

In February 1937, Senior Lieutenant Chibisov's detachment flew to the winter training camp for the first time.

In temperatures reaching -30^0 C. (-22^0 F.), they spent about a month in tents poorly heated by a potbelly stove. They had to sleep in their fur boots and overalls.

During flights, the MBR-2 cockpit was almost as cold as it was outside. The radio gunner and observer pilot in the nose of the plane were exposed to all the wind. Their fur overalls did not protect their faces and hands from frostbite. However, nobody in the detachment complained about the difficulties. In addition, none of the crew members became sick. Presumably, their fortitude boosted the defense mechanisms of their bodies beyond the maximum capabilities a person possesses under ordinary conditions.

By the end of the winter training period, the 2nd Detachment of the 10th Squadron was a strong, cohesive, hardened combat team capable of performing the most challenging missions. The airmen of the detachment were proud to be marine pilots and called themselves "naviators." This name, while not recorded in any official documents, expressed the true essence of the profession, which equally involves both the sky and the sea.

Maxim remembered everyone who served in the detachment by name for the rest of his life.

The subordinates who served under him also retained vivid memories of him as a strict and demanding commander, exacting mentor, and attentive and caring teacher. After many years, they continued to send warm, heartfelt letters in which they proudly recalled the months and years of their intense joint service.

Here is an example of one such letter:

> This is Navigator Pavel Filimonov, one of your former subordinates at Krasnaya Rechka. Perhaps you even remember me, as my fingers became frostbitten during cone shooting drills in an open cockpit. You were very concerned and rubbed my hands with snow. It's rare to encounter such sensitivity and attentiveness for people. We considered you a commander who should be emulated

in all respects. May you live as long as possible! January 1, 1983.

After receiving a reply to this letter, Pavel Filimonov corresponded with his former commander for several years and sent him touching poems filled with memories about serving at Krasnaya Rechka. The following is an excerpt from his poem "In the Far East":

> Our flight work eradicated carelessness
> And fiercely put an end to our flippancy.
> I recall friends who departed early for eternity—
> The ocean of air does not forgive mistakes.
> …
> We flew with oxygen and "shaved,"
> At nights, we "crawled" among the searchlights,
> We left for long-range flights,
> And swam in the clouds like in milk.

The detachment commander not only showed attention to his subordinates during service but also tried as best as he could to help them in their daily lives, and they highly appreciated this.

Soviet citizens lived very modest lives in the 1930s for the most part. Airmen, who were considered the elite members of the armed forces, received decent salaries by the standards of the time; however, their earnings melted away due to the high cost of living in the Far East.

The young men who served in Maxim's detachment found an easy way to make some extra money. On the days when they did not have to fly, they would unload flour from barges. This event, which was typical of the times, was also chronicled in Filimonov's poems:

> Taking a standard load on your shoulders from the hold,
> With a terrible creak and oncoming snickering,
> Carrying it as one thought eats away at you:
> When will these bags ever end?!
> Moving like a robot and covered in flour,
> You see only white shoes before you.
> But at least we did not drop bread crumbs,
> When we hurriedly ate our dinner.

Having exerted all our strength on unloading,
And received new stamina in the canteen,
We went to our homes and sweetly fell asleep.
The sky awaited us in the morning.

When going to these jobs, the pilots tried to cover their military uniforms with large raincoats. They were afraid of damaging their honor as naviators, the honor of their division, and the honor of their commander in front of strangers.

Another former colleague, Dmitry Khibin, wrote in a letter,

> Upon arrival in the city of Yeysk in 1936, where the Stalin Naval Pilot School was located, I was designated as a pilot in the 10th Aviation Squadron, in the detachment of the MBR-2 seaplanes. There I met with the air unit commander of this detachment, Maxim Chibisov. By that time, he was already an experienced, strong-willed and capable fighter, a thoughtful and sincere Commander Pilot. We, the youngsters, the youth of the ocean of air, from our first days of contact with our tall, fit and amiable Commander, felt a special respect and trust towards him. As young naviators training for the highly responsible duty of protecting the Far Eastern airspace, we broke in new types of land-based and sea-based fighter aircraft (R-5, Sh-2, MBR-2) both day and night with particular enthusiasm and pride for the great confidence shown in us. In everything we did, we followed the example of our senior comrades and, above all, Max Chibisov and Zhora Poplavsky. Following the military train to Khabarovsk, along with our Squad Commander Max Chibisov, we continued to knock together our young, boisterous and cheerful team of Far Eastern airmen over the course of 25 days while riding the rails. In everything we did, we always felt the strong, strict and friendly hand of our Max. On the uninhabited taiga banks of the Ussuri and the town of Krasnaya Rechka near Khabarovsk, our seaplane aviation group, armed with the MBR-2, worked tirelessly both day and night in difficult climatic, geographic and

living conditions on mastering flying techniques and the tactical use of the seaplane in the harsh Khabarovsk territory and the turbulent Far Eastern skies from the summer of 1935 to the fall of 1939. It was during this time that our combat training and great sense of camaraderie were continuously enhanced.

During those anxious, distant years, our Amur Red Banner Military Flotilla was commanded by the renowned naval commanders, Admirals Oktyabrsky and Golovko. Possessing special commander and human qualities, our Max rose very quickly—in the youthful eyes of this naviator, i.e. from 1935 to 1939—from air squad commander to air detachment commander and on to commander of the 117th Naval Aviation Regiment. I must say that, despite the considerable distance in our official positions, we—his subordinates—always continued to feel his father-like attention to us in everything we did as well as his caring involvement in our flight skills and our everyday lives. And it was not only Maxim—our Commander, our senior comrade—who enjoyed the great respect of the entire aircrew, but his feisty wife, Rosaly. We young pilots (Khibin, Morozov, Volodin, Zabrodin, Filimonov and others) would frequently gather in their cozy apartment for a cup of tea (always tea) and to listen to popular and our favorite records on the gramophone. We were fortunate in that during those years aviation was broadly developing and boldly taking off in terms of the emergence of new and more advanced fighter aircraft and weapons. This enabled us, naviators, along with our fighting comrades of the Red Army Air Force to actively learn and be victorious. Our beloved Commander and teacher, Max Chibisov, led the way in this regard as well as he skillfully taught his winged subordinates how to successfully master challenging types of piloting on the MBR-2 seaplanes and on ski-based and wheeled landing gear at any time of the day or night and how to operate seaplanes during year-round flights in the harsh Far Eastern skies. We successfully completed the program for the broad and complex combat use of types of military equipment that were entirely new to us without any minor damage let alone any "accidents." May 20, 1986.

4.3 Events of the Time

Rosalia Chibisova (third from the left) in a group of women - Voroshilov's Sharpshooters, 8ᵗʰ of March 1937.

These were immensely difficult, wonderful, and terrible times. It is impossible to unequivocally paint them in black or white tones.

The Soviet Union, which had become similar to one giant construction site, quickly took on the image of an advanced industrial superpower. The culture of the Soviet people was rapidly developing. Scientific discoveries were made, heroic deeds were performed, and world records were set.

Then there were the horrific atrocities committed by the authorities, which even surpassed the unforgettable madness of Ivan the Terrible in terms of their scale and brutality.

It was difficult to accept that such evil could be the work of human hands. To many people at the time, these deeds seemed like some sort of strange and terrifying disease that had engulfed the enormous body of the Soviet Union and filled the lives of a great number of Soviet people with sorrow and suffering. It was assumed at the time that the main focus of this disease was in Moscow, at the big building on Dzerzhinsky Square,[4] where a small man had established himself as boss after appearing out of nowhere.

Nikolai Yezhov was the people's commissar for internal affairs, and he managed an enormous staff of henchmen who spread death and pain among Soviet citizens. For this reason, the ailment that struck the Soviet Union at that time was called "the Yezhov terror."

Several decades later, a more correct term appeared: the Great Terror. After all, Yezhov was only one of the perpetrators of the evil deeds the authorities committed against the people.

In terms of the number of innocent victims killed, the year 1937 stands alongside the bloody years of the Civil War with their orgy of dekulakization. In terms of its tragic consequences for the country as a

---

[4]   The headquarters of the NKVD, the predecessor of the KGB.

whole, this year is unparalleled in the entire history of the Soviet Union. A mass of humanity was eliminated—shot, imprisoned, and ground into concentration camp dust—including the elite part of the mass needed to govern the state, develop the nation, and protect it from external enemies.

One can get a sense of the atmosphere in which Soviet officer Maxim Chibisov and his contemporaries—people of the 1930s—had to live and serve by looking back at the chronicle of events from that time. Here are a few episodes from that chronicle:

On March 17, 1937, the Soviet Union passed a law concerning peasants and collective farmers that effectively deprived them of the right to free movement.

On May 1, the first convoys of ships sailed along the Moscow-Volga Canal, which was built in record time.

On June 11, the press reported the USSR Prosecutor General had arrested several top Red Army officials: Mikhail Tukhachevsky, Iona Yakir, Ieronim Uborevich, Robert Eideman, Boris Feldman, August Kork, Vitaly Primakov, and Vitovt Putna.

On June 20, Valery Chkalov, Alexander Belyakov, and Georgy Baidukov made the world's first nonstop flight from Moscow over the North Pole to Portland, Oregon (USA). They flew 8,504 kilometers (5,284 miles) in 63 hours and 16 minutes on an ANT-25.

On July 2, the Central Committee of the All-Union Communist Party (of Bolsheviks) issued a directive on mass repressions against the "enemies of the people" (although these repressions had already been under way for several years). After eliminating the top Red Army commanders, they went after the people who had served with them, those who were acquainted with them, and even those who had tried them in court. In just two years—1937 and 1938—all of the military district commanders were replaced, in addition to 90% of their deputies, 80% of the top personnel of the corps and divisions, and 91% of the regiment commanders and their deputies.

On the eve of the war with Germany, of 899 senior military officers (including the first five Red Marshals), 643 were declared "enemies of the working people," and 583 of them were shot. The ground forces alone lacked 66,900 officers and were forced to call up reserve command personnel, who were nowhere close to meeting the requirements of the time in terms of their training and experience.

On July 12, Mikhail Gromov, Andrei Yumashev, and Sergei Danilin made a nonstop flight on an ANT-25 over the North Pole from Moscow to the United States, traveling 10,148 kilometers (6,306 miles) in 62 hours and 17 minutes.

On August 12, during a nonstop flight from Moscow to Fairbanks, Alaska (USA), over the North Pole, Sigizmund Levanevsky, one of seven pilots to earn the title Hero of the Soviet Union for rescuing the members of the Chelyuskin ship, disappeared without a trace. The search for the Soviet polar ace, which proved fruitless, turned into an international event; even pilot Hubert Wilkins became involved in the search in the American part of the Arctic with a PBY-1 flying boat that was purchased for him from the company Consolidated. This reconnaissance plane, which was ultramodern for the time, had caught the attention of Soviet specialists a year earlier. On April 9, 1937, the Soviet foreign trade organization in the United States, Amtorg, signed a contract with Consolidated on the acquisition of a license to produce similar aircraft in the Soviet Union.

On October 21, famous Soviet aircraft designer Andrei Tupolev was arrested. He was accused of wrecking Levanevsky's flight over the pole to America as well as spying for Germanyand was denounced as theleader of the Russian Fascist Party. In Butyrka Prison, this world-renowned scientist found himself in the company of former people's commissar for justice Nikolai Krylenko and the highly decorated Felix Ingaunis, who had commanded the air force of the Far East Army prior to his arrest.

In early 1938, the Great Terror subsided slightly. There was talk of excesses in the battle against "the enemy of the people." The Central Committee, with immodest publicity, passed a special resolution condemning the lawlessness in the NKVD. Some of the people who had been arrested were released from camps and prisons; however, most of them would soon find themselves behind bars again.

Then there was another high-profile trial, this time against the members of the Anti-Soviet Block of Rights and Trotskyites led by Nikolai Bukharin. This was followed by another wave of arrests, trials, and expedited sentences.

The final act of the Yezhov terror was the removal of Yezhov himself, who was dismissed as people's commissar for internal affairs and then arrested, convicted, and shot in early 1940. But even after Yezhov was declared an enemy of the people, the mass repressions continued (although not on the same scale as during the Great Terror years) right up until Stalin's death and the exposure of his cult of personality.

4.4 Officer Comrades

Trial of M.N. Tukhachevsky. Last photograph, June 11th 1937.

The conviction of a large group of top military officials led by Marshal Mikhail Tukhachevsky resulted in disastrous consequences for the USSR Armed Forces.

Tukhachevsky was an outstanding commander and military theorist. As first deputy people's commissar for defense, he actively promoted programs for upgrades to the armed forces with new military equipment so they could be prepared for the future war with fascist Germany, during which he believed—and he was far ahead of his time in this regard—the decisive role would be played by aviation, tanks, and mechanized formations.

According to the memoirs of Georgy Zhukov,

> [Kliment] Voroshilov, the people's commissar [for defense] at the time, was incompetent in this role. He remained a dilettante in military affairs until the end and never had a deep or serious understanding thereof … At that time, Tukhachevsky, who was a true military specialist, was responsible for a large portion of the work in the people's commissar. He had clashes with Voroshilov and hostile relations developed between them. Voroshilov disliked Tukhachevsky very much.

Tukhachevsky attempted to get Voroshilov dismissed and openly accused him of an inability to manage the defense agency. In the end, however, Stalin supported his old comrade, whose loyalty the leader did not doubt. By getting rid of Tukhachevsky and his associates, Stalin's incompetent appointees in charge of the Red Army essentially botched preparations for the war.

Following Tukhachevsky's conviction and execution, the repression flywheel in the army and the navy began spinning with unprecedented intensity. But this all had begun much earlier—when the state security services finished destroying what was left of the political opposition and, encouraged by the top party and government leaders to remain active, started searching for so-called "enemies of the people" among segments of society that were loyal to the regime, including the military.

Maxim's diaries contain an entry pertaining to the events of late 1936:

> In late October, major changes were made to the command staff in the 110th Brigade ... A large number of people from the command staff were appointed to serve in the NKVD agencies: political department chief K. Voinov, Squadron Commander Reneisky, Detachment Commander S. Puzanov (12 as), A. Glyadeiko (10 as), Intelligence Chief S. Chinkobadze and pilot A. Malyshev.

After this, there are no more comments at all about the fate of his colleagues who were taken "to serve" in the NKVD agencies (which actually meant arrest, generally followed by a conviction). Any speculation on such topics, even those contained in notes of a purely personal nature, could get the author of such notes killed under certain circumstances from which nobody was safe at that time.

Maxim's daughters recall his stories about how "arrests began at Krasnaya Rechka in 1937 among senior and mid-level commanders. Almost all of the leadership was essentially wiped out." He believed this was one of the reasons for his subsequent rapid promotion up the chain of command. At that sad time, he knew he could share the fate of his predecessors in positions of command. Some of his former colleagues who were victims of the repression yet miraculously survived told stories after they had been released about how they communicated in the prison cells by tapping on the walls to exchange news. One day, Chibisov's incarcerated colleagues had related "there was a rumor that Chibisov had been arrested. Thus, sitting in prison and understanding the situation, they had no doubt that he would be brought in sooner or later."

The entire officer corps was subject to the sweeping purge, from top to bottom. Every single military unit—from the regiment level up—was impacted by the repression of a commander, a political officer, a chief of staff, or all of them together.

What did the fellow officers themselves think about this situation? Did they really believe the security services did not make mistakes and were truly weeding out all the traitors and spies? Did they not understand the scale of the damage caused to the combat capabilities of the army and the navy?

Several decades later, when everything was open, disclosed, and permitted to be published, Maxim's daughter Elena asked her father to comment on an article written by Konstantin Simonov that claimed 78% of the armed forces command staff were subject to repressions during the years of the Great Terror. She asked Maxim if he was aware of what was going around him during that frightful time.

Major General Chibisov corrected Simonov's figures, saying, "It wasn't 78%, rather 90% ... My dear child, how could I not have known this? I lived at that time, this was my life, and that's the way it was."

He was aware of everything and kept this terrible knowledge to himself without letting it out—not in the 1930s, when any careless word could have resulted in disaster, and not later in life, when it became fully safe to expose the iniquity seen during the cult-of-personality era and even profitable for those willing to disclose its details.

At that time, though, in 1937, he was doing what he was supposed to do: serving the nation. He flew a lot and was a member of the squadron political bureau. He participated in the garrison activities and was actively involved in sports: cross-country skiing, cycling, and target shooting. He devoted a great deal of time to independent studies on general subjects since he was already thinking about entering the academy.

Back in ancient times before rifles existed, when armies went out into battlefields in tight ranks and columns, the ability to withstand fire was regarded as a particularly valuable combat quality. A good example of this can be found in *War and Peace*, in the description of one of the scenes from the Battle of Borodino, when Andrei Bolkonsky's regiment withstands artillery fire for several hours and loses a third of its men without having fired a single shot at the enemy. Each of the soldiers in this regiment sees the cannonballs and bombs turning the bodies of their comrades into a bloody mess and stands there expecting the same fate. Based on their dispositions, however, they have to remain in place and in combat formation without moving forward or backward. Fulfilling this task is much more difficult than simply rushing at the enemy lines using a bayonet attack.

In the same way, Maxim and his colleagues, along with the entire officer corps of the Soviet Union, found themselves "under fire" during the years of the Great Terror. They all witnessed the deaths of their comrades and knew their own downfall could come at any moment. There was no opportunity to step aside—each person had to maintain his position in the formation.

Only it was not the enemy shooting at them but, rather, their own. The agencies designed to protect the state and public acted as if they were run by fierce haters of the Soviet Union.

Maxim avoided the tragic fate to which several thousand commanders of the Soviet Armed Forces were subjected. One could say he was lucky. But there are also objective reasons for this good fortune.

During the first and most awful repressions against military officials, Senior Lieutenant Chibisov fell under the category of low-ranking officers who were sorted out during the general procedure according to their personnel files. In this regard, everything was as it should have been, including his social background, biography, and track record. He had no friends or patrons among the senior command staff; therefore, he was not considered a promising project for those who built up and untangled the imagined cases involving group conspiracies and betrayals. However, anything could have happened at that disastrous time: a denunciation by any ill-wisher or something else that could have attracted the attention of the enthusiasts from the state security services, who were capable of sculpting investigative storylines from nothing. But fate protected Maxim from unpleasant incidents during the most critical period of the military purges.

The officers who safely made it through these purges went on to have a good chance of survival. Many of them moved up the chain of command quickly.

Such was the fate of Maxim Chibisov. He did not actively aspire to attain higher ranks, but the circumstances spontaneously pushed him up the steps of the career ladder.

**[Small Pic illustration chapter05.tif, 42 mm h.
x 30mm v., Centered at top of page]**

CHAPTER 5

Major Maneuvers

5.1 Combat-like Conditions

In July 1937, a major war erupted in Eastern Asia. The Japanese Army seized Beijing, Tianjin, and several other major cities and quickly penetrated deep into inland China. The conquest plans and appetites of the rulers of the Land of the Rising Sun were not limited to Chinese territories. This was well understood in Moscow.

The Far Eastern group of Soviet forces was hastily fortified and replenished with men and equipment. In August 1937, the formations of the Special Red Banner Far Eastern Army and the Amur Flotilla conducted large-scale training exercises in conditions that were as close as possible to actual combat, during which the Soviet forces had to withstand the enemy as part of a full-scale military conflict.

According to the established procedure, Marshal Vasily Blyukher of the Special Red Banner Far Eastern Army was supposed to oversee the maneuvers; however, he was unable to do so because of circumstances related to his involvement in the disgraceful, farcical trial of Tukhachevsky, Yakir, Uborevich, and other prominent military commanders. As one of the members of the tribunal, Blyukher had become completely demoralized and virtually lost the ability to perform the duties of a commander, which came to light the next year—1938—during the famous Battle of Lake Khasan.[5]

The exercises were commanded by Major General Markian Popov, who would later go on to head the First Red Banner Army of the Far Eastern front and hold senior command positions on the fronts of World War II after 1941.

The training exercises covered a wide area from Blagoveshchensk to Khabarovsk. Senior Lieutenant Chibisov's squadron conducted reconnaissance during the exercises and was in charge of locating the imaginary enemy's troops and military equipment on land and its fleet on the rivers. Maxim later recalled the exercises:

Major General M.M. Popov. 1941.

The conditions for performing the missions were extremely unfavorable. For instance, the

---

[5]   Marshal Vasily Blyukher, a hero of the Civil War, had commanded the Special Far Eastern Red Army since 1929. He became famous for his successful offensive actions during the Sino-Soviet conflict on the Manchurian Chinese Eastern Railway, where Soviet troops used tanks in battle for the first time. However, during battles near Lake Khasan in July–August 1938, he demonstrated an unusual level of indecision and an inability to lead the troops.

At the beginning of the conflict, he sent a panicked telegram to Moscow, demanding the prosecution of the border detachment chief for advancing their positions three meters beyond the Soviet border, which allegedly triggered a conflict. When the Japanese occupied the elevated points of Zaozernaya and Bezymyannaya, there was a long delay in the army's response, which proved to be ineffective. At the insistence of a commission sent from Moscow (headed by SFERA Main Political Department Chief L. Mekhlis with Lavrenty Beria also being a member), actual command over final stages of the operation was transferred to SFERA Chief of Staff G. Shtern, who managed to expel the Japanese from their positions. The Soviet losses from this operation were twice that of the opponent. Following an investigation of the incident, Blyukher was charged with sabotage, espionage, and conducting a military-Fascist conspiracy. He pleaded innocent. In November 1938, he died during interrogation at Lefortovo Prison. In March 1939, he was retroactively stripped of his title as marshal and sentenced to death.

basing site in the channel ... was not at all prepared to receive the squadron. Once I got the squadron in the air, though, I led it to the designated ... place. We landed fine and prepared to begin the combat operation. But we immediately realized that we would have to do this in primitive conditions. The improvised air field was lacking the most basic equipment. Not only were there no boats, there were no floating crafts of any kind. There were no buildings and there weren't even any regular army tents. The crews had to sleep in the planes. The weather also added complications. Rain and fog had followed us in. The land-based air fields with natural cover were out commission, so the entire burden fell on the seaplanes.

The squadron's zone of action was the vast territory running along the Amur near the area where the Sungari River flows in from the Chinese side. The Japanese had based substantial forces from its river fleet in the waters of Sungari, from which point it was easy for its combat boats to enter the Amur. For this reason, there was a high probability that all types of provocations could be expected in this area since the Soviet forces were occupied with combat training and the Japanese commanders might be tempted to take advantage of the opportunity to test the nerves of their northern neighbors, as they often did at that time. Therefore, the reconnaissance pilots under Maxim's command had to not only monitor the actions of the imaginary enemy but also keep an eye on the other side of the Amur, where a very real enemy was stationed.

Summarizing the results of the training exercises during a meeting at headquarters, Major General Popov cited Senior Lieutenant Chibisov's squad as one of the units that distinguished itself and rated its actions as "excellent."

The commanders expressed gratitude to the squad, and several flight crews were awarded with gifts. Maxim was given a particularly valuable gift: a double-barreled shotgun produced at the famous Tula Arms Plant.

The following entry appeared in Senior Lieutenant Chibisov's personal file:

> Good combat training, satisfactory knowledge of aircraft hardware and engine. Knows flight theory well.

Respected among his subordinates. Disciplined. Tactful. Has no flight accidents or breakages. His squadron has two forced landings and one minor breakage caused by technical personnel. His squadron flies day and night.

In late October, the flight navigation results were reviewed at a meeting of the 10th Squadron's command staff attended by 10th Air Brigade Commander P. Sanchuk. Once all the achievements were marked, the shortcomings were identified, the objectives were set, and the goals were defined, the air brigade commander read out a degree from the People's Commissar for the Navy dated October 20, 1937, on the appointment of Senior Lieutenant Chibisov as commander of the 12th Squadron. This post turned out to be vacant following the departure of Lieutenant Colonel G. Repeysky.

According to Maxim's memoirs,

> he did not expect a promotion. But when ... his name was read out with the appointment to the post of commander of the 12th Air Squadron in the same brigade, he felt a pleasant rush of blood to his face and, while trying to contain his inner excitement, approached the table where Air Brigade Commander Sanchuk, the chief of staff and the political officer were sitting ... Everyone at the table stood up, warmly congratulated him on his new appointment, and wished him continued success.

5.2 A Special Mission

Nobody was surprised that a senior lieutenant had been appointed to replace the lieutenant colonel as commander of the 12th Squadron. Such were the times: yesterday's company leaders were forced to take command of regiments, and the regiment commanders who survived the purges became army commanders.

Taking over the position of lieutenant colonel (or, at the very least, major), the senior lieutenant took on an enormous amount of work. Brigade Commander Sanchuk ordered him to take command of the squadron in two days.

As was his habit, Maxim thoroughly scrutinized the minute details of the resources entrusted to him. Everything required careful supervision—both the aircraft and the people who flew the planes.

It was the people that had the highest priority above all. It was imperative to demand from them the highest performance of their full range of professional skills, from piloting skills to military bearing and using a sidearm. They had to be provided with decent living conditions to the extent circumstances allowed. Squadron Commander Chibisov was just as thoroughly involved in the lives of his subordinates as he was in the technical condition of the fighting machines in his squadron. Here is a portion of his diary dating from that time: "The detachment commanders report on the quartering conditions of the military personnel. The detachment commanders and the service directors report on the condition of families and their requests … The club director reports on the condition of the club's work."

Among other things, it was time to urgently start preparing the squadron equipment for winter conditions. Headquarters had warned that it would be necessary to move to a new base after the first snow. The families would remain at Krasnaya Rechka. The restationing was to begin on December 12.

Squadron Commander Chibisov informed his subordinates of their orders:

> There is little time before departure and much to do. Therefore, each person must plan their time in a way so as to gather everything needed for the journey without ruffle or excitement: personal things for yourself and the most common parts for the machines. Take into account that the trip could last until spring. Over the remaining time, the planes need to be flown and piloting technique needs to be practiced. Remember that the flight will be difficult and long … Don't forget to provide your families with everything they need. If you need help, talk to the detachment commanders. They will contact me if necessary. Any talk of re-stationing outside of the air field is categorically prohibited. Warn your family about this.

The next three days were tense. The squadron commander began each morning by listening to reports on preparations for departure. He then had to resolve a number of organizational issues, lead training flights, and fly around in his own plane as well. On the eve of departure, November 11, Maxim gathered the staff officers, detachment commanders, and support service directors. After making certain the squadron was fully prepared based on the reports, he declared, "The flight procedure is as follows: we take off in units with an interval of 1 hour 20 minutes and follow the route Krasnaya Rechka-Sofiysk. This is the first phase.

"You will learn the route of the second phase in Sofiysk, where refueling will take place. The first unit will take off at 8:00 a.m. and the second at 9:20 a.m. I will assume the flagman position ahead of the first unit."

They flew at an altitude of 2,000 meters (6,562 feet) for more than four hours to Sofiysk. The weather was good, and the radio connection with the takeoff and landing airfields was stable. They began their descent once they approached Sofiysk. Maxim's flagman plane landed first and was followed by the others.

During refueling, the navigator arrived with the weather report. A vast cyclone with strong winds and heavy snow stood in the path of their flight route. Maxim quickly gathered the flight crew, announced that the squadron was flying to Nikolayevsk-on-Amur, and asked them to open their flight charts and carefully study the area over which they were preparing to fly.

> Judging from the weather report, the upcoming flight will be made in conditions of extremely poor visibility. We will have to fly along the banks of the Amur, which is surrounded by hills. Towards the end of the route, the river makes a sharp turn: in order to follow it, we will have to make a turn at a 65–70 degree angle. Be careful here—you must stay alert! Because by taking this course we will commence approach within 20–30 minutes. We will encounter other dangerous areas on the road as well. Therefore we will split up now so that each crew, first of all, can carefully calculate the flight distance and time between these points and, secondly, determine whether it's worth flying in such weather. Assemble by my plane. I'll give you ten minutes to think about it.

The commander was supposed to make the final decision himself. For him, however, it was crucial that all of his subordinates clearly have an idea of what to expect on the flight and what actions they would have to be prepared to take in advance. At the designated time, everyone once again approached the flagship plane. The general consensus was to fly.

The squadron commander said as he looked toward the runway,

> Okay then. The planes are fueled. The takeoff and flight formation remains the same. Upon arrival in Nikolayevsk, I will be the first to land. Then the units led by their commanders will land. Prepare for a landing in difficult conditions. Pay close attention to the accuracy of your calculations and a good landing profile. Do not linger on the runway after landing. Don't forget that other crews are coming in to land after you. Any questions? No? To the planes!

Maxim did not leave a description of the subsequent flight in his diaries. He limited himself to praise of the weather service for providing accurate information. He also noted that all the crews fulfilled the flight to and the landing in Nikolayevsk "correctly and without any trouble."

The flight of the 2nd Detachment was not as smooth.

The commander of this detachment was F. Koptev, who had followed Maxim's steps up the career ladder. At one time, they commanded squads in a single detachment, which was later headed by Chibisov with Koptev being bypassed. Then one of them became a squadron commander, while the other was once again close behind, having been appointed detachment commander.

Following the always-one-step-ahead Maxim, Koptev led the 2nd Second Detachment to Sofiysk not quite as smoothly but safely, and his detachment refueled there. After receiving the unfavorable weather report, the commander decided to postpone departure until morning. But the cyclone intensified during the night. After taking off with his detachment in the morning, Koptev should have returned to Sofiysk after assessing the risks of the flight, but he decided to push through anyway. One can only imagine the concern felt by Squadron Commander Chibisov in Nikolayevsk when he learned of Koptev's takeoff from a radio report and realized that half his squadron was in a dangerous situation.

The squadron commander's mind was put at ease only once the aircraft of the 2nd Detachment appeared out of the dense clouds over Nikolayevsk. All six planes landed on the ice one after another. But troubles also occurred, as Squad Commander Vinogradov made a blunder: he was unable to even out his Chetvertak upon landing, and his right landing ski broke as a result.

On the whole, the squadron's flight to the new base ended successfully.

The aviation unit, which had been urgently redeployed to the lowlands of the Amur, was to complete a mission that went beyond the scope of the normal training exercises. This is how Maxim described it in his later memoirs:

> During those years, the Japanese militarists were constantly staging provocations on our Eastern borders. There were incidents both on land and at sea. One such incident occurred in the Strait of Tartary. In late October 1937, the Japanese cruiser Yubari crossed the Soviet border and, stopping across from the village of De-Kastri near a naval base, turned its turret guns towards the village. The coastguard signaled to them: "You have entered Soviet territorial waters and must leave immediately." The cruiser responded by raising a flag that means "I don't understand" in international maritime language. This "misunderstanding" lasted for several weeks. The Soviet command decided to deploy a squadron of fighter planes from Vladivostok to De-Kastri once winter navigation became possible (once the ice froze at the Krasnaya Rechka airfield) and relocated our 12th Squadron of seaplanes to Nikolayevsk, which was a two-hour flight from the events, as reinforcement for the fighters. As soon as the Soviet aircraft began flying over the Japanese cruiser from all different directions, the Japanese immediately "understood" and decided to go home.

Japanese ultra light cruiser Yubari, sunk by U.S. submarine Bluegil near Palau in 1944.

Heavy snowstorms had cut Nikolayevsk-on-Amur off from the rest of the world. The snowdrifts reached heights of 1.5 (4.9 feet) to 2 meters (6.6 feet).

The snow drifted so much that two-story homes and telegraph poles were hardly visible. The dormitory that housed the pilots was located just more than two kilometers from the airfield. This distance proved to be impassable for vehicles. Each day, regardless of the weather, the pilots waded to their planes through the trenches and paths burrowed in the deep snow in their heavy, bulky flight gear, using their flight maps to find their way. The standby crews were dealt the worst hand: awoken by the alarm, they had to traverse this path in a hurry. However, the young men, led by the 30-year-old squadron commander, proved to be stronger than the -40⁰ C. (-40⁰ F.) temperatures and torrid winds. In fur jumpsuits movement difficult, massive boots, and fur mittens, they rushed to the planes in order to manually heat the Chetvertaks and soar off into the skies, which changed constantly at that time of year.

The standard for flight readiness upon combat alert was strict under all weather conditions: 15 minutes for the standby crew and 45 minutes for all the rest. It was impossible to start frozen engines in this short time. The pilots would pour six to eight buckets of hot water into the fillers of the planes' coolant systems in order to heat them up quickly. This was performed with the use of a simple arrangement: a drum built into a boiler that was heated around the clock with coal or wood. If necessary, this contraption was dragged out to the plane on special skis and then returned to its special place after the engine was started.

Based at Nikolayevsk-on-Amur for about three months, the 12th Squadron patrolled the airspace over the Strait of Tartary and Sakhalin in some of the most difficult weather conditions imaginable. Over the course of such arduous practice, the professional skills of the squadron's flight and technical personnel improved immensely. They gained highly valuable experience in rapid relocation and prolonged service in the field.

In late March, the squadron commander received a ciphertext from the commander with an order: return to the main airfield base in three days, on March 25.

They returned to Krasnaya Rechka in the same formation in which they had flown to Nikolayevsk: two detachments, with a refueling stop in Sofiysk. Maxim once again flew as the flagship. The weather conditions were pleasant on the first leg of the flight, but then a strong headwind began gusting when they took off from Sofiysk. This was followed by dense clouds. On orders from the commander, the planes descended to 1,000 (3,281 feet) to 1,500 meters (4,922 feet) and made their way to Krasnaya Rechka along the lower edge of the clouds. At the end of the flight, they saw the sun peeking through the stratocumulus clouds, and the rain stopped.

The squadron commander gave the command to get in formation for a victory lap over their native airfield, and then he landed first. From the air, the pilots could see that nearly half the village had come out to greet them. The women and children looked toward the skies and waved. Brigade Commander Sanchuk observed the squadron's arrival from the airfield command post. After the planes had landed and he heard Squadron Commander Chibisov's report, he said, "Good going! And you landed nicely!"

Upon hearing the command "At ease!" the crew members parted and walked through the airfield, glad to be returning to their homes and families.

The squadron crew were given the next day off. After that, they all returned to work as if going to a parade: in their brand-new naval air force uniforms and in an upbeat mood.

The commanders assessed the squadron's performance in the winter conditions as "excellent." According to his later memories, Maxim was satisfied at the time that he had been able to handle the role of squadron commander. The commanders were of the same opinion. In late March 1938, another evaluation document was added to Naval Air Force Senior Lieutenant Maxim Chibisov's personal file: "Handles the work of air squadron commander well. Over a short period, he managed to get the air squadron through the conditions of the north. He fully meets the requirements for air squadron commander. 110th Special Air Brigade Commander Sanchuk."

Not long after this, Maxim wrote in his own diary:

> In late March, Brigade Commander P. Sanchuk received a new appointment in the security agencies, and the brigade was temporarily put under the leadership of Major M. Selivanovsky, who was in charge of the brigade until April 10. Colonel Sanchuk's departure somehow left the flight personnel gloomy since people had already

grown accustomed to him even though he had only commanded the brigade for a very short time. Everyone was speculating: who would be appointed commander, and would he come from within or be sent from another unit?

5.3 Vertical Rise

The winter maneuvers of the 12th Squadron received due recognition not only at the brigade level but also in the circles of the top brass.

The incident in the Bay of De-Kastri had been a blatant and deliberately planned provocation, along with others, through which the Soviets' Japanese neighbors were probing the vulnerabilities in the defense of the Far Eastern borders of the Soviet Union.

A cruiser is no fishing boat. The intrusion of such a ship into another nation's territorial waters creates a situation that, in the language of international law, is referred to as casus belli, or a justification for war. Soviet leaders, however, were primarily concerned about the worsening situation in Europe and, at the time, were trying to avoid a military conflict with Japan. But that was exactly what the Japanese commanders were counting on.

The Japanese had chosen the most appropriate place for a provocation: a bay, which was easy for ships to approach. The Pacific Fleet had an auxiliary base there, but the territory around that section of the coast was underdeveloped and had no reliable land-based connection with the main centers of the Primorye and Khabarovsk regions.

In the bay, a sort of rehearsal was held for one of the scenarios of an invasion of Soviet territory by Japanese troops. This scenario presumably involved troops storming the shore, securing a convenient bridgehead from which an offensive could be further developed, and meeting up with the Kwantung Army, which at that time would storm the Soviet defensive lines on the Amur and Ussuri.

Based on the Soviet response to the impudent actions of the Yubari cruiser at the hypothetical landing site of the invading army, the Japanese naval commanders were supposed to assess their chances for success in such a situation.

The response to the provocation was somewhat delayed but was effective.

The command of the Amur Flotilla, whose zone of responsibility included the coast along the Bay of De-Kastri, had no ships at their disposal capable of matching the cruiser's firepower. They could have requested assistance from the Pacific Fleet (to which the flotilla was operationally subordinate) and had two or three powerful naval ships sent from Vladivostok. The flotilla commanders, however, decided to make do with their own forces and mobilized aviation. The maneuvers of the 12th Squadron let the Japanese know they were prepared to meet the enemy on the sparsely populated coast with all the hallmarks of Russian hospitality.

The successful experience gained from using aircraft to simulate combat against the naval forces of a potential enemy, which mimicked the actions of a bridgehead being seized on Soviet territory, was probably actively discussed among navy officials. The Amur Flotilla staff were proud of the successful operation. The command of the Pacific Fleet were also satisfied: thanks to the pilots, they did not have to deploy heavy ships to De-Kastri and break up the fleet's forces that had assembled near Vladivostok.

The top naval commanders had become familiar with the name of Squadron Commander and Senior Lieutenant Chibisov. Meanwhile, Maxim was giving serious thought to furthering his education at that time.

He heard that a Maritime Department had opened at the Voroshilov Naval Academy in Leningrad. After making some inquiries, he realized the department was almost an ideal fit for him. Training was conducted in strict accordance with his military specialization. The length of studies was acceptable: three years and three months. Of course, they primarily accepted regiment and brigade commanders, but they might take a squadron commander as an exception. What could be better than living and studying in Leningrad, a city that was wonderful in all respects?

Maxim submitted a report to Amur Flotilla Commander Filipp Oktyabrsky with a request to be sent to Leningrad for studies.

He dreamed of studying in Leningrad,

Admiral F.S. Oktyabrsky, 1939.

but he had to put that dream on hold. One day the 12th Squadron received an unexpected visit from Amur Flotilla Commander Filipp Oktyabrsky himself, accompanied by acting Brigade Commander Selivanovsky.

Squadron Commander Chibisov,

> upon seeing the car approach and the flotilla commander get out, immediately went to meet the commander and reported, "Comrade Commander, the flight crew of the 12th Squadron is preparing aircraft for flight navigation as planned. Senior Lieutenant Chibisov reporting."
>
> After listening to the report, the commander asked where they could sit down and speak in private. Maxim invited him to an office area and they sat down for a talk. The commander began the conversation with questions about how the winter navigation had proceeded in Nikolayevsk-on-Amur and about the morale and health of the personnel. Maxim answered each question calmly and confidently. The commander appeared to be happy with the squadron commander's report. He expressed gratitude to the squadron personnel for their hard work in Nikolayevsk-on-Amur. Oktyabrsky reported that Colonel Sanchuk had departed, therefore the issue of appointing a new commander of the 110th Aviation Brigade had been raised. During their discussions, the flotilla commanders had settled on Maxim as the top candidate and wanted to appoint him commander of the 110th Aviation Brigade. He said they had come to deliver this proposal and asked how Maxim felt about it.

After listening to everything and briefly pondering the situation, Maxim began to decline, citing the fact that he was not prepared for such a position, but Oktyabrsky insisted. Maxim remained unconvinced. Then the flotilla commander "said with a more imposing tone, 'Think more carefully about it until the morning, and then call me by phone at my office in the morning.'"

Following a sleepless night, Maxim firmly decided it would be better for him to remain in his squadron. He called the Amur Flotilla commander and informed him of his decision. Oktyabrsky was displeased and replied "in the form of an order: 'within three days take command of the 110th Aviation Brigade and on the fourth day report on the performance of this order!' Maxim could only reply in one way: 'Yes, Comrade Commander. I shall take command of the 110th Aviation Brigade!'"

Filipp Oktyabrsky, a talented naval officer from the younger generation like Chibisov, had taken over the Amur Flotilla in February 1938, replacing I. Kadatsky-Rudnev, who had "departed" along with a large group of senior commanders.[6] At the time of Oktyabrsky's appointment, the flotilla was drastically lacking in senior personnel. In addition, Major Selivanovsky, who had replaced Sanchuk, was given a promotion—one must assume to replace another one of the departed. The entire Pacific Fleet endured enormous losses of personnel.

With two Pacific Fleet commanders falling victim to the repressions[7] one after the other, the fleet was taken over by Nikolai Kuznetsov. He quickly gained credibility among the sailors and naval pilots as an outstanding leader and a good person who was firm and did not bend, even before the top brass. Despite all the difficulties with the troop situation at the time and all the might of the state security agencies, Kuznetsov was not afraid to protect his subordinates from tyranny. Such was the case with Captain E. Chernoshchek, who was arrested on trumped-up charges. Kuznetsov interceded on his behalf and secured his release.

Admiral N.G. Kuznetsov, 1938.

---

[6]   Ivan Kadatsky-Rudnev, a first-rank flag officer and the commander of the Amur Flotilla, was arrested in 1938.

[7]   From 1932 to 1937, the Pacific Fleet was commanded by first-rank flag officer Mikhail Viktorov. In 1937, he was appointed commander of the USSR Navy in place of the arrested V. Orlov. By late 1937, 1,400 of Viktorov's subordinates had been dismissed as part of purges (many of them were repressed). Viktorov himself was arrested in April 1938, convicted, and executed in August of the same year. G. Kireyev was appointed to replace him as Pacific Fleet commander. In January 1938, however, he too was arrested, and he was convicted and executed in July 1938.

Chernoshchek was an assistant to the Pacific Fleet's head of operational staff. If Admiral Kuznetsov had not intervened, the officer's arrest could have been followed by arrests among his colleagues. The greatest threat was faced by Operational Staff Chief M. Klemensky, who could easily have been suspected of "harboring an enemy of the people" and then "organizing a criminal group." This would have resulted in a chain reaction affecting all the new persons named. By protecting Chernoshchek, Kuznetsov prevented another large-scale extermination of Pacific Fleet personnel. This story evoked a broad reaction among Navy officers.

One of Kuznetsov's most active supporters was Filipp Oktyabrsky, who had to restore the command structures of the Amur Flotilla, which had been depleted by the mass arrests. In appointing Senior Lieutenant Chibisov head of the aviation brigade, Oktyabrsky had to secure the support of the Pacific Fleet command. Admiral Kuznestov, who was barely 34 years old at the time, was not afraid of entrusting the aviation forces to the 32-year-old squadron commander, who had managed to excel in performing complex assignments.

The decision adopted by Oktyabrsky and approved by Kuznetsov was not subject to cancellation because of Chibisov's initial rejection of the position of aviation brigade commander. To accept the new appointment served him favorably since it meant he was not a careerist, that he had a very responsible attitude toward service, and that he did not have a superiority complex.

The newly appointed brigade commander was only a senior lieutenant, a rank that was highly inappropriate for the commander of a major aviation unit. This discrepancy had to be fixed. The Amur Flotilla commander issued a nomination for a promotion in military rank, and the Pacific Fleet command signed it. Senior Lieutenant Maxim Chibisov was officially appointed brigade commander and assigned the extraordinary title of captain by an order on the 110th Naval Aviation Brigade. The order was read out to the personnel at a dress parade. The new commander was given a report by the headquarters chief and Senior Lieutenant Sharko.

CHAPTER 6

The Naval Aviators Take on the Enemy

6.1 Regiment Commander

Captain Chibisov became burdened with new worries. Commanding a squadron was an anxious job by itself, let alone a brigade that included three squadrons (the 10th, 12th and 16th) plus the 69th Special Aviation Unit with an entire special group of observer pilots stationed at a distance from the main divisions – at the airfield and village of Sofiysk instead of at Krasnaya Rechka.

However, Maxim was not a brigade commander for long, just a week and a half. His position was then renamed the commander of the 117th Aviation Regiment. This was not a demotion but the result of the restructuring of the Pacific Fleet Air Force carried out by Nikolai Kuznetsov.

The Pacific Fleet commander decided to turn all the naval air brigades into regiments, making the formations less bulky and more flexible in terms of management while preserving their combat strength. Chibisov approved of the Pacific Fleet commander's innovations and believed they would be beneficial.

Meanwhile, the memorable spring of 1938 brought Maxim more than career success. Less than a month after he was assigned the rank of captain, the following entry appeared in his diary: "May 13, 1938 was one of the happiest days of our lives. Rosochka and I had a daughter, Emma, who we had been waiting for so anxiously here in Krasnaya Rechka after the tragic death of Alenka. It's hard to convey how this event has inspired me and how much strength and energy it has given me!"

He would need a lot of strength and energy. Reorganizing the brigade into a regiment turned out to be a difficult task. The regiment included 60 combat vehicles, just as the brigade previously had. The 69th Special Aviation Unit was the only one that did not undergo any significant changes. The rest of the structure changed dramatically, taking into account the experience of the aerial battles in which the Soviet pilots had participated in China as well as in Spain, where Kuznetsov had been a military adviser to the Spanish government.

Under the new manning table, there were four squadrons instead of three. Thanks to this arrangement, a regiment commander had greater ability to maneuver his units during combat and reconnaissance missions. Each squadron consisted of two squads instead of the previous three. This was exactly the number needed for the continuous shift work of the squadron—the main tactical unit—within the sector of airspace under its control. There were fewer units in the squadron, but this number could be increased at any moment through the reassignment of reserve crews. Along with the reforms of the combat divisions, the organization and work of the support services also changed.

When practicing combat formation flying with the squads and squadron, Maxim spared neither himself nor the others. He not only commanded his regiment, which was his primary duty, but also flew constantly, showing the others how to perform combat missions by example.

Evidence of this can be found in his flight log. Captain Chibisov's personal flying time for the year was 172 hours and 11 minutes. The training missions he performed included bombing, aerial shooting, flights within squadrons, under-the-hood flights, managing the formation by radio, route flights, an air assault raid, an enemy reconnaissance flight, the bombing of moving targets, and high-altitude flights. Wearing an oxygen mask on a badly outdated Chetvertak, under the hood and for combat purposes, Captain Chibisov flew up to an altitude of 5,500 meters (18,046 feet), which at that time was a significant result that few naval aviators had achieved.

Measuring themselves against their commander, the pilots of the 117th Aviation Regiment tried to achieve the highest possible results throughout the combat training program.

Of course, there were also a few emergency situations, which usually resulted from the human factor. Maxim remembered once such instance well and, later, frequently used it as evidence of the certain truth that in aviation, each little detail is important and requires attention.

Yeliseyev, the navigator for the crew of pilot Dobranchuk, had carelessly packed his parachute, which exploded out of the pack following a powerful gust of wind during the flight. The parachute immediately filled up with air and pulled the navigator out of the cockpit, but instead of carrying him away from the plane, it got caught on the aircraft. The plane lost speed, fell into a tailspin, and flopped down onto the ground from a height of 200 meters (656 feet). The plane burst into pieces, with no chance of being restored. Thanks to their incredible luck, the crew managed to survive, but all, including the negligent navigator, received such serious injuries that their flying careers were over for good. The incident prompted Maxim to devote even more attention to strengthening discipline.

As a result of the hard work of the commander and his subordinates, the 117th Aviation Regiment turned into a model military unit with a high level of combat capability.

6.2 Major Meeting in Moscow

Comrade Stalin was known as a man who respected the military but feared them as a united, organized force. When his fear of the men in uniform became particularly acute, he subjected them to reprisals, but sometimes he intentionally humiliated them, appointing commanders from among his trusted backbiters, who were incompetent in the affairs over which they were put in charge. Then, when the Stalin-sponsored appointees discredited themselves and the fair name of the leader, he would get out of the way of the outstanding military professionals and allow them to triumph over the military officials who were in over their heads, causing more harm than good. Seduced by the leader's supreme trust, the military people once again began to freely express their professional talents, until the next episode of Stalin's maniacal suspicion ensued.

In December 1937, following a round of brutal purges, the Navy was put under the control of the newly established People's Commissariat for the Navy,[8] which was headed by people who had little knowledge about

---

[8] The People's Commissariat of the Navy, established on the core of the Navy Office of the Red Army under the People's Commissariat for Defense, existed from

naval affairs and were zealous seekers of so-called "enemies of the people", including political officer and first-rank army commissar Pyotr Smirnov (who told Pacific Fleet Commander Kuznetsov immediately upon arriving at the train station, "I have come to bring order and clean the navy of enemies of the people") and, following his resignation (and disappearance in February 1939), chekist Mikhail Frinovsky, a protégé of the People's Commissariat of Interior Affairs under Nikolai Yezhov.

N.I. Yezhov and M.P. Frinovsky, May 1938. Major perpetrators of the Great Terror in the USSR in 1936-1938. Both arrested in April 1939 for 'participation in conspiracy in NKVD' and shot on 4th of February 1940.

On account of his status and personal qualities, Kuznetsov was the only real leader for the navy men, who could not help but resent the work being carried out by the amateur commissariat officials whose sole concern was seeking out the supposed "enemies of the people" in the navy.

In December 1938, Yezhov was quietly relieved of his duties as people's commissar of interior affairs before disappearing into the bowels of the Sukhanovo prison of the NKVD.[9] Frinovsky's position was no longer as strong as it had previously been, and Kuznetsov was aware of this. Stationed in Vladivostok, he received information from the headquarters in Moscow. Stalin's attitude toward the Pacific Fleet commander was favorable or at least appeared to be. At the Eighteenth Congress of the All-Union Communist Party in March 1939, Kuznetsov was given the right to express sincere support on behalf of all Soviet naval officers for the Central Committee's leadership, led by Comrade Stalin.

In April 1939, the Main Military Council of the Navy planned to hold

December 1937 until February 1946. Serving concurrently as people's commissar and commander-in-chief of the Navy, Nikolai Kuznetsov directly commanded not only the sailors but also the shipbuilders as well as the manufacturers of naval weapons and naval aviation.

[9]   The Sukhanovo Prison of the NKVD was located on the grounds of the Saint Catherine Monastery (now in the Moscow-region town of Vidnoye).

a meeting at which officials were to discuss the general condition of the fleet and the prospects for its development. Serious issues were supposed to be resolved at the meeting, including issues beyond the scope of purely professional matters.

Kuznetsov and Admiral Filipp Oktyabrksy were to give speeches at the council meeting. They had an opportunity to strike a blow at the people they felt were destroying the Navy. However, Kuznetsov had no desire to attack Frinovsky head-on, as Tukhachevsky had unsuccessfully tried to do against Voroshilov. He knew such a speech could attract the attention of the mighty corporation of the state security agencies led by Lavrenty Beria, who was even more powerful and dangerous than Yezhov. It was impossible to predict beforehand whom Stalin would ultimately support in the event of an open battle between the People's Commissar of the Navy and the Pacific Fleet commander.

The battle had to be constructed using the tactical bullfighting pattern Kuznetsov had witnessed in Spain. In this dangerous and beautiful game, an angry bull is teased into a frenzy and then, amid the applause of the audience, is brought with graceful maneuvers to the inescapable and precise thrust of the deadly sword.

During the review of the results of the summer navigation season, the 117th Aviation Regiment was recognized as one of the most well-prepared in the Pacific Fleet Air Force and won the title of best unit among Navy seaplanes in the army-wide competition of fleets. For this reason, as they were planning to depart for Moscow, Kuznetsov and Oktyabrsky took Chibisov with them and entrusted him with speaking at the Main Military Council of the Navy on behalf of the Pacific Fleet seamen.

This was customary in the Soviet Union: the top performers among the rank-and-file workers were invariably recruited for various meetings of top officials to give speeches that reinforced public confidence in the policies of the party and the government. These same leading representatives of the lower classes were sometimes trusted with disclosing the views, feelings, and wishes of the masses. Thus, Captain Chibisov was granted a modest but not insignificant role in the upcoming meeting.

The huge forum of the USSR military and naval elite took place over the course of several days. According to Maxim's diaries, during the first two days of the council meetings, speeches were given by "commanders of formations and units, including Maxim, on the condition of the 117th Regiment [...] There was something significant to report: the regiment had taken first place among all Navy seaplanes. The speaker promised in the future to achieve even higher results in combat training."

Regiment Commander Chibisov made his speech as specific as possible, trying to share experiences that could be useful to others, and the audience appreciated this.

Stalin was not at the council meeting at the time, but he undoubtedly was following it and studying what the participants were saying. The leader, who loved to delve into the private and specific details of events, could have paid attention to the speech of the modest officer, who was merely a captain but already the commander of the navy's best regiment. The clear, concise speech filled with businesslike energy destroyed the repulsive image of the navy officer environment, which Commissar Frinovsky had pumped up in his reports, representing himself as an indispensable fighter against rampant sabotage and betrayal.

The other speakers primarily adhered to the constructive tone, stuck to the subject at hand, and did not get carried away with political generalizations.

Frinovsky realized his speech would not fit with the general tone set by the council participants. He was inwardly irritated but restrained his anger as he waited for the top Soviet officials to appear so he could cut the navy officials down in front of the leader, drag them through the mud, accuse them of every sin imaginable, and ultimately trample and crush them.

Stalin, Molotov, and other members of the Politburo arrived on the third day of the Main Military Council of the Navy, when Frinovsky made his speech.

According to Maxim's recollection,

> in his report on the status of the navy [the people's commissar] deliberately gave a low assessment on all issues, all the way down to its morale. Everyone in attendance was displeased with his report, which was followed by the speeches of the commanders and members of the navy's military councils. During the speech by Pacific Fleet Commander Kuznetsov, a veteran of the Spanish Civil War, Comrade Stalin asked the following question, "Comrade Kuznetsov, tell me, is our navy truly in as bad of shape as Frinovsky reported here?" Kuznetsov replied, "No, Comrade Stalin! The condition of our navy is not

currently as the people's commissar reported here. In fact, the morale of the personnel is high."

The denunciations made by the people's commissar had run up against a rebuke that was as firm and overpowering as a steel sword. The strike launched against Frinovsky from a few simple and concise words by Kuznetsov had hit its target: Stalin acknowledged the Pacific Fleet commander as the one in the right, and Kuznetsov continued on to the substantive part of his speech, revealing his view of the problems and prospects facing the navy. Kuznetsov said,

> With regard to technical infrastructure, it is growing and improving every day. New ships are being built, new weapons are arriving. We will have a large and powerful navy in the very near future. It's another matter that significant changes need to be made to its organization. Life itself requires this. For example, some new complex equipment arrives. Three years is not sufficient for the naval service to properly master it. Service for enlisted personnel needs to be increased to four years.

The Pacific Fleet commander was speaking about real problems and not imaginary ones. He devoted a large part of his speech to the need to maintain a consistently high level of combat readiness among the naval forces. Drawing from his military experience in Spain, he also proposed stepping up the organization of anti-aircraft defense for ships.

Everyone then turned his attention to the speeches of Molotov and Stalin, who focused on the prospects for developing the navy and training personnel. Through the words of the top leaders, the party and government expressed a willingness and a desire to do everything necessary to strengthen Soviet naval power.

Summing up the work of the council, according to Maxim, Stalin "said the conversation was beneficial as everyone expressed great interest and worked hard. On behalf of the party and the government, he invited the meeting participants to a gala evening at the Kremlin."

Maxim was impressed with the luxurious beauty of the Kremlin hall. The tables and chairs all had nameplates displaying the full names of the participants. There were forty-meter tables covered with bottles of wine and various dishes. Then Stalin appeared. The hall burst into applause. The leader proposed a toast to the "development of our Red Army and the great Navy!"

Later, Maxim would never deny how awestruck he had been by what he saw and heard in the Kremlin as a young 32-year-old. He did not try to appear any more sagacious than he had been at that time. In his memoirs, he openly described his feelings of celebration and joy from mingling "with the supreme wisdom of the state" and "the sudden historical perspective that spread out before me." During those years, he did not allow himself to doubt the wisdom of the top Soviet leaders. He believed in their ability to properly lead the enormous country, which had chosen the difficult path of building the most advanced, scientifically grounded socialist system.

This belief was the foundation of the worldview shared by hundreds of thousands of people who were by no means naive or ignorant and who held various senior positions in the government, the economy, and the armed forces. The outrages carried out based on the arbitrary decisions of the supreme leader were no secret for this section of Soviet society. In order to keep the faith and avoid turning into complete cynics and misanthropes, such people had to mentally separate the light and dark parts of the Soviet reality.

On the one side were a great country, the powerful Communist Party, and its wise leadership led by Comrade Stalin. On the other side were various crooks, informants, and people in over their heads. In their rush to obtain power, they performed dirty deeds and committed horrific crimes.

Moreover, it was imperative to believe the party and Comrade Stalin personally were relentlessly fighting the bad guys. This notion was clearly confirmed by the events that occurred in 1939 following the April meetings of the Main Military Council of the Navy.

Major M.N. Chibisov, 1939.

Frinovsky was relieved of his duties. Nikolai Kuznetsov was appointed people's commissar of the navy. After this, the sailors and naval airmen could serve under normal circumstances and train for the bitter trials they would face during World War II.

Thanks to Kuznetsov's intervention, several unjustly convicted officers were released and returned to duty. Among these lucky individuals was well-known Pacific Ocean submariner Georgy Kholostyakov, who would later become famous as an admiral during the war.

On April 23, 1939, 117th Naval Aviation Regiment Commander Maxim Chibisov was awarded the rank of major. This event was also, to some extent, a result of the changes occurring in the navy under Kuznetsov's leadership.

6.3 On the Verge of War

During a meeting on May 20, 1939, the Main Military Council of the Navy reviewed the plan for the construction of seaplanes for 1939–1940. Under Kuznetsov's initiative, the people's commissariat, in July of the same year, established a Naval Aviation department responsible for the state of combat and mobilization readiness of the naval air force units, including the flying boats.

Semyon Zhavoronkov, the first chief of the Naval Aviation department, decided to personally test the MBR-2 hydroplane in flight and selected the 117th Regiment, the best in naval aviation, for the tests.

Regiment Commander Chibisov made a highly favorable impression on Zhavoronkov. Slender, tall, and always proper in communication, the regiment commander was a great pilot and provided his subordinates with excellent training. During bombing and aerial reconnaissance exercises, they had maximized the capabilities of their Chetvertaks. But the low-speed MBR-2 did not have these same capabilities with its short-flight range.

When Zhavoronkov was getting ready to leave following his introduction to the seaplane regiment, he and Chibisov had a memorable conversation.

"Thank you for your service!" the Naval Aviation department chief said as he stopped by the ladder of the plane that had been sent to pick him up in Krasnaya Rechka. "Have a good flight! But you need to go farther."

"Thank you, Comrade General!" Chibisov replied with the tone of a regiment commander. "I can go farther on the Chetvertak if it's only one way. If I need to return, I will need another plane."

"That's the problem, Major. We shall solve it!"

After visiting Chibisov's regiment, Zhavoronkov raised the issue of building new seaplanes with the People's Commissariat for the Navy. Seizing on the department chief's initiative, People's Commissar Kuznetsov sent a petition to the Defense Committee under the USSR People's Commissariat for the assignment to the Navy of the aircraft plants and design bureaus headed by Beriev, Chetverikov, and Golubkov, where they were preparing for test flights of the new seaplanes MDR-2, MTB-2, Che-2, and KOR-1. Unfortunately, they were only good for short-range reconnaissance.

At the Taganrog Aviation Plant, Beriev was preparing to launch a new model suitable for long-range reconnaissance. This aircraft was not the brainchild of the Soviet design school. Under the abbreviation of GST (Russian for "transport seaplane"), it was the Soviet analogue of the solid-metal PBY-1 flying boat manufactured by the American company Consolidated, which Amtorg had signed a licensing agreement to produce in 1937. Resembling a giant albatross, the PBY-1 was designed for reconnaissance in the open sea. Two powerful Wright Cyclone engines ensured high-speed flight for up to 30 hours. The flying boat was equipped with instruments of which Soviet pilots could only dream: the Sperry autopilot, a radio direction finder and a remote reading compass.

The GST was a bit simpler than the PBY-1, but it fully complied with the global standards of the time. The necessary equipment was supplied from the United States for its production, and Soviet naval aviators had the opportunity to use an excellent aircraft for long-range reconnaissance.

However, after the USSR and Germany signed the non-aggression pact in 1939, particularly following the start of the Soviet-Finnish War, relations between the Soviet Union and the United States (as well as England and France) sharply deteriorated, and the American experts were recalled from the Taganrog Aviation Plant.

Polar pilot's I.I. Cherevichny's GST flying boat.

The manufacturing process slowed down as the country switched to domestically produced components. The Taganrog plant would not produce more than 100 GST flying boats before the end of 1941.

During this time, Maxim's 117th Regiment continued their combat service on the good old Chetvertaks. Only slight improvements were made to their equipment and weaponry.

The position of commander and the growing amount of staff work did not prevent Maxim from flying on a regular basis. October 1939 marked seven years since the first entry appeared in Maxim's flight log. Over this time, Major Chibisov had flown a total of 1,631 hours and 4 minutes. He had flown 1,474.25 hours during the daytime, 101.56 hours at night, and 54.43 hours under blind (instrument only) conditions.

Based on the results of regular inspections that were conducted by a special Naval Aviation commission, the 117th Regiment was recognized as the best unit among the navy's boat-based aviation for the second year in a row in 1939. The commission assessed the regiment's combat readiness as "excellent."

Meanwhile, hotbeds of military conflicts were heating up considerably in both Europe and Eastern Asia.

The Japanese military elite had dragged their country into a union with the fascist powers, Germany and Italy, as part of the so-called Anti-Comintern

Daughter Emma at the hands of her grandmother Anna. To the right - Rosalia Borisovna, Yevpatoria 1940. Daughter Emmochka at the hands of her grandmother Anna. To the right - Rosalia Borisovna, Yevpatoria 1940.

Pact directed against the USSR. In summer 1938, when the situation worsened in Czechoslovakia, which Nazi Germany had targeted following its capture of Austria, Tokyo decided it was a good time to once again probe the strength of the Far Eastern borders of the Soviet Union.

In July 1938, the Kwangtung Army crossed the border near Lake Khasan and occupied the hills Bezymyannaya and Zaozernaya. The first attempt to dislodge the Japanese from the occupied territory ended unsuccessfully. After calling up reserves, using artillery, and involving aviation, on August 11, the Soviet forces finally expelled the enemy from their positions and retook control over the USSR state border in the area.

Three squadrons from the Pacific Fleet were involved in the battles; however, the Pacific Fleet command did not activate the 117th Aviation Regiment, preferring to keep this promising air unit as a reserve in the event the conflict expanded.

In 1939, Chibisov's regiment was assigned a mission: to patrol and do reconnaissance in the area of the Strait of Tartary and to observe the Soviet-Mongolian border. During fighting that erupted on the Khalkhyn Gol River, the 117th Regiment was put on a heightened state of alert: the command had not ruled out the possibility that the Japanese would go on the offensive near the Pacific Fleet's zone of responsibility after unleashing war in Mongolia.

The battle that took place that summer in the Mongolian steppes undoubtedly influenced the outcome of World War II, even though the scale of the Battles of Khalkhyn Gol were relatively small compared to the later major battles: the Japanese army lost approximately 25,000 people, while the Soviet forces lost 7,974 soldiers.

The results of this battle, however, forced the Japanese leaders to significantly modify their strategic plans. Mindful of what had happened at Khalkhyn Gol, the Japanese, in 1941, began launching attacks on the colonies of the United States, England, and the Netherlands in Southeastern Asia instead of on the Soviet Far East. This had far-reaching consequences, particularly during the critical days of the battle outside Moscow, when the fate of the country hung in the balance.

The Far Eastern soldiers who were involved in the Battles of Khalkhyn Gol as well as those who did not take part but were ready to do so at any moment made a notable contribution to the future victory of the Soviet people even before the actual start of World War II.

6.4 Fighting Brotherhood

In fall 1939, the following commanders were appointed at the initiative of People's Commissar for the Navy Nikolai Kuznetsov to lead the naval aviation units at the fleet level: Vasily Yermachenkov (Baltic Fleet),

Vyacheslav Rusakov (Black Sea Fleet), Alexander Kuznetsov (Northern Fleet), and Pyotr Lemeshko (Pacific Fleet).

Major Chibisov was on the list of candidates for senior positions within the Pacific Fleet Air Force command hastily formed by Lemeshko. In early October, the commander of the 117th Aviation Regiment was urgently summoned to Vladivostok. He was received by Fleet Commander Admiral Ivan Yumashev, who had replaced Nikolai Kuznetsov in this position. He immediately began speaking about a new senior appointment. Maxim did not specify the title of the position offered to him in his diaries. Apparently, it was a fairly high position within the Pacific Fleet Air Force.

However, Maxim was not attracted to the career opportunities opening up at that time. He was a passionate flier, a master and an expert in flying a wide variety of aircraft, and he never had any interest in administrative staff work.

Moreover, he still believed he lacked theoretical knowledge, even for the position of regiment commander. He tried explaining this to the Pacific Fleet commander.

According to Maxim's memoirs, Yumashev began offering him reassurances

> "You have enough knowledge ... The command believes in you. I highly sympathize with you ..." Hearing these words and realizing that everything could be decided here once and for all, Maxim took a chance and said, "If you truly hold me in high regard, send me to study instead. I think this would be better than being in a position of command without sufficient education." The commander briefly pondered the request, apparently weighing the pros and cons of each option. Eventually, however, he said, "Okay! Starting from the New Year, you will depart for Leningrad to study at the academy."

Admiral Yumashev's decision on the issue was final. General Lemeshko would be losing an excellent commander in Chibisov, but just like Yumashev, he respected Maxim's decision to further his military education.

Amur Flotilla Commander Arseny Golovko, regarded as a strict and demanding leader after replacing Filipp Oktyabrsky, who was appointed to the Black Sea Fleet, gave Major Chibisov an excellent recommendation for admission to the Voroshilov Naval Academy, in which he stated,

> The regiment commander has been in command for over a year ... During his command, Comrade Chibisov achieved dramatic improvements in the work of the regiment. In 1939, the regiment did not have a single crash. There were no accidents with aircraft. In 1939, a large group of young aircraft observers (18 people) and pilots (37 people) joined the regiment. Over the course of the year, they were put into service and flew under combat training day and night as part of the squadron. All of this work was performed under very difficult conditions: the squadrons were located at different airfields. The regiment did not receive satisfactory supplies. In addition, it should be noted that two squadrons were working on a special mission from the People's Commissariat of the Navy, were isolated from the base in the north for three and a half months, and successfully performed the mission. Overall, he is a great commander who promises to be a leader of major formations in the future. He fully merits being sent to the Naval Academy for studies in the air force department.

Maxim described his farewell with his dear 117th Aviation Regiment in his memoirs.

> Nobody in the regiment knew I was leaving for the academy yet. Accordingly, they did not understand why on one fine day the regiment chief-of-staff lined up all the personnel on the airfield. At first, everything was like usual. The chief of staff gave the command, "Attention!" I took my report and went out to the middle of the formation, greeted everyone and, after receiving a "Good day to you!" in response, I gave the command, "At ease!" Apparently, at that moment everyone else noticed my inner anxiety ... Everyone continued to stand there at attention ... "Comrades!" I started. "Dear comrades! Four

years have passed since our joint service began. We have managed to do a lot over this time. And yet we have not accomplished 100% results for combat training. After all, that is why we are here at Krasnaya Rechka—to achieve this goal. If a pilot, navigator or radio gunner is unable in peaceful conditions to strike a cone on the first try or hit a target during bombing, what can be expected from such a crew in modern warfare? Indeed, it does not appear to be that far off. Therefore, each person must tell himself: stop pointlessly going back and forth, needlessly wearing out expensive equipment, and burning fuel. Those who are incapable of air navigation should switch to a non-flying job without delay. The rest have no excuse or right to be dead weight. You must study day and night. There is no reason to let a crew take to the air if it hasn't been trained on the ground. No commander has the right to sleep soundly until his subordinates can confidently perform the combat missions they are assigned.

"Our long work together gives me hope that you will all manage. Moreover, I am confident that you will fulfill my instructions. I thank those who served faithfully and successfully with me in a crew, squad, detachment, squadron or regiment. Today we bid farewell. The commander of the Air Force has approved me as a candidate for admission to the aviation department of Voroshilov Naval Academy ... From this time on, the duties of commander of the 117th Aviation Regiment shall be transferred to my deputy in the unit, Colonel V. Vasilyev ... And one last thing: goodbye, comrades! I wish you health and success!" After these words, the orchestra struck up a march.

The regiment reacted to their commander's speech with silence. Despite the command to disperse, they remained in the formation for some time. The aviators of the 117th Regiment were shocked by what they had heard.

Maxim had served five years in this combat unit and held every command position from top to bottom. He would go on to maintain cordial relations and correspond with his fellow soldiers from the 117th Regiment, as evidenced by his diary entries.

Unfortunately, Maxim's diaries lack information about the circumstances surrounding the emergence of the aforementioned Colonel Vasilyev within the 117th Regiment and contain only a dry reference to the fact that he did indeed succeed Major Chibisov as commander.

One might wonder why, when high-ranking officers were lacking everywhere, this colonel ended up in a relatively low (non-colonel) position, especially a deputy major. If he had been a chief of staff or some deputy for administrative affairs, one could assume Vasilyev was a worthy officer but a poor pilot (and, consequently, had to yield to the major). However, he was deputy commander of an aviation regiment; therefore, he was a first-class pilot.

Was Colonel Vasilyev one of the few officers who was subjected to the repressions but survived and, by the will of capricious fate, received his freedom and once again joined the ranks? Such men were frequently appointed to positions that were modest compared to their titles. A classic example is author Konstantin Simonov's Brigade Commander Serpilin, a typical yet literary character of that time, who, upon being released from a camp, was only given command over a regiment.

This assumption would explain why Colonel Vasilyev ended up as a deputy of Major Chibisov. At the same time, one can't help but admire the senior commanders, who nominated the aggrieved officer in a roundabout manner to a position worthy of his title. What people Lemeshko, Golovko, and Yumashev were! After all, they sent a colonel who, while rehabilitated, remained under the watchful eye of the state security agencies not to some hole-in-the-wall but to the best regiment, whose commander was poised to soar upward. And what about Maxim? Indeed, he took in this unusual deputy with no fear that the colonel, particularly with his high patronage, might attempt to go behind his back. In addition, it appears nobody was afraid, collectively or individually, that if Vasilyev was arrested again—a likely prospect in those times—investigators would

Rosaly Chibisova (last on the left) in an officers' wives chorus. Leningrad, 1940.

attempt to find out who had sent an "enemy of the people" to command such an exemplary regiment. It was clear who had done so: Chibisov had recommended him, Golovko had consented, Lemeshko had appointed him, and Yumashev had approved him. It had been group-based collusion with all the resulting consequences.

Such a story was not as rare in those times as it might seem. Such were the people who made up the better part of the officer corps and its core: they didn't speak too much, but they understood one another through subtleties, and in their deeds, they were guided by the notions of honesty and duty. Sometimes they risked their lives for the nation, but they would also do so if they had to save their military friends, for they remembered the sacred oath of Suvorov: "Perish yourself, but rescue your comrade!"

It was a long way from the Far East to Leningrad at that time, but Maxim wasted no time, as Rosaly later recalled. He spent all his time on the train with his math and Russian textbooks. Looking for a quiet place to study, he would sit in the hallway of the train or the conductor's room, and at night, when their neighbors in the compartment quieted down, he would send Rosaly to the upper bunk and keep watch over Emma while continuing to study his textbooks. He remained anxious both night and day about passing his upcoming exams. He was also worried about whether or not he would be able to put a roof over the heads of his family in Leningrad. After all, there were three of them.

However, everything came together remarkably smoothly. After passing his exams, Major Chibisov was enrolled as a first-year student at

M.N. Chibisov (the first on the right at the first row) amongst the students of Voroshilov Naval Academy, 1940.

Voroshilov Naval Academy. He also resolved the issue of housing. They initially stayed with relatives of one of Maxim's fellow soldiers, and three months later, a room opened up at the academy's family dormitory.

While living in the dormitory, the Chibisovs felt the atmosphere of the military family fraternity. They were perfectly happy in a small room with a communal kitchen among the friendly surroundings of similar families.

During his second year, Maxim was given a private room at the municipal housing facility; however, the officers' wives from the dormitory maintained their friendship.

The study period at the academy had been reduced to two years at that time: the events of the time required the hastened training of professional military personnel. World War II was raging in Europe. Over the time Major Chibisov completed his condensed training program, the war with Finland came and went, with Leningrad serving as one of the frontline cities.

As a result of this brief but bloody war, the border with the not-so-friendly neighboring Fins was pushed back beyond the Karelian Isthmus by more than 100 kilometers (62 miles) to the northwest. After Estonia, Latvia, and Lithuania were annexed, the Soviet Union had excellent harbors on the Baltic Sea, where the squadrons of the Russian Empire had been based since the time of Peter the Great.

The People's Commissariat for the Navy made developing the newly acquired Baltic bases a top priority. A large number of ships and submarines were transferred to Liepaja and Tallinn. Airfields were quickly built on the islands of Saaremaa and Hiiumaa, blocking entrance to the Gulf of Riga.

In March 1941, while flying around to Naval Aviation department facilities in the Baltic Sea, Naval Aviation Chief Semyon Zhavoronkov stopped briefly in Leningrad, where he gave a speech at the naval department of Voroshilov Naval Academy. He spoke about the aircraft the Navy's aviation regiments were to be equipped with. At first, the naval aviators would be provided with regular army planes slightly modified for navy purposes. According to Maxim's diaries, Zhavoronkov assured the audience that "the units will soon be receiving the first prototypes of the latest aircraft, which in terms of their features are only slightly inferior to the best foreign models."

However, while speaking in private a bit later (in a group that included Maxim), Zhavoronkov cautiously acknowledged that there were serious problems with the quality of the aircraft being

Chibisov spouse with daughter
Emma. Peterhof, 1940.

supplied: "some of them [were] outdated," while the new models "[weren't] quite ready," posed difficulties during operation, and still required some "fine-tuning," which would take time, he said. "And time is now the most important factor," he added wistfully. Zhavoronkov also gave some parting advice: "Take a closer look at the article in yesterday's *Pravda*."

He was referring to an editorial dedicated to the anniversary of the Eighteenth Congress of the All-Union Communist Party, in which the author noted that Comrade Stalin had "unraveled plans to embroil the USSR in the war and would encourage our country to fight for the interests of the English and French capitalists."

In light of the actual military and political circumstances taking place by spring 1941, this biting article implied the following conclusion: the peaceful respite that had been provided to the Soviet Union by the Molotov-Ribbentrop Pact was coming to an end. There would be a war—one on one with Germany, which had strengthened immensely following the defeat of the English and French coalition on the battlefields of Western Europe.

Major Chibisov completed his second year of studies at the academy, unaware he would be unable to defend his graduation paper. Rosaly happily attended sewing classes, sang in the Academy's choir, and was an active participant in all shooting competitions. Maxim was proud of his wife's achievements and her title of "Voroshilov sharpshooter". On Sundays, the family frequently traveled to the suburbs of Leningrad when they had free time.

We still have family photos of them at the fountains of Peterhof. One typical picture shows little Emma with her bows and pretty dress, Rosaly sporting a stylish haircut, and a smiling Maxim in a snow-white naval jacket.

Maxim's peaceful smile, however, concealed his tense concern about what inevitably would follow. Neither he nor his comrades—military professionals—could grasp the scale of the threat looming over the country.

Only a little time remained until the start of what Russians call the Great Patriotic War.

CHAPTER 7

The Travails of Tallinn

7.1 Start of the War

Around 4 a.m. on June 22, 1941, the Soviet border patrol outposts along the Bug River noticed in the still-dark western sky what appeared to be scattered stars flickering and slowly increasing in size. The intermittent hum of hundreds of engines came a bit later. The situation quickly became apparent: an aerial armada was approaching.

Brazenly and arrogantly, even turning on their marker lights and headlights, the Nazi planes had come to bomb Soviet cities and troop locations concentrated in dangerous proximity to the western border.

Moscow received credible intelligence about the intent of the Nazi commanders to launch war just a few hours before the first bombs were dropped on Soviet territory. However, precious hours were wasted as the directive to put the troops on combat alert was prepared by People's Commissar for Defense Semyon Timoshenko and Chief of the General Staff Georgy Zhukov; coordinated with Stalin, who, until the last minute, refused to believe war had begun; and then communicated to the troop commanders. The Red Army units and formations located on the country's western border were caught unaware by the German attack. This is one reason the number of Soviet casualties was so high, particularly among the aviation units. Over the first day of the war alone, the Soviet Air Force lost approximately 1,200 planes at airfields, which were not prepared in time to repel the attack from the skies, and in unequal aerial battles.

The German planes did not fly to Leningrad that day. The city continued to live peacefully until around noon on June 22, when Vyacheslav Molotov came on the radio with an announcement about "treachery unprecedented in the history of civilized nations." The war had begun.

Major Chibisov's family was living on Vasilyevsky Island at that time. Several times a day, as soon as the air-raid alert sounded, Rosaly wrapped her daughter in a blanket and ran to the basement of the nearest church. Soon the kindergarten that three-year-old Emma attended was moved to one of the suburban cottage areas. It was believed things were safer in the countryside, where there were no military factories. Then officials decided not to return the children to Leningrad at all and to send them to the Urals by train.

Selfstudy of the students of Voroshilov Naval Academy. Major General M.N. Chibisov is third from the left, 1941.

Meanwhile, Rosaly was mobilized along with other citizens to dig trenches around Leningrad. The front was rapidly approaching, and it became urgent to evacuate the members of the city's population who were unfit for combat. In this regard, the leaders of Voroshilov Naval Academy decided to evacuate to the Urals the mothers of the children who had previously been sent there, allowing them to take only one suitcase of their most essential belongings.

Major Chibisov was under the command of the academy leadership until the order was issued on his deployment to a combat unit. In anticipation of this order, he anxiously monitored the progress of the military actions via the pieces of information released through the newspapers and radio programs.

The reports were confusing and contradictory. The same newspaper would state that the enemy had suffered a serious defeat yet also report on the battles near Pinsk, Dvinsk, and Minsk. All one had to do was look at a map to realize the Germans were advancing rapidly.

According to Maxim's memoirs, on the third day of the war, his heart sank when he heard the latest report from the just-organized Soviet Information Bureau: the Soviet Air Force had "shot down 381 German planes" but had "lost 374 aircraft" itself. At that time, he still did not know the whole truth about the Soviet planes that had been destroyed on the first day of the war, but as a military professional with an almost completed higher education, he felt the situation was clear: the Soviet Air Force had suffered enormous losses. The cheerful report that the Germans had lost more planes did not inspire confidence.

Superiority in the air is the decisive factor for success in modern battles of mechanized armies. This is what the students were taught during their lectures at the Naval Academy, and Major Chibisov—an officer with considerable experience—was also well aware of this fact.

One thing was entirely clear: the Luftwaffe had taken control of the air. Such was the beginning of the Great Patriotic War. Though the Soviet Union had been preparing, it proved unprepared in many respects. Nobody expected such a tragic turn of events in the initial battles, such horrific defeats and losses, or such a rapid advance by the enemy forces.

The German tanks and mechanized columns rushed toward Smolensk, Kiev, and Leningrad. For the Academy students, waiting out the raids in the bomb shelters was unbearable. They realized they belonged in the sky, in the battle, and they were eager to get to the front, using any excuse they could.

In the latter part of July, the long-awaited order arrived on "the appointment of Major M. Chibisov deputy commander of the 10th Mixed Aviation Brigade of the Red Banner Baltic Fleet Air Force." Upon receiving the letter, Maxim hurried to the Red Banner Baltic Fleet (RBBF) naval aviation headquarters in Peterhof, where the chief of staff and chief personnel officer immediately brought him up to speed.

The 10th Brigade, as part of the 13th and 71st Fighter Regiments, the 73rd Bomber Regiment, and a separate squadron of seaplanes, were based near Tallinn. One of the squadrons was operating out of the Hanko naval base in Finland. Its area of responsibility covered almost the entire Gulf of Finland.

Following the annexation of Estonia by the USSR, Tallinn became a major operational base for the RBBF. Officials believed it would be easier for ships and submarines to enter open waters for combat missions from this base than from Kronstadt. For this reason, a large part of the RBBF were transferred to Tallinn, although the most powerful cruisers and battleships remained in Kronstadt, where they were safeguarded based on the long-term prospect of gaining supremacy at sea.

The Tallinn base was of paramount importance for maintaining communication with the Moonsund Islands, where the advance units of the Baltic Fleet and naval aviation were stationed. The long-range bombers, which were based at the airfield on Saaremaa Island, were capable of flying to Berlin.

On June 29, 1941, People's Commissar for the Navy Nikolai Kuznetsov signed the Directive to the Military Council of the Red Banner Baltic Fleet on the Defense of the Islands of Saaremaa and Hiiumaa, which stipulated the need to retain these islands "under any conditions on the land front."

When this directive was issued, Tallinn was separated from the advancing German forces by hundreds of kilometers and the natural boundary of the Western Dvina, which had stopped the army of Kaiser Wilhelm II in 1915. In July 1941, however, the Germans effortlessly crossed over this easy-to-defend boundary, which was left unprotected by the Soviet forces, and then turned their tanks north toward Tallinn and Leningrad.

On August 7, 1941, when Major Chibisov was finishing up business in Peterhof, the German forces entered the Gulf of Finland just east of the Estonian capital. The land link between Tallinn and Leningrad had been severed, and communication was only possible by sea or by air.

During a flight to Tallinn, the plane on which Maxim was flying twice came under fire by enemy ships, and upon its landing, the wings of the Li-2 transport aircraft looked like a colander from all the bullet holes.

7.2 Battle in the Baltic Sky

Major Chibisov reported to his new superiors, and the brigade commander hurriedly briefed the newcomer on his duties and the current situation (which turned out to be more complicated than it appeared from the Baltic Fleet Air Force headquarters).

In his diaries, Maxim wrote,

I flew to the airfield of the 13th Fighter Regiment and made my way to the brigade headquarters, where Brigade Commander Maj. Gen. Nikolai Petrukhin, Chief of Staff Popov and Baltic Fleet Air Force Deputy Commander for Political Affairs L. Purnik were stationed. I reported my arrival to the brigade commander. Everyone there was under serious stress. They welcomed me, informed me about the extremely difficult situation on the ground as well as the missions being performed by the aviation brigade, and briefed me on my new duties. The situation was as follows: the Nazi forces were rushing headlong from all directions to capture Tallinn. They also wanted to prevent naval squadron ships from leaving the Tallinn naval base and encircle them on the ground and the air. Mines had blocked the squadron and transport vehicles from exiting the naval base into the Gulf of Finland. The defensive position in Tallinn was becoming more tenuous with each passing day and even hour. A large number of technicians and junior specialist had to be sent to defend Tallinn on the ground.

The 10th Naval Aviation Brigade was the sole aviation unit among the forces defending Tallinn. The brigade was in charge of protecting the city from attacks by land and by sea, conducting aerial reconnaissance, and making preventive strikes against enemy ships and planes in the areas where they were based.

In addition, the command of the 10th Aviation Brigade used their squadrons to maintain an air umbrella over Saaremaa and Hiiumaa.

Brigade Commander Petrukhin and his new deputy, Chibisov, appropriately split up the assignments among their divisions.

The air patrol of the Tallinn fortified zone, squadron ships and airfields on Moonsund Islands was performed by the forces of the 13th Aviation Fighter Regiment under the command of Hero of the Soviet Union Col. I. Romanenko on I-16 aircraft and the 71st Aviation Brigade on I-15 bis and Chaika (I-153) aircraft under the command of Col. G. Koronets. Both fighter regiments engaged in combat actions to repel enemy air attacks and shield squadron ships, transport vessels and aircraft at airfields near the naval base. In addition, assaults were sometimes made by the enemy land forces. The 73rd Bomber Regiment, using SB aircraft under the command of Hero of the Soviet Union Col. A. Krokhalev, struck at German warships, landing troops at sea and on land as well as enemy aircraft at airfields. The reconnaissance squadron of MBR-2 hydroplanes under the command of Major S. Mukhin conducted aerial reconnaissance of enemy ships at sea both day and night in addition to bombing gatherings of enemy troops and ships. One of the squadrons from the 13th Regiment was engaged in fierce fighting out of the Hanko naval base located on the Finnish coast.

At one point, when the long-range artillery began shelling the squadron ships in the inner harbor, one of the shells struck the Kirov cruiser right in front of my eyes. A column of smoke began to rise from the hole in the cruiser, which along with the other squadron ships continued to maneuver around the inner harbor of the naval base at high speeds. The entire Kirov team was inside the cruiser and of course fighting to save the ship. It took several hours for them to put out the fire.

The Germans were unable to bomb the squadron from the air: the pilots of the 10th Brigade had fulfilled their number-one mission and shielded the ships from enemy air attacks.

The enormous losses suffered by the Air Force during the first days of the war forced the Soviets to use seaplanes to attack advancing enemy columns. The pilots of the MBR-2 squadron dropped bombs from low altitudes and showered the enemy with machine-gun fire. However, the use of the slow-moving MBR-2 during the daytime without fighter protection led to huge losses. In August 1941, the pilots switched to nighttime bombing missions. The planes were occasionally used for anti-submarine warfare (which is actually what the MBR-2 was created for) in summer 1941, primarily on the Hanko–Tallinn, Moonsund–Tallinn, and Tallinn–Leningrad routes, but their search area was limited to 50-70 nautical miles, which negatively impacted their efficiency.

The MBR-2 from the Moonsund group was widely used as a minesweeper due to the almost complete absence of ships of this class in the RBBF. Bombs were used to destroy the mines. "During the aerial battles and attacks, all the brigade pilots displayed exceptional skills. Not afraid of losing their lives, they entered into battle with the superior enemy forces and came out victorious," Maxim said in describing the actions of the 10th Aviation Brigade in his later memoirs.

His diaries contain the names of the actual fighter pilot heroes: Antonenko, Brinko, and Golubev. Each of them shot down more than ten enemy planes. But the description of the feat performed by pilot I. Gorbachev of the 71st Fighter Regiment made a particular impression.

> While flying on a MiG-3 over the Irbe Strait a long distance from his airfield, he shot down a Ju 88 bomber, and upon returning noticed that he was being attacked by four Me-109 fighters in pairs from both sides. Gorbachev's plane soon caught fire ... Following the attack, two of the fighters passed him and were flying lower than Captain Gorbachev's plane. He decided to ram one of them and instantly pushed the control stick away from him! The plane immediately went into a nosedive and crashed into the enemy aircraft ... With his face and hands covered in burns, Gorbachev groped to open the cockpit canopy and tumbled out. A few seconds later his parachute opened ... He plunged into the salty water. With great effort, he freed himself from the parachute harness, but he was unable to remove his shoes and lightweight flight suit. A burned face and hands as well as severe headache did not break Ivan's spirit as he fought for his life in order to return to the unit.

The heroic pilot remained in the water, clinging to the bloated corpses of two German soldiers. The Irbe Strait was filled with such bodies after the Germans had conducted an unsuccessful landing operation not long before this event and suffered major losses. Observers from the aviation regiment's guard duty had seen Gorbachev's plane go down and his descent on the parachute. They dispatched a boat for the pilot, and soon he was taken to his regiment and then to the hospital. Maxim wrote, "After recovering, he continued to smash the enemy. But he did not live to see the great victory. On October 10, 1942, he died a heroic death during aerial combat. I shall never forget him!"

During the difficult, unequal battles with German aviation forces, the 10th Naval Aviation Brigade suffered irreplaceable losses. The crews left in the unit had to perform six to eight combat flights per day.

Maxim's diary entries from that time only briefly mention his own combat flights. Such flights were not within the scope of duties of a deputy brigade commander, who was supposed to be in charge of combat operations and not a direct participant. However, given his vast experience as a military pilot and his habit of always setting an example for his subordinates in everything, he could not remain on the ground.

He flew bombing missions on the seaplanes of Major Mukhin's squadron. It was difficult to evade enemy anti-aircraft artillery in the slow-moving MBR-2, and when the fast German fighters appeared, the Chetvertak became easy prey. Therefore, the seaplanes were used as bombers at night. Maxim was a virtuoso at flying under minimal or zero visibility, and he took full advantage of this skill during the battles for Tallinn.

During this time, he also had to "fly on SB bombers that existed in Krokhalev's regiment," as he casually mentioned in his diaries. The SB aircraft were used successfully in Spain in the 1930s, but by the start of World War II, they were already hopelessly outdated. While flying on them—during bombings, not training—Major Chibisov demonstrated for his subordinates how flying skills could make up for the shortcomings of archaic aircraft.

7.3 Berlin under Attack

On August 8, the day Major Chibisov arrived in Tallinn, the Soviet bombers from the Kagul airfield on the island of Saaremaa carried out their first air raid on Berlin.

Naval Aviation Commander Semyon Zhavoronkov made the proposal to strike at the enemy capital soon after the first mass air raid by the Germans on Moscow. He immediately received the support of People's Commissar for the Navy Nikolai Kuznetsov. They carefully planned the operation; made the necessary calculations; and, on July 28, submitted the plan for the strike at a meeting with Stalin. The supreme commander-in-chief gave the go-ahead, after which the necessary preparations were made under strict secrecy.

The operation was entrusted to the 1st Mine and Torpedo Aviation Regiment of the Baltic Fleet Air Force. This regiment was equipped with DB-3 bombers, which, according to calculations, were capable of flying to Berlin and back (approximately 1,800 kilometers both ways, including about 1,400 kilometers over sea), but would be test the limits of their capabilities. To ensure at least some extra flight distance range, all unnecessary components were removed from the aircraft, even the fuselage upholstery. The bomb load also had to be restricted: two bombs weighing 250 kilograms per plane or one bomb weighing half a ton but no more.

They were bombing Berlin in August 1941. First row (left to right): Captain A. Drozdov, Captain D. Borodavka, Major General N. Chelnokov, Colonel Y. Preobrazhensky, Commissar G. Oganezov, Major General P. Khokhlov, Captain A. Pyatkov.

Late on the evening of August 7, 1941, an air group comprised of 15 DB-3 aircraft under the command of Colonel. Yevgeny Preobrazhensky, the commander of the 1st Mine and Torpedo Aviation Regiment took off from Kagul airfield on the island of Saaremaa and headed toward Berlin. At 1:30 a.m.one thirty in the morning, the first bombs rained down on the enemy capital. After performing their mission, Preobrazhensky's group returned safely to Saaremaa, having lost only one plane, which had been shot down by German anti-aircraft defense.

The navigator on the flagship in the raid was Pyotr Khokhlov (later a lieutenant general in the Air Force and a Hero of the Soviet Union), who, in 1982, published a book of memoirs titled *Over Three Seas*. Maxim cherished this book, reading it multiple times and each time making notes in the margins with a pencil.

The material damage in Berlin caused by the raid of Preobrazhensky's group was not enormous compared to the psychological impact of the bombings: the Germans already viewed themselves as the winners of the war, yet suddenly, they were hearing the roar of exploding bombs and the ominous air-defense sirens in their own capital.[10]

The next raid on Berlin was carried out on August 10 by the 81st Bomber Aviation Division of the High Command Reserve under the command of well-known polar pilot and Hero of the Soviet Union Mikhail Vodopyanov. This division was equipped with the TB-7 and Er-2 long-range bombers, which at that time were some of the newest developments of the Soviet aviation industry. According to calculations, these aircraft could depart from the airfield in the city of Pushkin outside Leningrad, reach Berlin with a considerable bomb load (up to 4,000 kilograms (8,818 pounds) per plane), and return home. However, with the kinks still being worked out in the mass production of these planes, they were not fully ready structurally and had not been flight tested. The polar pilots who formed the backbone of the division had yet to fully master this combat equipment.

On August 8, the commander of the 81st Aviation Division, which was based in Kazan, received the following order from Stalin personally:

> Comrade Vodopyanov, I order the 81st Aviation Division led by Division Commander Comrade Vodopyanov over the night of August 9–10, or on one of the following days depending on the weather conditions, to carry out a raid on Berlin. During the raid, in addition to high-explosive bombs, you must also drop incendiary

---

[10] German radio reported in August 1941 that the raids on Berlin had been carried out by British aircraft. The British denied this information. When it became clear Berlin had been bombed by the Russians, the Germans were shocked. After all, Joseph Goebbels had already declared to the whole world that all Soviet aircraft had been destroyed. Luftwaffe Commander-in-Chief Hermann Göring had assured everyone, "Not a single bomb will fall on the Ruhr!" (V. Rimant, *The First Bombing of Berlin in August 1941*, glorimuzeum.ucoz.ru; "The Bombing of Berlin by Soviet Aircraft in 1941," *Wikipedia*).

bombs of small and large caliber on Berlin. In the event your engines give out on the way to Berlin, the city of Konigsberg shall be the backup target for bombing. J. Stalin, August 8, 1941.

However, technical and organizational setbacks began during the redeployment of the aircraft of the 81st Division from Kazan to Leningrad. Officials managed to deliver twelve TB-7 and 28 Er-2 aircraft to the staging airfield in Pushkin. Following a thorough inspection of their technical condition, 10 TB-7 and 16 Er-2 aircraft were permitted to take part in the operation.

Flight preparation of a DB-3 bomber from the 1st Mine and Torpedo Aviation Regiment of the Baltic Fleet Air Force. Pictured at the wing close to the airplane cockpit is the commander of naval aviation and the Hero of the Soviet Union Y.N. Preobrazhensky

On the evening of August 9, all the aircraft began taking off one after another to make their way to Berlin. But once again, problems arose. After one of the planes had its landing gear damaged by a drainage pipe near the edge of the airfield and another had two engines fail immediately after takeoff, Air Force Commander Pavel Zhigarev, who was responsible for the operation, canceled the takeoff of the remaining planes. But seven TB-7 and three ER-2 planes under the command of Vodopyanov continued to

Berlin. Six planes flew to the enemy capital, and two returned to the airfield in Pushkin. Another made an emergency landing in Torzhok, but the rest were lost. Two of the planes crashed because of engine failure, while several aircraft were seriously damaged by the actions of Soviet frontline anti-aircraft defense systems, which for some reason were not warned about the departure and subsequent return of their own bombers.

After the bombing, Vodopyanov managed to get his plane, which had been heavily damaged by antiaircraft fire, to Estonian territory, where he landed in a dense forest away from the road along which the German forces were traveling. The plane's crew—Commander Vodopyanov, copilot E. Pusep, and navigator A. Shtepenko—were not injured during the landing. Pusep, an Estonian, found a guide among the local residents: a shepherd boy. With his help, the pilots found a Soviet military unit in retreat. They returned to the plane with help and blew it up. Then they made their way through the front line. After this odyssey, Pusep received the Order of the Red Banner for his bravery and resourcefulness. Meanwhile, the renowned ace Vodopyanov was forced to resign from top command positions: with the rank of general, he flew combat missions as an ordinary aircraft commander, and he was later sent to an aircraft factory as a military representative.

The subsequent air raids on Berlin were performed by naval aviation forces from Saaremaa Island. In total, nine strikes were made on Berlin. A total of 33 planes dropped bombs on the enemy capital. Another 37 bombers unable to reach their primary target dropped bombs on other German cities.

Hitler ordered his generals and admirals "With the joint efforts of ground forces, the air force and the navy to eliminate the naval and air bases on the islands of Saaremaa and Hiiumaa, above all the airfields from which raids are being made on Berlin."[11] In executing this order, the Luftwaffe carried out massive bombing raids on Saaremaa, but the Kagul airfield continued uninterrupted operations. The air umbrella maintained over Saaremaa by the fighters of the Petrukhin-Chibisov brigade proved to be sufficiently strong.

The final air raid on Berlin was made on September 4, 1941. By this time, Tallinn had already fallen, and Colonel. Preobrazhensky's pilots were unable to obtain fuel and ammunition. Having used up all of their military resources, they flew back to Leningrad.

---

[11] "The Bombing of Berlin by Soviet Aircraft in 1941," *Wikipedia*.

7.4 A Doomed City

Fierce fighting broke out on the outskirts of Tallinn on August 5 after German forces from the Army Group North, led by General Field Marshal Wilhelm Ritter von Leeb, reached the approaches to the city from the south. Within two days, the Germans had taken up position on the banks of the Gulf of Finland to the east of the Estonian capital, which had been turned into a besieged fortress.

According to Maxim's memoirs,

> the squadron ships at the Tallinn naval base and the transport vessels in Kupecheskaya harbor were in a critical position. The 10th Aviation Brigade, comprised of two fighter and one bomber regiments and a squadron of seaplanes, was stationed in a confined area that was hastily put together near the bottom of a narrow spit that entered the Baltic Sea.

Suffering heavy losses both in terms of manpower and equipment, the Nazi forces tried as quickly as possible to break the defense of our troops, seize Tallinn, and prevent our ships and transport vessels from leaving the Tallinn port.

The situation became more complicated as the ring of defense provided by our forces shrank rapidly. The front line could already be seen with the naked guy. It was particularly stressful when the German lookout posts, which were raised up on small air balloons, adjusted the trajectory of their artillery strikes. Our attempts to neutralize these balloons were unsuccessful because as soon a plane began to take off, the enemy balloon would instantly descend. These balloons (which we called lookout baskets) generally rose to a height of 50–75 meters (164 – 230 feet).

The grave position of the Tallinn naval base defenders was exacerbated by several circumstances in the Baltic theater of military operations.

Admiral Kuznetsov, who had led the People's Commissariat for the Navy during the two years prior to the war, managed to accomplish a great deal over this time. Of course, he could not solve all the navy's problems at once, but he established a clear mechanism for managing the naval forces and fine-tuned it during training exercises.

On the night of June 21–22, Kuznetsov issued an order declaring "alert level number one" for the navy. This order was immediately communicated to the commanders of the military units and ships, who knew in advance what to do in such a situation. The alerted crews took their battle positions. The enemy planes trying to attack the naval bases were met with heavy fire by the ships and land-based anti-aircraft units.

During the first German raids, not a single ship from the USSR Navy was lost, even in the Baltic ports, which were subjected to particularly heavy bombing. However, the further actions of the RBBF proved to be ineffective. "Events unfolded so rapidly that all the preliminary operational plans turned out to be unrealistic," Kuznetsov recalls in his memoirs. "The Baltic Fleet sailors had to perform completely different assignments in connection with the situation that for now was not going in our favor."

Analyzing the initial period of the battles, Kuznetsov noted with self-criticism that the Chief of the Naval Staff and the People's Commissariat of the Navy virtually ignored the military intelligence data from the RBBF, which one week prior to the start of the war "had discovered suspicious unidentified ships … and reported on the violation of our air space and on the active ship traffic between German and Finnish ports." After the outbreak of hostilities, "most of the orders for commanders in the field arrived very late." Largely because of this slow reaction to the enemy actions, the Baltic Fleet lost the initiative, which they would be unable to regain until 1944.

Renowned military historian Andrei Platonov notes that the assignments given to the Baltic Fleet during this period were purely defensive in nature. "In order to fulfill them properly, they should have set up mine and artillery positions at the approaches to the Gulf of Finland and the Gulf of Riga and hidden behind them. That's all! There would have been no battle for the enemy's communications and no active operations against the forces of its fleet." One can understand the desire of the naval commanders not to subject the huge warships to unnecessary risk by sending them out to sea when the enemy was clearly superior and had managed to fill the waters of the Gulf of Finland with its own minefields first (some of them even in the final hours of peace). But did this strategy contribute to the unified network of Baltic Fleet bases, from Liepaja to Tallinn, being transformed into a chain of isolated and besieged fortresses that had no reliable connections with one another or with Leningrad and essentially were unable to perform their primary objective of serving as base stations for military operations at sea?

At any rate, the fate of these strongholds was decided by land battles and not at sea: they were all quickly overtaken by the advancing Nazi forces in the tragic summer of 1941. No land-based fortified defensive positions had been established anywhere beforehand.

Clearly, the fleet command initially underestimated the threat posed to the Soviet naval bases in the Baltic waters by the offensive carried out by the German land forces.

Platonov reveals the root cause of this, pointing out that all the preparations by the RBBF to fight off an enemy attack were made under the assumption that the land-based military actions would unfold favorably for the Soviet Union. At the same time, the RBBF forces, particularly the naval units, had a low level of combat training, which Platonov claims is solely attributable to the fact that a number of officials were neglecting their duties: members of the Military Council, the commanders of groups and units, the combat training division of the navy staff, and more.

It should be noted that at the start of the war, the Baltic Fleet commanders were not the only ones who were inadequately performing their official duties.

Individuals who were incompetent due to a lack of experience and professional training held various senior positions at all levels of the Soviet Armed Forces. This was the result of, among other things, the reshuffling that had occurred prior to the war, when the victims of political repressions were almost always replaced by those who had previously held lower positions. Many of them did not have the ability to adapt quickly to their new jobs. For others, their rapid career success went to their heads, creating the same negligence about which Platonov bitterly wrote.

As for the fleet's preparations being made exclusively under favorable projections of military actions for the Soviet Union, this cannot be regarded as a flaw specific to the RBBF commanders. When World War II began, engulfing Western and Central Europe, the top Soviet leaders convinced themselves, the army, and the people that if the USSR entered the war, military operations would be conducted on foreign soil, and victory would be achieved without significant losses.

The expression "a war with little bloodshed on foreign soil" was repeated like an incantation at meetings and political classes, and it was still being used even when the USSR found itself one-on-one with the vastly strengthened Third Reich, which had trampled all the countries of Europe from the Atlantic to the Bug and Neman rivers. Thus, the RBBF commanders were only fulfilling directives from above in terms of their combat exercise and training.

Under these circumstances, Tallinn was not prepared in advance for land-based defense operations. Fortifications only started being built around the city in the second half of July. Land troops, naval forces, and civilians worked together to build them; however, construction was never completed.

The Soviet forces defending the Baltic Fleet's naval base in Tallinn included the 10th Rifle Corps of the 8th Army, marine detachments, and a regiment of Estonian and Latvian workers—a total of 27,000 fighters. The actions of these forces were supported by the gunfire of coastal batteries and squadron ships in the harbor as well as strikes by the 10th Aviation Brigade against advancing German forces.

There were not sufficient forces in Tallinn to establish a strong front along the entire line of defense even though anyone who could hold a gun in his hand was thrown into the trenches. The 10th Aviation Brigade's technical and auxiliary personnel who were not directly involved in aircraft maintenance were also sent to the front.

The German command sent four infantry divisions (with up to 60,000 soldiers) reinforced by artillery, tanks and aviation to counter this force. However, despite the enemy's considerable superiority in manpower and resources, its progress was halted on August 10. This temporary and partial success was achieved by the heroic efforts of the city's defenders – the Red Army, sailors as well as Estonian and Latvian workers and volunteers. The Germans were forced to call for reinforcements. On August 20, they resumed their offensive along the entire front with the main thrust coming from the east in the coastal area, where the engineering support for defense was much weaker than in other parts of the front.

On August 25, the Soviet forces retreated to the main line of defense on the outskirts of Tallinn. The German forces now had the opportunity to fire on the city and the port with no obstructions. At the same time, the situation outside Leningrad also took a serious turn for the worse: Field Marshal von Leeb's forces had broken through the Luga line of defense and were rapidly advancing toward the outskirts of Leningrad. Due to the enemy's breakthrough to Leningrad and the need to concentrate all the forces of the Northwest Area to protect the northern capital, the general headquarters of the supreme commander-in-chief decided to relocate the Tallinn fleet and garrison to Kronstadt and Leningrad.

The last Soviet troops departed from the Estonian capital on the night of August 28, 1941. The defense of Tallinn, which continued for 23 days, diverted the forces of several of von Leeb's divisions for this period (and even a bit longer). This weakened the charge of the Army Group North in other areas. The defenders of Tallinn were unable to hold on to their own city, but they helped defend Leningrad.

7.5. Exodus from Tallinn

From the moment the Germans broke through to the Gulf of Finland, it was clear that the resources needed to defend the Tallinn base would soon run out and that the base would have to be evacuated to keep from losing all the squadron ships. The best thing would have been to prepare for evacuation in advance, gradually remove everything not required for the city's defense, and prepare to destroy everything that could not be removed, while continuing to fight off the enemy attacks and containing the German divisions that had besieged the city.

However, in order to implement such a plan, a decision was required at the level of the People's Commissariat for the Navy and the Baltic Fleet command, and Tallinn was receiving contradictory orders from the two authorities.

On July 14, the RBBF Military Council received Directive No. 16 from Deputy People's Commissar for the Navy Admiral Ivan Isakov indicating, along with operational assignments, the procedure for destroying the facilities of the Tallinn naval base in the event it had to be evacuated. However, Northwest Area Commander Kliment Voroshilov canceled this directive on July 17. The measures for implementing the directive had basically been drawn up and even approved with Isakov by this time. But the RBBF Military Council prohibited any preparations for the evacuation of Tallinn until the last moment. What happened there? Perhaps, following Voroshilov's reprimand, the naval authorities were more fearful of their boss's wrath than the risk of losing the entire Tallinn fleet.

Evacuation preparations only began on August 26, when Baltic Fleet Commander Vladimir Tributs issued the corresponding order based on a decision adopted by the general headquarters of the supreme commander-in-chief.

The ships had to evacuate amid battle and under the attack of enemy aircraft. The greatest threat came from the powerful minefields with which the Germans had blocked the Gulf of Finland. Numerous minesweepers were needed to navigate the minefields, but a third of these vessels assigned to the Tallinn naval base had been destroyed in battle.

Prior to the general evacuation, the Baltic Fleet managed to remove from Tallinn almost the entire arsenal, part of the ship-repair enterprise, about 15,000 tons of technical equipment, approximately 17,000 women and children, and roughly 9,000 injured. However, a large proportion of the civilian population had to be evacuated along with the troops.

After receiving the evacuation order, the command staff of the 10th Aviation Brigade headquarters held a meeting at which they identified the objectives for the aviation unit who would have to provide air protection for the ships to leave the Tallinn naval base. Major Chibisov was put in charge of the evacuation of the brigade personnel as well as its property and equipment.

Under his plan, which was adopted at the meeting without any modifications, the bulk of the personnel, including the pilots with no aircraft and the families of servicemen, were to be sent on the squadron's warships that had air defense systems and could protect themselves from an aerial attack. The equipment was to be placed on transport vessels. The aviation regiments and squadrons—or, more precisely, what was left of them—were to be relocated on the surviving aircraft. The bomber regiment departed first, while the fighter divisions left at the last possible moment.

Remaining one-on-one with Chibisov following the meeting, Petrukhin suddenly began speaking to him in an informal manner:

> "You know, Maxim, we need to organize the work
> so that the brigade will be capable of conducting combat
> operations immediately at the new location."

"Well, if you're talking about the property, we will find a place on the transport vessels for the most necessary items. Everything else will have to be destroyed. The most important thing is to evacuate people. Every last one of them."

"Exactly … We should be the last ones to leave—either based on our conscience or our sense of duty. For instance, if we stayed with the cover group, it would be a lost cause. What good does it do to add ten more rifles to two revolvers? We would only be stepping on toes while rushing around the airfield at the last moment and checking whether everything has been done, whether the airfield runway has been mined ... In short, my suggestion is that we send everyone off and the two of us remain here. We'll check everything quickly and fly out on the UTI-16 'shuttle.' What do you think, Maxim?"

"What is there to think about? As for the cover group, I agree: if a battle begins, we will only lose people in vain. One thing is not entirely clear, Nikolai: how will we take off from the mined runway?"

"Nonsense! It's a tiny plane and the takeoff is short. We'll go along the side."

"In that case, it would be better to roll it out to the area by the pier beforehand and take off from there."

On the eve of the evacuation, the 10th Aviation Brigade received a visit from Baltic Fleet Air Force Lieutenant General Mikhail Samokhin. He apparently wanted to assess the fighting capability of the aviation unit, for which there were high expectations in Leningrad, given that the city was being subjected to mass raids by the Luftwaffe on a daily basis. After giving several instructions concerning the aviation brigade's relocation to the new base, the airfield near Oranienbaum, Samokhin flew to Leningrad. On his return trip, he had to use the shuttle plane of the 10th Aviation Brigade's staff since the commander's own plane had been damaged. After seeing off his superior, Major Chibisov thought to himself, "Thank God Samokhin departed on time. At least we won't have to worry about the commander when the general evacuation begins. Petrukhin and I will manage somehow."

Commander of the 10th Aviation Brigade of Baltic Fleet Air Force in 1941 General N.T. Petrukhin. Post-war photo.

The deputy commander of the 10th Aviation Brigade held talks with the sailors, after which the squadron commander, Vice Admiral Drozd, ordered 60 of the brigade's servicemen and their families to be placed on the Kirov flagship cruiser. Everyone else—technicians and servicemen from the airfield's security service—were put on board the *Ivan Papanin*. The most necessary items of the brigade's military equipment were also loaded onto this ship. The other matériel somehow fit on various transport vessels.

The aviation regiments and squadrons—or, once again, what was left of them—were to fly out on the surviving aircraft.

The evacuation began at 11 a.m. on August 27 under orders from the RBBF commander. The first people loaded onto the ship were the injured, followed by the fleet's administrative staff, military hardware, and the most valuable equipment. The gold reserves and members of the Estonian SSR government were put on the Kirov cruiser, the squadron's flagman vessel. General boarding then began for the troops and civilian evacuees.

Commander of the Baltic Fleet Air Force in 1941-1946 General M.I. Samokhin. Post-war photo.

At 6:00 p.m., the demolition teams began destroying the base facilities and equipment. The city and port came under intense fire from the enemy at that time. The Luftwaffe were carrying out raids in groups of five to ten planes. Soviet ships and coastal batteries maintained barrage fire against enemy positions. The pilots of the 10th Aviation Brigade continued their regular combat operations: they provided air protection for the troops and ships under evacuation, battled with German planes in the sky, and dropped bombs on German troops advancing on the city.

Only a few bombers broke through to the area over the harbor. One Ju-88 was shot down. Leaving behind a trail of black smoke, it crashed into the bay, not far from the brigade's position. The crew ejected and were picked up by a Soviet boat. The German pilot, navigator, and radio gunner were taken to the brigade headquarters. The Germans appeared disheartened. During the interrogation, they named the unit and location of their airfield, after which they were handed over to the army command headquarters.

On the far outskirts of Tallinn, where the enemy assault groups were particularly active, several reconnaissance balloons were raised. Adjusting to the target, the long-range enemy artillery struck the anchored ships and transport vessels positioned near the pier. The fighters of the 10th Aviation Brigade managed to destroy the enemy's "sight" —the air balloons—and the final phase of loading the troops onto the ships was relatively quiet.

The personnel, equipment, and hardware of the 10th Aviation Brigade were placed on the squadron ships in accordance with the plan but with a few adjustments, about which Major Chibisov reported to Petrukhin. Maxim noted that no place could be found on the *Ivan Papanin* for the brigade commander's vehicle because the transport vessel was almost overflowing.

> "Well, there is no reason to give it to the Germans," Petrukhin said. "Let's start with the car! So as not to mess around, let them drive away and crash into the corner of the hangar. Everything else that has wheels must be wiped out in the same way. They had promised demolition men, but at the last moment said: do it yourselves. How we're going to incapacitate the runway now is beyond me … Oh yeah! Give orders for the UTI to be rolled out to the runway …"

"Nikolai, you probably forgot, but our piloting equipment inspector Samokhin flew to Leningrad on the UTI."

"Damn! I've been so swamped … Let's resolve the problems one by one. It would be good to bomb the runway. It's too bad that Col. Krokhalev's bombers have already taken off …"

"It's okay. We'll manage on our own."

"On our own?! But how?"

"Maj. Mukhin's hydroplane squadron is already in the air. But two of his MBR-2 stayed behind because of damages. The mechanics are working on it. I think they'll have it fixed by evening. At the very least, we can fly out on one. Incidentally, I'll ask them to mount the bombs. We'll hit the runway with them when we depart."

Loading was completed by the morning of August 28. Toward the evening, the squadron entered the outer harbor and headed for Kronstadt. After providing cover for the squadron until the last minute, the fighters of the 10th Aviation Brigade disengaged from combat and flew toward Leningrad as ordered.

Petrukhin and Chibisov remained on the deserted pier of the Tallinn port. They still had to destroy the airfield's runway and the equipment they'd been unable to load onto the transport vessels. The brigade commander and his deputy planned to perform this risky operation with their own hands. Then they were to take off and make their way to Leningrad on the slow-moving MBR-2 if the Germans did not shoot them down.

They were not overly concerned with their own fate at that moment. For the first time after several days of unbelievable stress and extreme fatigue, they felt relieved. With the departure of the ships and the last air squad, the enormous burden of responsibility for the fate of the base, the brigade, and the people was lifted from their shoulders.

The night before, Maxim had written a letter to his wife and packed up his most valuable personal belongings, including his officer's dagger with a long strap. The result was a bundle that resembled a roll of maps. Major Chibisov gave the letter, along with a request to deliver or forward it to his Leningrad address, to Colonel Romanenko, who was flying to Oranienbaum with a few of the squads left from his fighter regiment. He gave the package with the dagger to one of the brigade staff officers aboard the *Ivan Papanin* at the last moment.

Maxim had little doubt the letter he had sent to his wife via Colonel Romanenko would be his last. Only the pair of MBR-2 hydroplanes swaying on the waves gave him some hope of salvation.

By this time, the Germans were already moving about the city. Maxim assumed from the sound of gunfire and the roar of the motors that they would probably approach the bay after dark. He and Petrukhin had a little time left to destroy the airfield. But first they were forced to witness the first act of the tragedy playing out in the waters of the Gulf of Finland.

The German bombers attacked the squadron leaving Tallinn before dark. Several ships were damaged, and four of them sank. This was followed by the powerful explosion of the mines planted by the enemy at the exit from the Tallinn harbor. The first mine was tripped at 6:30 p.m when the *Krisjanis Valdemars* transport vessel went out of the mine-swept corridor in an attempt to avoid the falling bombs. The command ship *Vironija* was also damaged by a bomb, hit a mine, and sank. The rescue ship *Saturn*, which was trying to help the *Vironija*, also went down. The explosions went on and on.

This all took place in broad daylight, right in front of Maxim. Even several years later, he was still unable to forget the horror and despair of those minutes: "How was I to feel when I saw how the people whom I had just seen off, helped load their things, and embraced as we bid farewell did not even make it out of the bay. The ships exploded and sank right in front of my eyes while I stood on the shore in utter despair and was ready to cry out of helplessness and sorrow."

After passing through the most dangerous minefields near Cape Juminda with considerable losses, the squadron dropped anchor. It was not known where the mines were in the subsequent stages of the route, and the commanders decided to wait for dawn so as not to lose ships to random mines in the dark.

Early in the morning, the caravan of ships got into cruising formation and continued on. There proved to be no major minefields on the way to Kronstadt, but continuous attacks by the Luftwaffe began at 7 a.m. on August 29, and the first pair of Soviet fighters only appeared at 8:45 a.m. Then all the fighter planes available to the Baltic Fleet command were sent to the skies, but these forces were not enough to fully protect the caravan, which was spread out over a vast area throughout the entire route.

The Luftwaffe's most severe attacks were on slow-moving transport and auxiliary vessels that had no air-defense systems. Of the 75 such ships transporting the bulk of the evacuated soldiers and civilians, 43 were destroyed and 32 survived, many of them with serious damage. The losses among the warships and boats were not as significant: 15 of 127 ships.

Approximately 10,000-12,000 soldiers and civilians were killed during the evacuation from Tallinn to Kronstadt, according to data from various sources.[12]

Historians have offered a wide range of assessments concerning the Tallinn evacuation. Based on the horrifying number of losses, it is sometimes compared to the infamous Tsushima massacre, in which 27 Russian ships were destroyed and 5,000 sailors were killed. However, this comparison is not entirely correct. In the Battle of Tsushima, Admiral Rozhdestvensky's squadron was annihilated, and Russia was basically left without a navy. The squadron that broke out of Tallinn in 1941 maintained its fighting

---

[12] The minimum estimate for the number of victims of the Tallinn evacuation is 5,000 people, while the maximum is 15,000. However, both of these figures are presented in the publications of authors who took extreme positions in interpreting the results of this event. According to Andrei Platonov in his book *The Tragedy of the Gulf of Finland*, the total number of victims (military and civilian) was approximately 11,000, but this figures does not count the members of the naval command.

ability despite all the losses. The ships that made it to Kronstadt and the troops taken from Tallinn—several thousand experienced fighters—made a significant contribution to the defense of Leningrad.

The ship *Ivan Papanin* was among those lost in the Tallinn evacuation. Knowing this, Maxim later was never able to escape the feeling of guilt regarding those he had sent on the ship. After all, he had wanted to save their lives and failed: they'd ended up on a ship swallowed by the cold and indifferent waters of the Gulf of Finland.

However, the destruction of the ship, fortunately, did not claim the lives of everyone who had boarded it in Tallinn.

On the night of August 28–29, the *Ivan Papanin*, with more than 3,000 people and 200 vehicles on board, passed through the minefields of Juminda as it followed the minesweepers, and on the morning of August 29, it headed toward Kronstadt. It was traveling in a group of large transport vessels, of which only the lead ship—the *Kazakhstan*—ultimately managed to reach the final destination. The remaining transports in the group fell victim to attacks by the Luftwaffe.

Two bombs struck the *Ivan Papanin* when it was 19 miles west of the island of Hogland. A fire broke out, and about seventy people were killed. But the command managed to get the burning ship to Hogland and run it aground. Roughly 2,500 passengers and crew members were saved by landing on the island. From there, they were taken to Kronstadt. Gusts of wind dislodged the abandoned transport vessel from the rocks the next morning and carried it away to sea. On September 30, it was sunk once and for all by enemy aircraft 10 miles from the northern Hogland lighthouse.[13]

Some of the servicemen from the 10th Aviation Brigade who had been on the *Ivan Papanin* and survived the bombing of the ship as well as all the subsequent trials of the war tracked down Maxim several years later and began corresponding with him. He turned out to be their savior, although he was unaware of this for many years.

However, the fate of the young officer to whom Major Chibisov gave the package with the dagger remains unknown. Apparently, he was killed.

---

[13] The story of the destruction of the *Ivan Papanin* is described in a similar manner in various publications (see "The End of the Baltic Fleet's Tallinn Breakthrough," otvoyna.ru>tallin3htm; "Transport VT-505 Ivan Papanin (RBBF)," wreck.ru>baltika/20htm).

7.6 An Airfield for Two

Late on the evening of August 28, 1941, the two commanders of the 10th Aviation Brigade stood on the deserted pier of the Tallinn port in a daze, watching the destruction of the squadron ships they had just seen off.

Soviet army left Tallinn, August 31st 1941.

At that moment, several Junkers appeared in the sky. Most of them flew over the bay and went off in pursuit of the Soviet ships, but one squad broke off from the main group and began bombing the port. Clearly visible from above, the seaplanes were among the first targets of the bombing.

No longer planning to use their aircraft and giving up all hope of being rescued, Petrukhin and Chibisov rushed from the dock to the airfield, careful to avoid the areas where bombs were falling. By the time they made it to a group of abandoned vehicles, it was already dark, although not dark enough for them to be imperceptible to the sharp eyes of a professional pilot. Without delay, both commanders began fulfilling what they firmly believed would be their final mission.

But what could they do without explosives or grenades? The only thing they could do was use the vehicles that were still in working order, which they raced, crashed, crushed, crumpled, and flattened. When telling the story of this event several years later, Maxim recalled, "We were overtaken by some sort of joyful and at the same time evil fervor. Essentially left alone with death, two respectable, hardened guys, who were used to dealing with serious problems and managing large groups, were jumping from one vehicle to the next and racing around on motorcycles like boys."

Headlights in the distance forced them to regain their senses. It was the Germans. The brigade commander and his deputy ran back toward the dock. It seemed this was the end. The only thing left to do was use the last round in the revolver they always had at hand. But lo and behold, floating in the darkness on a small wave near the quay wall was a Chetvertak. It was riddled with shrapnel, but from its external appearance, it looked suitable for flight.

After hopping behind the wall, Major Chibisov tried to start the engine. The seaplane started up with unexpected enthusiasm. Petrukhin checked the ammunition, which was in place. Their next actions were performed with no words. They warmed up the engines, took off, and gained altitude. Instead of heading out to sea, Maxim confidently steered the plane back over the airfield, where the enemy was already taking up position.

Deserted pier of the Tallinn port. September 1st, 1941.

They dropped flare bombs during the first lap and took out the enemy on the next round. The runway, the hangars, and the vehicles that had not already been turned into scrap metal disappeared under the explosions. The two remaining commanders—who had essentially planned to be suicide bombers—bombarded the ground targets not just professionally but also from the heart, as the saying goes.

Having released the bombs, they quickly gained altitude in the much lighter aircraft and turned sharply toward the sea.

Not expecting an aerial attack in an area they had just occupied, the Germans were in such disarray that they did not even open fire immediately on the attacking plane.

Maxim was an experienced pilot with an impressive flight record in difficult, including blind conditions. He was able to find and maintain the proper course with zero visibility.

Everything that had taken place seemed like some sort of miracle: two officers left in a city captured by the enemy, having voluntarily chosen the fate of suicide bombers, managed to win their final battle in this city, fulfill their mission, and fly away from death on a slow-moving seaplane while avoiding a meeting with the high-speed German aircraft.

This all occurred on August 28, Maxim's birthday, which he had completely forgotten about while between life and death in the Tallinn bay. Several years later, on his 70th birthday, in the presence of numerous guests, he noted that August 28 was a birthday for him in two ways and gave his wife a long, meaningful look.

On August 28, 1941, Rosaly was evacuated to the Urals. That day, she could not sit still as she cried and prayed frantically for her husband. Having spent the entire night on her knees in front of icons in a village home, she fell asleep on the floor, leaning up against the bedpost.

In winter 1942, when fate granted the Chibisovs a brief meeting, Rosaly told her husband she had appealed to the heavens to save her husband's life on his birthday. From then on, Maxim was convinced his wife had saved him with her prayers and love.

Notes

Admiral Vladimir Tributs, in his memoirs, writes about the Tallinn evacuation, "Historians have different opinions of it. Some consider it solely as a breakthrough in the heroic epic of the Balts, while others are inclined to see it as a tragic event and search for the reasons for this. I don't share either of these positions. The breakthrough was one of the biggest operations conducted by the Baltic Fleet during World War II. The Nazi command had no doubt that the Baltic Fleet would [be] fully annihilated during the breakthrough by the Luftwaffe and mines. On the eve of the breakthrough, the Nazi command boastfully told the whole world that not a single ship would manage to leave Tallinn. The enemy miscalculated in its hopes to destroy the fleet. The objectives set by the commander-in-chief of the Northwest Area—to evacuate the troops from Tallinn and break through to Kronstadt—were fulfilled" (Vladimir Tributs, *The Baltic Fleet Sailors'* Fight – Moscow. Military Publishing, 1985).

CHAPTER 8

At the Front and the Rear

8.1 In and around Leningrad

Early on the morning of August 29, 1941, the plane of Major General Petrukhin and Major Chibisov splashed down in Lake Izhora, near Oranienbaum, at the new deployment site of the 10th Aviation Brigade. The joy, surprise, and questions of their fellow soldiers knew no bounds.

The Special Department of the Leningrad Front paid particular attention to the new arrivals. The commanders had to explain the circumstances of their fantastic escape from the enemy-occupied territory in great detail. The story may have seemed implausible, but all attempts to find something suspicious in the adventures of the two pilots were firmly rejected by Baltic Fleet Commander Lieutenant General Samokhin, who needed intelligent and courageous, not to mention lucky, commanders.

The situation in Leningrad was growing more complicated with each passing day. Field Marshal von Leeb's divisions were advancing on the city from the south, while in the north, the Finnish army had occupied the Karelian Isthmus and progressed to the old border, passing near the distant Leningrad suburbs. Shlisselburg fell on September 8. A handful of sailors heroically held out in an old citadel on an island near the origins of the Neva River after closing a convenient crossing to the right bank of the river. At that time, though, the Germans captured positions on the southern banks of Lake Ladoga, and Leningrad's land connection with the outside world was severed.

The situation appeared so ominous that Stalin sent General Georgy Zhukov, an outstanding expert in crises, to rescue Leningrad.

The Germans fiercely stormed the defensive positions of the Leningrad front until the end of September, trying to find their weaknesses. It was time for the citizens of Leningrad to muster the courage they had never abandoned.

The Baltic Fleet played a vital role in fending off the enemy attack. Thousands of soldiers brought together in the naval infantry brigade took up advance positions. The naval combat formations, which were steadfast in their defense and fiercely brave in attacks, became the strike force of the Leningrad front. The navy's most formidable weapon was its artillery. The large-caliber, long-range weapons shot targeted fire (as in naval battles) and smashed the combat formations of the advancing enemy into crumbs from long distances.

The ships, which were turned into stationary batteries, appeared to be easy targets for bombing attacks by the Luftwaffe. Protecting the ships from the air once again became the top priority for the 10th Aviation Brigade, which only had a few combat vehicles and pilots left following the battles for Tallinn. This small amount disappeared within just a few days of fighting. But the ships managed to survive the period of brutal and mass air raids that devastated Leningrad during the German offensive.

Erecting a human wall, the Soviet soldiers did not allow the enemy to break through to the famous city in which a foreign conqueror had never stepped foot. The Germans had only a few kilometers to go until they reached the outskirts of Leningrad, but this stretch proved to be insurmountable. On September 25, 1941, von Leeb reported to Hitler that it would be impossible to advance farther on Leningrad.

By this time, only part of the initial maintenance personnel of the 10th Aviation Brigade remained, in addition to pilots without planes. There was no hope of new aircraft being delivered; therefore, the 10th Aviation Brigade and a few other aviation squadrons were forced to disband. The flight crews and aviation equipment were distributed among other units. The RBBF Air Force was reduced to the 8th Bomber Aviation Brigade, the 61st Fighter Aviation Brigade and the 15th Detached Naval Reconnaissance Aviation Brigade.

Having only been in the besieged city for a few days, the commander of the Leningrad front, Georgy Zhukov, reported to the General Staff: "I have received 268 planes of which only 163 are serviceable. The situation with bombers and attack aircraft is very poor. We have six Pe-2 aircraft, two Il-2 and Ar-12, and eleven SB planes. I beg General Headquarters to send at least one regiment of Pe-2 and a regiment of Il-2."

The Leningrad front received only a small portion of the requested aircraft. In fall 1941, the situation outside Moscow had deteriorated sharply, and General Headquarters were sending all the reserves there. Soon Zhukov would also be redeployed to save the capital. The fate of the Soviet Union and its right to exist on the map were decided on the fields outside Moscow.

Meanwhile, Leningrad faced a grueling winter in 1941–1942, which would later go down in the history books as an example of the heroic durability of the Red Army soldiers and city residents, who withstood the severest test of hunger, cold, shelling, and bombing. The harshest days for the Leningrad residents came after November 8, when the enemy seized the city of Tikhvin and severed the last railroad line by which cargo had been shipped to Lake Ladoga to supply Leningrad.

In Leningrad, with a work card, one could receive 250 grams of low-grade bread containing all kinds of admixtures; 125 grams were issued for a worker, child, or dependent card. With such rations, hundreds of thousands of citizens were on the verge of starvation. Seeing this, the pilots of the 10th Brigade, despite an official ban, secretly shared part of their meager ration allowances with the city residents. At that time, they were receiving 600 grams of bread per person and on some days only half that amount.

The situation with food somewhat improved after the Germans were driven out of Tikhvin[14] and the ice road built over Lake Ladoga was put into operation (after December 22). Workers and technical personnel began receiving 350 grams of bread per day, while clerks, children and dependents were given 200 grams. The daily rations for pilots were also increased by 100 grams. Maxim remembered these bread rationing figures from the time of the blockade for the rest of his life.

---

[14] Tikhvin was liberated on December 18, 1941, during an offensive in which decisive success was achieved by the 4th Army under the command of Army General Kirill Meretskov (see the Russian versions of the articles "Tikhvin Offensive" and "Kirill Mertsekov" on *Wikipedia*).

He was tormented more by thoughts about his family than hunger or service-related concerns during the blockade. He did not receive any information about them until the end of 1941: Were they alive, how were they, and where were they?

Maxim tried to convince himself that his wife and daughter were alive and well.

8.2 Military Family

Emma Chibisov remembered her mother's stories about how she was taken to the Urals as a little three-year-old, to the distant city of Molotov (present-day Perm). It was a long journey with numerous delays. Sometimes they would wait at stations for several days, as the numerous trains carrying refugees and the wounded would get backed up. The adults accompanying the groups of children did the best they could to make the trip less difficult for the young travelers. To distract the kids from the horrors of the war and from thinking about their parents, the adults created a children's concert brigade, which was invited to perform in the ambulance trains. The children enjoyed this activity and gladly sang, danced, and acted out skits. Emma was the youngest actress in the brigade. Thanks to her parents and her tenacious memory, she knew several poems and songs. Her best act was always a huge success: poems about a shiny teapot:

> We had a shiny teapot,
> It shined like nothing else.
> And every time we looked at our teapot
> It was like gazing in a mirror.
> It reflected everything:
> The furniture, the wallpaper,
> The window and the city outside the window,
> And much, much more.
> In April, spring came to the garden,
> And everything blossomed splendidly.
> In June, the war began,
> And everything changed.
> Driving down our street were
> Armored cars and machine gun carts

Dust-covered infantry and cavalry
And tanks, tanks, tanks.
One morning, the fighting quieted down.
Three Fritzs entered our home,
And saw their shameless faces
In the teapot's reflection.
And the Germans began to rob the house,
Breaking the cabinets and sofas,
And boiling their filthy tea
In our dear teapot.

These touching patriotic children's poems were always rewarded with wild applause and a loaf of bread or bottle of milk, which was immediately shared by all the young artists.

Rosaly was evacuated along the same route her daughter had just traveled and saw with her own eyes the signs of the barbaric bombing of the railway lines, which had yet to be cleared. She tried not to think that her daughter could be among those killed, but terrifying thoughts nevertheless crept into her mind: *If Emma wasn't killed, she probably got lost. After all, she's still so small and can't say anything about herself. Where should I look for her now?*

Evacuation of the civilian population from the besieged Leningrad was conducted by a DC3 aircraft.

When Rosaly reached the city of Molotov, she learned that the children from Leningrad were being housed in nearby villages. The stressful search lasted for two months. Finally, she learned that the children's group from Voroshilov Naval Academy were located in Polazna, a village 45 kilometers (28 miles) outside Molotov. Rosaly traveled there together with other women who were searching for their children.

The day finally arrived when the mothers would see their children. The identification procedure was not supposed to traumatize the homesick kids, and viewings were arranged in the courtyard of the kindergarten.

"When a pale, skinny little girl with a boy's haircut, wearing a familiar little coat, came out in the courtyard, my heart sank," Rosaly recalled later. "This child looked nothing like my rosy, cheerful, plump little girl. I realized that my daughter had died, and her little suitcase had been given to another child. At that moment, I could only think of one thing: *I lost one daughter, and now I've lost another. Who knows if I'll ever have more children? I don't know if my husband is alive. But this little girl is also alone. I'll take her and raise her as my own child* … I slowly made my over to her. Most of all, I was afraid of fainting. From worrying and the fear of what awaits us as well as hunger. And suddenly, I hear, 'Mama!' The little girl—of course, *my* little girl!—rushed towards me, hugged me tightly, and buried her face in my neck so that I couldn't even look at her little face or eyes. She kept repeating, 'Mama, Mama, Mama.' I still couldn't believe that I had found Emma. But I understood one thing right away: from now on, I would have to do everything with my daughter in my arms, because she would never again let me out of her sight even for a second. And that's exactly what happened."

Rosaly and Emma were put up in a spacious house with an attic and a large cellar. The house was divided in half by large outer entrance halls. One of them was occupied by three families from Leningrad, who had come to Polzana earlier. These were also the wives and children of pilot officers. At first, the owner did not want to take in the new guests, citing a lack of space. However, Rosaly's natural charm and her story about happily being reunited with her daughter did the trick. Grandma Klava, as the house owner was called, housed Rosaly and her daughter on her side of the house. Soon they were joined by another familiar person. While searching for Emma, Rosaly had found her older brother Isaak among the list of refugees. He had been evacuated, along with their entire family: their mother, Anna; his son, Boris; and his wife, Sina, who was expecting their second child and soon gave birth to a boy named Vladimir.

Just before the Crimea was occupied, Rosaly's relatives had fled from Simferopol in fall 1941 and found refuge in the city of Molotov upon arriving in the Urals. The long journey in a freight car had aggravated Anna's peptic ulcer, so Rosaly brought her mother to her place so she could take care of her.

8.3 Eaglet School in the Besieged City

Following the disbanding of the 10th Aviation Brigade, the commanders decided to set up a new bomber aviation brigade while maintaining the Banner and the previous numbers. The brigade's personnel were to be comprised of experienced and combat-hardened naval pilots. This backbone was to be primarily fortified by the muscles of the young pilots, who had to be properly trained to perform combat missions for the fleet's future operations.

Of the aircraft sent to the Leningrad front at Georgy Zhukov's request in fall 1941, the new 10th Bomber Aviation Brigade received a pair of battle-scarred bombers: an SB and a Pe-2. But the commanders were happy with these aircraft since they now had planes to train the reinforcements who were arriving.

Major Chibisov took responsibility for training the pilots. Training was almost no different from combat: the brigade's "classroom" was located in direct proximity to the front, and anyone taking to the skies could easily encounter the enemy.

At first, Maxim personally tested the aircraft received by the brigade. He had studied both planes at the academy and had flown on the SB during the fights over Tallinn.

The SB plane (in Russian, short for "high-speed bomber") was developed in 1934 by the Arkhangelsk Design Bureau. During the war in Spain, it was considered a fast and maneuverable machine. In 1941, however, the war in the skies was fought at completely different speeds than the war in Spain. In this war, the SB appeared slow-moving and outdated. The German fighters easily took them out if they appeared in the sky alone. In the battles for Tallinn, the SB planes were primarily used as night bombers. One thing was clear to Maxim: it would be impossible to fight very effectively on this plane, but it was entirely suitable for training pilots.

The other plane, the Pe-2, developed by the Petlyakov Design Bureau and often called Peshka, left a good impression. This model went into production in early 1941 and, at that time, was the latest brainchild of the Soviet aviation industry. It was initially designed as a fighter. Its overall bomb load did not exceed 600 kilograms (1,323 pounds), and its flight range was up to 1,300 kilometers (808 miles). However, thanks to its powerful motor, small size, and pure form, the Pe-2 easily achieved speeds of 540 kilometers per hour (336 miles per hour) and had a high level of maneuverability. Having tested the plane under various conditions and performed aerobatic stunts, Maxim concluded that it could successfully elude anti-aircraft fire and, if necessary, act without the support of a fighter.

The strength of the Pe-2 was its ability to strike targets at dive angles of 50 to 60 degrees, which enhanced its bombing accuracy by several times. In short, it was a high-speed dive-bomber.

While analyzing the enemy's actions, Maxim paid attention to the quality of the Germany aircraft and the skills of the pilots. He saw the enemy had machines that were reliable, fast, and adaptable to air-combat maneuvering. Based on how controllable they were and how stably they behaved under critical conditions, it was apparent that flying and fighting in them was very convenient.

Bomber Pe-2 from the 73rd Bomber Regiment before a take off.

The German pilots made full use of the capabilities of their aircraft. As Maxim noted,

> almost all the Luftwaffe pilots were tactically well trained. Each one sought as quickly as possible to be the first to find the enemy and go undetected as long as he could. The Germans tried to launch most attacks from the direction of the sun. They dived rapidly so they could end up behind and below the plane they were attacking—in this position our pilots could not see the attacking plane from the cockpit. They shoot first and surely conserve ammunition.

Major Chibisov also noted numerous battle-tested techniques employed by the enemy.

For a while, Maxim assumed the Soviet pilots were being confronted in the skies by highly qualified professionals. Imagine his surprise when he learned during the interrogation of a Junkers crew shot down over the Tallinn bay that the highly qualified German pilots were conscripts who had worked in civilian professions prior to the war and entered the army during mobilization. The Luftwaffe flight personnel had been trained quickly and efficiently en masse.

The Soviet pilot training system was not as advanced, and during the first part of the war, the Soviet pilots were inferior to the Germans in terms of their flying prowess. This factor was complemented by the superiority of the quality of German aircraft compared to their Soviet counterparts. Major Chibisov was unable to influence decisions on the retooling and modernization of the unit entrusted to him, but he put all of his professional skills as well as all of his instructor and commander experience into training the young pilots who arrived at the brigade.

This training took place under extreme conditions. The blockade rations did not provide sufficient calories for recuperation after exhausting work on the ground and in the air. Other times, Maxim struggled to walk to the plane, climb up onto the wing, and get his body into the cockpit. This was a familiar feeling for any pilot in the besieged Leningrad. After making a flight, most pilots experienced darkened eyes, dizziness, and bleeding from the nose.

However, with each flight and each training session, Maxim's students began to fly better and with more confidence. Their rapidly increasing professionalism inspired hope: soon the enemy could forget about easy victories in the Leningrad skies. Maxim prayed to fate that his brave but not-yet-fledged eaglets would not be thrown into battle before they were ready. He was less concerned about the few brigade veterans who had already fought in the skies over Tallinn. He had constant bitter thoughts about how, without reliable, modern planes, his students had little chance of victory in their battles against the formidable opponent. To escape these difficult thoughts as well as worries about his family, Maxim took refuge in his work. From his outward appearance, none of his colleagues could have guessed the pain he was carrying around in his heart. He maintained a clean and neat appearance, his endurance was amazing, and all his actions on the ground and in the air were distinguished by his confidence as well as cool and accurate calculations.

In the middle of January 1942, Maxim's personal file contained an appraisal sheet with the following description:

> Strong-willed, energetic commander who works every day to enhance his overall and tactical level. Demanding of himself and his subordinates. Concise in his instructions and their monitoring ... Politically competent. Soundly assesses the situation and reacts properly. Tries to apply his knowledge in practice under the conditions of war. Rank and position are fully consistent.

Maxim's first military award was the Medal for the Defense of Leningrad, although he only received it in December 1942, when he was already far from the blockaded city on the Neva.

On February 2, 1942, Major General Petrukhin received an order: he was to transfer command of the brigade to his deputy and place himself under the orders of the Baltic Fleet headquarters. Under instructions from People's Commissar for the Navy Admiral Kuznetsov, the decision had been made to redeploy the 10th Aviation Brigade to the Far East.

Having devastated the US fleet at Pearl Harbor, the Japanese were conducting offensives in the Pacific Ocean at the time and seizing one territory after another. There were fears that Tokyo's leaders, in the ecstasy of their victories, would respond to Germany's calls and strike at the Soviet Union. Strong naval aviation units were required to fend off a possible attack on the Far Eastern borders. The battle-hardened 10th Aviation Brigade was to be one of these units after its pilots and aircraft were replenished.

Under Order No. 0274 of the Pacific Fleet commander, dated February 18, 1942, Major Chibisov was appointed commander of the brigade.

CHAPTER 9

Never Part with Your Loved Ones

9.1 A Wartime Rendezvous

The 10th Aviation Brigade redeployed from Leningrad was temporarily stationed in Saransk, where it was to be replenished with naval pilots from various fleets before departing for the Pacific Fleet.

In early 1942, the Soviet Union, with hope and joy, received reports from the Information Bureau indicating that the Red Army had defeated the Germans outside Moscow and were advancing as part of a broad front, liberating one city after another.

Maxim had his own reason to rejoice: he had finally managed to establish contact with his wife. He now began to regularly receive news about his family and sent word that he was alive and well.

Maxim's diary entries give no indication of how he found his wife's address. Perhaps he met an academy worker in Saransk who knew about the evacuation routes for employee families, or he might have been informed by one of his colleagues whose relatives had also been found. Or maybe some degree of order was established in the services responsible for evacuation. The addresses of the military families evacuated from Leningrad appeared at the Urals enlistment offices (lists and the temporary addresses of Leningrad residents were collected in Molotov, which greatly helped in establishing contact between people who had been separated by the war). The evacuees began receiving letters from their husbands, fathers, brothers, and sons who were protecting the nation. Military supply vessels transferred money from the salaries of the soldiers to the addresses of their families.

In one of the letters, Maxim suggested Rosaly meet him in Saransk.

In the chilly month of February 1942, Rosaly packed for the long trip with the active participation of the apartment owner, Grandma Klava. She put on all the warm things they could find in the house, kissed her daughter and her mother, and set off on the journey.

Emma, who still was not four years old, remained with her grandma Anna, who had gained back some of her strength and could walk and play with her granddaughter. The young girl's retentive memory later allowed her to recall some fragments of those times—for instance, her grandma read her stories at bedtime, and she had large gray-blue eyes.

Rosaly traveled to Saransk on post-horses, with long waits at the transfer stations. Trains were operating as they could, but any sort of schedule was out of the question. Nevertheless, she managed to overcome all the hardships of the trip and arrived to meet her husband.

They were together for two straight days. Two nights in the officers' dormitory were not enough for them to say everything they wanted to tell each other. In their endless and intense conversations, which seemed to stop time and return happiness to them, they took refuge from the war, the horrors of what they had survived, and their anxiety about the future. They almost had to whisper and even speak under the blanket since there was always someone else in the room: the brigade commander did not have an opportunity to occupy an individual room due to the Spartan-like life of his military unit, who were waiting for the order to depart to the Far East.

They did not mind the presence of other people. They were young, strong, and full of the brief and vivid happiness that had come their way after long months of separation.

The atmosphere in the dormitory was relaxed and even fun. Relations among the officers were free of the normal servility to rank and seemed simple and uninhibited. The pilots—frontline men scorched by the fire of fierce battles—fooled around and exchanged jokes. Rosaly later retold a few of the jokes with some embarrassment.

They also discussed serious issues. During one such conversation, Maxim casually mentioned that his brigade would soon be receiving new planes, which worried Rosaly. In her experience as a pilot's wife, she knew what kind of unpleasant surprises could be expected from untested aircraft.

They also spoke about how the 10th Aviation Brigade would be a mine and torpedo brigade, although Rosaly did not quite understand what that meant.

For her return trip, Rosaly was to take a plane directly to Molotov, which would save her time and energy but also made her nervous.

Her first stressful situation came in Saransk, at the snowy airfield to which Maxim and his friend the deputy political officer accompanied her. Rosaly was walking along the airfield between the two large figures, when Maxim's friend asked if Rosaly had ever flown before. She admitted she would be getting on a plane for the first time and, of course, was afraid. The deputy political officer then asked, for no apparent reason, what time it was. Rosaly replied, glancing at the watch her husband had given her not long before the war. Maxim's friend innocently remarked, "It looks like your watch is gold!"

"It is gold," Rosaly replied proudly. She was indifferent to such trinkets but appreciated her dear husband's gift.

The deputy political officer then loudly whispered Maxim's ear (so that Rosaly could hear), "Maxim, losing the watch would be a pity! A plane is a precarious thing, as you know!"

Rosaly was so terrified that it took a while for both pilots to calm her down while explaining the specifics of army humor.

There was no passenger seat in the small military plane, so the division commander placed his wife in the tail, in the seat of the radio gunner, where she unexpectedly found herself in the company of a small mouse that apparently considered itself a crew member. This "helping hand" quietly chewed on a cracker for the whole trip and paid no attention to Major Chibisov's wife, who trembled from fear and cold.

Shortly after the meeting with his wife, Major Chibisov departed for the Far East with his brigade. Rosaly did not receive any news from him until late March. From the new field post office number, she guessed that her husband had reached his place of permanent deployment. She did not know the exact location (it was a military secret), but the contents of the letter allowed her to presume it had been sent from roughly the same places the Chibisovs had left a few years earlier for Leningrad.

9.2 Division Commander

While in Saransk, the 10th Aviation Brigade became fully manned by senior commanders. They were all experienced commanders who had fought with success – some in the Black Sea and some in the Baltic Sea: Chief of Staff N. Sokolov, Commissar G. Medvedev, Aviation Regiment Commanders Y. Pashkov and B. Takhtarov, and others.

The situation with equipment was much worse. The only aircraft left in the fleet besides the Pe-2, which had appeared recently but was far from new, were outdated plane models that had been patched and re-

Commander of the 10th Bomber Aviation Brigade Lieutenant Colonel M.N. Chibisov (extreme left) arrived at the airfield of Suchan Valley, the base of the 33rd Bomber Regiment, headed by Commander Y.K. Pashkov.

patched—the legacy of the squadrons and units evacuated from Tallinn.

The city of Suchan (present-day Partizansk) in the Primorye Territory was designated as the brigade's permanent place of deployment.[15]

Major Chibisov had to re-assimilate to the conditions of life and service in the Far East. Much had changed over the previous two years, but the Pacific Fleet was still commanded by Vice Admiral Ivan Yumashev, and the naval air force was headed by Maxim's old acquaintance Pyotr Lemeshko.

The garrison settlement Nikolayevka, which looked like a small village, was located near the airfield at which the brigade was based. After receiving replenishments from the Pacific Fleet aviation units, Major Chibisov completed the formation of the 10th Bomber Aviation Brigade,

---

[15] The name Suchan comes from Chinese (*su* means "river" or "water," while *chen* means "fortress"). The town of Suchan was renamed Partizansk after the Sino-Soviet border conflict that took place on the island of Damansky in March 1969.

which was comprised of the 33rd and 34th Bomber Regiments and the 19th Fighter Regiment.

Maxim's former student Colonel V. Zhdanov, who had risen from a common pilot to an aviation regiment commander, later recalled,

> Much of the credit belongs to Maxim Chibisov for essentially transforming the just formed brigade into a formidable fighting force right before our eyes. Energetic, well-rounded and possessing excellent organizational abilities, he was rightly considered a thoughtful, understanding commander and enjoyed a well-deserved reputation among the military personnel. And he was so good at conveying his wealth of experience to us young pilots! Maxim was always with us and knew almost everyone—all the way down to a common sailor—by their last name. It was amazing how he was able to find good qualities in each person and help him to develop. For many of us, he not only gave us our start in the skies, but in life as well.

Torpedo bombers were the most formidable weapon in the naval battles of World War II. With their speed, ships could not escape a rapidly diving plane firing a powerful torpedo at its target from a short distance. The impact of such a torpedo was similar to a shot at close range. But the attacking aircraft had to fly directly at the target during the last trajectory segment without deviating to the right or left so that the torpedo did not miss the ship after being dropped. The pilot could not maneuver in the air and was exposed to defensive fire from naval weapons during the dive and when coming out of the dive.

In a duel between a warship and a torpedo aircraft, it was highly probable that both participants would be destroyed. However, according to the canons for naval tactics during the first half of the twentieth century, such an outcome was considered a victory for the attacking side since the loss of the plane, even along with the crew, was more than justified by the damage inflicted on the enemy.

During the fighting, the pilots from the mine and torpedo units were supposed to display extraordinary bravery as well as an ability to act coherently and properly under conditions of fatal risk while breaking through the veil of enemy fire. These skills were acquired over the course of intensive training. Such training was intended not only to ensure success in battle but also to provide the torpedo aircraft pilots with an additional chance to make it out of the battle alive.

The commander of the 10th Bomber Aviation Brigade spared no effort or time in training his subordinates in the science of victory and survival.

The brigade personnel trained intensely for almost the entire second half of 1942. Zone flights, precision bombing, patrols on land and at sea, studies of the matériel and area of combat operations were the kinds of activities the crews practiced from day to day along with the brigade commander. He trained his brigade persistently, intensively, and purposefully for the upcoming battles.

In June 1942, Major Chibisov was conferred the rank of lieutenant colonel under an order from People's Commissar for the Navy Nikolai Kuznetsov, a recognition of his achievements in building a highly efficient fighting unit.

On August 20, 1943, the 10th Bomber Aviation Brigade was transformed into the 10th Short-Range Bomber Aviation Division (10th SBAD). Lieutenant Colonel Chibisov was in charge of making this division a combat-ready aviation unit, and he never eased up on himself or his subordinates.

A reliable group of professional pilots had taken shape around Maxim. He remembered each of them well even several years later. In his diaries, he listed them by name: Deputy Division Commanders Bogomolov and Semyonov; Chief of Staff Sokolov; Regiment Commanders Pashkov, Kovalenko, Tikhmirov, and Takhtarov; and others.

The division started receiving new Pe-2 bombers. Maxim's dream had finally come true. Wasting no time, he and 33rd Bomber Regiment Commander Y. Pashkov, who were the only ones with experience in piloting this plane, began training the command staff initially and then the rest of the flight personnel.

Soon the training in the bomber regiments was put entirely in the hands of their commanders. Maxim remained in charge of the final technical polishing of the future aces as well as check flights and the most complicated flights: at night and under conditions as close as possible to combat. The crews were flying with more confidence, and the tactical interaction between the units and squadrons became increasingly clearer.

But the division commander was still not fully satisfied: the naval component remained a weakness for the aviation unit.

Nothing else seemed to cause any complaints. The division almost had enough dive-bombers for combat actions both on land and at sea. The fighter regiment was still waiting for the arrival of the latest Yak-3 aircraft. However, the division lacked a necessary component to become a truly effective fighting unit within the fleet: a detachment of seaplanes.

General Lemeshko, to whom Lieutenant Colonel Chibisov had repeatedly appealed regarding this issue, one day cryptically said, "Just wait—you will get your seaplane detachment. You will have flying boats that are capable of fulfilling the relevant objectives."

Lieutenant Colonel Chibisov did not ask for clarification about exactly what kind of boats would be sent, since he understood that the commander was hinting at something secret. *They will tell us when they think it is necessary*, he thought.

9.3 In the Urals and the Distant Polazna

The family of Brigade Commander and Division Commander Chibisov survived the harsh daily challenges of wartime in the Urals village to which they had been evacuated.

Anna's heath was deteriorating. She could hardly eat any of the food her daughter managed to find. Money had no value at that time, but barter trade was flourishing. At the market, refugees exchanged the things they had brought for farm products, such as eggs, poultry, potatoes, and honey. The Chibisovs had nothing extra to trade, but Rosaly had returned from Saransk with a supply of tobacco, which was a mandatory part of the pilots' rations. Maxim, who had never smoked in his life, had the idea to save all the tobacco he received and give it to his wife when he saw her. She began trading the tobacco for food.

In order to somehow survive, Rosaly persuaded the village council to allocate her a small piece of land. Numerous evacuees took such plots, calling them "new land." With bloody blisters on her palms, the senior military commander's wife dug up the plot by hand and planted a bucket of buds in the garden, which, in the fall of 1942, yielded a bumper crop: two whole sacks of potatoes!

After growing potatoes on her "new land," Rosaly shared the wealth with her neighbors. One of them, Elena Galyamova, was a sailor's widow who was raising two daughters alone. Much later, in the early 1960s, she visited the Chibisovs and reminded Rosaly of the story with the potatoes: "You saved my children from hunger. I will never forget that. And I want your daughters to know this!"

For Emma's fourth birthday in May 1942, Rosaly invited over the neighborhood children. She baked Urals *shanezhki* (a type of custard-filled pie with potato filling instead of curd). Someone gave the kind hostess flour, and she received eggs and milk in exchange for tobacco. It was a glorious feast! It was interspersed with performances by the children, who read poems and sang songs, and they also played bingo. Forever afterward, Emma remembered her mother's words: "A birthday must be celebrated each year regardless of the circumstances."

A month later, Anna fell ill. She was not eating anything and could not even swallow a hard-boiled egg. She quietly passed away in July 1942. This was a huge blow for Rosaly.

On that sorrowful day, Emma asked her grandma to read to her like she always did and wanted her to open her eyes. After putting her daughter to bed that night, Rosaly began making preparations for her mother's burial.

She reached an agreement with a local carpenter, who promised to build her a coffin, again in exchange for tobacco. But she was supposed to find the boards for the coffin on her own. The carpenter told her exactly where she could steal them, but he refused to come along. His fear was understandable, given the severity of the punishment for so-called anti-social actions under martial law.

Nothing could stop the brave officer's wife. She went to the village and singlehandedly dragged the lumber she needed back to the house.

Shortly thereafter, Rosaly became seriously ill. The hard work with which she exhausted herself every day had taken its toll. After all, she would take any work she could get on the collective farm since it was the only way to receive half a dozen eggs, a liter of milk, or a piece of butter.

The well-educated city girl, who was unaccustomed to heavy farmwork, had to get up before dawn and take care of the cattle all day as she substituted for sick collective farmers. Then she would rush home to her dear and equally helpless mother and daughter.

When Anna passed away, Rosaly's physical exhaustion was compounded by nervous breakdowns. For instance, she continued to cook soup or porridge for three, but she would not eat anything herself and would reproach herself for not paying enough attention to her sick mother. By fall 1942, her condition worsened. The doctors gave her a terrifying diagnosis: open-cavitary pulmonary tuberculosis.

After studying the results of her x-rays, the doctor inquired about Rosaly's family status and then told her, "I'm not going to speak to you as a patient but as a person who is caring for the sick. It is imperative to urgently stop the process in your lungs and let the cavities cicatrize. We don't have any medicine for tuberculosis here, but there is a natural remedy. You need to drink at least one three-liter jar containing a mixture of suet, honey, garlic, and aloe juice. If we don't stop the process in your lungs before the ice on the Kama River starts to break, you'll be gone with the ice drift, and your daughter will become an orphan."

Rosaly did everything she could to recover. She obtained lard from some peasants in exchange for tobacco, and she found garlic. When she tried to buy honey at the market, the saleswoman said she was only interested in trading for specific items. Rosaly brought the woman to her home and opened her small suitcase. The lady selected a piece of crape and a lace silk shawl. Grandma Klava was also involved in the conversation and helped to barter aloe paper in exchange for felt boots.

As it turned out, however, the main difficulty was not preparing the healing mixture. The hardest part was forcing oneself to swallow at least one spoon of the supposed miracle potion, since it was disgusting. There were some bitter days filled with physical and mental anguish. It was all seen as some sort of huge injustice by the higher powers. After an entire year of the desperate fight for survival, separation from her husband, and the loss of her mother, the disasters kept coming for Rosaly Chibisova!

In the winter of 1942–1943, all tobacco products disappeared in Molotov and the surrounding area, and Maxim's military-issued tobacco rose sharply in price. Thanks to this "capital," Rosaly somehow managed to get through what proved to be the most difficult months for her.

She also received a great deal of help from Grandma Klava, a simple peasant woman who had taken four women and children into her home and done everything possible for a person in her condition to help them survive the difficult time of war with no husbands and far from their native homes.

When ringing in the new year in 1943, Grandma Klava's guests sang a song they had composed themselves in her honor, which started with the following verse:

In the Urals and distant Polazna,
On Factory Street, number six,
Among many very different people,
There is a remarkable person.

For the rest of her life, Emma would remember the words to this song as well as the address: Factory Street, house 6.

In 1994, more than half a century later, Emma visited Perm on business. She stopped by Polazna and managed to find the miraculously preserved house where the evacuees had once lived. Unfortunately, she was unable to find the graves of Grandma Klava and her own grandmother Anna. Too much time had passed, and too many changes had occurred.

9.4 Assembling the Family

Even though he was fully immersed in his official duties, Maxim could not help but worry about his family, who were separated from him by several thousand kilometers. Upon learning of his wife's illness, he asked that an extract from her medical records be sent to him, and after seeing the frightful diagnosis, he could not sit by idly.

Contrary to his principles, he appealed to the Pacific Fleet commander with a personal request for the first time. Ivan Yumashev, who was already a full admiral by this time, granted permission for Lieutenant Colonel Chibisov's family to move to Nikolayevka.

In late summer 1943, Rosaly and Emma arrived in Vladivostok. They were met there by a naval officer since Maxim could not leave work. The five-year-old Emma recalled that he immediately began teasing her. Upon hearing snippets of the adults' conversation—"The Suchan River is flooded after the rain. Emma may not be able to wade through it. We'll have to go around"—the young girl immediately retorted, "Of course I can't wade. I don't even have any rubber boots, just shoes." The adults laughed. This funny episode became part of the Chibisov family chronicles and was frequently retold to friends and loved ones.

When they arrived in Nikolayevka, Maxim was frightened: his wife looked like a walking skeleton. It appeared she had just returned from a concentration camp instead of evacuation.

With her family reunited, Rosaly's health gradually began to improve, and soon she managed to find a job. The family got into a normal routine in the military settlement and comfortable commander's apartment. Maxim was at work, Rosaly was in a familiar position at the bank, and Emma was in kindergarten. Everything was almost as it had been prior to the war.

But then a new problem arose. Doctors began finding problems with Maxim's body—like a combat machine constantly subjected to extreme forces. He had experienced signs of gallstones in the past, with pain in his lower right side. He patiently endured the pain and did not go to the doctor, fearing he would be forbidden to fly. In late 1943, the attacks became more frequent. Concealing his painful illness from his fellow soldiers, he continued to perform his commander duties at full speed. He continued to fly and never even considered serious treatment. But he went on a diet and gave up alcohol completely.

Rosaly Borisovna and Emma Chibisov, 1941.

When they stopped by the officers' parties, Maxim and Rosaly would switch their glasses without anybody noticing. He would drink mineral water, and she would rescue her husband by consuming all the alcohol. At the end of the evening, they sometimes had to wait for everyone to leave. Then he would take his rescuer by the arm, and they would slowly return home. In the morning, Maxim would laugh and praise his wife: "Rosaly, you saved me again. If I had drank that much, I definitely would have had another attack."

9.5 Special Mission

Lieutenant Colonel Chibisov's aviation division was not thrown into the fire of battle in 1943 or 1944, one of the fortunate consequences of the great turning point in the war. Following the decisive battles outside Stalingrad and Kursk, the Soviet Army was advancing steadily, and Germany's ultimate defeat was expected to take place in the near future. After victory over the primary German enemy, war still lay ahead with the Japanese military, which had been threatening the Soviet Far

East for decades. Maxim understood that his division was being kept on standby, replenished with personnel, and equipped with powerful combat machinery specifically for the war with Japan. In preparing for this war, he created an exemplary aviation unit capable of dealing a powerful blow to the longtime enemy at any time.

(wrap text under photo): Commander of the 10th Short-Range Bomber Aviation Division Lieutenant Colonel M.N. Chibisov (at the center) with his subordinates, 1944.

In early July 1944, however, Lieutenant Colonel Chibisov was urgently summoned to the fleet headquarters in Vladivostok. After returning to Nikolayevka, he rushed home, where he shocked his wife with the news:

M.N. Chibisov with his wife and daughter prior to the departure to the USA, 1944.

"Rosaly, they're sending me to Moscow on a special mission."

"When?" she asked.

"The day after tomorrow," he replied.

Maxim had to quickly hand over the divisional affairs to his deputy, Vasily Bogomolov. He had almost no time left to say goodbye to his family. He hugged his wife and daughter, found a minute to take a picture of the three of them together, and took off without indicating when he would return, although he himself knew little about his mission.

Rosaly once again had to resign herself to waiting patiently for news from her husband. He had left, and it seemed as if he had disappeared into the unknown. He did not send a single letter for several months.

Emma often woke up at night around that time and found her mother crying by herself in the kitchen. Rosaly continued to work at the local bank, take her daughter to kindergarten, and work her second shift in the garden during the evenings. When there was a threat of war with neighboring Japan, she would maintain a night watch with the other pilots' wives.

After a while, Rosaly began to sense a change in her status: she was no longer the first lady of the garrison but only the wife of a former division commander, with all the ensuing consequences. Some of Maxim's fellow soldiers with whom the Chibisovs had been family friends lost interest in their former commander's wife. Two pilots were housed in her three-room apartment on the second floor of their three-story house.

Then Emma suddenly came down with the measles, the same disease that had claimed the life of the Chibisovs' first daughter, the joyful two-year-old Alenka. Rosaly did not leave her daughter's bedside for days, and in the dimly lit room, she fed her a potion, which was actually heated red and sweet wine, which, according to the household myths of that time, contributed to the outbreak of the measles rash. Emma would never forget the name of this potion: Madera.

CHAPTER 10

Journey over Three Seas

10.1 Lend-Lease

The reason Lieutenant Colonel Chibisov was summoned to Moscow was considered more important than commanding a single division and training it for combat. It was so top secret that Maxim no longer had the right to maintain contact with his family until the end of the war and even a little bit longer.

He had been appointed head of a special air group that was to handle the delivery of aircraft from the United States for Soviet naval aviation under the Lend-Lease Program.

Lend-Lease was by no means viewed as a type of charity. It's no accident that the law on Lend-Lease adopted by the US Congress on March 11, 1941, at the initiative of President Franklin Roosevelt was given the title "An Act to Further Promote the Defense of the United States." This law granted the US president the authority to transfer, exchange, lease, lend, or otherwise supply military supplies or military information to the government of any country if its defense against aggression was vital for the defense of the United States. The countries receiving aid under Lend-Lease signed bilateral agreements with the United States stipulating that the matériel destroyed, lost, or expended during the war would not be subject to payment at the war's end.

Forty-two countries received US aid under the law on Lend-Lease, with the largest supplies going to the United Kingdom. Roosevelt announced his willingness to provide such aid to the Soviet Union on June 24, 1941. Official negotiations on Lend-Lease between the USSR and the United States began on September 29 after Roosevelt sent his representative Averell Harriman to Moscow.

On October 1, 1941, Harriman signed the first protocol on supplies to the Soviet Union. On November 7, Roosevelt signed a document extending Lend-Lease to the USSR.

Missions from the United States and United Kingdom then traveled to Moscow. The negotiations resulted in the signing of the Moscow Protocol, which officially documented an agreement under which the Soviet Union would urgently purchase $1 billion worth of weapons from the United States. The scale of such purchases increased in the future, and by the end of the war, the total was estimated at $11 billion.

In order to implement this agreement, the Governmental Procurement Commission (GPC) was established on a permanent basis and set up headquarters in Washington.

The GPC employees were in constant contact with the US Department of Defense, representatives of the naval and air forces and engineering corps, and other structures supplying weapons under Lend-Lease.

The aviation group of the GPC was primarily staffed with graduates of the Zhukovsky Air Force Academy. They typically had combat experience as well as experience in accepting military equipment at Soviet enterprises.

Their work required them to frequently visit US aviation plants, study the aircraft being supplied, and inspect their quality and completeness. The GPC was also in charge of considering claims concerning the incompleteness of the equipment supplied or discrepancies with the inventory ordered. Such instances were not uncommon, particularly during the early stages of the Lend-Lease supplies.

The most difficult task was actually delivering the Lend-Lease cargo to the Soviet Union.

The heaviest cargo was shipped from the United States to the USSR via the Pacific Ocean on Soviet ships. The Japanese, who owned the Kuril Islands, controlled all the straits leading to the Soviet Union's Far Eastern ports. They were supposed to let vessels sailing under the Soviet flag pass through under a neutrality treaty signed by the two countries; however, numerous obstacles were erected, Soviet transport vessels were often searched, and sometimes they were sunk, allegedly mistaken for US ships. Only nonmilitary cargo was permitted to be delivered along this route.

Another supply route ran from the United States via the sea and ocean to Iranian ports. From there, the Lend-Lease cargo was shipped by land to the Caucasus. In terms of its length and time, this route seemed like a journey around the world. It was particularly inconvenient for the delivery of aircraft. At the Persian Gulf ports, the planes were partially disassembled, their wings were removed, and then they were shipped along the unstable Iranian railways to Baku, where they were reassembled and had any damages caused during transit fixed.

The fastest route for shipping military cargo was from the US East Coast across the northern Atlantic Ocean to England, then to Iceland, and on toward the shores of the Soviet Union, ending in either Murmansk or Arkhangelsk. The bulk of the military cargo delivered to the USSR from England and the United States traveled along this route, which only took 10 - 14 days. The only drawback was that this route required the transport vessels to pass close to the coast of Norway, where the Germans maintained sizeable naval and air force groups.

To fend off attacks from the sea and the air, the Allied transport vessels traveled in large caravans escorted by warships. Even with such convoys, however, the German bombs and torpedoes destroyed a significant part of the ships and cargo. One out of every six transport vessels in the northern convoys was sunk by the Germans in 1942–1944. The losses were even higher during the initial stages of these operations.

In May 1942, a plane carrying a Soviet governmental delegation headed by Stalin's closest ally, Vyacheslav Molotov, departed along the route of the northern convoys, only in the opposite direction: to England and then to the United States. This transatlantic flight by the Soviet delegation to England and the United States and then back to the USSR was fraught with great danger, as they had to fly over the Barents Sea in an area frequently patrolled by Luftwaffe fighters. Endel Puusepp, a famous polar pilot and participant in the bombing of Berlin, piloted the plane carrying Molotov and his colleagues and received the star of Hero of the Soviet Union for this flight.

Molotov signed the Anglo-Soviet Treaty in London, and in Washington, he managed to reach an agreement on the extension and expansion of supplies under the Lend-Lease Program. However, the issue of transporting these supplies soon became a serious problem.

In June 1942, two-thirds of convoy PQ-17—given this name because it was the seventeenth convoy sent—were destroyed in attacks by German submarines and torpedo bombers. Only eleven of the initial thirty-five ships sent made it to the Soviet shores. Hundreds of sailors were killed, and cargo valued at more than $500 million was lost. After this, the British Admiralty decided to temporarily suspend the northern caravans. The next convoy, PQ-18, was sent in October and also suffered enormous losses. The use of this route was then discontinued until spring of the following year.

Meanwhile, battles were unfolding on the Soviet-German front that would essentially determine the outcome of World War II.

In winter 1941–1942, the Soviet Army had achieved its first victories while basically fighting with old reserves. The Battle of Moscow was won by the heroism of the Russian infantry and the strategic talents of Zhukov. But due to a chronic lack of tanks and aircraft, the offensive launched by the Soviet forces became bogged down by spring. The strategic advantage had once again shifted to the Wehrmacht. In subsequent months, the country's fate would be decided in fierce battles raging between the Don and Volga rivers. During this period, the Soviet defense industry was still only evolving after recovering from the losses suffered during the first months of the war. Under such conditions, any aid from abroad in the form of military equipment, weapons, ammunition, and materials for weapons production was invaluable.[16]

---

[16] The estimates of the impact of the Lend-Lease Program are contradictory. Nikolai Voznesensky, the chairman of the USSR State Planning Committee during the war years, said in his book published in 1948 that "the proportion of these supplies with respect to domestic production [was] only about 4% during the war economy period." It is unclear how this percentage was calculated. Voznesensky, who was arrested as part of the so-called Leningrad Affair and shot in 1950, never managed to provide any comments about this assessment of the Lend-Lease Program, but one must assume it was highly understated for political reasons.

Under Lend-Lease, the Soviet Union received 22,150 planes, or approximately 15% of the total amount produced by Soviet aviation factories during the war years. The ratio of imported armored vehicles to domestic ones was roughly the same. Incidentally, the foreign (primarily English) armored vehicles delivered to the USSR were not particularly popular (due to weaknesses in their combat performance) in contrast to the US planes (there were no complaints about the Airacobra heavy fighters, while the Boston bombers and other aircraft also demonstrated their worth). In addition, the Studebakers manufactured in the

At the time, the Soviet Union needed supplies of aircraft more than anything else, particularly fighters and frontline bombers. Thousands of these planes had been enveloped in flames in the skies in 1942. Soviet aviation industry workers made heroic efforts to increase aircraft output, but the Luftwaffe had factories conquered by the German forces working on its behalf all throughout Europe.

V.M. Molotov at the airfield in Dandy, England, 20th of May 1942.

United States became an essential part of the Soviet Army's truck fleet, and all the top military brass traveled on the Willis vehicles provided under Lend-Lease. Once the Soviet factories began manufacturing a sufficient amount of military equipment, weapons, and ammunition, their work was supported by Lend-Lease supplies of technological equipment, materials, and semi-finished products that the strained Soviet economy was producing in insufficient quantities.

Food was also supplied to troops and the population at a time when the Soviet Union's main grain-producing regions were occupied by the Germans.

Thus, the Lend-Lease supplies actually made a tangible contribution to the victory over the Fascists in terms of material support.

Anastas Mikoyan, who served as people's commissar for foreign trade and was responsible for accepting supplies from the Allies during the war, expressed his opinion on the matter quite succinctly: "Without Lend-Lease, we would have probably continued fighting for an extra 12–18 months" (G. Kumanev, *The People's Commissars of Stalin Speak*, Smolensk: Rusich, 2005, 70).

It should also be noted that the Lend-Lease Program was very beneficial for America (in purely financial terms, without even taking into account the political component). US Senator Walter George explained to his colleagues why money needed to be spent on Lend-Lease as follows: "The nation is currently approximately $8 billion per month. If not for those preparations we made during these months to buy time, I am convinced the war would have continued for another year. We spend up to $100 billion per year on the war; in addition, we could have lost an enormous number of the nation's best sons. Even by shortening the war by six months, we are saving $48 billion and spending only $11 billion, while no value can be placed on the blood of our soldiers and the tears of our mothers" (Lend-Lease article from the Russian version of *Wikipedia*).

In summer 1942, Stalin sent Roosevelt a letter stating, "We are in desperate need of supplies of modern fighter aircraft (for example, the Airacobra) … The Germans proved to have large reserves of aircraft. In the south, the Germans have at least twice the superiority in the air, which makes it impossible for us to provide cover for our troops."

In order to receive aircraft as soon as possible, Soviet leaders agreed to temporarily forego supplies of tanks, artillery, and ammunition. US officials were prepared to respond to their ally's appeal, but the routes utilized at that time were not suitable for the prompt delivery of planes. Therefore, both sides made it a priority to establish a direct air route from the United States to the Soviet-German front through Canada, Alaska, and Siberia. The advantages of this route, called the Northwest Staging Route in English and AlSib (for Alaska–Siberia) in Russian, compared to the sea-based routes were obvious: the aircraft delivery time was reduced, and losses were minimized.

The length of the route from Fairbanks, Alaska, to Krasnoyarsk was 6,500 kilometers (4,039 miles).

Numerous new airfields had to be built along the Soviet part of this route (in Ulekal, Markovo, Anadyr, Tanyurer, Pevek, Khandyga, Chaybukha, Omolon, Kedon, and Seymchan), as well as seaplane stations (in Gizhiga, Magadan, and Chaybukha). In addition, drastic improvements had to be made to the existing Siberian airfields. The construction of the infrastructure required for this air route in the harsh conditions and undeveloped, sparsely populated areas of the Far North was completed in an incredibly short period due to the war: just under a year from the design blueprints to the start of operations on the Northwest Staging Route.

On October 1, 1942, Soviet pilots flew the first A-20 and B-25 bombers and P-39 Airacobra heavy fighters (which were praised by numerous Soviet pilots during the war, including the renowned ace Alexander Pokryshkin) along this route to the front.

The Northwest Staging Route not only compensated for the reduction in aircraft supplies caused by the suspension of the North Atlantic conveys but also made it possible to supply almost twice as many US planes to the USSR. The Soviet Union received 1,485 planes in 1942. While these aircraft might not have been the decisive factor in the aerial battles fought toward the end of the Battle of Stalingrad, they nevertheless played an important role.

In 1943, supplies under Lend-Lease increased significantly, totaling 700,000-800,000 tons per month starting in May.

The convoys also resumed in the North Atlantic with increased protection from the British Navy. The Northwest Staging Route was operating at full capacity.

The Soviet Air Force received 5,320 US-manufactured aircraft in 1943. The national aviation industry was also continuously increasing the production of fighter, frontline bomber, and attack aircraft. As a result, Soviet aircraft began to overpower the Germans in air warfare by the fall.

The Soviet aviation industry, however, was incapable of producing certain types of high-quality machines at that time, in particular long-range seaplanes.

The only Soviet plane of this type was the GST, an analogue to the US-manufactured PBY-1, which had been produced at the Beriev Taganrog Aviation Plant prior to the war under a license acquired from the company Consolidated. Due to an embargo on imported components in late 1939, the production of these planes had to be scaled down, and the few that had been produced were distributed to all the fleets (most of the GSTs ended up in the Northern Fleet Air Force, in which a seaplane aviation group had been formed to provide protection to convoys). Such aircraft were desperately needed, and it had proven impossible to resume production of the GST at the Beriev plant, which had been evacuated after Taganrog was captured by the enemy, first in Omsk and then in Krasnoyarsk.

Given the needs for such planes by naval aviation and also considering the prospect of the Soviet Union's entering into a war with Japan (about which Stalin had agreed with Roosevelt and Churchill in Tehran), Soviet leaders requested a consignment of PBN and PBY flying boats from their overseas allies. Soviet experts had been familiar with their prototypes since before the war, but the USSR became particularly interested in these seaplanes after the British Navy used them to establish reliable protection for the northern convoys against attacks by German submarines.

President Roosevelt agreed to grant the request from the Russian allies.

Seaplanes OS2U Kingfisher, PBY Catalina and Hall PH at
the airfield in Elizabeth City, USA. March 21st 1942.

10.2 The Wonderful Catalina

As the first US allies to receive the long-range seaplane, British pilots
were enthralled with its flight and combat features as well as the aesthetic
form of the plane, and they gave the plane a nickname, as is customary in
the Royal Air Force: Catalina.

They used this plane successfully for long-range reconnaissance and
to hunt for submarines. The Catalinas escorted the convoys traveling to
Murmansk and Arkhangelsk, landed troops, were involved in rescuing
crews from sinking ships, and also shot down aircraft (the winged beauty
was indispensable for this purpose).

The US Navy, which followed the example of the English in using the
nickname Catalina, most frequently used the planes for landing operations.
The PBN-1 Nomad and PBY-6A were improved versions of the Catalina
(the latter was amphibious, with three-wheel retractable landing gear that
enabled the plane to land on and take off from both water and land). They
reached a respectable speed of 288 kilometers per hour (179 mph) and could
fly 4,500 kilometers (2,796 miles) without refueling.

It is to be noted the PBN-1 Nomad had a number of design differences
from the PBY-5a that was being produced at that time. In order to avoid

disruption of existing Catalina production, it was decided the PBN-1 seaplanes would be built by the Naval Aviation Factory at the Naval Shipyard in Philadephia, PA.

The Catalina had excellent aerodynamic and nautical abilities. Side floats were attached to the ends of its long wings. During landing, the ends of the wings folded out into a vertical position, and the plane turned into a trimaran that was stable even on waves. During takeoff, it glided delicately along the water and spread its broad wings after separating from the water. With such wings and powerful engines, the Catalina could carry a considerable bomb load and take on an entire detachment of paratroopers. An airmobile command post or a mini-hospital could fit in its relatively wide (up to three meters) (10 feet) frame.

In addition, the Catalina was equipped with the latest communications and navigation equipment, which was of particular interest to Soviet experts since the domestic aviation industry was significantly inferior to its US counterpart in this regard.

It was no surprise that the Soviet leaders sought to obtain this wonder of US technology as something that would be required in the upcoming battles and also be useful as a model for the subsequent development of the Soviet military and industrial complex.

Majestic Catalina

The United States quickly resolved the issue of manufacturing and supplying the Catalina to its Russian allies since the Americans expected the USSR to enter into war with Japan. The project for these supplies was strictly confidential and given the code name Zebra. As head of this project, Roosevelt appointed Vice Admiral Patrick Bellinger, a veteran of Pearl Harbor and the Naval air force commander in the operational zone of the Atlantic Fleet.

In the top US leadership circles, there were numerous opponents of such close cooperation with the Soviets. Several senior officials at the Pentagon believed that along with the Catalinas, the Russians would receive too many US military secrets. In March 1944, Project Zebra came to a halt.[17]

President Roosevelt once again had to intervene to resolve the problems that had arisen, but soon the first 48 Catalinas (primarily intended for the Soviet Northern Fleet) were handed over to the Soviet representatives at the military base in Elizabeth City on the Atlantic coast. Meanwhile, U.S. factories were already working on the next consignment of seaplanes for the Soviet Union.

A special group of 26 crews with high levels of training and flight experience with the MBR-2, GST, and Che-2 was established to ferry the aircraft across the ocean. The Northern Fleet Air Force and Pacific Fleet Air Force allocated ten crews each for the group, while the Black Sea Fleet provided six crews. Colonel Viktor Vasilyev was appointed commander of the group, while Major N. Piskaryov was appointed his deputy. The latter appointment was somewhat of a surprise since Pacific Fleet Air Force Flight Inspector Lieutenant Colonel Ignatyev was supposed to perform the duties of deputy commander. However, he was dismissed just before the flight due to an accident on a Che-2 plane he had inspected. The plane had taken off from a land-based airfield. While descending in the operational area, the pilots had overcooled the engines, which had given out when they increased the throttle. The pilots, unable to restart the engines and fearing they would be unable to properly calculate the landing, had decided to put the plane down in the water of Sukhodol Bay with its landing gear extended. The plane had been destroyed upon impact with the water, and

---

[17] Gregory Gagarin spoke about some of the peculiarities of the US military bureaucratic machine: "In our Department of the Navy, any action required authorization from ten different admirals and their subordinates, who had their own bureau in Washington. In order to replace even the tiniest screw, these ten admirals had to sign the authorizing document. We even deliberately kept one lieutenant—I can't remember his name—in Washington, and any time such an issue arose we would call him and say, 'Please go to the bureau. We need to get a signature from so and so.' And this lieutenant would run around to ten offices collecting signatures. Moreover, none of the admirals wanted to be the first to sign it." It was difficult to work with such a decision-making system and easy to slow down any process, as demonstrated by opponents of Roosevelt's policy toward the USSR.

the check pilot had been killed. Ignatyev had been suspended from flights and replaced by Piskaryov from the Northern Fleet Air Force, who had only recently been discharged from the hospital following injury.

To help the commander of the special group, Naval Air Force Flight Navigator Colonel Mostsepan, Engineer Lieutenant Colonel Kokarev, Engineer Major Korobkov, and others were appointed. It was decided to split the flight crews into three groups and send them to the aircraft acceptance base in Elizabeth City in North Carolina. The commander and his group were flown from Murmansk to England and then on to the United States. The Pacific crews arrived in Krasnoyarsk by train and then traveled to Fairbanks on passenger flights. The Black Sea crews went to Murmansk and then traveled to the United States by sea.

The first ten Pacific Fleet pilot crews arrived in the United States on C-47 and C-54 transport planes on April 2, 1944. Waiting for them at the seaplane station in Elizabeth City were 25 PBN-1s that had been built at the US Naval Aviation Factory in Philadelphia and were ready for takeoff.

Naval Aviation Factory, US Navy Shipyard, 1941, Attribution : U.S. Department of the Navy. Bureau of Aeronautics., Public domain, via Wikimedia Commons.

Since the pilots from the special group had previously flown on single-engine MBR-2 seaplanes for the most part (only a few pilots had flown on the transport seaplanes), the incoming Soviet crews received intensive training from US Navy squadron commander Lieutenant Harper; his deputy in the flying unit, Holtz; pilot Lieutenant Stauers; and squadron engineer Lieutenant Hodge. Interpreters were sent from the Soviet embassy, while the Americans later began using their own interpreter.

From left to right. 1st row: V. Tertsiev, M.khrolenko, F. Danilov. 2nd row: I. Genkin, translator from the USSR Embassy, V. Vasiliev, Commanding Officer of the Special Operations Group, S. Chernack, U.S. Navy Commanding Officer, Project Zebra in front of the Wright Brothers Memorial.

In the study group, the Soviet specialists were surprised by the somewhat unusual approach of the American experts to aviation equipment. Soviet engineers were used to constantly digging around in engines, adjusting them, flushing them, and so on. They were astonished when the US engineers refused to open the engines. It turned out they did not know where the main engine parts and components were located.

The expertise of the Americans was limited. Previously retrained English and French pilots had smashed a few planes, perhaps due to the

Pilots' cockpit of Catalina. At the bottom you can see a bombardier's space equipped with a Norden sight.

insufficient training methods of the American instructors, which differed slightly from the practices accepted in Soviet naval aviation, involved taking into account the specific features of the aircraft and the individual qualities of the trainee, and were aimed at providing retraining in the shortest possible period. The pilot under training was given greater independence, starting from the first flight. When practicing piloting techniques, particular attention was paid to performing flights with one feathered engine and then switching it on in the air. This was new for the Soviet pilots since the engines on Soviet aircraft still did not have feathering systems at that time. The Soviet aircraft did not even have autopilot systems.

The capabilities of the plane were such that the instructor could take not one but three pilots on a flight and work with them during the morning hours. Later in the day, the instructor would take up another three pilots. Another pilot under training sat in the right-hand seat during the training flights. Particular attention was paid to flying in blind conditions (under the hood) and, when possible, flying in clouds. The pilots were also trained in maintaining the course of the flight based on the radio beacon, which was the type of condition they would face during a transcontinental flight. The instructor pointed out their errors over the aircraft intercom and only intervened in extreme cases. On the third day, six pilots would usually fly on their own.

A crew was considered prepared if the pilot flew the plane confidently, could manage flying in difficult weather both day and night, and could maintain a given flight mode even with only one engine. The navigator was to be capable of independently guiding the plane to its destination in the event it was separated from the group. In addition, the navigators studied bombing and small arms at a special US Navy school in Norfolk, Virginia.

For the Soviets, successful retraining was a matter of prestige, as it generally gave the impression of a certain level of professionalism. Already, within 20 days after arriving, the Pacific Fleet group was ready to ferry the aircraft, the onboard equipment had been tested, and two six-hour training flights had been conducted over the Atlantic. The American instructors gave glowing reports about the Soviet pilots. The instructor who flew with Piskaryov could not conceal his delight and, after three flights, stated there was nothing new he could teach the Soviet pilot.

Despite their readiness to ferry the aircraft back to the Soviet Union, the pilots had to wait about a month for the group commander and other crews to arrive. Only after they had been trained—this time by their own native instructors—did they commence immediate preparations for the 7,200 kilometer (4,500 mile) flight along the Northern Route: from Elizabeth City to Gander (Newfoundland) to Reykjavik to Murmansk. The estimated flying time at a cruising speed of 185 kilometers per hour (115 miles per hour) was 45 hours. As part of an agreement, each plane was to have an English pilot (who performed the navigator's duties) and radio operator. The Soviet pilots handled landing and takeoff, while the English pilots were in charge of obtaining permission to land both the main and alternate airfields, determining the best places for cloud breaking, and using radio equipment. This seemed fair, given the vast experience of the English pilots, some of whom had crossed the Atlantic Ocean more than 50 times.[18]

On May 25, 1944, the lead group of 25 seaplanes began making its way across the North Atlantic to Murmansk.

---

[18] Noting the important role played by the British Royal Air Force, Gregory Gagarin wrote, "All the flight routes were coordinated between the U.S. Navy and the Royal Air Force. The Atlantic headquarters of the Royal Air Force was located in Montreal. Despite the fact that the United States had airbases and the necessary resources in many areas where Soviet aircraft could land ... the Soviet crews used the British airbases. In addition, each crew departing from Elizabeth City that flew along the Northern Route included three members of the Royal Air Force (a pilot, navigator and flight engineer) who accompanied the Soviet crews all the way to the last stopover before the final flight to the USSR. These British crews had great experience in transatlantic flights and were subordinate to the Royal Air Force transport aviation command. It should be recognized that the Royal Air Force pilots were the ones who made the main contribution to training the Russian seaplane crews and preparing them to fly over the ocean."

The Northern Route was not particularly advantageous in terms of the safety of the aircraft. There was a good chance they would encounter German Bf-110 fighters along the way. In addition, they had to make a significant portion of the flight in poor weather conditions, passing through low-pressure areas where thick clouds and the icing of the aircraft were inevitable. Some of the crews had to fly in turbulence at an elevation of 40 meters (130 feet) over the stormy sea, using the radio altimeter readings. The exhausted pilots were forced to turn on the autopilot function. As one of the crew members wrote in his memoirs, they declined hot lunches, even though the planes had electric stoves, food stocks, and water. They had plenty of other troubles to deal with. For instance, on the trip from Elizabeth City to Newfoundland, defects were discovered in the attachment of the antennae. They had to be reinstalled and secured more firmly. During the second leg of the flight, one of the most experienced navigators made an error with the compass bearings. Two hours prior to the landing in Reykjavik, he reported to the crew commander, "We passed Iceland." The commander decided to turn around and return. Fortunately, during the flight across the Atlantic Ocean—the most difficult and lengthy part of the journey—the Soviet navigators received support from their British allies. The British pilot accompanying the crew attempted to explain that they needed to turn around, but his Russian colleagues did not speak any English. The Englishman requested help with an urgent radiogram to Reykjavik. Soon a British fighter caught up to the Catalina, which had drifted far out to the ocean, and signaled for it to follow the fighter back to the base.

The more-than 2,400 kilometer (1,500-mile) flight from Reykjavik to Murmansk took from 15 to 22 hours (depending on speed and wind direction) and was the most dangerous part of the flight since German planes were always in the air over the north coast of Norway, watching for the transport convoys of the Allies. Avoiding encounters with the German fighters, the Catalinas proceeded at a low altitude, parallel to the rugged coast, almost touching the water at times. So as not to attract the enemy's attention, the crews maintained radio silence and had no contact with Murmansk. This resulted in all the other problems being compounded by difficulties with orientation.

Unfortunately, an incident occurred during the first ferrying of aircraft: a plane commanded by the leader of a group of Soviet ferry pilots, Colonel Vasilyev, disappeared. Upon splashing down in Murmansk on June 16, the commander of the first squad of Catalinas, Major Piskaryov, reported to the Northern Fleet Air Force headquarters that Colonel Vasilyev had been trailing the squad of Captain Ivanov. However, when Ivanov's squad arrived safely in Murmansk, Vasilyev was not among the group.

It later came to light that immediately after takeoff in Reykjavik, an engine had failed in one of the planes, flown by Captain Boychenko, who had been forced to make an emergency landing. After seeing this from the ground, Vasilyev, a special group commander, decided not to take off but to wait for the problem to be fixed and then to fly in tandem. When Boychenko's plane overtook the Catalinas on the way to Murmansk the next morning, it became clear that something had gone wrong with the commander's plane.

Boychenko said he and Vasilyev had been flying in tandem over the dangerous zone near the Norwegian coast, when they'd encountered thick fog. The crews had decided to break radio silence and maintain constant communication so as not to get split up in the fog. In his final radio transmission, Vasilyev had reported to the wingman that his plane was flying at a course of 66 degrees and an altitude of 500 meters (1,640 feet), and he could see water below them. Suddenly, Vasilyev had given the order "Descend!" and the connection had been lost. Vasilyev had not responded to any further calls.

The Soviet and English pilots' searches for the crew conducted over a ten-day period from June 18 to June 28, 1944, were unsuccessful. It could only be assumed the plane either had been shot down by German fighters or had deviated off course and collided with the mountains on the Norwegian coast. A commission immediately set up at the headquarters of the Northern Fleet Air Force on June 28, 1944, stated that the seaplane had gone missing along with its crew, which included commander Colonel Vasilyev, navigator Colonel I. Mostsepan, copilot Lieutenant Colonel N. Romanov, flight mechanic K. Chichkan, and flight radio operator N. Kuznetsov.

V. N. Vasilyev

I.F. Moscepan

N.P. Romanov

E.K. Chichkan

A.M. Skvortsoy

Catalina's crew № 02826.]

All the other planes that had flown together with Vasilyev arrived safely in Murmansk and began fulfilling the orders of the Air Force command. The members of the difficult journey proved themselves as steadfast and courageous pilots and immediately began preparing for the trip to bring over the next batch of PBN-1 aircraft.

Place of the crash of V.N. Vasilyev's crew. Andotten cliff in Norway.

Once it became clear that Vasilyev would not be returning, questions arose about who would become the new leader of the operation to deliver flying boats to the Soviet Union. Such a person could only be a qualified pilot with excellent knowledge of the machinery and vast experience in flying over water surfaces. Naval Aviation Commander Semyon Zhavoronkov nominated Lieutenant Colonel Chibisov, whom he knew as an ace pilot with combat experience and extensive flying hours on seaplanes and, most importantly, as an experienced commander who had repeatedly demonstrated a remarkable ability to rapidly and efficiently build new units from scratch.

Naval Aviation Commander-in-Chief Nikolai Kuznetsov, who also knew Lt. Colonel Chibisov well, approved the appointment and signed the appropriate order.

10.3 Special Operations Group

While in Moscow, Maxim stayed with his brother Alexei, who lived on Nizhny Novgorod Lane at the Abelman outpost. His brother lived with three other family members in a cramped fifteen-square meter (161square feet) room. Lieutenant Colonel Chibisov had to sleep on the floor, using his fur coveralls as a mattress.

He vanished to the Air Force headquarters from the early morning until the late evening, delving into the specifics of the upcoming mission.

The general plan for the operation to ferry the Catalinas was discussed in detail in Moscow at meetings chaired by Naval Aviation Commander and Marshal of Aviation Semyon Zhavoronkov and attended by new operation leader Lieutenant Colonel Chibisov and Guards Major Nikolai Piskaryov, who was urgently summoned from the United States and had served as a deputy to the late Vasilyev.

There were three routes for ferrying the seaplanes from America to the Soviet Union.

The route to Murmansk through the northern Atlantic (the Northern Route) was the shortest, but it was unsafe, as Lieutenant Colonel Vasilyev's death had demonstrated.

The Eastern Route, which partially overlapped the Northwest Staging Route, was best suited for ferrying the seaplanes to the Pacific Ocean Fleet. Using this route, the planes were to fly from the Elizabeth City base on the Atlantic coast to New Orleans and then head west to the Pacific port of San Diego, passing over the southern United States. From there, they were to travel north along the Pacific coast via San Francisco and Seattle up to a base on Kodiak Island in Alaska. Then the aircraft were to fly over the Bering Sea to Anadyr and then on through Soviet airspace to Sukhodol Bay, outside Vladivostok. The trip covered a total of 12,850 kilometers from Elizabeth City to Anadyr and 18,450 kilometers to Vladivostok.

PBN-1 from the 118th OMRAP Airforces of the Northern Fleet. Guba Gryaznaya, 1944

Fighters and bombers had been ferried through Anadyr

since late 1942 for ground forces, but seaplanes had never been transported along this route before.

Another route, the Southern Route, which was entirely unfamiliar to Soviet pilots, passed over the central and southern Atlantic and then flew along the North African coast or bypassed Africa from the south in the general direction of Iraq and Iran before finally ending in Baku. This was the most convenient route for aircraft intended for the Black Sea Fleet.

All of these routes were to be used in the upcoming operation for the phased redeployment of Catalinas to various fleets.

Upon arriving from the United States, Guards Major Piskaryov provided Maxim with the details about the procedure for accepting aircraft and the training of the ferry pilot crews.

The former commander of the special group, along with his subordinates and the American members, had worked hard. Acceptance of the aircraft, like all other organizational and technical issues, was regulated by instructions prepared by experts from the two countries and approved by Naval Aviation Commander Colonel General Zhavoronkov. According to these instructions, the Catalinas built at the Naval Aircraft Factory at the US Navy shipyard in Philadelphia and delivered to the airfield were to be accepted in two stages.

At first, the technicians inspected the completeness of the equipment, weapons, instruments, and spare parts. Then they tested the engines on the ground. The crew who were to ferry the aircraft to the Soviet Union then took it for a test flight, during which they thoroughly inspected the operation of control equipment, navigational devices, the de-icing system for planes and propellers, and the radio and autopilot capabilities. They also determined fuel

Major N.F. Piskaryov

consumption at that time. Particular attention was paid to the propulsion unit. Defects were documented, conveyed to the Americans, and generally eliminated unconditionally. Following the final test flight, a delivery and acceptance statement was drawn up to include all the property associated with the plane.

The crews were trained in accordance with the proven method. The special group was divided into six detachments, and final adjustments were made for each crew on an individual basis. The crews repeatedly tested the engines, navigational equipment, autopilot, and de-icing system on land and during test flights. They paid special attention to the training of navigators, including the theoretical fundamentals of radio and celestial navigation, among other things.

Shortly before the departure date, the navigators received maps and planned the route, specifying the main and alternate airfields, radio beacons, broadcasting stations, and radio direction finders. Attached to the maps were images of alternate airfields, emergency landing areas, and information on the prevailing winds as well as ascending and descending currents.

The incident with Colonel Vasilyev and his crew was also addressed at the meeting with Zhavoronkov. The events leading up to the mysterious disappearance of the Catalina off the coast of Norway were reconstructed as part of the discussion. Experts from Naval Aviation headquarters put forward several versions of the accident: the plane could have gone down due to engine failure, it might have gone off course and crashed into the cliffs along the Norwegian coast, or it could have been shot down by the Germans. Lieutenant Colonel Chibisov was also asked to give his opinion on the incident.

For a number of years, it remained unknown what had happened to the lost crew. According to news that came in 2007 from a Norwegian reconnaissance group, the remains of the crashed Catalina were found in the Haswick commune of Finnmark Province. An old Norwegian fisherman who had witnessed the Catalina's crash said that at about 6 o'clock in the morning on June 19, 1944, a large hydroplane crashed into the top of the Andotten cliff at the seaside on Soroya Island, on the far-northern part of Norway. Had the Catalina been flying 10 meters (33 feet) higher, the crash would not have happened. Germans who came to the place where the hydroplane had crashed found three bodies of high-ranking pilots, whom they thought to be Americans. All documents found at the place of the accident, aviation equipment, and armament were taken by Germans, whereas fragments of the plane were thrown into the sea. The wings of the Catalina, which remained on the shore, served as a kind of monument memorializing the killed pilots and marking the place where the accident happened.

Drawing on his vast piloting experience, Maxim proposed two versions of the death of Colonel Viktor Vasilyev and his crew, which generally coincided with the aforementioned expert opinion. First, their plane could have been knocked off course in the fog and smashed into the cliffs near the North Cape while flying over the Norwegian coast at a low altitude. Per the other version, which Lieutenant Colonel Chibisov believed was more probable, perhaps Vasilyev broke radio silence when approaching the Norwegian coast, the Germans got a fix on the plane's location, and their fighters overtook the Catalina and shot it down. Maxim expressed these observations verbally as well as in writing in a brief submitted to the Naval Aviation commander. Zhavoronkov agreed with the opinion of Chibisov and other experts, who believed the missing plane had been shot down by Germans in all likelihood. Perhaps the marshal had specific grounds for this assumption. According to some reports, some information had been leaked on US territory, and the Germans might have known the flight dates and routes of the Catalinas and been waiting for them near the North Cape. However, due to the thick fog, the enemy managed to detect and shoot down only one plane.

Both Chibisov and Zhavoronkov firmly rejected the possibility that Vasilyev had committed treason, gone over to the enemy, or breached his duty in any way. Thus, the colonel's good name was not tainted by even a shadow of suspicion.

Colonel Vasilyev's death resulted in tighter secrecy. The members of the Special Operations Group, who were bound by written nondisclosure obligations, were deprived of any opportunity to send news to their relatives. The traditional "I'm alive, well, and serving," plus a vague hint at a distant trip, was the last news the wives, children, and parents of the pilots received from the front. For the next year and a half—all the way up until their meeting after the war—the pilots turned into "missing persons" for their families.

Despite all the measures of secrecy, however, some vague information about the death of the leader of a special operation apparently leaked out, without specifying the exact name of the deceased. Spreading by word of mouth, the news reached the Nikolayevka garrison in the Far East, where Rosaly Chibisova learned of it. The rumor spread that a Pacific Fleet pilot had been killed—either a colonel or a lieutenant colonel, the commander of a special group who had been performing a secret mission. People suddenly began whispering behind Rosaly's back and taking pity on her. The moral burden of the surrounding environment became unbearable for Rosaly.

The most difficult part was the uncertainty and lack of information about her husband.

In total disarray, Rosaly traveled to Vladivostok and made an appointment with Lieutenant General Lemeshko.

"I am Lieutenant Colonel Chibisov's wife," she said.

"I know," the Pacific Fleet Air Force commander replied.

"Please tell me the truth about my husband!" she said.

"You will still not be receiving news from him for a while, but I swear that he is safe and sound," he responded.

That was all General Lemeshko could say. With this news, Rosaly returned to Nikolayevka. What else could she do other than hope and wait?

10.4 Over Seas and Countries

Once all the issues that needed to be dealt with in Moscow had been resolved, Major Piskaryov flew to Krasnoyarsk along with the group of pilots designated to ferry the Catalinas to the Pacific Ocean Fleet. From there, their journey continued along the well-traversed Northern Staging Route through Yakutia and the Bering Strait to Alaska.

Under orders from Marshal Zhavoronkov, Lieutenant Colonel Chibisov, along with a group of 25 pilots and specialists, set out for America via the Southern Route in order to get a closer look at the path on which the Catalinas intended for the Black Sea Fleet would be traveling in the near future.

They left Moscow for Astrakhan and made their way to Baku from there. Maxim flew over the Caspian Sea at the helm of a Catalina that had just arrived from the United States. He immediately took to the aircraft, which demonstrated excellent landing and takeoff capabilities as well as seaworthiness and was easily manageable. Regretfully parting with the seaplane, Maxim boarded a Li-2 plane in Baku and took off for Tehran.

From the Iranian capital, their group traveled on the Douglas C-54 Skymaster transport aircraft with stops in Cairo, Egypt; Tripoli, Libya; and Lyautey, Morocco. The flight took a total of four days.

Traveling abroad for the first time, Maxim left colorful sketches in his diaries "from land and the air."

In each country he flew over, he paid attention to whether it had a well-developed highway and railroad network or heavy industry. He was struck by the architecture of the Eastern cities and did not fail to note that some of them were "fantastically beautiful." At the same time, he could not help but notice the dirty streets, the torn clothes of the workers, and the many beggars.

Each city had an abundance of stores and "all kinds of taverns." Having grown up in the Soviet Union, where people were at their jobs during work hours, Maxim was amazed by the "large number of loafers sitting around in cafes and bars."

Liberal manners, unusual for a Soviet citizen, prevailed in the foreign capitalist countries. This could even be seen in the behavior of the American pilots during the flight: "They quite frequently put the auto pilot in control, while sitting around and talking to each other, joking, and laughing. They overwhelmingly use radio guidance and beacons."

All over the world, pilots make up a special international community whose members are capable of instantly recognizing one of their own and immediately determining who is an ace and who is a novice. This assessment is based on imperceptible signs that are known only to the professionals—how a person looks at the sky, how he climbs into the cockpit, and how he takes the helm.

When Maxim flew from Tehran to Cairo, the Douglas pilots immediately sensed the Russian officer was a "real aviation boy" and entrusted him with the helm of their plane.

He made particular mention of this moment in his diaries: "During this flight, I was fortunate enough to fly the plane for three and a half hours. The American pilots behaved rather informally as if we had been flying together for a long time. It was pleasant and even flattering. We actually had no problems at all—not with learning the machine or with orientation."

At that time, Maxim still did not know any English, so he and his colleagues communicated solely with gestures. After a few hours, Maxim began to feel the stress of his first flight on an unfamiliar aircraft: "I had been flying the plane for quite a while. It was shaking hard. I became a little weary." During the fourth hour, fatigue truly set in. "I handed over the controls. I ate something, got comfortable, and slept for about forty minutes." Considering the Americans once again gave the controls to Maxim after Cairo, it appears they enjoyed riding with the Russian pilot.

Once the North African coast was behind them and the wide expanse of the Atlantic Ocean opened up directly in front of them, he wrote,

> We are flying with the course set for the Azores. The ocean is the greatest expanse of water, where the weather conditions change rapidly and most unexpectedly. Thunderstorms, fog, squalls—these are among the things that we most certainly will have to experience. But for now overhead is a moonless starry night with small cumulus clouds. The four-engine giant C-54 cuts powerfully through all air masses. It seems as if it has no barriers.

Maxim was flying on the latest brainchild of the Douglas firm: the C-54 long-range military transport plane, which had outstanding features for that time, including a speed of 451 kilometers per hour (280 miles per hour) at an altitude of 4,265 meters (14,000 feet) and a flight range of 4,023 kilometers (2,500 miles). The US military department took a rather reverent approach to this powerful beauty, which ruled out not only the possibility of deliveries under Lend-Lease but also basic familiarization with this miracle of technology, the pride of the American aviation industry.

After entering US airspace, the following description appeared in Maxim's diary: "We are flying over big cities. They are major industrial centers and they all tend to be conveniently located on the shores of rivers, lakes and the ocean ...

Transport aircraft C-54 Skymaster

There is a lot of green in the cities and around them. Beautiful forests." Gradually the landscape began to change. The cities gave way to wilderness and boundless farms: "The land below has a very pleasant appearance. The farms are situated like small islands and surrounded by well-planned fields ... Each farmstead includes vast land for farming and generally a section of forest. The land plots are bordered by nice highways."

On August 14, 1944, Maxim Chibisov and his team arrived at the air base in Elizabeth City, where the Soviet specialists in charge of accepting the Catalinas were deployed. They had crossed three seas: the lakelike Caspian; the Mediterranean, the cradle of ancient civilization; and the Atlantic, the great ocean separating the Old World from the New World.

10.5 Allies and Comrades in Arms

Approximately twenty specialists were involved in Project Zebra on the American side. The unit was headed by Vice Admiral Patrick Bellinger, a highly influential person in the Washington corridors of power and also a renowned pilot. In 1919, he was a member of a group of American pilots who made the first transatlantic flights.

In December 1941, Bellinger was a witness to the tragedy that befell the US Navy at Pearl Harbor. As a true patriot, he was a fundamental supporter of Roosevelt's policy to strengthen the anti-Hitler coalition. As a true military professional, he admired the Russian allies, who had broken the back of the German Wehrmacht. He also believed America would need the Soviet Union's help to settle accounts with the Japanese for Pearl Harbor.

Vice Admiral P.L. Bellinger

Captain George Owen was subordinate to Bellinger. According to the official chain of command, he was followed by Lieutenant Commander Stanley Chernack, head of the Elizabeth City base. This officer was Maxim's main associate from his first day until his last day in the United States. Chernack later admitted he had liked the tall, quiet, persuasive, and "handsome Russian colonel" since their first meeting. Maxim was known by this complex yet accurate nickname by all the personnel at the Elizabeth City base.

The thirty-year-old Chernack was an American of Ukrainian descent; his parents had traveled abroad after the 1905 revolution. He did not speak any Russian.

He and the "handsome Russian colonel," who still did not know English at the time, communicated with the help of an interpreter, twenty-two-year-old Gregory Gagarin, a descendant of immigrants from a rather famous aristocratic family in pre-revolutionary Russia.

Gregory Gagarin later described in great detail for the authors of this book how Maxim worked with his colleagues and subordinates.

Formation of American Catalinas

I met Maxim Chibisov in August 1944 ... I first saw Maxim when he came into our hut at the base, where we were sitting at a table covered with a pile of papers. The special group commander was a little shorter than me (I am 6'2" or almost 190 cm). I can still recall the strength of his enormous hand that he offered me for a handshake.

Lieutenant Gregory Gagarin

When Gagarin was asked which of the Soviet commanders was the easiest to work with, he replied,

I worked with Vasilyev for almost three months and with Chibisov for approximately a year and a half. In my mind, Vasilyev was a strict but very pleasant, calm and collected person. He said very little and never raised his voice, but at the same time I think that he was a good commander. It was easy for me to work with him, although he did not allow his subordinates to relax. For example, I don't remember the crews under him being able to watch movies at the base, where Hollywood reels were frequently shown. Chibisov was understanding of such matters: "Do you want to watch the movie? Fine, go to the gym." A huge screen was stretched out there. I usually sat next to Maxim in order to translate the scenes he did not understand. It was the same with trips to the city: we never knew how Vasilyev would spend free time with his crews or whether he would give them rest time in general. Perhaps this was because for the first six weeks our Soviet colleagues simply had no free time at all and therefore almost never left the airfield and rarely visited nearby Elizabeth City. Once Maxim Chibisov took over the group, we quickly realized that this energetic individual aspires to see and learn as much as possible and wants to provide his subordinates with the same opportunity.[19]

The interpreters also included Lieutenant Rushinsky, an ethnic Ukrainian. He was well versed in machine guns and bombing devices, while Gagarin was a professional engineer in electrical and radio engineering. Their colleagues, Kallick and Hodge, who spoke Russian at a slightly lower level, also helped out as much as they could.

Some of the translators—Kostritsky, Sesak, Barton, and van Burgh—were sent to bases located in South America and Africa along the ferrying route for the Catalinas.

The aircraft maintenance group was headed by Lieutenant William Stauers. The pilot instructors Hodge, Crossman, and Gilchrist were in charge of training the Soviet ferry pilot crews.

---

[19] Special mention must also be made of the enormous support to the mission by Georgy Gagarin, who was directly and actively involved in numerous negotiations to coordinate the routes and the times of the flights in this tense environment. In September 1945, he was specially flown to Montreal to reach agreement with the Royal Air Force on the resumption of aircraft ferrying along the Northern Route. In Paris, he personally greeted the last five planes to fly to the USSR under the command of Lieutenant Colonel Chibisov. They saw each other for the final time on this trip on October 24, 1945.

Sargent S. Krivitsky

Lieutanant Y. Stauers

Lieutenant K. Hodge

Lieutenant O. Gilchrist

Junior Lieutenant
S. Kallick

Sergeant Krivitsky served as a logistics manager or supply chief. He spoke Russian with difficulty but willingly. In particular, he told the story of how he ended up in the military service. He came to the United States after World War I. At the border, the immigration officer asked him, "Do you have a profession?" He replied in the negative. "What are you going to do here?" the officer asked.

"I don't know," he replied.

"Would you like to serve in the US Navy?" the officer asked.

"Why not?" Krivitsky responded.

The photographer Berenson also spoke a little Russian.

Navigation specialist Lieutenant Brownyard served as the cartographer. With his help, the Soviet pilots learned how to navigate coastal and ocean geography and also received vital maps for future flights. Brownyard prepared a personal map for Lieutenant Colonel Chibisov. After the war, Maxim brought it to Moscow, and it remains in excellent condition to this day.

The special group that Maxim Chibisov had the opportunity to lead in the United States in July 1944 included approximately 150 specialists.

The commander relied most on his deputy for political and flight affairs, Major Piskaryov. Maxim wrote about him in one of the preserved documents: "As if on a

Commander of the special operations group Colonel M.N. Chibisov and the head of the Project Zebra Lend Lease Program Captain George Owen.

business trip abroad, Comrade Piskaryov proved himself to be a faithful, vigilant officer. As a political worker, he was sensitive and attentive to his subordinates. He was also a strong-willed, pro-active and decisive pilot … He was the first to pave the way for all the new routes from the U.S. to the USSR."

Special responsibility in the team was assigned to the following crew commanders: Piskaryov, Spiridonov, Zamyatin, Manykin, Chesalin, Antonov, Boychenko, Kravtsov, Ivanov, Tarasenko, Leonov, Abramov,

Pogorelsky, Yakovlev, Petrushin, Chikov, Kartashov, Yeroshenko, Dorofeyev, and Medelyan.

Technical issues were handled by the engineers Tertsiyev, Salnikov, Turmilov, Shapkin, and Genkin (as a representative of the Government Procurement Commission, the latter was responsible for the second signature on the aircraft acceptance statements alongside the signature of the special group commander, Maxim Chibisov).

At the diplomatic level, Chibisov's group received support from Lieutenant Colonel V. Maximovich and Lieutenant Colonel M. Khrolenko, who worked at the defense attaché office of the Soviet embassy in Washington, DC.

The first person with whom Maxim had an opportunity to interact closely at Elizabeth City was engineer Colonel Kokarev (from the first team of specialists). An excellent pilot and a man with extraordinary personal courage, Kokarev had an uncanny understanding of machinery in addition to being an open and friendly person. He accompanied his new comrades to dinner and helped them settle into their new surroundings.

The living conditions were decent on the whole. All of the Soviet ferry pilots were put up in a dormitory with roughly twenty people in large rooms. The commanders were housed in the visiting officers' quarters with two people in each room. As the leader of the special group, Lieutenant Colonel Chibisov was provided with an individual apartment.

Maxim later described his first day in Elizabeth City in the energetic style of a news reporter. Along with a group of his pilots and specialists, he departed in a military-provided vehicle for Elizabeth City, a "small suburban town" that had "almost no industry" but did have "nice architecture, paved streets and a large number of stores." They had to stop in the shops to purchase some soap, toothbrushes, and other essential items. At the local department store, the Russian visitors had their trousers hemmed and their service coats adjusted since "a Soviet officer must look good, especially abroad!"

The day after arriving in the United States, Maxim was supposed to fly to Alaska. There were reasons for the urgency with which this had to be done.

During the seaplane ferrying operation headed by Colonel Vasilyev, 24 Catalinas were delivered to Murmansk along the Northern Route (another plane was lost, as mentioned). Following Vasilyev's death, his group ferried the planes that remained in Elizabeth City along the same

179

route. These Catalinas were distributed among the fleets and immediately put into combat operation, where they performed excellently. Meanwhile, the Soviet Union was already preparing for a war with Japan under the strictest secrecy. For this reason, the second consignment of seaplanes intended for the Pacific Ocean Fleet needed to be sent over immediately. They were to follow the Northwest Staging Route, along which the fighters had been ferried: from Kodiak to Anadyr and then through Magadan to the final destination in the Soviet Far East.

However, the Americans decided to ferry the Catalinas through US territory on their own to the Kodiak military base in Alaska, after which the Soviet crews were to take control of the aircraft. The reasoning behind this decision was clear: the Americans did not want any foreigners—even allies—present at their top-secret military facilities. In fact, this was fair: the Americans were categorically forbidden from flying in the Soviet skies, and this gave them grounds to respond to the Soviets in kind.

Catalinas resting at the Lake Worth in Texas

Most of all, Maxim did not like the fact that the planes would once again be put into someone else's control following acceptance. What would happen with the aircraft as they were ferried to Kodiak? What condition would they be in when he received them? Who would bear legal responsibility for planes that were already Soviet-owned but were being flown by Americans? The next day, the following entry was made in his diary: "I had a restless sleep and awoke before dawn … In the morning I was introduced to Lt. Commander Chernack, the manager and organizer of the aircraft shipment on the U.S. side. He told us that the plane would arrive in Kodiak at 3:00 p.m. We decided to see the city during the remaining time."

CHAPTER 11

In the Land of Endless Cyclones

11.1 It All Began on Kodiak Island

From Elizabeth City, Lieutenant Colonel Chibisov's special group flew to San Francisco on a C-54 transport plane. Already familiar with the aircraft from his flight to the United States, Maxim was once again given the opportunity to pilot the plane, although with backup from the American crew. Once in San Francisco, they switched to a brand-new Catalina that had come straight from the factory, and the Russian pilots—under the control of their American colleague—flew the plane along the Pacific coast to the US naval base on Kodiak Island in the Gulf of Alaska, where the crews and some of the seaplanes ready to be shipped to the Soviet Union through the Bering Strait were stationed.

The rest of the aircraft had been delayed for various reasons back in Elizabeth City. In addition, some of the Catalinas ferried to Kodiak by the American pilots had been damaged to varying degrees. This was the result of the somewhat irresponsible manner in which the Americans treated the aircraft, which had already been formally accepted by the Soviets.

In any event, the Russians had to wait a long time for the Catalinas to arrive from Elizabeth City, as the defects discovered in Kodiak had to be urgently repaired on the spot.

Prior to the arrival of the Russians, the local airfield had only accepted light single-engine seaplanes. The hosts were unable to predict how

---

such heavy machinery would handle during takeoff and landing. Such information was particularly important to know since the pilots would be taking off from a confined area of water in a valley between high mountains.

The special group leaders, Chibisov and Piskaryov, had to conduct reconnaissance of the area, examining the bay from a boat, taking note of shallow areas during low tide, and drawing up a rough diagram for takeoff. The first test takeoff on a Catalina at full force revealed the unpleasant nature of the local air currents: after the planes parted from the water and gained altitude, the wind pushed the planes back toward the mountains. Due to this factor, Maxim reached an agreement with the base command that each crew should make a few test flights before departing for the Soviet Union.

Kodiak base (c.1990s) A – Seaplane Base, Б- Catalinas towing designated area, B - direction of planes take off.

By August 20, the special group had done everything they could possibly do in terms of preparations at Kodiak. Maxim believed the crews were fully prepared for the flight, but the biggest problem was that they did not have maps to follow after crossing the border. There was also no information about radio communications with the Soviet side.

Maxim had zero information about who would be there to meet the Catalinas on the Soviet shores or how this process would work. Apparently, following Colonel Vasilyev's death, there had been some sort of breakdown in the resolution of organizational issues. Nobody had been handling these issues until Maxim came along, and he only had an order from Marshal Zhavoronkov demanding an immediate start to the shipment of the Catalinas intended for the Pacific Fleet. The order ended with the phrase "All relevant instructions for receiving the aircraft have been given."

With fall approaching, the weather along the route they were to take worsened every day, particularly the northern part of the route from Kodiak to Anadyr. It was difficult to predict when the bay in Anadyr would freeze, and in the event the cold came early, the flight would have to be postponed until the ice melted. Captain Maident, the base commander at Kodiak, became increasingly persistent in his inquiries about when the Russians were planning to launch the ferrying operations.

The special group commander was forced to make the decision on his own authority. During a meeting with Maident on August 23, Chibisov requested assistance in facilitating communications and providing alternate airfields on US territory. The Americans proposed five Alaskan airfields. They just as promptly resolved all issues concerning the specific route, flying conditions over US territory, and the regulations for radio communications.

Chibisov designated August 25 as the departure date for the first Catalinas from Kodiak. He understood how risky it was to fly along an unexplored route. Maxim's first impulse was to fly the plane himself. It was not in his nature to delegate an assignment that, in terms of the degree of risk, was comparable to flying over enemy territory. He probably would have done so if not for Guards Major Piskaryov, who, as a highly experienced pilot, volunteered to lead the flight and persuaded Chibisov that the special group could not be left without a commander at such a critical moment.

11.2. A Top-Secret Mess

At noon on August 25, two crews, led by Piskaryov and S. Spiridonov, took off in their Catalinas and set course for Anadyr. Piskaryov recorded the details of this flight in his memoirs.

The bay in Kodiak was shrouded in dense fog. It was impossible to take off. We spent about two hours waiting. Finally, the fog lifted from the water. The shores of the bay became visible. We tested the engines at the airfield. Then the planes with working engines were lowered into the water. We took off. After the plane separated from the water, we almost immediately entered the fog. Gaining altitude, we made our way through several layers of clouds. We set our predetermined course. Spiridonov's plane was not visible.

Under the wings - mountains of Kodiak Island.

Meanwhile, the top layer of the clouds was driving us higher and higher. It was getting hard to breathe. In the end, we had to go down. We descended into the "milk bowl," thinking that we had already passed over the mainland and were over the sea. Suddenly, during a break in the clouds we saw mountainous land rapidly drawing nearer. I managed to warn Spiridonov on the radio, "We can't go down, there are mountains here! Increase altitude!"

We had to continue flying in the clouds, but at a safe height from the surface. After a few hours, we ran into a cloudless area. Below us was the Bering Sea. In front of us to the right was St. Lawrence Island. That meant we were about to cross the International Date Line, where the date changes on Earth. We would get to Anadyr on the 26th.

Piskaryov's radio reports contained valuable information that proved essential to the next crews as they prepared for their flights.

However, the vanguard of the ferrying group encountered many obstacles and not just because of the changing weather and harsh conditions of the far north. In his notes, Piskaryov wrote,

Nobody was there to meet us in Anadyr. The bay around the town is huge. There were some houses visible in some spots along the shore. Where were we supposed to land? I was at my wits' end. I flew at a low altitude. Upon closer look, I saw a radio tower. This is probably it, I thought. There were no other visible signs of an airfield. We landed on the water. We dropped anchor about fifty meters from the shore. There was nothing with which to transport the crews to the shore—no floating devices. Thanks to the foresighted Americans, we found rubber lifeboats onboard the Catalinas. We inflated them, got in the water, and somehow made it to the shore. We were right about the so-called airfield. But once we landed, we were immediately convinced that nobody had prepared for the arrival of the Catalinas at this base. At the same time, it became clear that nobody had heard about any maps for us.

Above the Aleutian Islands.

Piskaryov reported all of this to his commander in Kodiak by radio. Chibisov was pleased the first two crews had made it safely to the first destination. At the very least, communication had been established with Anadyr. The rest of the situation, however, was not encouraging: there had been a serious breakdown in the system for accepting the seaplanes on the Soviet side.

Pacific Fleet Air Force Commander Pyotr Lemeshko had come up with the idea of ferrying the Catalinas from Anadyr through Magadan to their permanent base, while his deputy, Alexander Kuznetsov, was in charge of implementing the operation. It was assumed there would not be any major difficulties since the Northwest Staging Route had already been successfully traveled.

But the fighters previously ferried along this route had been transported from Anadyr to Yakutsk. All the work performed by the Anadyr airfield personnel focused on supporting this route and only for land-based machines. The airfield authorities, who were not affiliated with the navy, were unaware of the arrival of the Catalinas because the operation was top secret, and the Pacific Fleet Air Force commanders had not informed their colleagues from ground force aviation about it. There was no clear interaction between the various levels of naval leadership. Therefore, an unfortunate and dangerous mishap took place with the map routes.

In his memoirs about the flight from Alaska to Chukotka, Piskaryov writes,

> We saw a transport ship in the sea headed towards Provideniya Bay. It later turned out that this vessel, which had departed from Vladivostok, was carrying an aviation support group led by Col. M. Nizhegorodtsev that had been sent to receive the Catalinas in Anadyr. They also had the flight maps for our further route on to Magadan and Vladivostok. But the ship captain had not received any instructions from his superiors and did not drop Nizhegorodtsev's group off in Anadyr. He took the group to Provideniya Bay. So we were left with no flight map.

The most important result of the reconnaissance flight was understanding that it was possible to make it to Anadyr. After this, the vanguard pairing of Piskaryov and Spiridonov had to travel the route to Magadan and beyond. Surely, they thought, they would be met somewhere along the way by command

Catalinas at the Soviet Seaplane base at the Far East.

representatives who were somewhat aware of the situation.

Such a flight seemed impossible without route maps. However, the trailblazing pilots found a solution, as Maxim noted in his diaries:

> Nikolai came up with the idea of using weather maps instead of flight maps. We got them from the meteorologists. Of course, it's difficult to discern much about the Magadan region there. But the guys updated them, surveying everyone at the Anadyr airport who had previously been in Magadan. Based on these stories, they managed to reconstruct a few things, for example, the shape of Nagayevo Bay and where they could expect to land.

Piskaryov later recalled,

> The conditions in Anadyr were dreadful. Departure was scheduled for the next day and we had to fill the planes with fuel. But how? The tanks were on land, while the Catalinas were in the water 50 meters (164 feet) from the shore. What were we supposed to do? We got some rope, tied it to the planes, and dragged them as close as we could to the shore. We hooked up a hose onboard and spent the entire night pumping gas with hand pumps, all the while cursing our superiors wholeheartedly for organizing such a "warm" greeting. But apparently such is the fate of reconnaissance officers, test pilots and everyone else who draws the lot of being the first: don't expect any comfort or ceremonious speeches, rely solely on your own experience, will, intuition and fortune … On the morning of August 27, Magadan suddenly broke in over the radio and gave permission for our two Catalinas to land. Prior to taking off at 10 a.m., we surrounded the airport director and strongly "urged" him to ensure better preparations to receive and serve the following crews. For starters, at least install buoys from empty drums for the seaplanes to park in the water. We also reported the most important thing to Kodiak: Anadyr is not capable of accepting more than six planes at a time.

11.3 Breakthrough to Magadan

Six more Catalinas took off from Kodiak for Anadyr. Maxim did not leave the command post in Kodiak for a single minute and thus felt close to the crews at all times, recording each radio communication, which he later described in his diaries:

> The flight passed over Alaskan territory in the clouds at a high altitude. Severe icing began up there and the planes began losing altitude. After receiving a radiogram about the aircraft being forced to descend, I immediately realized that this wasn't safe. At that time, the Catalinas were flying over mountains with elevation of up to 2,000 meters (6,562 feet) in some places, plus they were right in the middle of a cyclone in an area where turbulence and icing are the strongest. Fortunately, the deicers were able to handle the load. I didn't even have a chance to enjoy this fact when one of the crews came over the radio with an emergency report: "We are traveling at an altitude of 3,500 meters (11,484 feet) but descending. A piece of ice broke the cockpit glass. The captain is wounded with shards of glass. The turbulence is worsening."

This was a critical moment, but with his sixth sense as an experienced pilot, Maxim determined that his crews had already overcome the most difficult part of the journey: "I felt that the guys were losing heart and essentially had no real way to support them. So then I spontaneously dictated a short radiogram: 'My friends, hang in there! You're on course! The cloud front is coming to an end. The most difficult part is behind you. See you soon. Chibisov.'"

Maxim's intuition had not deceived him: soon all six

Lieutenant Colonels M.N. Chibisov and V.V. Tertsiyev teaching american pilots to play backgammon. USA, Elizabeth City, 1944.

crews emerged from the cyclone, and a while later, they splashed down safely in Anadyr. Reporting upon arrival about the flight, one of the pilots admitted that the commander's radiogram had come at just the right time. From the moment the crews received it, they became confident that they were just about ready to move out of the cyclone.

Meanwhile, the lead pair of Catalinas piloted by Piskaryov and Spiridonov were making their way to Magadan. In his memoirs, Piskaryov wrote,

> It all began when the radio antenna stopped working because of the ice. It was a good thing that at least the deicing boots held up. They reliably broke the growing ice away throughout the whole trip. We didn't receive any instructions from the Anadyr airport director about maintaining radio communication with Magadan: he simply didn't have any, he only had information about communications with the civilian airports of Seymchan and Markovo. So communication with the capital of the Kolyma region was conducted through them, i.e. through a long chain of intermediate conversations that consumed a lot of time. About two hours before Magadan, we emerged from the clouds and found ourselves in the midst of a low fog creeping across the water. Hoping for the best, we inquired about the local conditions. Then came a radiogram stating that Magadan would not receive us. They suggested landing somewhere about 200 kilometers outside the city near Lake Mayorichi. There was no trace of this lake on our weather maps. Should we have flown back to Anadyr at night? What was the point? Plus we didn't have enough fuel. We reported to the command post in Magadan that we would nevertheless prefer to land near the city. In response, an authoritative voice roared over the radio: "I strictly forbid you from landing! I order you to land at Lake Mayorichi!" It was the voice of General Alexander Kuznetsov, who had been sent to Magadan to arrange the acceptance of the Catalinas from us and their redeployment to Vladivostok by crews from the Pacific Fleet Armed Forces. Thus, the boss's orders were clear: it

would have to be Lake Mayorichi! But we didn't know where it was, what the weather was like there or whether anyone would meet us there. It was an almost hopeless situation: there was no sense in going back and we weren't permitted to go forward. But we had been taught: "Never go back!" So that's what I did, on my own authority. Before reaching Magadan, we noticed a fog-free lagoon. After consulting with one another, we decided to sit there for a while until the weather in Magadan improved. Remembering the course, we set the radio altimeter at a safe altitude of 50 feet, headed away from the mountains and towards the sea, and prepared for landing as we passed through the fog. Both planes simultaneously crossed the coastline and the radio altimeter lamp switched on, signaling that our altitude was less than 50 feet. We continued to descend, but there was still no water. What were we to do? A few seconds could mean death. Where was the water?! Then finally the front step hit the crest of a wave, and the plane once again began skidding and porpoising over the water. Gradually the speed declined. The plane came to a stop. However, the rough waves would not let up. They swept over the wings and the surface of the plane. Water was inside of the plane. We were forced to turn on the emergency pump. We had to seek shelter.

We taxied to the shore in search of the lagoon. But how were we supposed to find it? I didn't know. Evening was approaching and it would be dark soon. Then through a stroke of good luck, I saw a fisherman on the shore with a boat. This was our salvation. With his help, we made it to a quiet backwater and dropped anchor. After a long,

Colonel M.N. Chibisov, Lieutenant G. Gagarin, Major A. Shapkin, Lieutenant Colonel V. Tertsiyev, Captain I. Genkin, Major I. Salnikov. USA, Elizabeth City, 1945.

stressful flight and a rough landing, the crews needed to rest. We ate dinner, put men on duty and went to sleep.

At night in the dense fog, which just would not dissipate, we heard the sound of a boat motor. We soon learned that it was General Kuznetsov, who was searching for us on a coast guard motor boat. We gave him a signal with our searchlight and that's how he found us. The general boarded the boat. He was extremely angry and made no attempt to conceal it:

"You were ordered to land at Lake Mayorichi! Why didn't you obey this order?"

"Comrade General, we didn't know where the lake was located," I replied.

"Show me your map," he said.

"We don't have any maps," I said.

"What do you mean you don't have any maps? You were supposed to receive maps from the support group in Anadyr."

"The group still has not made it to Anadyr."

"How did you fly without maps?" he asked.

"We used weather maps from the meteorological center," I replied. The navigator showed the general our handmade maps and he realized that he had been unfair to us.

Awaiting suitable flying weather conditions, 1944.

The fog rose by ten to fifteen meters only by the middle of the next day, August 28. By that time, the water from the lagoon had almost all been washed out with the tide. The Catalinas were tilted and sitting on the bottom. In the evening, reports of improved visibility came in from Magadan. The tide began to rise, and it became possible to take off.

In his memoirs, Piskarev wrote,

"We'll fly at a low level, Comrade General!" I suggested to Kuznetsov.

"Let's go!" he replied.

I had the general sit in the right pilot's seat with the expectation that, as an expert of these shores, he would show us when we had to make the turn to Nagayeva Bay. I took off first and Spiridonov was behind me. After picking up speed, we jumped out of the lagoon. I still wasn't able to break away from the water when suddenly a sand bar appeared out of a rolling wave directly in front of us. Well, I thought, you can only die once …

"Hold on, Comrade General," I yelled. "We're going to be jumping along the waves now!"

I seized the moment and, not having reached the speed needed to take off, jumped over the sandbar from one rolling wave to another. One jump. Another. A third. The Catalina was hanging in the air. The afterburner was holding it back. We turned left and began flying over the lagoon at a low altitude. Now the most important thing was to warn Spiridonov. From above I watched his Catalina take off after managing to yell over the commander's radio: "Turn off more to the left! The river flows into the sea there and it's deeper!" I was relieved to see that Spiridonov's plane separated from the water after slipping into the bay through the channel and avoiding the sandbar. I waited for him to catch up to my plane and we set course for Magadan.

On August 29, following the trailblazers, the next six planes arrived in Magadan from Anadyr. Four of the crews immediately went back to Kodiak for the next batch of seaplanes. Two crews remained in Magadan to train the Far Eastern pilots who had urgently arrived to fly the Catalinas brought from the United States through Soviet airspace. They later ferried the aircraft to Sukhodol Bay.

11.4 Air Transport Conveyor Line

All the sections of the Kodiak–Anadyr–Magadan–Vladivostok flight route had been traveled. Soon all the Catalinas from the consignment intended for the Pacific Fleet were being ferried one group after another along this route.

The flight conditions along the route were such that Maxim probably would have had an easier time flying himself than managing the ferrying process. He felt responsible for each plane and for the life of each departing crew member.

The following is a diary entry from August 29, 1944:

I woke up at 4 a.m. I slept very badly. I had some crazy dreams. I got up at 6:30 a.m. and went to the command post. Along the way, I stopped by the weather station to find out the weather report. Nothing good was expected. At any rate, there was a prevailing cyclone over the first half of the route. But the future forecast was even worse. I made the decision to send them. As the planes were preparing to take off, I was terribly worried. Of course, this feeling wouldn't go away until they landed in Anadyr. The connection with the planes was stable. Except one leader was silent for two hours and didn't respond to any calls. Based on their reports, the others all seemed to be in formation. I say "seemed" because they were flying in a "milk bowl" and could only determine each other's location through command communications. During the third hour of the fight, Zamyatin turned up. Finally! He reported, "I am flying alone. I'm flying blindly. Altitude is 16,000 feet." After a while I received a similar radiogram from Manykin: "I can't figure out where the formation is! I'm flying blindly. Altitude is 16,000 feet." I was sitting in the operations room on pins and needles. I hadn't heard from Chesalin's crew for a long time. Where was he? What had happened to him? After six hours of flying, the clouds finally cleared. Zamyatin came over the radio. He reported that he was flying above the clouds together with the squad commander. After a while, we received the following information: "We are traveling in a squad above the clouds. Altitude is 14,000 feet ... 10,000 feet. We have begun our descent!" And finally: "We are preparing for landing!" That was it! The flight was completed. Now the next ones can be prepared. It has already been decided that it will be the squads of Kravtsov and Antonov.

On August 30, the weather did not bode well either. There was another cyclone along the flight route, and the pilots would have to fly blindly against a strong headwind with the potential threat of icing. After consulting with the crew commanders, Maxim gave orders to postpone departure and start preparing the matériel.

On the next day, August 31, he wrote,

> I woke up very early this morning like I have all these days. I immediately went to the control post to get the meteorological report. The weather was tricky: there was a cyclone raging in the second and third zones. The detachment commanders assured us they were ready to fly. I didn't want to risk any people. I checked the forecast once again. The weather was good in the first zone. I consulted with the commanders. I decided not to cancel departure. I released Antonov first. He was followed by Boychenko. I put Kravtsov in the rear. The latter was highly offended as to why he hadn't been first. He came to me with a complaint. There was no time to debate it. Therefore, I explained it in simple terms—such is my decision and we'll hold off on the "debriefing" until you return. Then I ordered everyone to take their places.

From the radio reports, we got the following picture of the flight: Antonov's squad was scattered in the thick clouds, while Kravtsov's group was all flying above the clouds. Their altitude was 18,000 feet. Antonov's squad was 4,000 feet below them, flying in a "milk bowl." During the fourth hour of the flight, I ordered Antonov to gain altitude and travel at the same flight level as Kravtsov's squad. Now all the crews were flying above the clouds.

The lack of communication with Boychenko was very concerning. My nerves were at their end. Things became easier when the first five crews reported that they were preparing to land in Anadyr. Then the rest joined them. In the end, Boychenko turned up as well. His Catalina splashed down in the water last. That was all! Another day of suffering had ended for me.

On September 1 and 2, departure once again had to be postponed due to bad weather. On September 3, Maxim released Pogorelsky's squad, who arrived safely in Anadyr.

All the planes at the military base on Kodiak Island had been sent. Now they just had to wait for the American pilots to ferry the new consignment of seaplanes from Elizabeth City and for the Soviet pilots to return from the USSR.

Despite his workload, Maxim found time to read daily reports from the various theaters of war. Every day without fail, he would mark the advances of the Soviet troops toward the west on a big world map hanging in his room. He collected information from the New York–based newspaper *New Russian Word*. Oddly enough, this relatively small Russian-language newspaper had considerably more detailed information about the events on the Soviet-German front than major US publications.

M.N.Chibisov (last on the left) giving the instructions before a long haul flight. The pilots of the group: L. Yakovlev, I. Levchishin, Dyachenko, Commander of the squad L. Ivanov and onboard technician V. Zaychenko. USA, Alaska, airfield Kodiak, September 3rd, 1944.]

The special group commander told his comrades about the two August dispatches he received marked "From the Soviet Information Bureau." The first one indicated that the troops of the 2nd Soviet front had launched an offensive deep into Romanian territory. The second said that units from the 3rd Belarusian front had reached the border with Germany in the area of Eastern Prussia. This news was greeted with jubilation. A chorus of "Hurrah!" thundered throughout the officers' mess room, echoed in the dormitory of the noncommissioned personnel, and spread out to the airfield, drowning out the roar of the engines from the next batch of Catalinas that had been brought to the pier.

At that time, the US-manufactured flying boats were already being used in battle by the Soviet Navy.

On August 29, 1944, during an operation to seize the German-occupied Romanian port of Constanța, advance detachments of paratroopers were dropped off using Catalinas. Flying to the shore before dawn, the seaplane pilots shut off the engines and silently glided along the coastal strip in the dark, unbeknownst to the German air-defense systems. Having demoralized the enemy with a surprise attack, the aerial assault occupied the coastal positions and created favorable conditions for the subsequent landing of marine units from the Black Sea Fleet. Constanța was taken in one day with minimal losses for the Soviet forces.

Catalinas would later be used to deploy advance paratrooper groups at the Bulgarian ports of Varna and Burgas, although no fighting took place there, and the locals met the Soviet troops with flowers.

Starting from July 1944, after the American seaplanes arrived at the Northern Fleet, it became possible to ensure continuous air patrols of the Kara Sea. From this time on, the German submarines could no longer plunder fearlessly, as they previously had, on the most important section of the Northern Sea Route.

The Catalinas were also used in air battles near Murmansk, mainly for reconnaissance and rescue operations. For example, on August 19, 1944, the flying boat of Major Melnichenko rescued the crew of a Pe-2 bomber that had been shot down over the Barents Sea as the rescuers successfully repelled an attack by German fighters.

Thereafter, as new consignments of the American seaplanes arrived in the USSR, the scope of their usage continued to expand. In this way, the special group led by Vasilyev and Chibisov made a tangible contribution to the victory over Nazi Germany and its allies.

In the middle of the first week of September, General Kuznetsov personally contacted Lieutenant Colonel Chibisov by radio and conveyed Zhavoronkov's gratitude as well as the marshal's request to hasten the completion of the ferrying project.

Even without this request, it was clear that all the planes should be in the Soviet Union by September 15. Fall had arrived, and bodies of water were already beginning to freeze in the northern latitudes. Nonflying weather was approaching for the seaplanes. If they were delayed in Kodiak much longer, the Catalinas could end up stuck there until the next spring.

Meanwhile, the weather complications were compounded by

organizational problems. The planes arriving from Elizabeth City had to wait for the Soviet ferry pilots, whose return was often delayed for various reasons.

Sometimes they got a chance to fish in one of Kodiak's lakes.

There were already cyclones along the route—not a single day went by without them. The question of whether or not to release the planes became increasingly acute. The crews were ready to take the risk. However, the commander nevertheless bore responsibility for making the decision. The closer they got to the departure of the last Catalinas, the higher the tension became at the command post in Kodiak.

On September 11, 1944, Maxim wrote the following entry in his diary:

> Sunday. I got up at 6:30. I went to the meteorological station to find out the flight weather. Everything was calm in Kodiak and departure was possible. But the weather was complicated along the flight route with half of it covered by a vast cyclone. Of course, there was a strong tailwind blowing, which would reduce the flight by 2–2.5 hours. But this didn't make it any easier. I instructed the crew commanders to carefully study the weather maps for the trip. Then I asked for their opinions. I saw that they were ready to fly. I decided to release eight planes in pairs

with intervals of 45 minutes. In total, it turned out to be two full squads and one partial one. I sent the crews of Ivanov and Tarasenko first. Second was Leonov's squad: the crews of Zamyatin and Abramov also took off along with his Catalina. Third to take off was Pogorelsky's (the leader) squad with the wingmen Yakovlev and Petrushin.

The flight was different for each crew. The first pair took the Northern Route, flying in clouds for approximately half the flight. Then the second group flew above the clouds and valiantly fought off icing for an hour and a half. I was grateful that they maintained a good connection. There is nothing worse than uncertainty!

Leonov's squad soon fell apart with each plane continuing its flight alone. For me, this was extremely bad: if someone disappears from radio contact, you can no longer ask his "neighbor." This threesome flew in the "milk bowl" for four hours, with severe icing, of course. Leonov and Abramov maintained radio communication with me. Zamyatin vanished into thin air. It's better not to recall what I was thinking! Things got a little bit better only after I received final confirmation from Anadyr and the "debit matched the credit": the same number of planes that had taken off had splashed down. Prior to this, we had to set our wits to work with Pogorelsky's squad. It all started when the autopilot in Captain Petrushin's Catalina malfunctioned almost immediately after takeoff. I ordered him to return to the airfield. Pogorelsky and Yakovlev were flying along the southern part of the route and ended up almost in the center of the cyclone, which scattered them far apart. Both continued to fly blindly for the remainder of the flight. It's a good thing that I managed to maintain a normal connection with both of them. But true "miracles" began to take place during the second half of the route, especially towards the end. According to all the calculations on the ground as well as the information from the crews that were ahead, I was certain that Pogoreslsky's plane should already be approaching. Then suddenly I received a message from him: "I'm flying above the clouds!" He then stated his coordinates, according to which he still had another hour and a half to fly to Anadyr.

A similar situation took place with Yakovlev, only his time remaining to the landing spot was supposedly half an hour shorter. I asked both of them to update their position, thinking to myself: they are probably circling somewhere near Anadyr but lost their orientation due to the cloud cover.

I ordered them both to descend and pass through the clouds. Just in case, I warned them that the cloud cover over Anadyr was 1,500 feet and visibility was 3 miles. Yakovlev fulfilled the command and 40 minutes later reported that he was preparing to land. But Pogorelsky remained silent. Another hour passed. And then another 20 minutes. Not a peep. My nerves could not handle the silence. Finally I heard those long awaited words: "I'm going in for landing!" Where had he been this whole time? I'll find out when he arrives. I had already had to worry about Yakovlev during the first leg of the flight as he flew in the "milk bowl" over the mountainous part of Alaska. At one point, he reported: "I'm

Crew of Senior Lieutenant A.M. Medelyan (third from the left), Senior Lieutenant P.M. Belyaev, Second pilot Lieutenant P.A. Lobzhanidzhe, First flight engineer Captain M.Y. Kuznetsov, Second flight engineer Senior Lieutenant K.S. Pecherin, radio operator Sergeant V.V. Nadvikov.

flying blindly, the plane is iced over, altitude is 5,000 feet." For those more familiar with the metric system, that's only 1,800 meters. Some of the mountains he was flying over reached as high as 6,000 meters (19,700 feet)!

Commander of the squadron P.A. Lobzhanidzhe. Post-war photo.

I immediately ordered him to gain altitude and promised him that in an hour he would reach the sea, where it was calmer and the weather was better.

I calmed the other guys and remained worried myself until Pogorelsky, who was the sixth to descend on the bay in Anadyr, reported: "I see another one of ours behind me!" It was the Catalina flown by Zamyatin. So all seven planes made it to Anadyr. The eighth, Captain Petrushin, returned to Kodiak on my orders. Once the damaged autopilot is repaired, he will fly with the next group.

I passed on my gratitude to all those who

had safely flown back to Soviet territory. I left the command post with the happy feeling that my stress was over for today.

Maxim Chibisov in the company of his good friend Mikhail
Khrolenko during the rare days off in Kodiak.]

PBY-6A Amphibians of the Pacific Fleet Air Force.]

11.5 Farewell, Kodiak

On September 12, the last consignment of Catalinas traveled the difficult path over Alaska and the expanses of the Bering Sea and landed in Anadyr before preparing to fly on to Magadan the next day. Pacific Fleet pilots would then take the planes over the Sea of Okhotsk. All of the Catalinas assigned to the Pacific Fleet were assembled outside Vladivostok.

Lieutenant Colonel Chibisov's special group had fulfilled their mission in Kodiak. The Soviet Union had received thirty large seaplanes, which the Pacific Fleet desperately needed.

Before departing from Kodiak, the Soviet pilots went to see the work in the aviation repair shops. Having observed the repairs to the aircraft, Maxim concluded, "If any problems are discovered on the way from Elizabeth City to Kodiak, high-quality repairs are guaranteed here."

On September 14, Lieutenant Colonel Chibisov and the specialists working with him at Kodiak flew to Anchorage. Waiting for them there were a group of ferry pilots returning from the Soviet Union, led by Major Piskaryov, who had brought the special group commander a package from General Kuznetsov. The general reported to Maxim that he had once again been authorized to convey to him and his subordinates the personal gratitude of Colonel General Zhavoronkov for their considerable efforts. Relaying the marshal's words, Kuznetsov wrote, "Now a new high-profile government assignment awaits. The Soviet Embassy in Washington will give you detailed instructions upon arrival at your location of permanent deployment."

It was nice to receive such gratitude. But there was something lacking in this message to Maxim. He realized what that was only once on board the C-54, which took a steep turn over the Anchorage airport and headed south, first to Seattle and then San Francisco. After settling in the tail end of the fuselage on a folding bed, Maxim wearily closed his eyes. Only a month had passed since his arrival in the United States. He had been dealing with so much work and so many concerns that the basic desire to have a good sleep seemed like some sort of unattainable dream. Now, during this long flight, he finally had the chance. But as soon as leaned back in his chair, his mind began racing with disturbing thoughts he had previously managed to block out due to the avalanche of work. Of course, his first thoughts were about his home and his family. How were they doing there without him?

It's a shame that none of his superiors thought of providing Maxim with at least a few words about his family. Such news would have been the most precious award he could have received at that time.

CHAPTER 12

American Engineering and Russian Persistence

12.1 Between Washington and Elizabeth City

Along the way from Kodiak to Elizabeth City, Maxim stopped for a few hours in Washington for a meeting with Lieutenant Colonel V. Maximovich, the assistant Soviet naval attaché in the United States, who, through diplomatic channels, oversaw deliveries of American aircraft to the USSR. Maximovich informed Chibisov of his next government assignment.

Chibisov's special operations group were to open up the new southern ferrying route, which had a total length of more than 18,000 kilometers (11,200 miles)—nearly half of Earth's equator. The seaplanes intended for the Black Sea Fleet were to fly along this route, which spread halfway across the globe, from the United States to Brazil and then cross the Atlantic Ocean at its narrowest point. From there, the route passed over North Africa and the Middle East and then turned through Iranian airspace in the direction of Poti or Baku, from which the seaplanes were transferred to Sevastopol.

Two months earlier, during his flight to the United States on board the C-54 transport plane, Maxim had become familiar with the main aspects of the Southern Route, except for the airfields in Brazil, which the mighty Douglas had bypassed in flying directly over the Atlantic to the United States from Morocco.

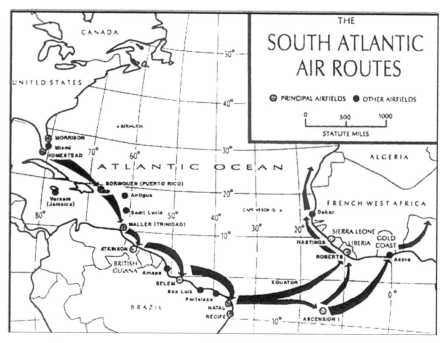

Shipping route of the seaplanes for the Black Sea fleet along the southern route Elizabeth City - Sevastopol in October 1944.

In terms of the performance by the Catalinas, this route meant more than 100 hours of flight time (half of which would be at night) and approximately ten stops. The flight time and requirements for fuel and other consumables could not be accurately calculated in advance, as the ferry pilots could expect to run into a wide range of unforeseen circumstances during the long flight: thunderstorms, heavy rain, strong winds, turbulence, and powerful ascending and descending air currents that could push the aircraft up and down by up to 500 meters (1,640 feet). Encounters with such obstacles sometimes muddled all calculations.

This route was to be used to ferry not only PBN-1 Nomad seaplanes, which Chibisov's special operations group already knew well, but also Catalina aircraft of the PBY-6A model, amphibious, with retractable landing gear that could land both on water and on land.

The amphibious capability was considerably superior to the previous model in terms of its onboard equipment. The most valuable component of its equipment was the radar, which enabled the crews to see one another, as well as surface targets, at great distances.

Thanks to the availability of radars on the PBY-6A aircraft, special bomb sight units could be installed for precision bombing, an effective innovation. After such planes appeared in the US Air Force, the American pilots could detect and destroy enemy submarines effectively even at night.

Knowing something about the wonderful sight unit from his American colleagues, Maxim asked Maximovich whether it would be possible to obtain something similar on the amphibians. The assistant attaché shrugged uncertainly and replied that while perhaps people might have heard about this miracle, nobody had seen it, at least none of their fellow countrymen. The military diplomat believed that they should focus only on the new Catalinas and that everything else was "a bird in the sky versus a bird in the bush."

Upon returning to Elizabeth City, Lieutenant Colonel Chibisov discovered that the situation with his "birds" was far from favorable. In his diary, he wrote,

> September 18, 1944. First of all, I checked out what they sent from the [Naval] Aircraft Factory. It's quite an unenviable situation. Not a single plane is ready for departure. Three planes have no tails: I was told they were allegedly smashed by a storm. As for another four aircraft, they reported that they are "in the process of being prepared for ferrying." As a result, there is nothing to send. I spoke with my colleagues and the Americans. We outlined a timeframe for their preparation. I stated that all seven planes should be ready by September 25, 1944. The Americans promised to meet this deadline. I ordered the flight crews to commence training. During the day, we held sessions on piloting techniques: takeoff, calculations, landing, flying under the hood. At night, we studied takeoff, landing, zone flights and route flights for three hours.

After coordinating things in Elizabeth City, Maxim once again rushed to Washington, where he had to complete work with technical documentations for the new Catalinas, for which he had brought along his chief assistant on technical issues.

After compiling a plan, I had peace of mind when I went to Washington, the Governmental Procurement Commission and to see Maximovich at the embassy. I took Tertsiyev with me. We arrived in the evening and stayed at a hotel. In the morning, we went to see Maximovich and read the documents. Then, Tertsiev and I went to the GPC. We didn't manage to accomplish much there in a day. There was too much idle talk. We postponed the discussion of some of the planned issues until the next day. In the evening, I wanted to fly back to the acceptance base. But Rudenko instructed me to wait for Mazuruk's group. I had to stay for a third night.

12.2 The Specially Protected Pilot Mazuruk

The aforementioned Ilya Mazuruk was one of the pilots who landed the famous North Pole-1 expedition led by Ivan Papanin on drifting ice back in 1937. Since that time, he had been known as a great hero of Soviet polar aviation.

He had held a number of senior positions during World War II and commanded a ferry aviation division supplying aircraft along the Northwest Staging Route. Mazuruk was then appointed deputy director of the aviation unit of the Northern Sea Route Authority, and in that capacity, he departed for the United States along with a group of pilots and technical specialists to ferry four PBN-1 Catalinas back to the Soviet Union for his department, a routine practice that Chibisov's special operations group had already mastered by that time.

Although this mission was to be performed by the famous Mazuruk, his group was put under the special care of General Rudenko, the head of the Government Procurement Commission (GPC), who was responsible for all the operations associated with the Lend-Lease Program.

Under an agreement with the Americans, Mazuruk's group was to receive four Nomad seaplanes at the Elizabeth City base and then ferry them back to the Soviet Union on their own. The group consisted of experienced pilots who were accustomed to severe Arctic conditions. The second most authoritative member of this group after Mazuruk was Vladimir Malkov. He had probably flown on every single seaplane in the

Soviet Union, including the GST transport seaplane and even the US-produced Consolidated boat, the prototype for the improved Catalinas. A few of these aircraft had been used in the Soviet Arctic before the war.

However, Mazuruk's team did not possess the knowledge and experience needed to successfully fulfill the Catalina ferrying mission. None of the polar explorer aces were familiar with the procedure for accepting the aircraft. In addition, this would be the first time any of them had ever flown the PBN-1 seaplane model before. This was made even more complicated by the fact that Mazuruk's polar crews would have to fly over the unfamiliar Southern Route.

Maxim wrote the following entry in his diary,

> September 22, 1944. In the morning, we met at Khrolenko's and went to see General Rudenko together with Mazuruk. We discussed the details of preparing the polar pilots for ferrying, including the issue of training flights with the crews. I volunteered to personally take part in testing the piloting techniques for the flying boats along with the flight crew under a wide range of conditions (including those found on the Southern Route).

The famous polar explorers were included in the general group for crew training to ferry the Catalinas.

Mazuruk's group was based in Washington for about a month before flying to Elizabeth City for acceptance and training, where Maxim gave the group the proper attention: "October 9, 1944. I took out Mazuruk's pilots. Then I let them drive on their own. I began training hard by myself at night."

The polar aces completed the training program just as well as the other pilots who had undergone the accelerated course in Elizabeth City. As required, they received detailed preflight instructions signed by Guards Major Piskaryov and documented briefings about actions to take on the route.

A couple days later, Maxim wrote in his diary, "October 12, 1944. I flew with the young pilots during the day. The next two nights I took Mazuruk's group around in circles. The first night I made 32 landings. The second night it was 29. All the pilots are ready to fly on their own."

On the night of October 31, four PBN-1 Catalinas took off from the airfield in Elizabeth City and headed out over the Atlantic Ocean. Mazuruk and Malkov flew the first plane. To the delight of General Rudenko, nothing went wrong for the famous aviators, and they safely made it to their destination.[20]

12.3 The Southern Route Conveyor

Meanwhile, the ferrying conveyor was operating in full swing. After returning from Washington, Maxim noted in his diary,

> Upon arrival at the base, I began inquiring what had been done in accordance with the plan. It turned out that nothing had changed in my absence. The bosses had not let my guys fly at night, citing a strong wind—a "cross wind." The planes with no tails remained in the same condition. No progress. I had to have a serious talk with Chernack, who cited objective factors. We revised the plan once again. We outlined it definitively and firmly: by September 27 ten planes should be ready for departure (ten because another two had just been brought in that day with minor defects). Looking ahead, I should note that all agreements once again remained on paper. I waited another day. There were only seven planes ready. I hadn't designated any new dates. What was the point? Chernack had his story and the regular reply, "I'm trying! But at present you only need five planes." In short, at every step there [are] more hindrances than progress.

[20] In his memoirs about his visit to America, Ivan Mazuruk did not say a single word about the Soviet specialists from Elizabeth City who trained his group to ferry the Catalinas, but he did provide a detailed description of his meeting with a certain congressman named Willkie, whose help was supposedly needed to receive the seaplanes that had been delayed by the Americans for some reason. GPC Director Rudenko (according to the author of the memoirs), of course, was powerless to do anything, but the heroic Mazuruk managed to secure the transfer of the Catalinas. He arrived, saw, conquered, and flew off without requiring any help from his fellow countrymen working in America (see narod.ru>mazuruk.html).

Left to right: Commander of the Special Operations Air Force, Lieutenant
Colonel M. Chibisov, American Lieutenant Commander S. Cherniak, Hero of
the Soviet Union Colonel I. Mazuruk, Deputy Chief UPA GUSMP Lieutenant
Colonel F. Danilov and attaché of the USSR Navy Lieutenant Colonel M.
Khrolenko by the monument to the Wright Brothers, Kitty Hawk, 1944.

I took over the organization of the night flights myself. I decided that by hook or by crook the guys had to have an opportunity to fly as much as possible in order to gain experience for night flights in various conditions.

> September 28, 1944. The flight along the Southern route to the USSR is scheduled for today. The first pair of planes will be flown by Abramov's crews. We met with the British navigators who are flying with our guys and helping with navigation during the transatlantic leg. The departure went well, but some unexpected problems arose with tracking their progress. It proved to be extremely difficult to obtain a basic weather report from the American meteorologists. There were also complications in obtaining information about the flight progress. The Americans were perplexed—and almost laughing—about my plan to monitor each radiogram sent by the crews. Before I would have been offended. But now I understand: they are different and in their work they don't allow anything personal, no emotions. That's how things are done here: they send off the planes from the airfield and that's that! Afterwards, they couldn't care less! But I cannot do that. So, I was trying to do everything in my normal way. During the day, I struggled to get information about the location of the planes and at night there was no sense in even trying! The American communications operators said that they were entitled to rest at this time. Fourteen hours after takeoff, I nevertheless managed to obtain information that our planes had landed in San Juan (Puerto Rico). So, the first step had been made: the first pair of planes had safely made it through the first leg of the route!

This was followed by entries about the departure of the Kartashov-Zamyatin crews on October 1, 1944, and, three days later, the Pogorelsky-Yakovlev crews. The rest continued training with the piloting techniques. Once again, his diary contained the familiar words "Day—takeoff, calculations, landing, flights under the hood" and "Nights—circuit flying." The training particularly focused on flying in blind conditions, which was logical since the flights across the Atlantic, which would take 16-18 hours, would mainly be made at night.

It should also be noted that the flights along the southern route presented obvious difficulties for the Soviet crews simply because of its newness— Soviet naval pilots had never flown at such subequatorial and equatorial latitudes, which featured high temperatures, humidity, thunderstorms, and fog. Prior to departure, the crews had received detailed maps, data required for communications, photos of the airfields, and information about radio navigation equipment, along with the necessary explanations in Russian. The plane balance was calculated during each leg of the flight. In addition to the difficulties, the pilots also experienced some happy moments during the transatlantic flight. For instance, when they crossed the equator, the pilot performed a pull-up maneuver symbolizing that an obstacle had been overcome, and those who had crossed the equator for the first time were "baptized" and treated to a shot of rum.

While training crews for the long and difficult flight, Maxim soon realized it would be necessary to accept the Catalinas and train the pilots at the same time. The time factor was becoming increasingly critical. With this in mind, the decision was made to start inspecting the aircraft immediately during their transfer from the Philadelphia factory to Elizabeth City. During the 25-hour flight over the Atlantic Ocean, engineers managed to examine all the electrical equipment and both motors in addition to shooting from the machine gun if they wished. This made it possible to reduce the acceptance period to three days. Of course, there was a risk involved, but everything went smoothly.

Gregory Gagarin later recalled that as an interpreter, he had to spend two months in headphones on the floor of the cockpit between pilots Crossman and Hodge, who taught their Soviet colleagues the tricks of controlling the flying boats. One of the first to master these skills with Lieutenant Gagarin's help was Maxim Chibisov, who then personally trained all his subordinate crews for the flight across the ocean.

Starting from late September, Major Turmilov, an engineer and the special group's top radar specialist, was actively involved in training the flight crews based on Maxim's orders. Presumably, this was when the first amphibious PBY-6A Catalinas arrived in Elizabeth City with the latest radar equipment of that time.

12.4 The Amazing Norden

In mid-October, two PBY-6A amphibians arrived from the Floyd Bennett Field factory in Brooklyn, New York, with antennae that had never been seen before. This event was recorded in Maxim's diary: "October 15, 1944. Two new planes have arrived for the crews of Leonov and Chikov. We started studying its hardware, the plane equipment and particularly the sight." Why was their attention drawn specifically to the bombsight? Because all the other equipment—the radio direction finder, the autopilot, the attitude indicator, and even the brand-new radar, which had only been installed on these versions—were analogues of equipment that had already been tested in practice. But the Soviet pilots had never encountered a bombsight like the one installed on the newly arrived planes.

Norden sight, 1944.

Maxim realized this was the same sight about which he had been pestering Maximovich a month earlier. He read the name of the hardware on the data sheet (as best as his English allowed him): Norden. The documents contained no other comprehensible details. Certain knowledge of technical English would be required to properly understand them. They had to get in contact with the Government Procurement Commission to request that someone be sent to assist them. Maxim examined the hardware every which way with Turmilov and other experts but without much success. He left the following entry in his diary: "We encountered great difficulty when studying the Norden sight. There were no manuals, so we were basically poking around blindly. The GPC specialist never showed up."

Without waiting for the specialist, Maxim decided to take a risk: he would go up in the plane and attempt to jump straight to the implementation stage while bypassing the theory. His diary also contains an entry on this event:

> Chikov, the navigator Levin, the American specialist [apparently, the interpreter Gagarin] and I flew together. We prowled around the skies for three and a half hours until we were sure the navigator had properly mastered the aircraft's navigation. He had to sweat quite a bit over the change in course. But the first and relatively positive result had been achieved. Everyone was pleased with the radio direction finder, which is capable of accurately guiding the plane to its destination.

The next day I flew with Leonov's crew. We worked hard just like the first time. We flew for about four hours and also ensured that we could confidently keep the plane on a combat course. Of course, we got carried away and in poor visibility went too far out to sea. And this is precisely when the radio direction finder came in handy. Later Chikov, Levin and the navigator Fomin also flew. Based on their report, I gathered that they had also managed to figure out the device. This is how we mastered the new equipment in three days. On the fourth day, the Americans returned both Amphibians to New York, explaining that they needed to be moved away from a coming storm. The weather really did become nasty: rain poured for days along with a strong wind of up to 20 meters per second (45 miles per hour).

According to Maxim's diary, the planes returned to Elizabeth City on October 21. By that time, the commander had managed to find a description of the bombsight and was once again making regular calls to Washington.

This time, a specialist was sent promptly. It was 26-year-old Air Force

Captain Igor Lebedev, who came from a military family and was a graduate of the Zhukovsky Air Force Academy. Since fall 1942, he had been working at the Government Procurement Commission as a military representative. Igor was involved in accepting various types of American planes, mainly the A-20 Boston bombers, and sending them to the USSR.

Lebedev had a good command of English and was already familiar with the local aviation equipment.

Upon being summoned to Elizabeth City, he was actively involved in work with the Norden sight. The proverbial calling card of this unit, which operated on principles of radar, was a specific type of antenna device. Captain Lebedev had already seen something similar during his trips to US factories. Later, he recalled,

Senior operational engineers of the air department of the USSR Government Procurement Commission in the USA Capt. I.P. Lebedev (left) and Lieutenant Colonel V.I. Bakhin.

> At a local airport, I immediately noticed a magnificent A-20 bomber adorned with a "bouquet" of antennas. I began asking about it. Most of the Americans I knew shrugged their shoulders, while some of them evaded a reply, clearly trying to distract my attention from the plane. Such a reaction led me to believe that it was some sort of new highly important equipment.

The Americans had not installed Norden sights on the A-20 bombers sent to the Soviet Union. So how did this device end up on the Catalinas handed over to Chibisov's special group?

While returning from Elizabeth City to Washington, Igor Lebedev, according to his memoirs,

> kept going over options in his head about how such an outcome could have taken place. There was only one real possibility: we received the Catalinas from the U.S. Navy

and the Bostons from the U.S. Air Force. The two offices had an antagonistic relationship at that time. Thus, there was probably a lack of coordination in their work. The Air Force decided not to give us the Nordens, while the Navy, faithfully fulfilling the Lend-Lease supplies, sent us Amphibians with this installation. Of course, an accident can't be ruled out either: perhaps the machine with the special equipment was shipped by mistake. At any rate, we were obviously lucky! [...] Upon returning to the aviation department, we proposed a plan of action to the GPC leaders. The essence of the plan was as follows: it was above all necessary to ferry the Catalinas to the Caucasus with the night vision device and instruct to the crew to send an urgent telegram confirming their safe arrival as soon as they land. After the telegram is received, someone must go to the Pentagon with a request to install Norden devices on all A-20 bombers sent to the Soviet Union under Lend-Lease. The GPC leaders approved my plan.

The launch of Operation Norden was casual and almost imperceptible. Maxim made brief entries about this event in his diary: "November 1, 1944. All three of my crews are prepared for departure. I am releasing Capt. Popkov first" and "November 2, 1944. The crews of Leonov and Chikov were supposed to fly out, but it had to be postponed due to the weather." Leonov and Chikov were supposed to ferry the Catalinas equipped with the Norden sight. Finally, it took place: "I released Leonov and Chikov. They took off on November 3, 1944. The main concern now is how will they fly!"
This was followed by a few more typical entries:

November 4, 1944. I gave instructions for the planes ferried from the factory and accepted by us to be lowered into the water. I then left for Washington. Turmilov had gone there a day earlier. I took the navigator Fomin with me. We will work on the sight. Salnikov was instructed [to] inquire about the issue of communications. I received information about their trip: everything is fine for now.
November 6, 1944. I spent half the day at the

procurement commission again. Then I had a long talk with Khrolenko and Maximovich.

November 8, 1944. Attaché Skryagin introduced me to Ambassador Andrei Gromyko, who was interested in our progress.

Apparently, there was interest in the Norden sight among some of the top officials in Moscow. The Soviet representatives in Washington and the special group commander were presumably being urged to ensure the immediate departure of the next batch of Catalinas equipped with this device as soon as they arrived in Elizabeth City. Even Ambassador Gromyko, with his established contacts in the White House and the State Department, was prepared to get involved if necessary.

12.5 On the Issue of Price

During the war, the Soviet Union lagged considerably behind Western countries in the production and use of radar equipment, despite the fact that during the first half of the 1930s, the designs of Soviet scientists were on par with the achievements of their Western colleagues.

However, the following wave of repressions dealt a devastating blow to a wide range of research and design teams working on radar technology under the patronage of Deputy People's Commissar for Defense Mikhail Tukhachevsky. By the time World War II began, the Soviet Armed Forces only had a small number of highly flawed radar stations.

The lack of radar technology had to be compensated for by the Lend-Lease Program.

Under the Washington Protocol of 1942, the United States alone sent more than 640 various types of radar stations to the Soviet Union, while the United Kingdom shipped more than 200 such units.

This equipment was highly effective during combat actions and also used to defend the Soviet home front from Luftwaffe attacks.

But the onboard radar units installed on the planes were classified as top-secret military equipment in both the United States and the United Kingdom, which were reluctant about supplying such technology to the Soviets. The Western allies did not always share such secrets even among each other.

The top-secret achievements of US military technical thought contained in the Norden sight were valued so highly and guarded so carefully that at the start of the war, the Americans refused to supply them even to the United Kingdom, their closest ally, despite Churchill's personal request to the US president. A controversy erupted when it came to light after the war that Roosevelt had given Stalin the secret device Churchill had been denied. It should be kept in mind, however, that by 1944, the secrecy of the Norden was highly relative, as samples of the sight had fallen into the hands of the Germans with the wreckage of bombers shot down over the Third Reich. Therefore, in the eyes of Roosevelt's White House, the transfer of such military technology to the Soviet Union would not harm the security of the United States.

Even under such conditions, though, it was no easy task to get Norden sights installed on planes that were to be delivered to the Soviet Union. It was something along the lines of "catching a bird in the bush," as attaché Maximovich's aide rightly noted. Thanks to a fortunate set of circumstances and Lieutenant Colonel Chibisov's persistence, his group managed to catch this bird, and he soon found himself in a snare that played out in full compliance with the rules of the art of diplomacy.

A detailed description of how this story unfolded is contained in the memoirs of interpreter Ivan Lebedev:

> We soon received a telegram about the arrival of the Catalina in the USSR. We prepared a memorandum for the GPC. General Piskunov was supposed to talk, but he didn't speak English. So he took me along. We arrived at the military department. When the sight was mentioned, the U.S. Air Force colonel who received us made a surprised face, as if to say he hadn't heard or seen anything about it. And then I, allegedly on behalf of my boss, said, "My general wishes to inform your command that we recently received the Norden device for night vision installed on the amphibious Catalinas from the U.S. Navy. It is already in the USSR. And it has performed very well at night along the front." The colonel looked like he was going to be ill when I added that I had personally seen the A-20 commercial machine with the same equipment and even indicated the airport where I had seen it.

After accepting the memorandum, the colonel then chose to end the conversation, promising that the issue would be considered and we would receive a reply soon.

After a while, a reply did in fact arrive at the GPC. It stated that we should consult with the company Douglas, which manufactured the A-20 Bostons under Lend-Lease, and resolve the issue of installing the Norden devices with them.

Three of us—two military representatives and I—went to the Douglas headquarters in Los Angeles. We were received by the head of the company, Donald Douglas. Before even considering the issue for which we had come, Douglas spoke with us over breakfast and came to the conclusion that we were "real aviation boys." Thus, he was in a positive mood from the start ... At any rate, when the most senior among us, Col. V. Bakhin, outlined the details of the request, Douglas replied, "Well, the Pentagon is the Pentagon, but business is business. Russia is important to the company as a trading partner. It pays regularly." He gave instructions for the new sights to be installed on all A-20 aircraft being supplied to the USSR.

Later, during the Cold War years, the story with the Norden sight seemed like a fantastic success for the Russian procurers of American military technology. There was even one version of the story according to which the Norden issue was decided at the highest level between Stalin and Roosevelt in conjunction with the issue of the US Air Force using airfields in the Ukrainian cities of Poltava, Myrhorod, and Pyriatyn as landing spots for heavy bombers making flights over Germany. In particular, US historian Robert Burgener, author of the book *On Borrowed Wings*, alluded to the possibility of such a link in his interview with the magazine *Ekho Planety* in November 1995.

However, the airfields in Ukraine were provided to the Americans back in the first half of 1944. Stalin made this concession to the allies based on the prospects for the opening of the western front.

The Norden operation took place a few months later. It was successfully achieved without the involvement of big politics and without any concessions in return from the Soviet Union.

The deal was made thanks to the attentiveness and persistence of the Soviet specialists working in the United States. They were aided by the "real aviation boys," the subordinates of Commander Lieutenant Chernack from Elizabeth City, and the businessmen from Douglas. They were guided not by instructions from top politicians but by normal business instruments and an appropriate understanding of allied relations between the United States and the Soviet Union.

12.6 Drudgery

In late October and early November 1944, Lieutenant Colonel Chibisov frequently traveled back and forth between Elizabeth City and Washington. In the capital, he worked hurriedly with the GPC and the embassy on the paperwork to send the Catalinas, and at the base, he had to train the crews on a daily basis, primarily at night.

Soviet pilots and British radio operators that provided communication and pass through of Catalinas over the allied territory. At the center of the bottom row - Gregory Gagarin.

The PBN-1 Nomad seaplanes were being sent along the southern route one after another. The supply of aircraft from the Philadelphia Navy Shipyard factory had finally been smoothed out, and planes were arriving at the acceptance base in Elizabeth City without any delays or flaws. But the Russians returning for each consignment had to take a long, circuitous route and were frequently late. The ready planes stood idle, and at times, there was nobody to fly them.

Maxim did everything he could to ensure the ferrying conveyor along the southern route operated with no interruptions.

On November 9, 1944, Lieutenant Colonel Chibisov held a highly productive meeting with General Piskunov. Maxim wrote in his diary, "The main subjects discussed were the progress and the flight of the last group of ferry pilots and the acceptance of new planes." In conclusion, he left a remark about his boss's reaction: "All matters were dealt with seriously. A statement was prepared for each issue and sent to the procurement commission."

The ferrying of the first consignment of 100 PBN-1 patrol naval bombers was close to completion. Maxim began preparing for the shipment of the next consignment, which was to consist of amphibious seaplanes.

At that time, stress and physical exertion once again took their toll on Maxim's health. He came down with either angina or the flu, his temperature rose to 39°C. (102° F.) and his gallstone disease returned. On November 12, 1944, he wrote,

> I spent the off day alone. Feeling sick, I laid in bed almost all day, although I forced myself to get up around 11 a.m. I went to see the guys at the hotel to talk with them and give them the "command" to fly to New York without me. I fell ill and started thinking about my sore spots. I needed to check whether there were any stones in my gallbladder and whether I should remove the mole that I've had on my neck since 1938.

Maxim spent the next few days going around to doctors to get x-rays and ultrasounds. He received instructions regarding his diet, a prescription for pain relief drugs, and recommendations for treating the gallstones, which he followed rigorously for several years. He was prescribed medicine. The tablets and pills of various form and color looked like candy and were also highly effective. He stocked up on them in large quantities and later brought them back to Moscow.

Maxim continued to take this medicine until 1950, and the pain did not bother him for another 35 years. When he turned 75 it was suggested he have surgery to remove the stones, but he replied, "We are so used to one another that as long as an acute attack does not occur, I'll go ahead and live out my days with them."

In late 1944, Maxim, despite his shaky health, still did not go easy on himself or anyone else. Each day, he settled multiple organizational situations, placed his commander's signature on acceptance statements, personally took out crews, and flew a lot on his own. The schedule for plane departures remained tight. Chibisov tried to finalize the shipment of the PBN-1 Nomads for the Black Sea Fleet as quickly as possible.

At the same time, preparations were underway to ferry the PBY-6a amphibians with the coveted Norden sight. He wrote several diary entries: "December 1, 1944. The crews of Kartashov, Spiridonov and Zamyatin returned after ferrying to the acceptance base. They all began to examine the new equipment on the plane"; "December 6, 1944. Spiridonov and Kartashov have taken off. The crews of Pogorelsky, Yeroshenko, Yakovlev and Dorofeyev have also arrived. Immediately after studying the new device, they began preparing them for the subsequent flight"; "December 9, 1944. Departure of Zimin and Yeroshenko"; and "December 11, 1944. I sent off Pogorelsky and Yakovlev."

The crews from Chibisov's special group had each crossed the ocean multiple times. Such work became the norm for them yet remained difficult and dangerous. They had to prepare each flight carefully, sparing no effort and not losing sight of a single detail. All kinds of different incidents could take place along the routes, from the simple, such as Yakovlev's airspeed indicator suddenly malfunctioning, to those fraught with serious consequences, such as Medelyan's discovery during one leg of his flight that

Catalina Commander A.M. Medelyan, Post-war photo.

gasoline mixed with water had been pumped into his Catalina. Luckily, both pilots made it to their goal. Moreover, Medelyan was once forced to urgently return to the airfield and land on a river channel that was no more than 35 meters (115 feet) wide in the pitch-black darkness of the southern night.

Those who had graduated from the school of Maxim Chibisov knew how to fight for the survival of their aircraft.

During the week leading up to New Year's in 1944, the Catalinas intended for the Black Sea Fleet departed from the Elizabeth City base almost every night. Maxim's diary entries reflect this fact without any fanfare:

> December 20, 1944. At 7:00 p.m. I began flying with Kravtsov and Antonov. I trained both for about two hours. After returning to base, I immediately prepared Popkov's crew for departure. The weather was favorable. I sent them off at 10:00 p.m.
>
> December 23, 1944. In the morning, I took out the second pilots—Belov, Sedov and Dorofeyev. They fly well. During the day, we prepared in full swing for the ferrying of two planes on which the crews of Kravtsov and Antonov are to fly … I sent them on the route. Thus, the ferried planes are spread out in a chain from Elizabeth City to Baku. Following the departure of Kravtsov and Antonov, we had a small banquet. We—that means Kokarev, Salnikov, Genkin and I. And on behalf of the allies—Fry, Chernack and Gagarin. The weather became much worse after December 27. The departures had to be suspended.

12.7 Russians in America

Based in the United States for a long time, Maxim began studying English intensely, both on his own and with a tutor. Classes were held twice a week for three hours. The Soviet pilots treated the language barrier as they would have any other combat mission. In their free time, they worked hard on their English, aware that a lack of language skills when flying on American combat machines could become a matter of life or death at any moment.

Even basic spoken English skills made it possible to get a more complete understanding of the country to which the circumstances of war had cast Soviet officer Maxim Chibisov.

The America of that time—wealthy, comfortable, and free—could overwhelm a person with its splendor, especially compared to the harsh realities of Soviet wartime existence. Maxim's diary entries, however, do not contain a hint of flattering admiration for American power or prosperity. He did not lament that people were living well in the United States while the Soviets were fighting and straining with all their might. He looked at America with the friendly, calm gaze of a person who knew his worth and highly valued his dignity as a citizen of a great, heroic country.

The hospitable hosts at the Elizabeth City base provided their Russian guests with a bus for regular trips to the city. The special group commander was given his own car, in which he traveled several miles on American roads. Thus, he did not see America only from the wing of his plane.

Lt. Colonel Chibisov with assigned Pontiac automobile in Elizabeth City, NC, 1944.

Maxim had the opportunity to visit the famous cities of San Francisco, Philadelphia, the exotic New Orleans, and the incomparable New York. But most of all, he liked the US capital of Washington, DC: "The city left a pleasant impression on me. Nice buildings, lots of green—in some places it feels like the streets were laid in the forest. An incredible amount of cars. The people are friendly. A huge number of stores. Good movie theaters of which there are also plenty."

On October 7, 1944, he left an entry in his diary about visiting the memorial to the Wright Brothers, the first conquerors of the sky. A pilot by vocation, Maxim could not pass up the iconic site for aviators in the town of Kitty Hawk, North Carolina.

America was a country with great aviation traditions, as proven by the quality of American aircraft and the highly professional staff at the base in Elizabeth City.

However, there were some peculiarities in the work style of the base superiors that never ceased to amaze Maxim. Particularly strange for him was their commitment to a "narrow specialization." When the Soviet pilots asked the American officers for an explanation about the motor unit or certain aircraft components, they replied that "for a pilot it's enough to know how to turn on, turn off and operate a given plane. And if something messes up, then you call the experts. You can't get by without them anyway." The American pilots had no inclination or ability to wriggle their way out of emergency situations on their own, a common practice for the Soviet aviators, who hadn't been spoiled with such service.

Pictured by the Wright Brothers Monument (left to right): F. Danilov, M. Chibisov, I. Mazuruk, S. Cherniak, M. Khrolenko and the photographer J. Berenson. Kitty Hawk (USA), 1944.

Following the example of their commander, the Soviet officers from Chibisov's special group approached their jobs with fanatical zeal. They studied the US equipment religiously and meticulously, and their dedication could not help but command the respect of their American colleagues.

In order to save time, which was sorely lacking on the transport conveyor, they accelerated the inspections of

Catalinas assembly point at Consolidated factory in San Diego.

the aircraft, although not to the detriment of the quality of the work performed.

Gregory Gagarin later retold a funny story about how GPC representative Genkin one day refused to sign an acceptance statement for a plane that cost $25,000, due to the fact that there was no chocolate in the food container. Gagarin had to run to the nearest store to buy several fifty-cent chocolate bars, after which, by his own admission, he gained a better understanding of "precisely what Russian meticulousness is."

The Soviet pilots also had free time when they could play chess at the local officers' club as well as volleyball, which was especially popular among the Russians.

Gagarin later recalled,

> One day someone from Chibisov's team suggested playing a game of volleyball with the Elizabeth City base hosts. We accepted the offer without even thinking about it. We trained once in a while, tossing the ball over a small net, but none of our guys had ever seen the Russians with a ball in their hands. And when the Russian pilots appeared in the gym in identical uniforms with a bouquet of flowers in their hands, the Americans, each dressed in their own way, gasped and then burst out laughing while giving me a questioning look as the interpreter, as if to say: "Flowers! What does that mean? Is that all she wrote for us?!" Sure enough, the "international match" ended miserably for us—we lost three games in a row. For the record, the judge of this "championship" was Chibisov.

Gagarin spoke about another funny episode as well. When the Soviet pilots saw the ocean for the first time, they naturally wanted to jump into the water. The Americans tried to stop their allies. "But you don't have any bathing suits!" they yelled.

"Nonsense," the Russians replied. "We'll swim naked!"

The Americans continued to object mildly, noting that this was a city, after all.

"Oh, come on," they replied.

The hosts didn't even have time to blink before the Russians fearlessly rushed off toward the waves, shocking the Americans with their identical military-issued grayish-blue long underwear.

Of course, all the special operations group members tried to buy something in America for their loved ones; after all, their daily allowances were issued in dollars. They mostly acquired simple things from local merchants, such as clothing, shoes, fabrics, whiskey, and cigarettes. Such purchases did not require special knowledge of English, although there were also some funny moments in such elementary shopping excursions.

It so happened that the Soviet pilots arrived in the United States with old-style dollars printed prior to the reforms carried out by Roosevelt, when the size of the bill was reduced by almost a third. The American merchants initially thought the old dollars were counterfeit and refused to accept them. Once the situation was cleared up, however, one of the clerks placed the pre-Roosevelt bills in a frame like a museum exhibit.

A few of Maxim's subordinates decided to make even more serious purchases in order to equip their homes in the Soviet Union with refrigerators, washing machines, and record players. Some of these purchases resulted in considerable problems in the postwar Soviet Union, when there was great dislike for anyone who could be suspected of greed or, even worse, kowtowing to the West.

As for Maxim, he demonstrated his usual restraint in his purchases. Toward the end of his time in the United States, his American friends were prepared, out of the kindness of their hearts, to give the "handsome Russian colonel" the Pontiac he had been granted for official use. They promised to ship his car to any Soviet port Maxim wanted. Of course, he declined the offer in the most polite manner possible. He said he already had three cars in the garage at home.

Naval pilots from the special operations squad that
delivered seaplanes from the USA to the USSR.]

Maxim liked how the American officers spent their leisure time: "with
a bottle of beer or wine. With the sound of the gramophone. Three or four
couples dancing." He frequently returned to this subject:

> They come with their families on Saturdays and have
> dinner at the officers' mess. After dinner they go to a
> movie, then dancing at the officer's club. They drink light
> alcoholic beverages, beer and Coca-Cola, a drink with
> a rather pleasant taste that is unknown to us but very
> popular here. The radio-gramophone with the record
> autochanger mechanism and the quiet rhythmic music.

The Soviet pilots were invited to these events as well. Chibisov wrote,
"The American officers and their families are friendly to us. Despite our
poor knowledge of the language, everyone tries to chat with us. Women
invite our officers to dance."

Chibisov was strict in his demand that his subordinates uphold the
high reputation of their team both during leisure activities and when on
duty. However, the "healthy-lifestyle" rules established in the special group
were nevertheless violated now and again, primarily with respect to alcohol
and smoking. Gagarin described one unpleasant story:

> Everyone knew that there was an officer in the special
> group who smoked too much. One evening, after drinking

a few glasses, the chain smoker passed out with a cigarette in his mouth. The bed started smoking. The American firefighters came and put out the fire. The room stank of smoke, dust and moisture. We wanted to relocate the culprit of the accident to a clean and dry room, but Chibisov, a proponent of strict discipline, objected: "No! He created this mess, let him stay in his place." Not surprisingly, the troublemaker never returned to America after ferrying the Catalina back to the homeland. Everyone understood this is how the "offender" had been punished.

But this was an exceptional case. On the whole, the Elizabeth City hosts remembered Chibisov's group as a highly professional team comprised of decent, appealing, and well-mannered people.

At that time, all of America demonstrated warm and friendly feelings toward the Soviet people.

On December 14, 1944, while on a trip to New York, Maxim and a few of his colleagues found time to go to the theater to see an ice show ("it was dancing on stage with skates" was the explanation he left in his diary). They enjoyed the spectacle: "Great show. Nice costumes. Healthy beautiful young artists. Masters of their craft. They even performed the most complex numbers well."

Prior to the start of the show, the host announced that allies of the United States—the valiant Russian officers—were in the theater. The crowd applauded. Maxim and his colleagues had to stand up and bow in all directions in order to respond to the ovation by the audience, which, of course, was directed not only at them personally but at the whole of the great nation they represented.

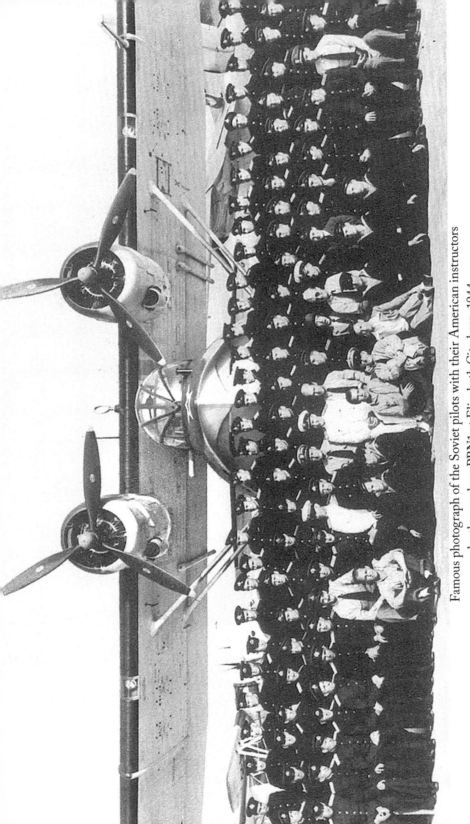

Famous photograph of the Soviet pilots with their American instructors by the seaplane PBN1 at Elizabeth City base. 1944.

12.8 The Last Year of the War

The commander of the Russian ferry pilots rang in the New Year in 1945 at the Soviet Embassy:

> We took a train to Washington. We got bored along the way. Kokarev, Kotov and Genkin were joking around and playing cards. Khrolenko was going over my "lessons." We arrived in Washington on the evening of December 31. We took a taxi from the train station and stopped by Misha's apartment. We cleaned up, changed our clothes and left for the embassy.

Things were formal initially as expected at such an institution. The counselor of the embassy read out a report. A short break was followed by amateur performances by embassy workers and their wives, who gave recitals and sang a total of eight songs. It left a rather gray impression overall. Not a single memorable performance.

At a quarter to twelve, we went to the table. Once everyone was seated, Ambassador Gromyko rose to speak. He touched on the latest events on the fronts of World War II. He recalled the end of the operation to liberate the Baltic countries, the Soviet offensive in Yugoslavia and the battles in the eastern parts of Czechoslovakia and the streets of Budapest. He then mentioned the Western front and the U.S. presidential elections in November, which Roosevelt had won for the fourth consecutive time. And at the end of his speech, he briefly summarized our achievements in the outgoing year of 1944, highlighting the successes of the Red Army.

Comrade Gromyko also made the first toast. This, of course, was a toast to the health of the leader, strategist and commander, Comrade Stalin. When the clock struck midnight, it was time for the next toast and everyone raised their glasses to the new year of 1945 and victory! After this, we started drinking as people made various toasts depending on their feelings and the company at the table. Then we sang and danced. Following the event at the embassy, our group left at 4:00 a.m. to resume the fun at the GPC. We didn't spend much time there. I was tired. I tracked down my coat in the cloakroom, got in the car with Misha Khrolenko, and went to the hotel. And that's how I rang in the New Year.

Maxim later recalled that by the end of the evening, he was overcome with not only fatigue but also sadness. After all, the New Year was a family holiday, and it wasn't particularly joyful to celebrate it inside the walls of a government building. Of course, to some extent, the Soviet Embassy in America was considered a small island of the homeland. This tiny island was inhabited by people connected by a common duty and cause; thus, they were not entirely strangers to one another. But the ones dearest to him—his wife and daughter—were so far away. His mind could not escape troubling questions, not during working hours or on holidays. How were they doing? Did they know he was alive and missing them? After all, he did not have the right to send word about himself.

From the first days of 1945, there was a forced break in the special group's activities, mainly due to the weather conditions. Gagarin recalled,

> The winter in January was exceptionally cold. The river near the factory in Philadelphia was covered with ice and the Catalinas couldn't take off even though they were ready to be transferred. As a result, roughly a month went by without any airplanes. The standstill was exacerbated by another factor: we had to wait a long time for the main group of Soviet crews to return.

Then an accident occurred as a plane crashed during takeoff. When the special group commander rushed to the scene of the accident,

> the plane was still floating in the water smashed and upside down. All that was left was the tail in which there was a live and unharmed person, the technician Borodin, who was calling for help. The rescue team began to cut through the tail, but they were too late and the merciless water swallowed the poor soul.

Floating crane lifting broken parts of PBN1 from the river.

Some of the details of this tragic event were burned into Gagarin's memory:

First of all, the Catalina was slightly overloaded. Secondly, the accident took place at night, to be more precise at 3:00 a.m. The water surface looked so still that it seemed like glass. The plane was carrying six Russian pilots and three officers from the British RAF (a pilot, navigator and radio operator). In order to help the crew with orientation, we used flares, which burn for roughly half an hour, to mark the takeoff path on the water. When the plane passed the last light, the pilot saw absolute blackness in front of him. He thought he was ascending too quickly. So he decided to keep the speeding plane parallel to the water without knowing where he was. He didn't even have a couple seconds to glance from the cockpit window down at the instruments (one of the most common and deplorable errors by pilots all over the world). Without managing to gain any altitude, the plane with all its might and weight literally became stuck in the water, split in half and sank to the bottom. Three or four guys (including one Englishman) were killed, while the rest were rescued. They were treated for fractures at the hospital for a few weeks.

In his diary, Maxim briefly reported,

> The commission from Washington that came to investigate this incident laid the blame for the crash and the death of five people on the pilot, who lost control. He was an English pilot and by no means a novice. But the fact that it wasn't our crew didn't make things any easier: after all, our comrades had been killed.

In early February 1945, the amphibious PBY-6A seaplanes with the Norden sights began to arrive from the Floyd Bennett Field factory in New York. A large number of the crews returned from the Soviet Union to Elizabeth City. It became possible to once again launch the ferrying conveyor along the southern route.

But this time, the first person to fly the route would be Colonel Chibisov. Under an order issued by the People's Commissariat of the Navy on January 16, 1945, Maxim had been promoted in military rank to Colonel for the timely and uninterrupted supply of the aircraft.

Pacific Fleet Air Force Commander Pyotr Lemeshko had nominated Maxim Chibisov for this rank back in January 1944, when he was the commander of the 10th Naval Aviation Division of the Pacific Fleet, and then again in the spring and summer of the same year. But the Far East officers were not quickly rising in rank at that time. The petitions for his promotion simply sat in the Moscow personnel offices for six months. Three petitions concerning Chibisov were delayed in this manner. Thus, Maxim became a colonel at a time when he was already a special group commander and working with senior military political leaders.

He was shown a copy of the order conferring his new title at the Soviet Embassy in Washington in late January 1945. He was told at the time that an urgent call had been made for him to return to Moscow.

Members of the Colonel's M.N. Chibisov special operations seaplane squad. Left to right: onboard technician G.V. Pasynkov, Commander of the squad P.A. Pankov, pilot of the unit G.Y. Yermilov.]

CHAPTER 13

Long Flights and the Adventures of 1945

13.1 From America to the USSR

The flight of the Catalina group from Elizabeth City to Baku under the command of Colonel Chibisov was completed in a ten-day period from February 15 to February 25, 1945.

Comparing the Southern Route with its Eastern and Northern counterparts, Maxim noted in his diary, "We were on the lookout for tropical heat instead of northerly winds, thunderstorms instead of icing and the black sand storms of the Southern Hemisphere instead of gray eastern fog."

The route, which stretched over 18,000 kilometers (11,200 miles), was split into ten stages, each of which Maxim recorded separately in his manuscripts. His description of this trip does not require any special commentary.

> Preparing for the flight was almost no different than for the two previous routes with the exception of training the navigators on orientation in the Southern Hemisphere. The classes were led by a Canadian navigator. In addition, we had to undergo intensive pilot training at night since a

large part of the route would pass over the Atlantic Ocean when it was dark.

Taking into account past mistakes, we carefully detailed the maps, marked all the radio stations on them, and stocked up on photos and descriptions of the main and alternate airfields. In accordance with the conditions set forth by the Americans, we had to ferry only two planes at a time instead of four.

I.N. Salnikov, M.N. Chibisov, american pilot Kostritsky and engineer I.M. Genkin at the airfield Belem. Brazil, 1945.

Each of the ten stages of the route had its own peculiarities. Not all my memories are equally clear, but looking back at the diary, I can recall everything as if it were yesterday.

1. Elizabeth City–San Juan (Puerto Rico)

The first stage passed along the Atlantic coast of North America. We had to cover a distance of 1,200 miles in 12.5 hours. There was not enough daylight for the trip. Departure was scheduled for night so that the landing would take place in the first half of the following day.

Landing in Brazil, in the mouth of the Amazon River close to Belem city, 1945.

The two planes took off from the Elizabeth City airfield at 11:00 p.m. Reaching an altitude of 3,700 meters (12,140 feet), we flew in the clouds. We saw flashes of lightning ahead and soon found ourselves in large cumulus clouds with an updraft. I was flying the plane myself, while the co-pilot

235

was an experienced American. When we got caught in the storm front, the turbulence was so strong that we could barely maintain control of the plane. It was being tossed from side to side, but we continued to gain altitude in an attempt to escape from the clouds. At an altitude of 4,301 meters (14,100 feet), it became difficult to breathe and the lightning was so blinding that our eyes saw nothing but darkness after each new flash. This continued for over two hours. Then it seemed like the turbulence had calmed down a bit. And suddenly a powerful updraft abruptly pushed the plane up to an altitude of 5,000 meters (16,400 feet). The plane was up on its tail. The instruments displayed an extreme increase in altitude and a loss of speed. We barely managed to hold on to the wheel and pushed it as hard as we could. One thing was clear: if the air current suddenly changed sharply at that moment, we would be unable to handle the controls and the plane would inevitably fall into a tailspin. Holding our collective breath, everyone watched the instrument readings. My American colleague and I understood one another without saying a word. We pushed again. The nose of the plane began to quickly descend. We reduced the speed, but the plane continued to dive. The instruments showed a speed of more than 200 miles and a sharp loss of altitude. In a few seconds, we dropped to 3,100 meters (10,200 feet) from 5,000 meters (16,400 feet). This happened instantly, thus the resting crew members fell to the floor and were then thrown to the ceiling.

I must admit that I had never been in a similar predicament even though I had seen a lot by that time. I will probably never forget that night flight through the immense stormy sky. The struggle against the elements lasted for more than six fours in total darkness, blind conditions, and using the instruments. The storm only ended at dawn. We came out of the clouds and couldn't believe that we were still alive. We needed to determine our position, but we had no communications—the radio station and the autopilot had broken down. We had to fly the plane manually without a moment's respite, based solely on celestial references.

When we approached the island of Puerto Rico, visibility was perfect as the sun was shining and blinding us from its reflection on the smooth sea. At this point, we realized that it wasn't over yet and that we would still be tested at the finish line: we would have to land on a smooth water surface with a strong uprush. Thus went the first twelve-hour leg of the route, which was far from extraordinary but, rather typical flight on the whole route.

2. Puerto Pico–Port of Spain

The shortest and easiest stage of the route with total length of 556 miles and estimated flight time of 5 hours 35 minutes. The flight took place during the day using radio beacons. The perfectly situated airfield in the Bay of Trinidad was well prepared to accept the Catalinas. Therefore, the landing of the crews did not cause any commotion.

3. Port of Spain–Belém (Brazil)

This stage with length of 1,100 miles (estimated flight time of 11 hours) mainly passed over water and was known to pilots for its thunderstorms and tropical downpours. We took off four hours before dawn. As expected, we battled storms for the first half of the flight. I remember the story of Captain I. Abramov, who was flying in tandem with the crew of Senior Lt. A. Medelyan: for six hours they were struggling with the water that had penetrated into the plane. The pumps had been working for a long time and the water was receding slowly. The electrical instruments, navigational equipment and radio station all malfunctioned. It seemed it would never end. And then, suddenly, two hours before Belém, the rain stopped. The sky became clear and blue, and the ocean was visible down below. At this moment, the crews crossed the equator for the first time, crossing over into the Southern Hemisphere from the Northern. According to famous naval and aviation traditions, the crossing of the equator is celebrated with a ceremony. In the British and U.S. navy, everyone receives 100 grams (3.5 ounces) of rum and symbolically makes a sacrifice to Neptune, the god of the sea, by throwing some item overboard. It's true what they say: this goofy exercise is contagious. Having heard plenty of stories from the Canadian instructors, our pilots quickly became versed in the ritual of sacrifice and tasting San Juan rum.

At the Belém base, crews were sometimes delayed by several days due to bad weather. All our pilots recalled the city as a lovely little place that was picturesquely situated in the mouth of the Amazon River. Of course, they also never forgot that the sea-based airfield almost always had a strong uprush due to which both takeoff and landing took place amidst the roar of waves striking the bottom of the planes. However, this never once bothered us during the ferrying of the Catalinas. We were always met, our planes were raised from the water, and the crews were immediately sent to the hotel to relax.

4. Belém–Natal

This route (with a total distance of 900 miles and estimated flight time of 9 hours) mainly passed over land along the Atlantic coast of Brazil. Compared to the others, this part of the route was relatively simple since we flew during the day and the weather was generally decent. However, another incident happened here which I'll never forget. At some point, the motor failed in the plane flown by Captain F. Yeroshenko at an altitude of 3,000 meters (9,840 feet). The plane began to gradually descend on one engine. The commander ordered all nonessential items to be thrown overboard. The plane continued to fall. At 900 meters (2,950 feet) they even threw out the retractable landing gear, but this didn't help either. Their descent continued. The situation was complicated by the fact that they were flying over land. The terrain was rough and there were no alternate airfields in the area. It seemed like there was no way out. And then, without any hope for success, Yeroshenko tried to start the malfunctioning engine just in case, and it worked. The plane and crew had been saved. They landed safely at the planned airfield at the mouth of the Rio Grande. Both engines were working smoothly. It turned out that oxidation had occurred in both magneto contacts due to salt water infiltration during take off and the engine had stalled. Once the contacts dried out, the sparks got through, and everything returned to normal.

5. From America to Africa: Natal–Bathurst

> Flying over the ocean is always a difficult test for
> which one must carefully prepare and we had done this in
> every respect: morally, physically and logistically.

The distance over the ocean was 1,612 miles and the estimated flight time under ideal conditions was more than 16 hours. Therefore, we had to depart in the evening just before dusk in order to land on the next day while it was still light out. I flew this route three times: in summer 1944 as the second pilot in the American crew on the C-54 Skymaster, then as the first pilot on Catalinas in February and October 1945. But the difficulties faced on this flight did not depend on the season. The airfield in Natal was located on the river bed of the Rio Grande with width not exceeding 90 meters (300 feet) as well as curves and large sandbanks. Thus, each takeoff involved weaving between the shoals, boats and floating logs.

On the eve of the flight, both crews had a difficult time falling asleep. All our minds were restless … We got up early in the morning and began preparing for departure. We took off at 8:00 p.m. without any incidents. I was the lead pilot and Georgy Kartashov was the wingman. Flying with me were second pilot Lev Yakovlev, navigator Dmitry Fomin and onboard technician V. Zaychenko. Night came quickly. We almost immediately entered into a thick layer of clouds. We tried to break through the clouds, but to no avail. This was the warm Atlantic front which the English pilots had spoken about. A storm began and it started to rain heavily. This was all reminiscent of the first leg of the Southern route (Elizabeth City–Puerto Rico) in the stormy skies of the Northern Hemisphere. While the turbulence here wasn't quite as strong, it was not a pleasant flight. It seemed like the night would never end. We had already been in pitch black darkness for five hours. It's hard to express in words how long these hours stretch on during the gloomy tropical night when there's not a single light in sight and nothing but the boundless ocean below you. Despite the seeming hopelessness of visual observation, we were constantly watching the sky, waiting for gaps in the clouds. Around 7:00 a.m., the heavenly bodies began to appear occasionally and briefly. Comparing their position with the map, we made adjustments to our course. About 8:00 a.m., we unexpectedly reached the coastline of the African shore. We flew along the coast and for a long time could not determine our location—visibility was almost zero. We were rescued by the radio beacon. The navigator took our bearings a few times and finally determined that we were slightly to the right of Bathurst. Soon we came out of the clouds and saw the bending channel of a large river in the distance. We had fully restored our orientation. We approached the mouth of the Gambia River, where we were supposed to land. It turned out that we had arrived an hour and a half earlier than scheduled. This occurred because we were flying with a tailwind for part of the trip.

The English base of Bathurst is close to the equator. It's very hot and humid here (45–50° F.) (113-122⁰ F.), the real tropics. In addition, there are frequent storms. There are no hangars for the seaplanes; the boats remain in the water and are repaired there. Two hours prior to our arrival, a storm had flipped over and destroyed two English seaplanes. Another storm could take place at any moment. There was no need for us to stay here and take a risk with the new planes. Therefore, despite being extremely tired, the crews agreed to fly out on the same evening.

The takeoff was surprisingly complicated. The wind was blowing from the ocean, the runway [on the Gambia River] was bumpy, and muddy, viscous water was being heaved up by high waves from the river, sharply striking the bottom of the boat. It was only after six porpoises that I was able to separate from the water and head towards Morocco in the dusk.

6. Bathurst–Port Lyautey (French Morocco)

In terms of duration, this stretch was slightly shorter than the flight over the Atlantic Ocean. The distance was 1,460 miles and the estimated flight time was about 15 hours. The route passed along the desolate west coast of Africa. There was only one alternate airfield (Dakar) along the entire route and only two intermediate beacons.

We took off in the evening, two hours prior to dusk. Our departure time coincided with the start of the ebb tide. In such cases, there is a high probability of running aground and damaging the bottom of the aircraft hull. Therefore, we were quick to steer away from the shore and quickly found ourselves in the open sea. We had to take off from a large wave, which is no easy task. The wave smashed into the plane a few times and it was only after five or six "porpoises" that I managed to break away. The plane got hung up and it seemed like I was about to fall back to the water again. I gave it some gas and the engines roared at full blast. The plane slowly started to gain altitude. Soon it became dark. This was my second sleepless night in a row and I felt fatigued. In order to stay awake, we constantly drank coffee and chewed American bubblegum, which at home I never even knew existed.

The weather was relatively decent for the whole route, but we hit a strip of thick fog on the approach to the airfield in Port Lyautey. We requested permission to land, but were denied. We were asked to wait until the fog rose. For two hours we circled over the water near the airfield, cursing the overcautious airport officials, and dreaming about only one thing: getting into a horizontal position. Later we learned that the airfield was located in a narrow river with a rapid current, thus the caution of the hosts was justified.

7. Port Lyautey–Djerba (Tunisia)

Following a long and well-deserved rest, we flew out of Port Lyautey at dawn the next morning. The route cut straight through the Atlas Mountains, the sandy deserts of Algeria and Tunisia and the Gulf of Gabes. We were supposed to cover 800 miles in eight hours. This was the shortest route. A few lakes were recommended as alternate airfields. However, while these lakes were marked on the map, they were actually dry as a bone this time of year.

A large part of the route passed over the lifeless desert. The main impression I got was a dull landscape and debilitating heat, even in the cockpit despite the high altitude. We were flying in nothing but our swimming trunks and joked that we were ready to go diving but for some reason the water was yellow.

Finally, the coastline appeared. We could see actual blue waters. It was the Gulf of Gabes and the long-awaited airfield located in the strait between the mainland and the island of Djerba.

8. Island of Djerba–Port Kasfareet (Egypt)

The next stage passed along the Mediterranean Sea and totaled 1,100 miles (estimated flight time of 11 hours).

We wanted to depart at night and land during the day, but the temporary and primitive airfield on the island of Djerba had such shallow water that a nighttime departure from this strip was rather risky. We had to start out at dawn. The weather was excellent and, according to the forecast, we would have good visibility for the entire flight, which is what occurred. We flew over areas that we had heard about in newspaper reports. This was the North African theater of war: Tripoli, Benghazi, Torbuk and Sallum. We saw the traces of battles as well as the remains of tanks, planes, vehicles and other military equipment.

Suddenly, in broad daylight and with good weather, my crew had to make an emergency landing. Halfway between Djerba and Kasfareet, I noted a thin stream of smoke coming from an engine. I called over the flight mechanic, we observed the engine, increased the speed, and the trickle of smoke with oil became more pronounced. We reduced speed and the plane started to descend. I consulted with the second pilot and decided to land. We landed right in the sea. A local boat came to meet us and towed us to the port. Fortunately, we had an American pilot onboard and I didn't have to explain anything. In the meantime, the mechanic started looking into the cause of the smoke leak. He quickly discovered that the coupling clamp around a fitting had become loose, fastened it, and said that we could continue flying.

I started the engines. Indeed, everything was in order. We took off and flew to the Libyan-Egyptian border. We initially flew over the desert and then the deep Nile. We passed over Cairo just before nightfall and reached the Gulf of Suez, where Port Kasfareet was located. Here we were able to land on a superbly equipped naval base. We were immediately granted permission to land and were given a luxurious reception: the planes were secured on crosses and the crews were taken to the city to rest and see the pyramids. We were invited to the English Officer's Club that evening and departure was scheduled for morning.

9. Port Kasfareet–Lake Habbaniyah (Baghdad)

This stage passed almost entirely over land through the Sinai Peninsula, the Dead Sea and the Syrian desert (total distance of 650 miles, estimated flight time of 6 hours 30 minutes). We were forbidden from using radio communications: citing the proximity of military operations, the English were afraid of the German reconnaissance aircraft based on the Greek islands.

Landing on Lake Habbaniyah was complicated by the fact that the airfield waters do not have a sufficient number of landing markers. When the sun is shining bright and the conditions are calm, it is very difficult to gauge height. People say that several planes have had accidents when landing on this lake.

10. Lake Habbaniyah– Baku—the final stop on the Southern route

Soviet pilots and American interpreter during a visit of the King of Iraq's palace.

The last leg of the route (approximately 500 miles) passed directly through mountain passes. The English advised us not to take this shortcut. Indeed, the route had not been traveled much and passed over high mountains with no landing sites or weather stations. The allies suggested another route—through Iran, Iraq and the Caspian Sea. But we were in a hurry and took the direct route.

We flew at a high altitude with poor visibility. At times, the engines were working at maximum capacity, the instruments said climb to ceiling, and we had to go even higher.

However, the most difficult part was landing on the Caspian Sea. There was a thick fog and raging wind over the Caspian. We had to wait for the fog to lift a little. Once this occurred, we could see the huge rocky waves pummeling the oil rigs. It wasn't a very pleasant-looking place to land. I spent a long time maneuvering through the rigs, waiting for the right moment. But I had no doubts that anything would happen to me here, after all it was my native land. I'll never forget the feeling I had at the moment when I stepped on land. I wanted to fall down and kiss the ground like my own mother. I remember how people surrounded us: I couldn't believe that they were all fellow countrymen. My native tongue sounded like music. It turns out a person needs so little for happiness.

13.2 Business in Moscow

Ultra long-range flight along the South route successfully accomplished.

Maxim spent one night in Moscow but was not able to sleep for a single minute. First, he went to see his brother Alexei and left his things there, and then he went to the Naval Air Force headquarters, where he spent most of the day. Colonel Chibisov had been summoned to Moscow for further consultations on the combat use of the new amphibians equipped with the Norden sight. Also at this time, Marshal Zhavoronkov awarded him two Orders of the Red Star, which Maxim had been unable to receive earlier while far away from the Motherland. He was awarded the first ruby star for his combat service during the defense of Tallinn and Leningrad and the second for his exemplary command of the 10th Naval Aviation Division and his sound training of flight personnel.

Colonel M.N. Chibisov, 1945.

Soviet forces were rapidly advancing on Berlin. The war in Europe had ended, and the day when the USSR would enter into war in the Far East was steadily approaching. The Pacific Fleet was anxiously awaiting the delivery of the Catalinas, which had already proven themselves during combat actions on other fronts. The decision was made to urgently deploy the new consignment of PBY-6A seaplanes using two routes: the eastern (from Kodiak to the Chukotka airfield of Uelkal and then along the well-trod path to Vladivostok) and the Northern Route (via Reykjavik to the Baltic nations and then across the entire country to the Pacific shores). The details of these air transport operations were discussed during the meeting at Zhavoronkov's headquarters, where Colonel Chibisov had been summoned all the way from America.

Once he had finished his business, Maxim rushed back to his brother's. His other brother in Moscow, Ivan, had also come over, and they all spent the evening and much of the night talking at the dinner table.

In his diary, Maxim offered a detailed and colorful description of this meeting with his family, which took place on March 13, 1945:

> I sorted out all the things I had brought, put together a small package for Rosaly and Emmochka, and put aside everything I would need for the return trip … At the same time, during the few intervals between conversations with my brothers, we happily had a few drinks … If there was a long pause, I would say: "The conversation is dragging for some reason" (my new phrase), after which someone would bring me a glass to "improve my speech." Alexei was pretty drunk and the situation was made worse by the fact that he had to go to work at 7:00 a.m. I gave him a "command" at 4:00 a.m. to go to sleep. He initially refused but then obeyed after some prompting. The older Ivan stayed with me despite the fact that he also had to rush off to work … Morning. My brothers are gone. March 14. I got my things together. A driver came to pick me up. I started checking my documents. The main one with the visa wasn't in the pocket of my leather jacket. I searched everywhere and rummaged through the garbage, but to no avail. My nerves were on edge. I tried to remember what I had been wearing. Finally, I thought about checking in the pocket of my summer protective jacket, where I found everything that I had spent an hour and a half searching for. Following such severe stress, my mood improved and my pulse returned to normal. I was amazed that I had been able to keep myself under control and not utter a single angry word in front of Lina, Alexei's wife. I will be very happy if I manage to get through moments like those with such composure in the future … I quickly got ready

and we went to the Izmaylovo airfield. We got in a C-47, started the engine, taxied and took off. After a sleepless night, I wanted to sleep but it was too cold in the plane. Nevertheless, I managed to sleep for an hour and a half. I woke up because I was freezing. I went to the cockpit in order to warm up.

Colonel Chibisov flew out of Moscow with two crews and the flagship specialist, Major A. Shapkin.

According to Maxim's diary entries, they made a stop in Mozdok and received an invitation to a party to honor the eldest farmers. There were Caucasus dancing and flowery toasts. The guests were impressed with the commitment of the respected elders to "acquire a few fighter planes using our own money and present them to the hero pilots of the Soviet Union." This was not empty boasting: Baltic naval aviation pilots had already received several planes acquired with such donations.

Next, following the same path he had traveled in July 1944 through Baku, Tehran, North Africa, and the Atlantic, Maxim returned to Elizabeth City. The flight was uneventful except for a day's delay in Port Lyautey, where the group were joined by Zamyatin's crew, who were returning to the United States.

While waiting for Zamyatin's plane, the Soviet pilots went to the movies. They were highly impressed by the American military newsreels, specifically a story about planes based on aircraft carriers. Assessing what he had seen with the eye of a professional, Maxim wrote,

> What features stand out? A high state of readiness for departure; the planes stand there with raised cockpit covers; the engines are all turned on at once; a mobile takeoff, one after the other, and rapid assembly in the air. Single-engine torpedo bombers flying in a coordinated tight formation. Features of attacks on surface targets: part of the group maneuvers to distract the enemy with gunfire while the rest of the group comes in to strike the target with a low-level attack. In most cases, such attacks lead to success. Return and landing. The braking system is well developed. The moment the planes touch the deck, the landing gear is caught by arresting wires stretched

across the ship deck and after "landing" the plane doesn't run more than 25 meters (82 feet). In the event the ship arresting wires don't catch the landing gear for some reason, the pilots hit the brakes so hard that the plane comes to a stop almost on its nose. The cameramen filmed two such instances. From these shots, one can assess not only the technical merits of the carrier and the planes, but also the psychological condition of the flight crew.

13.3 Amphibians for the Pacific Fleet

In early April, Colonel Chibisov was already waiting for planes and crews to arrive at the Elizabeth City base for the next round of ferrying. Relations with the Americans were constructive and friendly, as always. Therefore, the special group commander did not anticipate any new problems.

But problems arose. When the four planes to be ferried arrived in Elizabeth City, they were lacking components—and not just spare parts, engine tools, and other easily fixable flaws. The navigational radar had been removed from the planes, and the deicing systems had not been installed.

Taking Tertsiyev with him, Maxim urgently traveled to Washington and tried to sort things out with the deliveries via the Government Procurement Commission. Their reaction was not encouraging. A favorable reply was received only for the provision of spare parts and engine tools. The explanations given on the fundamental issues were unconvincing. The radar had been removed because the Soviet Union supposedly did not have the appropriate ground equipment to operate it. The reason provided for the removal of the deicing system was just as odd: the previous system was allegedly outdated, and its production had simply been discontinued.

But it would be impossible to ferry the Catalinas through Kodiak without a deicer. This had been proven by flights made the previous September, when planes under the weight of ice cover had descended

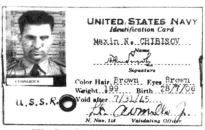

ID Card of Colonel M.N. Chibisov issued by the United States Navy in 1945.

247

almost all the way to the water—and that had been with deicers. Without such devices, the Catalinas simply could not function. Reporting these problems to Moscow, Maxim made the decision—with the support of the GPC leaders—not to accept the planes without deicing systems.

His diary contained the following series of entries: "Busy working on piloting techniques for the Amphibians. And waiting, constantly waiting for a decision from Moscow and a reply from the GPC—General Piskunov and Ryazantsev were supposed to go to the U.S. Department of Defense."

Soon the reply came from the GPC: the necessary deicing equipment was being manufactured and would start being installed on ten planes to be ferried to the USSR starting from May 1.

On April 17, a new gesture of goodwill came from the Americans as GPC employees were invited to visit the Consolidated factory in New Orleans, where various modifications of the Catalinas [type PBY-6a] were manufactured. The trip took place on April 19–22 with military representatives and Maxim, along with a few of his subordinates, traveling to New Orleans.

Maxim liked the factory: "The workshops are clean, well lit and equipped with a variety of cranes and good ventilation ... Many women are employed in production. They work in almost all workshops and sections." He enjoyed the process of checking the boat for leaks. "In a special pool, water is poured in the boat to the float line. It is kept in this position for a day. If there is no leak, the boat is declared fit and sent off for assembly and the installation of internal equipment."

On April 21, Maxim was invited to take part in the test flight of an amphibian that had just been manufactured.

> The pilot removed the landing gear on the water and went to take off. I was sitting in the navigator's seat and observing his actions ... I was invited to sit in the right-hand seat and fly the plane. Thus, I was at the controls, while the senior test pilot was in the left-hand chair. From my right-hand seat, I made four water landings. The surface wasn't smooth with a half-meter (one and half foot) wave. After the first splashdown, the plane twice jumped over the water. I successively landed on the front stepped hull, then the tail and then on both stepped hulls. The plane landed well and takeoff was also okay. We climbed up to

8,000 meters (26,250 feet). We gave it full throttle and headed off towards the horizon. Speed of 115–200 miles per hour. All the data was recorded by an intern who was monitoring the instruments. I made the fifth and final landing on land after releasing the special amphibious landing gear. My American colleague was pleased. And so was I. Following the test, the plane was sent for inspection and documentation as prepared for delivery to the client.

Maxim was pleased with the attitude of the workers toward the Soviets: "It's the same as in the rest of America—friendly and kind. Seeing Soviet officers in uniform, many of them gave us curious glances and showed a desire to ask questions and talk."

After blowing off some steam in the sky, on the ground, Colonel Chibisov returned to the problems concerning the supply of the new Catalinas. He studied the tactical and technical features of the seaplane with the factory's main military representative, Lieutenant Ellison. Maxim was particularly interested in data on the plane's fuel reserve, which was of paramount importance for determining its maximum range.

That evening, Maxim invited [Lieutenant Ellison] and his assistant to dinner so that in the presence of Tertsiyev and the interpreter Doronin, he could try to at least clarify, if not resolve, some business matters.

We drank a bottle of vodka and a bottle of cognac. We talked. Then we all went to have dinner. We sat and talked some more, after which we all went our separate ways ... The gist of the conversation can be summarized as follows: Our wish: to accelerate the production of the planes allocated for

Review of the airship construction. Left to right: I.N. Salnikov, M.N. Chibisov, Major Shavlyuk, V.V. Terciev, Captain Holtz, USA, Elizabeth City, 1945.

us as much as possible. The reply: "It doesn't depend on us—Washington arranges everything." The second request: organize the installation of the deicing system at the factory. The reply: "This system is manufactured and installed at other centers."

Based on the nature of the questions Ellison asked in reply—"Is Russia planning to fight with Japan, and will it buy products from the United States after the war?"—it was clear the US military continued to view the Russians as allies.

13.4 Stormy Winds from Washington

In the airship cockpit (left to right): Colonel V.V. Terciev, Major I.N. Salnikov, Colonel M.N. Chibisov. At the back American Capitan Holtz is pictured. Elizabeth City, September 20th, 1945.

The problems with the missing modifications on the Catalinas arose as part of the changes taking place in the Washington corridors of power.

Franklin Roosevelt had died on April 12 and been succeeded by Vice President Harry Truman, who was known for his candid phrase uttered back in summer 1941: "If we see that Germany is winning we ought to help Russia, and if Russia is winning we ought to help Germany, and that way let them kill as many as possible."

In 1945, there was a lot Truman did not like about the political legacy he had inherited from Roosevelt: the trust-based tone of Soviet-American relations, Lend-Lease, and the results of the Yalta meeting of the Big Three (Stalin, Roosevelt, and Churchill), during which the Western partners conceded too much to the Soviet Union in the opinion of the new US president.

On April 23, 1945, a week after arriving in the White House, new US President Harry Truman declared to the government and the armed forces command that he intended to pursue a "hard line" with respect to the Soviet Union.

On May 12, 1945, three days after Germany had surrendered, Truman signed an order suspending exports to the USSR. Someone then managed to explain to the president that fighting Japan alone would mean increasing the length of the war as well as the loss of American lives. Based on this rationale, Truman canceled the order on May 15. The US government expressed a willingness to continue sending cargo to the Russian allies and increased the volume of supplies as a way of compensating for "emotional damage."

Truman's anti-Soviet initiative, however, had already had a negative effect: it had energized the rabid enemies of the USSR who held numerous positions of responsibility in US government agencies. In the naval department, Vice Admiral Patrick Bellinger, who was in charge of Project Zebra, saw his position weaken. His boss, US Secretary of the Navy James Forrestal, was a fierce proponent of Truman's tougher policy toward the Soviets.

All of this could not help but affect the Lend-Lease Program, with which Chibisov's special group was involved.

Sensing the change in the American political climate and fearful of its rapid deterioration, Colonel Chibisov, in late April, once again got in touch with Lieutenant Ellison about the planes manufactured for the Soviets that still had no deicing systems.

After receiving a reply that the planes would not be equipped with these systems until June at the earliest, Maxim realized the planes that had already arrived at the base needed to be urgently sent to Alaska to be subsequently ferried along the Eastern Route to the USSR. If nothing else, the deicers could be installed at workshops at the Kodiak base. He did not waste any time in coordinating this issue with the GPC officials and urgently requested authorization from Moscow for this risky move.

He sent a group of experts led by Tertsiyev to Kodiak and began accelerated training for the flight with the crews he had available. Chernack and his subordinates at the Elizabeth City base fully understood the situation and helped their Russian colleagues as much as they could. But Maxim was already counting down hours instead of days.

Tertsiyev called the special group commander every day in anticipation of the planes and crews. A group of American pilots arrived in Elizabeth City and waited three days for the command to ferry the amphibians to

Kodiak. Chernack started to worry and said that he could not keep his guys sitting around idly for so long and that he would have to send them back soon. Maxim was already afraid he would never receive a reply from Moscow. But on May 2, the GPC reported that permission had been granted. Maxim gave Chernack the go-ahead to start ferrying the planes.

Then, on the eve of departure, more bad news came: the US Department of Defense had issued an order for the Norden sights to be removed from the planes. That evening, during a heartfelt conversation over a glass of tea with Chernack and his assistant, Maxim persuaded his American colleagues that they should release the planes and only then have a look at the order concerning the removal of the sights.

The Americans took a serious risk in providing this important service to their Russian allies. After all, their actions could have easily been viewed as a malicious breach of this order!

13.5 Ten-Ruble Notes for Kodiak

On May 3, the first consignment of five PBY-6A Catalinas intended for the Pacific Fleet took off for Kodiak Island. On May 4, another three planes departed, while all the crews involved in ferrying the planes, led by Colonel Chibisov, also left on the same day.

On May 7, they were greeted like old friends at the Kodiak base. Maxim even had a few shots of gin with the base commander, Captain Maident, to commemorate their reuniting. He also had a friendly meeting with Mr. John, the head of communications, who was in charge of the operators. He recalled that during the previous ferrying of aircraft along the Eastern Route, the Russian commander had spent both day and night at the command post radio center, worrying about his subordinates.

This time, the commander had much less to worry about than he had during the previous fall: the Eastern Route was already more or less established; the cyclones along the route did not rage as fiercely during the summer as they did when winter was approaching; and the crews had gained extensive flight experience, enabling them to cope with various difficulties on the trip.

The acceptance of the Catalinas by the Soviet side was also organized much better. On May 8, Colonel Chibisov flew to Fairbanks to resolve several organizational issues. On May 9, he received maps and radio frequencies for communication with Uelkal, the starting point for the ferrying of seaplanes on Soviet territory.

Taking advantage of any opportunity to further expand his knowledge, Maxim took a tour around Fairbanks and visited the local university. The next day, he returned to Kodiak.

As of May 10, not a single plane had arrived in Kodiak. They were stuck somewhere between San Francisco and Seattle. The special group commander was becoming increasingly concerned about this delay. On the same day, however, news arrived about Germany's surrender, pushing everything else to the side.

In his diary, Maxim wrote,

> I did not cancel flight training for the crews that day. But that evening I announced the assembly of all personnel on the occasion of the great victory over Nazi Germany. I asked Misha Khrolenko to speak first. He was followed by many others—everyone had something to say. It was so uplifting! That night I allowed the guys to each have 200 grams of wine at the officer's club. People were in a good mood. There were no incidents.

On May 12, the first two Catalinas ferried from Elizabeth City arrived in Kodiak. They were immediately sent to the workshop for minor repairs and preparations for departure. Another five planes arrived a day later. Assembling all the flight personnel, the special group commander began preparing the crews to ferry the plans, going over the route from Kodiak to Uelkal in great detail.

The first five planes took off on May 17, 1945, which Maxim recorded in his diary:

> I got up at 6:00 a.m. I checked the weather at the weather station ... We started the engines and checked the equipment. The first to be released were the crews of Spiridonov and Ivanov (flying in place of Dorofeyev whose radar had malfunctioned). The second to take off was the pairing of Antonov and Petrov ... The connection with all four was stable. I monitored them over the radio up until their approach to Uelkal when I heard that the crews were

in contact with the local command post. Following the report that they were preparing to land, I understood that the first ferrying operation had gone well … After lunch and before dinner, I flew with Abramov, Manykin and Bondarenko. We took off and landed seven times. There were two planes left: the one on which I had just taken the crews and the second was Dorofeyev's plane with the broken radar. All the rest were en route to Kodiak. For today, the work day was over.

May 18, 1945. I am anxiously awaiting the next planes. In the meantime, I found three bottles of whiskey for the American crews ferrying the aircraft to Kodiak. I thanked them from the bottom of my heart for successfully ferrying the planes and delivering them in good condition. We spoke and exchanged opinions. I got the impression they were touched by the attention I showed them. But, after all, they had truly done a great job!

There was a powerful cyclone along the route from May 19 to May 22, and Uelkal was not accepting planes. Another nine seaplanes arrived during this time. While the mechanics were preparing them to be ferried, the crews flew around in the aircraft that had been approved for departure. Maxim's diary entries reflect the strenuous work performed during these days:

May 19, 1945. I am scheduled to fly with captains Abramov, Manykin and Bondarenko. The weather was not cooperative in the morning and we only began after lunch. I made four flights with them and then let them train on their own. We flew well. Another four planes arrived, which they immediately began preparing to be ferried by Kravtsov and Medelyan. These aircraft were ready in a day. What was generally a good day ended sadly: Mikhail Khrolenko departed today. I was left without an interpreter and a friend.

May 20, 1945. Kravtsov's planes are scheduled to be prepared and taken out for a flight. Captains Abramov, Manykin and Bondarenko are ready for self-training.

They each made eight circle flights and one flight in the area with ground-based landings. In addition, Kravtsov prepared the planes for the flight. With this, the work day came to an end. I took a close look at the weather forecast for the next day. It didn't look good. A severe cyclone had moved into our area and stopped, which complicated the release of planes to the Soviet Union and the arrival of the next consignment of Amphibians in Kodiak. But I nevertheless scheduled the departure of Kravtsov's squad for May 21, 1945.

May 21, 1945. The flight did not take place due to the poor weather along the route and the landing area. Next up is Kravtsov's departure and training flights for Abramov, Manykin and Bondarenko.

May 22, 1945. Kravtsov's scheduled departure once again did not take place due to the poor weather. Uelkal is not accepting aircraft. But another five planes arrived in Kodiak.

Finally, the weather improved, and the commander gave the order for departure:

May 23, 1945. Kravtsov, Medelyan and Dorofeyev took off along the route. At first, the weather was favorable, then the dual layer of clouds closed into a single layer and began pushing them up against the water. They flew at a low level. They came out of the clouds over Uelkal. True to form, they continued to fly in formation despite the bad weather and didn't lose anyone along the way. The training in blind conditions hadn't been in vain! So, another consignment of planes has been sent to the Motherland.

Members of the seaplane crews from the special operations group of Colonel M.N. Chibisov. Left to right: crew Commander N.E. Dorofeyev, second pilot A.M. Tartakovsky, pilot P.M. Belyaev.

Then a sharp deterioration in the weather delayed flights for another four days.

> In Kodiak, there is a thick fog and drizzling rain. It's the same along the entire route. On May 25–26, the flights of squads led by Leonov and Manykin were postponed. But training continued. We also continue to accept planes—the American pilots delivered a new consignment of Catalinas to the base even in these squalid conditions.

The weather improved slightly on May 27: "Uelkal reported it was prepared to accept another batch of planes. But it remains overcast in Kodiak: drizzling rain that is ready to turn into snow at any minute, while along the route we are deceptively being lured by breaks in the weather."

So as not to risk people's lives, Maxim initially delayed the departure of the planes until noon and then canceled it altogether. About an hour and a half later, this proved to be the correct decision: "The departure airfield was shrouded in dense fog. A cyclone was raging along the route with wet snow. Uelkal immediately radioed to call off the flight." It is better not to think about what would have happened with the crews of the six Catalinas if not for the commander's inherent restraint and intuition, which the pilots themselves called a "sixth sense."

Over the next two days, the weather did not improve.

Departure continues to be postponed, but training is underway. Planes continue to be accepted. Fortunately, the American pilots are delivering a new batch of Amphibian Catalinas to the base even in these foul conditions. Once again, a huge Russian "spasibo" to them and a round of "friendly tea" accompanied by bottles of whiskey.

The mixed team of "real aviation boys" included nine Americans and three Soviets, not including Maxim, who drank symbolically but sincerely thanked the American pilots in his toasts for not letting them down.

On May 29, the commander created a major storm for his subordinates due to the negligence of the radio gunner Kozlov from Abramov's crew. According to the acceptance statement, their plane was listed as ready for operation and ferrying, but in fact, the onboard radar was defective. The radio gunner knew about this defect but supposedly forgot. Such forgetfulness could have proven costly in the air; therefore, Chibisov was merciless in such cases. Everyone received a reprimand, from the careless radio gunner to the flagship [lead] engineer Tertsiyev.

Meanwhile, the cyclone began sliding to the north, and on the last day of May, they managed to send another six planes to Uelkal.

I went to the weather station at 6:00 a.m. I checked the map and the weather forecast. I concluded that it would be possible to fly. I scheduled departure for 11:00 a.m. The crews prepared for the flight. I gave the order for Manykin and his squad to fly out first. He was followed by Levchishin and Bondarenko. They took off safely and started along their route. An hour later Leonov took off (he had been delayed due to a malfunction in his radio compass). It was a six-hour flight. The weather was good and they stayed above the clouds. Around evening they reported that they were over Uelkal. In the morning, we learned that all six planes had landed safely.

The last two Catalinas arrived on the same day. They had to be postponed due to leaks in the fuel tank. The American specialists worked hard to repair the defect in two days, and by June 3, these planes were also in Uelkal.

Maxim wrote,

> They flew in two crews (Antonov-Spiridonov and Ivanov-Petrov) in order to take another two planes from Uelkal and fly them to their destination. After that, they returned to America along with everyone else to prepare for the flight along the Northern route. They flew in good weather and safely landed at their airfields. Thus, I believe the campaign is over.

Another operation to ferry seaplanes to the Pacific Fleet had been completed.

| Captain K.T. Tedtoev | Engineer Major I.N. Salnikov | Colonel M.N. Chibisov |

This event was celebrated that same evening along with the Americans. Of course, they prepared excellent food and drink. In parting, Colonel Chibisov thanked the base command and its personnel for hosting them.

> This support was truly very significant and informal. They prepared the equipment for the flight of the Catalinas in exemplary fashion; they eliminated all defects smoothly, quickly and with excellent quality. Nobody hid anything from us. They even allocated a special room for us at the command post. And their meteorologists provided fresh reports at any time of day or night upon request.

Maxim wrote in his diary about his warm farewell with the base chief, Captain Maident:

> The meeting took place at his apartment. There were three of us—Captain Salnikov, the interpreter and I. The base chief was hosting a friend, the chief of transport from Seattle. Taking advantage of this opportunity, we outlined the plan for the redeployment of our "team," which was supposed to return to Elizabeth City through Anchorage. Both commanders promised to do everything they could to ensure this happens as quickly as possible. In parting, I gave each of them a bottle of whiskey ... In short, we were clearly happy with one another when we bid farewell.

Colonel Chibisov left Maident with a souvenir: a ten-ruble note.

Igor Lebedev, an expert on American manners, said there was a tradition in the US flying community of pilots giving friends commemorative dollars autographed by their colleagues since the dollar is the "idol of Americans. If you have a lot of dollars, you are a person with a capital *P*!"

The Soviet ten-ruble note given to Maident could be seen as a fully adequate sign of gratitude and appreciation for their support.

Maxim also gave a ten-ruble note with his autograph to a local Aluet hunter, who in return gave Maxim a talisman handmade from mammoth ivory, a pendant depicting a human head. According to the hunter, there were only nine such talismans left in the world. Seven of them were in the collections of famous American generals, and he gave one of the remaining two to the "handsome Russian colonel", along with wishes for happiness in life and success in business.

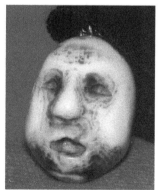

Amulet gifted to M.N. Chibisov by an Aleut.

On June 4, before leaving Kodiak for Elizabeth City, the Soviet pilots went on a fishing trip. The base command allocated a plane to take Chibisov, Salnikov, Tertsiyev, and three interpreters to a place where the fish were unfrightened. Much to the delight of those involved, the catch proved to be a bountiful one.

They fished, cooked fish soup on the fire, and ate heartily. They returned to the base with a couple of huge fish: one for the base commander and the other for his deputy in the flight unit.

| Engineer Colonel V.V. Tertsiyev | Flagship specialist Major A.N. Shapkin | Engineer Major P.I. Turmilov. |

Maxim later liked to recall how, in early June 1945, he and his comrades were invited to the town next to the Kodiak base:

> Upon learning about our presence at the base, a club of the most respected and wealthy citizens of the town invited me and several officers to visit. The meeting we attended was devoted to elections of the club's leaders— the president and council members. There were 14 candidates on the secret ballot and eight of them were elected. After the voting, I was asked to say a few words. I had to speak. First of all, I conveyed regards from my comrades and from our people on their behalf. I spoke about how the joint battle against the common enemy had united the Americans and the Russians and that we greatly appreciate their help. I emphasized—and, as I gathered, everyone was waiting for this—that we would have to work together to finish off the Japanese aggressors and that we would then have to cooperate, make friends, and build peace throughout the world. This was followed by a lunch at which the newly elected president made a speech in response. He noted that our people had put on a heroic display in the war with Nazi Germany and that

this heroism had forced the world to respect Russia as a strong power.

Colonel Chibisov and his comrades left Kodiak the next day, on June 5, 1945, and returned to Elizabeth City on June 8.

13.6 The Northern Route

Along the way to Elizabeth City, the Soviet pilots were delayed for a day and a half in San Francisco, where the founding conference of the United Nations was held from April 25 to June 26, 1945. Colonel Chibisov and his comrades wished to attend one of the sessions, but they were not allowed.

Maxim viewed the creation of the UN with cautious optimism, and this comes through in his diary entries: "Sure, issues of postwar settlement are being considered here. But for now everyone is fighting—some legally, some illegally."

Illegally referred to his view of some of the actions taken by the Anglo-American alliance, particularly by British forces in Greece against local resistance forces who had liberated much of the country from the Nazi occupiers and were vying to participate in reestablishing the government authorities. The Greek antifascist liberation movement was run by Communists who were supported by the Soviet leadership. Therefore, the Soviet Union was extremely sensitive to the policies of the occupying British forces in Greece.

On June 8, 1945, the Russian ferry pilots returned to the acceptance base. It was time to send the next batch of seaplanes to the USSR.

At this time, under the strictest secrecy, large units of the Soviet Army started being redeployed from Eastern Europe on special trains to the border with Manchuria. The Amur Flotilla and the Pacific Fleet were put on high combat alert. The seaplane fleet needed to be expanded considerably for reconnaissance missions during the anticipated campaign of the Pacific Fleet.

Under orders from Marshal Zhavoronkov, the next consignment of Catalinas for the Pacific Fleet was to be ferried along a special transatlantic route.

The first section of the route—from Elizabeth City to Gander,

Newfoundland, and across the ocean to Reykjavik—followed the [same] path along which Colonel Vasilyev's squad had ferried the Catalinas in 1944. However, instead of flying from Iceland over the Norwegian Sea to Murmansk, this time, the planes were supposed to take a more southern route in order to fly through Preston, United Kingdom, to the city of Kolberg on the Baltic Sea. From there, the route proceeded to Moscow and then on to Vladivostok through Kuybyshev (present-day Samara), Krasnoyarsk, and Chita. This route, with a total length of more than 16,000 kilometers (9,940 miles) and a flight time for the Catalinas of roughly 90 hours, was only slightly shorter than the southern route.

Upon returning to the Elizabeth City base and hearing Tertsiyev's report about preparations for the ferrying operation, Maxim wrote in his diary,

June 9, 1945. Morning. I listened to the report from Tertsiyev ... Verbally, things were proceeding like clockwork: everything was ready, approved, Moscow had seemingly given the go-ahead, and all that was left to do was determine the departure date. Once I started looking into the details though, it turned out that there was still a great deal of work to do.

It became clear that none of the planes were fully prepared for the flight, and the flight itself had not been approved with the U.S. military mission in Moscow or the Royal Air Force command, which were to provide assistance to the Soviet pilots on the Newfoundland-Reykjavik–United Kingdom leg of the trip. The issue of the flight being accompanied by a person with knowledge of the Russian language had not been resolved either since the appropriate US military department had not yet approved even the route or allocated interpreters.

Maxim rushed off to Washington and returned to Elizabeth City on June 11. His trip had not produced any results. "I received a reply—just wait!" he wrote in his diary.

The agonizing wait lasted for the next eight days, from June 12 to June 19. Maxim's diary is filled with monotonous entries: "June 12, 1945. I am sitting around waiting for the situation to be resolved. The preparation of the equipment is also just middling along ... The diplomats are silent"; "June 15, 1945. Update to the situation. No changes"; and "June 19, 1945. Still no answer. I'm waiting."

The break in the clouds came on June 20, when Maximovich came to the acceptance base with news that "everything was on the verge of being resolved." That day, Maxim made the following entry:

Chernack came by in the evening and reported that permission has been granted for the flight and that the interpreters could be sent to the four bases along the ferrying route, including Gander, Reykjavik and Preston ... Immediately, the question arose of how to transport the interpreters. I suggested the most natural option in this situation—to send them on our planes. But the U.S. department in charge would not give authorization. Chernack was furious. That same evening he flew to Norfolk to sort out the situation.

A day later, the issue with the interpreters had been settled. The departure of the first crews was scheduled for June 23. Maxim wrote in his diary,

We got up at 4:00 in the morning. The weather conditions were to be favorable along the route and at the first landing site. At 6:00 a.m., I released five planes at once ... Everything was fine for a while, but suddenly, after two and a half hours, I received a radiogram from Gander stating that the weather had deteriorated sharply and that they could not accept the planes. Would we really have to return them? Chernack proposed the option of landing at a base in Portland [Maine]. I agreed. But there were no interpreters there. Therefore, I flew there to arrange the meeting of the planes.

The first thing I saw upon arrival was that three of "my" planes were cutting circles over the airfield one after another. Where were the other two? Then I looked down and saw that they had already landed. So why where the others circling and not landing? I tried to get an explanation from the airfield base commander who came to meet me. It turned out that the front landing gear on Boychenko's Amphibian wouldn't deploy and he was trying to release it manually. I ran to the command post tower and spoke to all three of them. I permitted Yakovlev and Zamyatin to land and began suggesting different options to Boychenko. Eventually, the landing gear came out and he landed safely.

The nonflying weather became protracted due to the cyclone that had engulfed the coast. The group was stuck in Portland for four days. To pass the time, Colonel Chibisov and his comrades visited the cities of Brunswick and Portland. In his diary, Maxim noted that Portland was "a port city, a bit like Taganrog, and the nature of the surrounding area is very similar to our own: mixed forest and such familiar trees—pine, spruce, birch, aspen."

Of course, his mood was understandable. When there is a lot to do, there is no time to think. During such downtime, however, nostalgia immediately sets in.

On June 27, the weather remained poor. In the morning, it was completely overcast, with drizzling rain. But once the fog lifted, the commander immediately gave the order for takeoff while also establishing a strict order:

> Yeroshenko took off first, entered the clouds at 500 feet, and as soon as he passed through them after ten minutes at an altitude of 5,000 feet, he reported to me over the command communications. Now that the situation with takeoff was clear, I permitted Yakovlev's crew to depart. Thus, the crews got in formation over the clouds one after another and set their course. A proper send-off.

Fifteen minutes later, Colonel Chibisov took off in the opposite direction toward Elizabeth City in order to prepare the remaining planes and ferrying crews.

The ferry conveyor continued to operate erratically until late June. Sometimes the weather was not conducive for flying, sometimes the planes arrived with a delay, and sometimes they were not fully equipped. However, by late July, all the Catalinas from this consignment had safely made it to Vladivostok and joined the Pacific Fleet Air Force on the eve of the war with Japan.

A conference of the leaders of the United States, USSR, and United Kingdom opened in the Berlin suburb of Potsdam on July 17, at which the fundamental differences between the Soviet Union and its Western partners were revealed on issues concerning the postwar reconstruction of Europe.

Attempting to put pressure on Stalin, Truman announced triumphantly at one of the meetings that the United States now had "a new weapon of unusual destructive force." He was referring to the atomic bomb, which had just undergone its first test explosion in Alamogordo, New Mexico. Stalin was highly reserved in his reaction to this news.

Eventually, the victors over Nazi Germany managed to iron out their differences at that time. The American leaders agreed to a compromise on several contentious issues since the US military, despite obtaining the atomic bomb, very much wanted their Russian allies to enter the war against Japan. Stalin promised to do so in the near future.

On August 6, 1945, the atomic bomb was dropped on Hiroshima.

On August 7, Stalin and USSR General Staff Chief Alexei Antonov signed a directive on the commencement of military operations against Japan. Early on the morning of August 9, the Soviet Army launched an offensive along the entire line of contact with the Japanese forces in Manchuria and Korea. On that same day, another atomic bomb was dropped on Nagasaki.

Over 25 days of offensives, the Soviet Armed Forces crushed the million-strong Kwantung Army, occupied almost all of Manchuria and a large chunk of Korea, and seized the South Sakhalin and Kuril Islands. This short-lived campaign widely employed the tactics of landing forward detachments of attacking troops from ships and aircraft.

The paratroopers were the first to storm into Mukden, the capital of Manchuria, and take control of a POW camp, where the Japanese were holding hundreds of American and

Relocation of the marines to the Kuril Islands by the Catalinas of 16th Reconnaissance Aviation Regiment of the Pacific Fleet Air Force, 1945.

English military personnel, including senior officers and generals, who had been captured during battles in the Pacific Ocean.

The Soviet amphibious assault forces seized several Korean ports, the legendary Port Arthur, and the Kuril Islands. The Catalinas delivered to the USSR by Colonel Chibisov's special group under the Lend-Lease Program were used with great efficiency in these operations. The reliable and comfortable seaplanes performed many functions at that time: they conducted reconnaissance and hunted for Japanese submarines, they rescued the crews of aircraft that had been shot down over the sea, and they played the role of mobile headquarters and hospitals.

On September 2, 1945, Japan conceded defeat and declared its unconditional surrender.

Lieutenant General K. N. Derevyanko puts his signature under the Japan Surrender Act. A Catalina provided by the M.N. Chibisov (Special Operations) group delivered the Soviet Mission to Tokyo Bay]

13.7 From America with Love

Victory over Japan was celebrated on September 5, 1945, in the United States. Maxim, who was in Washington at that time, wrote in his diary,

> There were mass demonstrations throughout the whole city, the wide streets were filled with streams of people making their way towards the center. Everyone was singing and dancing. Orchestras played celebratory marches. Military personnel were literally swarmed with crowds forming instantly around them. Everyone wanted to touch the military uniform. People were shaking their hands, hugging them, kissing them, and even picking them up and swinging them in the air. Many of them chanted: "Long live the armed forces of the United States, Soviet Union and United Kingdom!"

Due to the Victory Day celebrations, all military aircraft were prohibited from flying for the next three days. According to Gregory Gagarin, "the command thus thwarted the possibility of even one drunk pilot being in the air!"

In honor of Victory Day, the American military officials decided to arrange a trip for the Soviet officers to Williamsburg, a historic museum town located 100 kilometers (62 miles) from the base. It was the site of one of the first English colonies in the United States and the place where the American Revolution began and where the country's main laws were written.

Gagarin later recalled this trip:

> After the tour, we went to a restaurant at the best hotel in town and ordered lunch. The hosts fed us well. Of course, they didn't know that you could find planes with red stars nearby at the airfield. But ... interacting with people in Russian military uniform was an unexpected and remarkable event for them. They actually arranged a rather "royal" welcome for us. And when we asked for the bill, the owners said, "Today is a huge celebration. For us and for all military people. So no money is required. Please accept this meal from us as a small gift!" Such was the absolutely sincere gratitude of ordinary Americans to Soviet soldiers.

For most Americans, the United States and the Soviet Union were still allies, but at the level of big politics, the phenomenon that would later be referred to as the Cold War was already taking shape.

The Lend-Lease Law passed under Roosevelt was supposed to remain in effect until June 30, 1946. In late August, however, the law was amended at Truman's initiative to expire on September 20, 1945. The delivery of aircraft to the Soviet Union under Lend-Lease was abruptly discontinued, even though the Americans were supposed to send another five PBY-6A Catalinas in accordance with the London Protocol. They had been delayed at the factory, partly through Chernack's fault, and had not been included in the last consignment sent to Vladivostok due to this delay.

Nobody intended to give the Soviet representatives the last five planes. There was also nobody to ferry them: following the amendments to the Lend-Lease Law, crews from the USSR would no longer be traveling to the United States.

However, Maxim felt it was his duty to obtain the remaining five planes with the latest modifications and send them back to the Motherland. In his memoirs, he gave a detailed account of how he managed to come to the only correct decision under difficult and adverse circumstances:

Going through the Washington top brass was pointless. So I decided to launch an attack on the local commanders. Initially, I had zero luck. The closest administrator was the base chief Stanley Chernack. I didn't put any special pressure on him, but simply reminded him that the delay in the delivery of the last five planes to the Soviet Union was his fault to some extent. Stanley Chernack generally had friendly relations with our pilots and with me personally. We had worked together for more than a year, and during that time he almost always tried to help us, and he had often helped us out in difficult situations. But this time his reply was dry and uncompromising: the decision had been made at the highest levels, therefore there was no way he could influence the situation. Then I asked Chernack for at least one plane for my crew. It seemed to me that he hesitated, but he didn't reply right away. It was getting close to my time to depart the base, so I decided to arrange a farewell dinner. I thanked Chernack for his help and support, found the suitable kind words, and organized a nice gift for him as a farewell and a keepsake, from one pilot to another, so to speak. I could see that Chernack wasn't simply pleased, he was genuinely moved. Then it dawned on me: perhaps it would be possible to reach an understanding in this manner, if not with the big bosses (and bureaucrats), then with our pilot colleagues—the "real aviation boys." I consulted with Chernack. He supported my idea and said that we could try to get in touch with a few officers from the General Staff of the U.S. Navy. I asked for his help and promised gifts for everyone on whom the decision depended. Chernack gave me five names. Not putting things off, I flew to Washington to coordinate the issue with Government Procurement Commission Chairman Gen. Rudenko and naval aviation attaché Maximovich. Both of them approved my initiative, prepared five nice presents, and sent a request to Moscow to make plans for the immediate departure of four crews to the U.S. in the event it became possible to ferry the remaining Amphibians.

That same day, upon returning from Washington, I gave Chernack gifts for his superiors. Three days later, I was invited to New York and given permission to retrieve the five long-awaited planes from the factory. Now I had to think of a way to get them to Elizabeth City right away. But how was I supposed to do that? Five unfamiliar planes! And I only had one crew available. Once again, Stanley came to my aid. He provided four American crews, who quickly delivered the planes to Elizabeth City.

But the main task had been accomplished: the tactical mission had been resolved by commercial means. And for my country, the result was rather sizeable—five brand new PBY-6A Catalinas with the latest technology stood at the base airfield waiting to be ferried to Moscow.

What sort of gifts could have initially persuaded Lieutenant Commander Chernack and then his superiors to actions that ran counter to the official political line of their government? What exactly could the rather poor diplomatic mission of the Soviet Union offer the well-off American officers? One of the selections from the standard Russian offerings of vodka and caviar? Goods made from exotic Russian fur? Perhaps some sort of souvenir, such as malachite boxes, cigarette cases, or watches with inscriptions?

At any rate, the value of such gifts was negligible compared to the assistance Maxim received in retrieving the last five Catalinas under the Lend-Lease Program from the American bureaucratic swamp, which had frozen over from cold anti-Soviet winds.

It was not a matter of the gifts, of course, but, rather, the sentiments of the American officers who helped Colonel Chibisov in addition to the aversion inherent in the American people against manifestations of injustice by those in power.

In the fall of 1945, Chernack and his fellow officers, like the rest of the American people, were still unable to give up the simple and clear ideas that had formed during the war. They firmly knew who their allies were and who their enemies were, and enemies needed to be fought and friends loved. The Russians were unequivocally considered friends. The nice guys from Chibisov's special group were not simply friends and comrades in the battle against the common enemy but also real aviation boys!

As a true "old soldier," Stanley Chernack gladly thumbed his nose at the bosses in big politics in order to help out his Russian friends.

Chibisov's special group finished up their business at the Elizabeth City base, where the Russian pilots' reliable allies served.

After the arrival of experienced crews headed by Abramov, Medelyan, Yakovlev, and Dorofeyev, two days were spent preparing the planes for the trip across the ocean. On the third day, after taking a group of Soviet specialists on board and bidding a warm farewell to their American colleagues, the crews of the five last Lend-Lease Catalinas set off for the transatlantic flight along the southern route.

The only high-ranking US official to say thank you to the Russian pilots was the head of Project Zebra, Vice Admiral Patrick Bellinger. Assigned this position by President Roosevelt, he still believed Lend-Lease had been an effective investment in his country's national security.

One day prior to their departure, Vice Admiral Bellinger arranged a farewell dinner for the crew members. In his welcoming speech, he highly praised the professional, business, and human qualities of the allies and wished them good luck. As an experienced pilot, he knew what a transatlantic flight was all about and sincerely wished his Russian colleagues a safe journey.

At that same dinner, Colonel Chibisov, who did not smoke, was given a cigarette case as a keepsake. Into this cigarette case, he inserted a sheet of paper that had been signed by the friends with whom he had worked in Elizabeth City.

Colonel Chibisov led the detachment of five Catalinas along the challenging route with a total length of more than 10,000 kilometers (6,214 miles) and flight time of roughly 100 hours. The planes flew in formation during all stages of the flight, and landings were made at land-based airfields.

From Elizabeth City, they flew to Miami Beach (500 miles, 5 hours), then to San Juan (700 miles, 7 hours), and on to Port of Spain (800 miles, 8 hours).

This was followed by the difficult flight to Belém in Brazil (1,100 miles, 11 hours), which passed over the infamous Bermuda Triangle. The planes ran into storm clouds there, and it took six and a half hours to pass through them.!

From Belém, they flew to Natal (800 miles, 8 hours) over Brazilian territory without any major problems. Then the trip over the Atlantic began: from Natal to the island of Fernando (400 miles, 4 hours) and then to Dakar in Africa (1,300 miles, 13 hours). On this section, the ferry pilots encountered showers and thunderstorms.

They took the familiar route from Dakar around the West African coast to Casablanca (900 miles, 9 hours). From there, they took a new route to Gibraltar (600 miles, 6 hours) and then to Paris (900 miles, 9 hours).

In the French capital, the travelers had a short break before the final sections of the flight: to Kolberg in Poland (500 miles, 5 hours) and then directly to Moscow (another 600 miles, 6 hours).

Chapter 14

Smoke of the Fatherland

14.1 Final Embraces of America

America—wealthy, generous, and friendly in relations with its Russian allies—in fall 1945, took full control over the fate of the people and nations on the western half of the Old Continent.

The headquarters of the American Expeditionary Forces were comfortably set up in Paris, which for centuries had been considered the European cultural capital. It became hard to tell who was most important in the famous city: de Gaulle's provisional government or General Eisenhower.

In that city, Maxim and his comrades experienced the pleasant taste of American hospitality for the last time. Their group was met by an old comrade, Lieutenant Gregory Gagarin, who was also fluent in French. He had spent his childhood in France and attended primary school there.

In fall 1945, Gregory arrived in France a week before Chibisov's group under orders from the thoughtful Vice Admiral Patrick Bellinger. Later, he recalled,

> According to the order, I had to check in with the Army. I showed up. I saw a colonel, the chief of some service. And I was in a naval uniform. "Who are you?" he asked. "Lt. Gagarin, a French translator," I replied.

"Why are you here?" he asked. "In a few days, five planes with red stars and Russian crews will be landing here," I answered. The officer knew nothing about this. "What are you planning to do?" he inquired. "Take care of them and make sure they have everything they need—fuel for the planes, food for the crews," I said. "What do you need?" the colonel asked. "Two things: a hotel to accommodate the Russians and transportation for them," I replied … He gave me two phone numbers after which I resolved all the problems in advance. I drove Chibisov, Tertsiyev and the other members of their team all around Paris and its famous outskirts for a week. For me, this was a pleasant nostalgic excursion to places I had known since my childhood. In parting, we embraced and wished each other all the best.

Crews of the special operations group of Colonel M.N. Chibisov with the Commander (front row, center). France, Orly airport, October, 1945.

Accompanied by such a wonderful guide as Lieutenant Gagarin, Maxim and his colleagues wandered around Paris, took in the opera *Luisa* at the Grand Opera House, and traveled to the fabulous Versailles, the residence of the French Bourbons.

Before the departure to Moscow, Orly airport, France. Colonel
M.N. Chibisov - in the middle of the row. October 1945.

In the 1990s, Gagarin traveled to Leningrad and tried to track down
Maxim Chibisov and his subordinates. Unfortunately, this proved to be
impossible, although many of the pilots from Chibisov's special group were
still alive at the time. Several of the American pilots and specialists who
signed the paper that was preserved in the cigarette case given to Maxim
at the dinner with Vice Admiral Bellinger were also still alive.

It is a shame the veterans of Chibisov's special group were never able
to meet up with the American veterans who had helped the Russians ferry
the Catalinas to the USSR so many years ago.

In mid-October 1945, the
rearguard detachment of the
special operations group led
by Colonel Chibisov landed
safely at Tushino airfield in
Moscow. There, five brand-new
Catalinas—the last aircraft of the
final consignment—were quietly
handed over to the Motherland.

G.G. Gagarin carefully kept through
his life the wings of the naval aviator
pilot gifted to him by M.N. Chibisov.

As Commander S. F. Zhavoronkov of the Naval Aviation Forces noted,
the special operation group and its 162 members successfully coped with
their task and fully justified the confidence given to them. Altogether, they
ferried 200 airplanes by the Lend-Lease Program. Thirty PBN-1 planes
were ferried from May 25 to July 26, 1944, by the northern route, which

strengthened Marine Aviation Forces of the North and Baltic fronts. From August 25 to September 11, 1944, another thirty PBN-1 planes were ferried by the Eastern Route from Kodiak through Anadyr to Vladivostok and enforced aviation regiments of Pacific Ocean Forces.

Another 59 PBN-1s were ferried from September 28 to March 28, 1945, by the longest route, the southern route, to reach Baku on the Caspian Sea. They became part of the Marine Aviation Forces of the Black Sea Fleet. After the end of the Great Patriotic War from June 23 to August 31, 1945, eighteen crews ferried twenty-eight PBY-6A amphibous planes along the route including Elizabeth City, Gander, Reykjavik, Prestwick, Kolberg, Moscow, Kuibyshev, Krasnoyarsk, Chita, and Vladivostok. Almost 30 PBY-6As were ferried from Kodiak over Uelkal to Vladivostok from May 17 to June 2, 1945. After World War II ended in October 1945, the last group of Russian pilots, under the command of Colonel M. N. Chibisov, ferried 5 amphibious planes from Elizabeth City by the southern route to Casablanca through Gibraltar, then to Paris, and finally to Moscow Airdrome Zakharkovo (now known as Tushino). In addition, after spending a probationary period with Colonel Chibisov in Elizabeth City, the group of pilots commanded by I. P. Mazuruk ferried to the USSR another 4 planes PBN-1s, to the Polar Aviation Agency. At this point, the top-secret Zebra operation was completed.

In late October, each member of the ferrying operation was presented with two government awards under a decree from the Presidium of the Supreme Soviet of the USSR for exemplary performance of the mission. Maxim Chibisov was awarded the Order of Lenin and the Order of the Red Banner.

Colonel Maxim Nikolaevitch Chibisov.

14.2 Personal Combat record of Colonel Chibisov

Maxim Chibisov began World War II as a major and ended it as a colonel. He took part in fighting at the start of the war, the most difficult period overall for the Soviet Union. He demonstrated outstanding qualities as a commander and an organizer of military work during the fierce battles for Tallinn and the defense of Leningrad. His military service was distinguished with government awards.

Recalled from the front, he put together a strong aviation brigade under extremely difficult conditions that later turned into a strike aviation division. In August–September 1945, this division took part in the war with Japan.

Maxim made a highly significant contribution to the cause of victory with his work in America as the head of the special group ferrying aircraft for the Soviet Navy.

He later summed up the results of this work in his memoirs, written around 1980, focusing, as usual, primarily on the achievements of his subordinates:

> Commanding people is a difficult and anxious job. I have held numerous positions of leadership in my life. But my work was never as multidimensional and intense as it was during the year and a half that I commanded the special [Project Zebra] group. After all, this work involved continuous flights along different routes with constant time constraints.

I flew on my own, tested the planes, conducted training sessions with the flight personnel, and monitored preparations for each flight. In addition, I was in constant contact and held negotiations with foreign experts: pilots, navigators and businessmen.

Looking back on those days, I have to mention my subordinates. They were excellent pilots, great friends, and courageous and loyal sons of the Fatherland. I got to hear rave reviews about them from the American pilots on multiple occasions. I was happy and proud that all my comrades served the country with honor. It could not have been otherwise since we never forgot that we were representing a great country and were part of a great people, who for the four extremely

Students of the Voroshilov Military Navy Academy by Catalinas of the Baltic Fleet Air Force. Tallinn, 1951.

difficult years of the war lived according to the principle: "Everything for the front, everything for Victory!"

After all, we were at war. The Motherland needed planes that could only be obtained overseas. Flying across the ocean at that time was not as common as it is today. During those years, each flight of this kind became a real mission, and our guys, like true patriots, did not hesitate to take any risk for the sake of defeating fascism.

They fulfilled their duty as civilians and soldiers—they helped the country replenish its aircraft inventory for all the fleets during the height of the war. The two hundred planes they delivered almost immediately entered into battle. Naval pilots performed hundreds of sorties on these planes. Across continents and oceans, the crews of the special aviation group covered a total distance of more than 124,000 nautical miles over various routes with overall flight time of approximately 12,400 hours.

They became highly proficient at piloting the new planes and mastered both the English and American flight support systems, radio equipment and other machinery. They then shared this experience with the flight personnel of the combat units that used the Catalinas in operational missions.

I must also mention the special contribution to the common cause by the Pacific Fleet personnel. I can safely say that thanks to their courage and perseverance in performing the missions to deliver and develop the new seaplanes for the Pacific Fleet, our pilots entered the war with Japan fully trained and technically armed. In 1944–1945, the pilots of the Pacific Fleet Air Force gained extensive practice flying in various conditions of the northern and southern hemisphere. They visited all the continents, passed through all the latitudes from the Arctic to the equator, and saw dozens of English and American air bases, and everywhere they went they proudly displayed the scarlet stars of the Soviet Union on their wings.

Colonel Chibisov's activities during his time in the United States as head of the special operations group also earned high praise from the USSR Armed Forces. This assessment was documented in an evaluation drawn up in connection with certain circumstances in 1946 that was signed by Major General of Aviation Alexander Shuginin. It reads,

> Performed a high-profile mission: commanded a group of crews who ferried Catalina planes from the U.S. to the USSR. Handled the mission in full, accepted and

ferried the planes in an exemplary manner, managed the group excellently, and was highly respected by both the ferrying pilots as well as the Soviet and American organizations involved in the ferrying operations. Thanks to the persistent and skillful actions of Col. Chibisov, several Catalina planes were received and delivered to the USSR even after supplies under Lend-Lease had been discontinued.

Colonel Chibisov's special group provided the USSR with approximately 200 seaplanes, which the Soviet naval aviation forces needed desperately.

The Catalinas delivered from the United States were used in battle by all fleets. They served as reconnaissance planes and naval bombers. They were used in landing operations and to rescue the crews of downed planes and ships.

Some of the seaplanes sent by Colonel Chibisov in the final wartime consignment through Newfoundland and Reykjavik in June–July 1945 ended up with the 117th Naval Aviation Regiment, the same unit in which Maxim had once climbed the career ladder from squad commander to regiment commander. His former colleagues fought the Japanese on the Catalinas, never suspecting that the fine aircraft had promptly arrived for them thanks to the energy, intelligence, and organizational skills of their former commander and fellow soldier.

14.3 Postwar Happiness

Still in the Far East, Rosalia Chibisova had yet to receive any news from her husband. She did not keep a diary but sometimes took pictures. Many years later, when she was already gone, Maxim wrote captions to pictures taken in 1944–1945, apparently recalling what his wife had told him about her feelings during their long separation.

> October 18, 1944: "Rosaly was sad, the stone had fallen out of her ring."
> March 1, 1945: "Oppressive sorrow, 20 hours, stifling tears."
> March 17, 1945: "Lonesome mood, crying all day."

On a special [secret] assignment, Maxim did not tell her anything about himself, not even on Victory Day or afterward.

In the spring, however, she received a package with presents thoughtfully put together by her husband. Maxim was not permitted to attach a letter to the package, but Rosalia easily guessed who had sent the gifts.

After waiting until fall 1945 and still not receiving any news from Maxim, the experienced officer's wife decided to make her way to Moscow, where the package had originated from and where she believed she would have the greatest chance of meeting her husband.

Pendant from America - a present for the beloved wife

Only military personnel with travel authorization were allowed to leave the closed Far Eastern garrison. However, it so happened that Colonel Kovalenko, who at one time had led a regiment under Maxim's command and then replaced him as division commander, was planning to travel to Moscow for a meeting. Rosaly persuaded him to take her and little Emma with him. He agreed and, at his own risk, had tickets issued for them as members of his family.

They set off on the long journey from Vladivostok to Moscow along the endless Trans-Siberian railroad. They rode in the general seating car. Emma caught a cold along the way and ran a temperature for all ten days. Rosaly bombarded her husband's brothers with telegrams about her upcoming arrival from every station.

The scene upon their arrival in Moscow is firmly etched in the memory of Emilia Chibisova, who by this time was seven years old and a first-grade student.

The train was approaching the Northern (now Yaroslavl) station. Not yet recovered, Emma was lying on the bed in a hat with her ears covered, looking out the window. Kovalenko was standing by the open door of the train car in his long black overcoat and naval cap. Before the train had even come to a stop, he jumped onto the platform and immediately embraced a tall officer in a naval uniform.

Exhausted from the trip, Rosaly sat next to her daughter, stressing about what to do next. She was frightened by uncertainty and the prospect of not finding her husband's relatives in Moscow. Observing the scene of the two naval officers meeting outside the window, she was initially still. But she perked up when she thought she noticed something familiar. Then she realized who the officer with Kovalenko was. She suddenly lost her voice and slowly, as if dreaming, whispered, "Darling, it's Papa!"

When the two men entered the coupe, Emma saw grown men shed tears of joy for the first time. The stern Colonel Kovalenko, whom nobody had ever seen laugh, burst into a huge smile. Maxim wrapped up his daughter and wife in his huge, warm arms and embraced them tightly. Rosalia was speechless and simply pressed her face against her husband's cheek and wept silently. He took turns kissing his wife and daughter and, speaking to Kovaleno, repeatedly thanked him for delivering such precious cargo.

Maxim had come to the train station in two cars with friends. They loaded his family's things into one car, which his pilot friends drove. The Chibisovs rode with Kovalenko. Maxim would not allow Kovalenko to go to his hotel and took him along to his brother's apartment for a celebration that included doughnuts traditionally baked by Alexei's family.

Maxim marveled at his wife: "Rosaly! Reading your telegrams, I repeated every day what a clever wife I have! I never even dreamed that you would come to Moscow on your own and save me the trouble of traveling to the Far East."

He had brought his family gifts from America: a cut of gabardine, dark blue polka-dot knitted fabric, and light blue and cherry-red velvet. Rosaly had not even been aware that velvet could be colored. In those years, for some reason, it was thought that clothes from such fabric, always black, were intended for stage performances. Maxim believed that a cut of fabric was more reliable than ready-made dresses (he could not bring himself to buy dresses for his girls). In Paris, he had bought his wife a perfume set he had picked out with the help of the kind Gregory Gagarin. The fragrance collection included Coty powder, the French perfume Lily of the Valley, hand and face cream, and nail accessories. In addition, as a souvenir of his time in America, he had brought back colorful postcards and a slide projector with pictures of America.

Slidescope with the views of America - a souvenir from the USA, 1945.

These souvenirs have been preserved in the Chibisov family and handed down to Maxim's daughters.

After officially reporting on his mission, he received thanks from his commanders and a month's leave. The Chibisovs spent the time in Moscow with their relatives.

They were overflowing with feelings of joy. They were all alive and well! They had won! Along with the rest of the country, they savored the sweet taste of the Great Victory. Maxim later recalled, "My dear Rosaly was beyond happy. She even displayed a childlike playfulness and a desire to sing and dance. And that's how this carefree month of my life passed—a month of long-awaited rest."

14.4 Officer's Lot

Once his leave was over, Maxim reported to the Naval Air Force headquarters for a new appointment. Commander and Aviation Marshal Semyon Zhavoronkov gave him a kind reception, according to Maxim's diaries.

> He thanked me once again for successfully completing the government mission to ferry the seaplanes from America to all the fleets of the USSR. And then he asked, "Where would you like to serve?" In reply, I asked, "What kind of vacancies do you have?" The commander thought about it and in conclusion said that senior officials had made the decision to establish the 19th Separate Mine and Torpedo Aviation Division of the Navy High Command Reserve, which would report directly to the Naval Aviation command. Division location: headquarters in the city of Kuybyshev with subsequent transfer to the Baltics; aviation regiments: 66th near the city of Chapayevskm, 67th near Tancha (Kazakhstan), and the 68th near Koporye in the Baltics.

During the conversation with the commander, Maxim inquired as to the condition of the regiments. The reply was "The regiments are in the process of formation. The personnel are living in private apartments and only the 68th Regiment has been partially accommodated in the remaining eight-apartment buildings at the Koporye airfield."

Translated from military to conventional language, the marshal's offer would have sounded something like this: "Here's a division for you that must be assembled from disparate parts and turned into a combat-ready unit. We understand that this work is hell, the responsibility is enormous, and we personally can't guarantee you any conditions. Oh, and we can't provide you with an apartment."

It was impossible to be insulted by this offer, and there was no point in requesting comfortable accommodations for his family. The country that had defeated fascism lay in ruins. The country had more heroes, recipients of government awards, and distinguished commanders than it did suitable apartments.

Of course, he could have humbly said, "Semyon, put yourself in my position. I have a family, and my wife suffered through tuberculosis. I can't live in a private apartment!" The marshal could have made a call over a government line to the Volga military district or the Kuybyshev regional committee of the Communist Party, and they probably could have made an exception and found an apartment for the mine and torpedo division commander. But how would Maxim then have been able to look into the eyes of his fellow officers who had no prospect of obtaining decent housing? Plus, Colonel Chibisov was not in the habit of requesting something personal for himself.

Given the postwar environment, Maxim agreed to command the 19th Separate Mine and Torpedo Aviation Division of the Navy High Command Reserve. He went home and explained the decision to Rosaly, who listened carefully but looked a little perplexed after he had finished. Judging from her appearance, she had mixed feelings. First of all, it was crowded with their relatives in Moscow, and they had already been staying with them for more than a month. Secondly, when she learned that the 19th Aviation Division had no apartments of its own and that they would have to live in a private apartment, according to Maxim, "I saw anger appear on the face of my Rosaly. Immediately, Rosaly asked, 'But what about us? Where will we live?' … I replied, 'At first, I will go to Kuybyshev alone, find a private apartment, and then you will come.'"

Maxim went to Kuybyshev, stayed at the headquarters temporarily, and enthusiastically immersed himself in his work. He flew in the aviation regiments, while Rosaly and Emma lived in Moscow for another two and a half months. They remained uncomfortable there and eventually moved to Kuybyshev in March 1946.

In 1945, the city of Kuybyshev, home to the alternate residence of Soviet leadership during the war, was overcrowded with people and institutions that had been relocated there from the western and central regions of the country. It was virtually impossible to rent even a small room for a family there. But Maxim applied his military smarts and found a solution. At the airfield, there was an enormous hangar in which he found an empty container that had been used to transport planes by rail. They divided the container in half with a sheet hung over a strong rope and had two sets of living quarters: one for the division commander's family and the other for the headquarters chief, Vasily Skomorokhov. They took turns cooking simple meals and spent the weekends and holidays together. The families became good friends and maintained contact even after their official duties sent Chibisov and Skomorokhov to different cities and military units.

Commander of the 19th Separate Mine and Torpedo Aviation Division Colonel M.N. Chibisov by the airplane Tu-2T prior to the take off from the airfield Bezenchyuk

While based in Kuybyshev, the headquarters of the 19th Separate Mine and Torpedo Aviation Division were in charge of manning the aviation regiments and training the regiment personnel for the new Tu-10 planes while also preparing for relocation to the permanent base.

14.5 Under the Baltic Skies

In summer 1946, the military units of the 19th Division were gradually relocated—by truck, train, and aircraft—to their permanent posts near the Baltic shores. The 66th Aviation Division headquarters were stationed in Novaya Ladoga; the 67th in the village of Plekhanovo, near the Volkhov Hydroelectric Plant; and the 68th remained in Koporye. Waiting for the arrival of the new Tu-10s, the crews began training on the Tu-2T torpedo bomber, which was similar in terms of design and piloting technique.

Colonel Chibisov's division units arrived at their permanent base

without incident and immediately began resolving organizational issues: accommodation for personnel, putting the units on alert, exploring the flight area, searching for private apartments, catering for all personnel, placement of children in schools and so on. Over the next two months, the division's main organizational issues were resolved. The division headquarters and aviation regiments have fully commenced ground and flight training in accordance with the plan.

Headquarters of the 19th Separate Mine and Torpedo Aviation Division in Novaya Ladoga. M.N. Chibisov is pictured at the center of the first row, 1947.

Novaya Ladoga, located at the point where the Volkhov flows into Lake Ladoga, was an ideal place for the headquarters of the strike air division of the Navy High Command Reserve since it had both a ground airfield and a water airfield for flying boats.

It was a small town (with a population of approximately 4,000 in 1945–1946), but it had a rich history. In 1763–1769, the Suzdal Infantry Regiment was deployed there under the command of Alexander Suvorov. Novaya Ladoga was where the future generalissimo compiled his famous Regimental Instructions, which contained the basic provisions and regulations for educating soldiers, internal service, and combat training.

From there, he departed for his military campaign against the Polish insurgents from the Bar Confederation, where he earned ranks, medals, and the glory of an outstanding military leader.

The barracks of Suvorov's regiment have been preserved in Nizhny Ladoga to this day (our ancestors knew how to build durable structures that would last for centuries). However, this housing stock was not sufficient to accommodate the arriving units of the 19th Aviation Division.

At first, life was difficult in Novaya Ladoga. The military personnel lived in tents all summer long. There was a shortage of vehicles, and problems arose with even the most basic living conditions, such as firewood and water supplies and building a bathhouse. Food was distributed in the hangar.

Emma Chibisova had started school in Nikolayevka, then studied in Moscow, and finished the first grade in Kuybyshev. She entered the second grade in Novaya Ladoga. In the winter, she had to walk two to three kilometers each day along the ice of the frozen Lake Ladoga to the local school. One time, in early spring 1947, she fell through a section of thin ice. Fortunately, she was pulled out, and instead of going to class, she was taken to the nearest farmhouse to dry off.

At any rate, life and work in Novaya Ladoga began to improve.

However, this continued only until April 1947. In April, an order was received from the naval aviation commander on the reorganization of the 19th Separate Mine and Torpedo Aviation Division, which was to be transferred to the command of the Red Banner Baltic Fleet Air Force commander.

14.6 Golgotha of the Victors

The year 1946 was marked by numerous disasters both natural and manmade in the chronicles of the Soviet Union.

Adding to the burden of postwar recovery was a fierce drought that destroyed crops even in the most fertile lands: the southern regions of Russia and the Volga area. Moreover, no help was to be expected from abroad.

One of the reasons for this was the famous speech made by Winston Churchill, the leader of the British conservative opposition at that time, on March 5, 1946, at Westminster College in Fulton, Missouri, in the presence of President Truman, during which he specifically cited Soviet Russia as the main enemy of the United States and the British Empire. Through Churchill's words, the Anglo-American alliance demanded strategic concessions from Moscow and threatened to use nuclear weapons, which America had a monopoly on at that time.

In an interview with *Pravda* newspaper, the leader of the Soviet people, Comrade Stalin, gave a proper reply to his former colleague in the Big Three, putting him on par with Hitler.

Soviet leaders had to seek additional funds to accelerate the national "uranium project." Scientist Igor Kurchatov and his colleagues managed to get a hold of the secrets to nuclear fission and catch up with the American nuclear scientists with their heroic progress. After miraculously surviving at a labor camp in Kolyma, Sergei Korolyov, who had been a member of the team of enthusiastic rocket scientists who had been picked apart in the wake of the Tukhachevsky case, created the structural basis for a future breakthrough in Soviet rocket science.

In the meantime, the great Russian minds and millions of dedicated workers, both voluntary and involuntary, worked hard to build the scientific foundation for a strategic deterrent, while the professional military strengthened the country's defense using the means at their disposal.

In this context, it was a rather logical decision to create the 19th Separate Mine and Torpedo Aviation Division of the Navy High Command Reserve. The division was stationed at the most appropriate place: near Lake Ladoga, which was close (by aviation standards) to the Baltic as well as the Arctic theaters of combat operations against the forces of a potential enemy.

The initiative to create this division came from the outstanding military leaders, People's Commissar for the Navy Nikolai Kuznetsov, and Naval Air Force Commander Semyon Zhavoronkov. In February 1946, however, the entire complex of the USSR military departments underwent a radical reorganization. The People's Commissariat for the Navy was abolished, and the land and naval forces were merged into the unified Ministry of the Armed Forces, which at first was headed by Joseph Stalin himself.[21]

---

[21] After the war, Stalin altered the configuration of the senior military leadership on several occasions. Apparently, he wanted the defense complex to be managed effectively while at the same time remaining under his full control (but in a way so that he did not have to get bogged down in the routine affairs of the military agencies).

The new minister—the greatest military leader of all time—did not tolerate any overly distinguished or independent subordinates close to him. Marshal Georgy Zhukov was summoned from Germany and appointed commander-in-chief of the land forces, although he was later dismissed from this post in disgrace and sent to the Odessa district (and subsequently harassed with investigations into his various sins). Admiral Kuznetsov, who was about as popular in the navy as Zhukov was in the army, was stripped of his powers as head of the independent department. Later, in early 1947, he was transferred from the position of Navy commander-in-chief to head of the naval school department of Leningrad, which was more or less a sign of disfavor. A year later, the renowned admiral was investigated and tried by a court. His rank was lowered, but at least he was not imprisoned or shot.[22]

In early 1946, Stalin personally took over as head of the Ministry of the Armed Forces, merging the People's Commissariats for Defense and the Navy into a single structure. A year later, he formally handed this bulky structure over to the command of Nikolai Bulganin, although he continued to manage the affairs of the army and navy de facto. Bulganin was dismissed in early 1949, and the Ministry of the Armed Forces was headed by Marshal Alexander Vasilevsky, a true professional who, unlike Zhukov, was not in the habit of making claims against or arguing with the supreme commander-in-chief. In 1950, Stalin apparently decided the highly loyal Marshal Vasilevsky could not be entrusted with authority over all the armed forces. The navy was removed from the ministry's subordination and transformed into the separate Ministry of the Navy, which was initially headed by Ivan Yumashev and then Nikolai Kuznetsov in 1951. Finally, after Stalin's death, his successors ultimately returned to the arrangement that had existed prior to 1937: a single Ministry of Defense was established and included both the army and the navy structures.

[22]   On January 12, 1948, Nikolai Kuznetsov and Admirals Lev Galler, Vladimir Alafuzov, and Georgy Stepanov were tried by the Court of Honor under the Ministry of the Armed Forces. They were accused of handing over some secret materials to the United Kingdom and United States in 1942–1944 without the permission of the Soviet government. The Court of Honor found them guilty and transferred their case to the Military Collegium of the USSR Supreme Court. On February 3, 1948, the Military Collegium found Kuznetsov guilty of the charges. However, due to his great achievements in the past, the collegium decided to waive criminal punishment for the former navy commander. At the same time, the collegium ruled to request that the Council of Ministers reduce Kuznetsov's military rank to a rear admiral. The other defendants were given various prison sentences (see the material on Nikolai Kuznetsov in *Wikipedia*).

The removal of the most authoritative naval commander of the war years was followed by the persecution of his closest associates and those who were involved with these associates in any way. The authorities then went after anyone who could be snagged for any suspicion.

The repressions in the navy were carried out in an accelerated manner and engulfed an increasingly broad circle of officers. Roughly the same process took place (and on an even larger scale) within the Army.

The repressions were not as massive in scale as they had been in 1937–1938. The personnel needed to defend the nation were not removed randomly, which indicated that the lessons of 1941 had not been in vain. The leader of the Soviet people did not destroy the officer corps but "tightened it up" as it was described at the time. He broke the professional hubris and obstinacy of the military as well as the self-will that had developed during the years of World War II.

Stalin not only put the squeeze on the supreme command of the armed forces but also humiliated them. In March 1947, he formally renounced his post as minister and transferred control over the military department to Nikolai Bulganin, who, during the war, had served as a member of military councils (i.e., had been responsible for the political and moral state of the troops) at various fronts and attained the rank of marshal without ever learning how to read military maps, as the army wisecrackers claimed.

Under Bulaginin, who held the post of minister until March 1949, the purge of the officer ranks took place with particular intensity. But there is no point in blaming the minister himself for the repressions of that time since he did not persecute anyone on his own but only signed the documents he was ordered to sign.

At that time, some military leaders who proved to be in dangerous proximity to the disgraced leaders of the military corps saved themselves by transferring from military to civil structures. Such was the case with Semyon Zhavoronkov. In early 1946, he made the transition to the chair of the deputy head of the Main Department of the Civil Air Fleet under the USSR Council of Ministers with surprising ease for a reputable marshal.

With Zhavoronkov's departure, the naval aviation structures were carved up once again based on the ideas of the new people flowing into the Main Command of the Navy. At the same time, Colonel Chibisov's division was not only assigned from the High Command Reserve to the command of the Baltic Fleet but also redeployed to new places based on the prospects for employing this formation exclusively in the Baltic region.

14.7 Gora-Valday

An order from the Main Command of the Navy issued in April 1946 identified the new places of deployment for the units of the 19th Aviation Division.

The 68th Aviation Regiment remained in Koporye. The 67th was transferred to Kronshtadt (this regiment was lucky as it ended up in a good place). The 66th was assigned to the Borki airfield outside Oranienbaum, where everything was in ruins after the war. The headquarters of the aviation division were also to be set up close to Oranienbaum, in the village of Gora-Valday on the banks of a lake with the same name, about 10 kilometers (6.2 miles) from present-day Sosnovy Bor.

The redeployment was to be carried out before May 25, 1947.

In his memoirs, Maxim wrote,

> Upon being notified about reassignment and, in particular, about another impending relocation, the division personnel reacted negatively since the new deployment locations had been destroyed during the war. But orders are orders and must be obeyed without question. The personnel understood all of this and began preparing for redeployment. Upon completing preparations, the division headquarters, aviation regiments and logistics units were relocated by May 25 and began settling in under extremely difficult conditions. Families endured particular difficulties with housing problems and supplies, including my Rosaly.

The division headquarters were established in a small village founded in ancient times by Izhorians (people of Finnish roots). It was originally called Harjavalta in the Izhorian and Finnish languages. Adapted to the Russian style, the name became Gora-Valday, or Kara-Valday. In the eighteenth and nineteenth centuries, the estates of several people who made significant contributions to Russian history, including Alexander Menshikov and Alexei Razumovsky, were located near Lake Kara-Valday (present-day Gora-Valday).

During the siege of Leningrad, the territory adjacent to Lake Gora-Valday was part of the Oranienbaum Bridgehead, which the Soviet troops managed to hold on to even after the Germans broke through to the Gulf of Finland near Peterhof.

Defense structures started being established in Gora-Valday back in the 1920s. The military town that emerged at that time belonged to the naval aviators after the war; in the 1990s, it was closed down completely, and now only a helicopter remains on the pedestal at the entrance to the former closed military facility as a monument.

It is a beautiful area, but life was harsh there in the early postwar years, as everything around lay in ruins.

However, the veteran pilots managed to get properly set up in Gora-Volday. The officers' families received housing—small houses with no windows, frames, or doors. Led by the division commander, the staff officers, all hardened from the difficulties they had faced during the war, set about fixing up the housing. The Chibisov family finally got their own spacious home.

In the spring of 1947, Rosaly was expecting a second child. Her pregnancy seemed like a miracle to the Chibisovs since both of them were past the age of their flourishing youth and had endured numerous hardships and diseases.

While pregnant, Rosaly traveled to Leningrad to tend to some affairs. She suddenly became ill there and was rushed to the hospital in an ambulance.

Maxim visited his wife whenever possible. The night before she was discharged, the doctors warned that she could have a miscarriage on the way back to Oranienbaum if she took a train or car, given the rough roads at that time.

As a seasoned pilot, Maxim acted decisively and unconventionally. He went to one of the squads of his division and personally flew a combat plane to a Leningrad airfield.

He carried his wife in his arms from the hospital room to the car and then from the car to the plane. He took off cautiously, and they flew back together, just the two of them. The loving husband then carefully landed the plane at the division airfield and gently carried his wife from the plane to the car and from the car to her own bed.

Elena Maximovna Chibisova was born safely on May 30, 1947. She was born in the place where her father had fought to protect the skies over the great city on the Neva. However, instead of Leningrad, her birth certificate was issued in Moscow, where the Chibisovs moved not long after the birth of their second daughter.

Fellow soldiers came to congratulate their Commander with the birth of the second daughter. Left to right: the headquarters chief V.F. Skomorokhov, deputy Commander of the flight training Kazakov, Commander of the 66th BAP Hero of the Soviet Union I.T. Karpenko, Commander of the air division M.N.]

14.8 From Naval to Polar Aviation

Maxim had to move to Moscow because he had been transferred to a new job at the Northern Sea Route Authority. Apparently, he decided to make this switch due to the situation taking shape in the leadership of the Soviet Navy.

In early 1947, Nikolai Kuznetsov was dismissed as commander-in-chief of the Navy and fell into disgrace for all intents and purposes. Stalin's disfavor extended to a wide circle of officials from the highest ranks of the Navy. It was expected the naval command would soon start being replaced and cleansed of "Kuznetsov's people." Maxim was well aware of how this process worked from his experiences in 1937–1938.

He could easily be considered a protégé of Admiral Kuznetsov dating all the way back to 1939, when the young Pacific Fleet commander confirmed the appointment of the young squadron leader as commander of an aviation brigade. At all the subsequent stages of his career, Maxim had always remained within sight of Nikolai Kuznetsov, who promoted the talented naval aviator up the career ladder and appointed him to a position in which he could do the most good for the country. A captain, then major, then lieutenant colonel, and finally colonel, Maxim was part of the cohort of unique professionals selected by Kuznetsov who comprised the chief naval commander's own team.

This was not a safe position for Maxim amid the conditions unfolding at the turn of 1946–1947.

As part of the anticipated investigation into the affairs of Kuznetsov's group, Maxim knew, investigators might be interested in the group's ties with the commander of the 19th Separate Mine and Torpedo Aviation Division. They would notice that this division commander had spent almost two years abroad, where he'd entered into close relations with Admiral Bellinger and other senior officers of the U.S. Army and Navy, according to the available data. This would open great opportunities for a further investigation and inquiry of Commander Chibisov himself.

On top of this, with the onset of the Cold War, the state security agencies had begun showing heightened interest in all persons who had any experience in dealing with the citizens of the United States and other Western countries. Some of the pilots who had ferried planes from America during the war began to encounter problems.

For example, pilots who were in the United States during the war under the patronage of the People's Commissariat for Foreign Trade were dismissed from the staff upon return to the Soviet Union and subjected to humiliating inspections that continued for several months. The inspectors, according to the recollections of witnesses, split hairs over every minute detail, forcing them to report for almost every single day spent abroad. Absurd suspicions arose with regard to any off-duty contact with Americans—for example, in connection with a visit to a film studio, where Soviet officers had a chance to meet the famous movie star Dina Durbin.

The group of pilots under the command of Chibisov did not have any serious sins or doubtful contacts that could discredit them. Therefore, diligent inspectors left

ractice of torpedo bombing from the airplane Tu-2T.

292

them without any consequences. However, some other cases turned out to be much worse. One of the subordinates under Chibisov, engineer Major I. N. Salnikov, attracted the attention of the special agencies after World War II when Marshal S. F. Zhavoronkov (then a commander of the Air Force Navy of USSR) visited the subunit where Salnikov served. Marshal Zhavoronkov did not forget a modest major who was introduced to him together with other officers of the special operation group in October 1945. He asked Salnikov to make a report about the special group work [Project Zebra] in the USA. The report presented by Salnikov caused a lot of interest from his colleagues who had never been to the USA. In his presentation, he gave high praise to technical parameters and construction of Catalinas. However, in the audience was one person whose duty was to oversee the behavior and attitudes of mind in the corresponding military subunits. This person sent his own report concerning Salnikov's presentation, in which he claimed that Salnikov had overpraised American technology and that his presentation itself had been made following Zhavoronkov's order. Since the State Security Agency was overwhelmed by such snitch information, Salnikov was brought to their special attention only in 1948, when the Cold War was already in full progress. Although Zhavoronkov had already worked in the Civil Air Fleet Agency, he remained under close observation as one of the prominent members of the disgraced Kuznetsov group.

Engineer Major Salnikov was arrested and kept in Lubyanka for 6 months and, after that, for 2 years in Butyrka prison. His interrogators tried to make him give evidence against Zhavoronkov that would prove his contacts with American intelligence services. But Ivan Nikolaevitch remained firm and did not provide any false evidence. However, his health and psyche were considerably damaged. After his interrogators decided he was not useful as a source of required information, they hastily framed him and sent him for 5 years to the labor corrective camp. He was released from this camp only after Stalin's death.

Salnikov was completely rehabilitated, and his military orders and ranks were returned to him. He lived a long life after that.

Such stories could not be stopped from spreading throughout the aviation community. Maxim Chibisov probably heard about them. Of course, he had developed a sixth sense to warn pilots about impending danger. Even under the most basic outcome, Colonel Chibisov could not help but worry about his future.

Perhaps he was mentally seeking some way out of the emerging situation, which was not entirely hopeless. After all, the longtime leader and Maxim's friend Marshal Zhavoronkov had escaped the persecutions that had come down on the Navy command by transferring to the Civil Air Fleet system.

Around this time, Major General of Aviation Alexander Kuznetsov flew to Gora-Valday to see Maxim. They had worked productively together when Maxim was in charge of the special group of ferry pilots sending Catalina seaplanes from the United States; Kuznetsov had been responsible for accepting the aircraft as a deputy commander in the Pacific Fleet Air Force. The latter then saw his career take a major nosedive: in March 1945, he held rather insignificant posts, running Navy educational institutions. But in 1946, his career once again took off. Major General Kuznetsov became deputy head of the Northern Sea Route Authority (NSRA), an autonomous agency under the USSR Cabinet of Ministers. Thus, in terms of status, he was almost a deputy minister.

Kuznetsov traveled to Gora-Valday to call on Maxim to come work for him and wanted to entrust the command of polar aviation to his old comrade. The amiable and eloquent Kuznetsov knew how to pitch the prospects of this highly responsible, challenging, and interesting work.

After weighing all the circumstances, Naval Aviation Colonel Maxim Chibisov accepted the proposal and agreed to be the head of the Polar Aviation Office (PAO) and a member of the collegium of the NSRA Main Department.

Chapter 15

Over the Arctic Skies

15.1 Flight to Moscow

Maxim recorded the conversation he had with his wife on July 1, 1947, shortly after she returned from the hospital with their new daughter in her arms.

She had barely recovered, when he told her the news:

> "In seven days, we have to relocate to a new duty station."

"Where?" she asked.

"To Moscow," he replied.

"But what about housing?" she asked.

"They promised to provide an apartment," he said.

"When will this all end? I still haven't managed to get settled properly in a regular home. I'm so tired of packing and unpacking things at old and new duty stations."

Maxim had to spend a long time gently persuading his wife that everything would be okay and ultimately promised, "Consider this redeployment to be the last." After this, she smiled, cheered up, wiped away the tears from her eyes, and came to grips with everything.

The prospect of life in the capital was supposed to encourage Rosalia to once again start packing, particularly since, according to Maxim's diaries, "packing went extremely quickly for us because we left all our furniture behind during redeployment." All of the belongings they transported consisted of three small suitcases as well as a baby carriage.

With this cargo, Maxim set off for another journey with his beloved Rosaly and two daughters: nine-year-old Emma and a still-unnamed daughter born in Leningrad (she received the name Elena, which was fashionable at that time, at the Civil Registry Office in Moscow). The seven days allotted for preparations went by quickly. During this time, Maxim had to hand over his duties as commander of the 19th Aviation Division and say goodbye to the personnel of the aviation regiments.

Colonel Chibisov's successor as division commander was Colonel Karpenko, a Hero of the Soviet Union.

On the appointed day, July 8, an officer arrived at the garrison from the airfield and reported, "Comrade Commander, a plane has come for you and is waiting at the airfield." It was time to bid farewell to the 19th Separate Mine and Torpedo Aviation Division, which Maxim had created and developed for the last two and a half years.

> The division personnel and aviation regiment commanders assembled to see us off from the garrison to the airfield … By the plane I received a warm farewell and wishes for further success in work, good health and happiness. We then boarded the Li-2 plane. We waved from the stairway as the roar of the motors deafened any words. The doors closed and the plane quietly and smoothly rolled out onto the airfield. We stopped by the edge of the runway, increased the motor speed, picked up speed, took off, and began to climb. Once at an altitude of 400 meters (1,300 feet), we made an honor lap over those who had seen us off and set course for Moscow.

The plane, which belonged to the Polar Aviation Office and had been specially sent to pick up Colonel Chibisov and his family, landed in Tushino, just outside Moscow, at the Zakharkovo airfield, which was equipped with a seaplane ramp on the Khimki Reservoir, where, in late fall 1945, the rearguard of the special ferrying group led by Maxim Chibisov had landed the last five Catalinas under the Lend-Lease Program following the trip from the United States. Now this airfield formerly belonging to the Civil Air Fleet had been transferred to the PAO of the NSRA.

Maxim was met personally by Alexander Kuznetsov as well as members of the PAO.

The Chibisovs and those who had met them were taken by car through Moscow to building 14/16 on Sadovo-Kudrinskaya Street. On the sixth floor of the building was the three-room apartment 61, which had been allocated for the new PAO chief.

Upon moving in, however, Maxim and Rosalia encountered an unexpected surprise: they had only been given two adjoining rooms with total area of 27 square meters (291 square feet).

The third room in the apartment, with floor space of 20 square meters (215 square feet), was already occupied by a three-member family. The Chibisovs, of course, were not happy with this option since Alexander Kuznetsov had promised a separate apartment, as someone with Maxim's status was supposed to receive. But his superiors, once again through Kuznetsov, comforted them, saying that the arrangement of two families in one apartment was temporary and that later everyone would be resettled as they should be. Neither Maxim nor Rosaly could have known at the time that their so-called temporary residence in the communal apartment— with two children in an area of 27 square meters (291 square feet)—would last for the next thirty years.

By agreeing to take the rooms offered to them, the Chibisovs fell into a bureaucratic trap of which they were unaware. At that time in Moscow, any family who had more than five [square] meters (54 square feet) of living space per person was considered well secured with housing, and there was no line to join for upgrades. Given the housing crisis in Moscow at that time, it was extremely difficult to do anything about this situation. It would have required going around to different chains of command, making requests, exerting pressure on people, and humiliation. Maxim Chibisov was not capable of doing this.

15.2 The Polar Aviation Office

The NSRA was established in December 1932, shortly after the triumphant success of the expedition led by Otto Schmidt, who had made a nonstop voyage along the entire Northern Sea Route on the *Sibiryakov* steam icebreaker without wintering for the first time in history. This expedition was so impressive that the government proposed that Schmidt and Valerian Kuybyshev, who was deputy chairman of the Council of People's Commissars at that time, draw up a plan for regular navigation along the Northern Sea Route.

According to the memoirs of Mark Shevelyov, one of Schmidt's closest associates, this project was created by a group of enthusiastic polar explorers. The document they prepared—the first version—included numerous orders for various people's commissariats and departments. When Kuybyshev and Schmidt presented their preliminary work at a Politburo meeting, Stalin, puffing on his pipe, asked, "Do you think all this can be done?"

They replied, "If the decision is made."

Stalin said, "Show me where exactly this Tiksi is."

Schmidt went up to the map and pointed the town out.

Stalin chuckled. "Well, of course! We have been scolding the People's Commissar of Water Transport every week for not being able to transport oil from Baku along the Volga as it should be, and you want him to start thinking about your Tiksi and building a port there? He thinks he is going to receive a reprimand tomorrow for transporting the oil, while for your cause, for Tiksi, he would face a reprimand in two to three years. He won't do anything in Tiksi."

Roughly the same conversation was held regarding the People's Commissariat for Posts and Telegraphs.

"The People's Commissariat for Posts and Telegraphs can't even deliver newspapers on time. How is it going to build a radio center in Dikson?! ... This won't do," Comrade Stalin said authoritatively. "The Arctic is a serious thing ... We need to create an organization that will be responsible for everything and knows that it is responsible for the Arctic and nothing else. We will hold it strictly accountable! ... Redo the papers and we will prepare a decree to create the Northern Sea Route Authority under the Council of People's Commissars, instruct it to establish a route from the White Sea to the Bering Strait, equip it, keep it in good order, and ensure safe navigation. This is sufficient for now."

This is how the concept of the NSRA was born.

With a special decree, this agency was tasked with developing the polar regions; managing all sectors of the local economy, including transport; building industrial enterprises; handling trade; procuring furs; and establishing cultural centers, schools, and hospitals. Stalin likened the Soviet polar organization to the British East India Company, which had all the attributes of a separate state and even its own troops. "But we should resolve everything peacefully. Therefore, no cannons for Schmidt!" With this joke by Stalin, work began on the systematic development of the polar regions.

One of the ideas contained in Mikhail Lomonosov's prophetic formula had been put into practice: "Russian power will grow through Siberia and the Arctic Ocean."

Of course, the NSRA headquarters were located not among the polar ice and snow but in downtown Moscow, on Razina (also known as Varvarka) Street. This organization's structure included offices for sea and river transport, polar aviation, polar stations, and hydrographic and geological offices, as well as departments for agriculture, trapping, fishing, trade, economic planning, finance, mobilization, and more.

The first chiefs of the NSRA, Otto Schmidt and his replacement, Ivan Papanin, were men of science who made it a priority to promote scientific and expedition research work, laying the foundations for the effective economic use of the Arctic's resources. This approach paid off: by the late 1930s, the flow of cargo along the Northern Sea Route began to grow rapidly, particularly after the start of the industrial development of the wealth of minerals in Taymyr, when the name Norilsk Mining and Metallurgical Combine first appeared on economic maps.

A special project was implemented in Norilsk, managed by the security services at Lubyanka instead of the NSRA at Varvarka. But without the transport support of the NSRA, it would have been impossible to implement the unprecedented construction beyond the Arctic Circle. The project involved tens of thousands of workers and various specialists who, for one reason or another, had "arrived at the command of NKVD agencies."

Their woeful work was not in vain: in the difficult year of 1942, the Urals metalworkers obtained their first batch of highly valuable nickel, which was urgently required to manufacture armor steel.

The enormous importance of the Arctic routes became fully apparent during World War II, when Murmansk and Arkhangelsk became key acceptance points for military supplies sent to the Soviet Union by the Allies. However, the system for defending the Northern Sea Route proved to not be entirely reliable, as the actions of German submarines showed in the Barents and Kara Seas as well as the raid by the *Admiral Scheer* cruiser, which broke through the Kara Sea all the way to Dikson.

In 1946, when the legendary Papanin was forced to switch to quiet research work for health reasons, both military and civilian seamen were competing for control over the vacant office on Razina Street. Following a brief battle among the staff, friendship won out, with a slight advantage going to the civilians, (who were supported by the curators from the State Security Ministry).

The new chief of the NSRA was Alexander Afanasyev, a former deputy minister of the Soviet Navy. However, the Navy leadership also obtained its share of bureaucratic influence as Alexander Kuznetsov, who had previously held senior aviation positions in the Baltic, Northern, and Pacific Fleets, was appointed as Afanasyev's first deputy.

As duties were distributed between the NSRA chief and his first deputy, the latter, as a professional pilot, was given authority over the PAO. But in order to effectively manage this office, the NSRA deputy chief needed a reliable, experienced leader on whom he could fully rely without fear of any ulterior motives. General Major Kuznetsov believed Colonel Chibisov would be an ideal candidate for this post, as he was a high-class professional; a clear-cut leader; and a decent person who would not let you down, betray you, or go over your head.

Head of the Polar Aviation Authority M.N. Chibisov (right) and the Chief of the Main Northern Sea Route A.A. Kuznetsov at the ice airfield during the high expansion expedition "North 2". April 1948.

15.3 The daily Routine of Heroic Service

Beyond the Arctic Circle, there were almost no railways or roads. Most of the cargo along the main section of the Northern Sea Route—from the White Sea to the Chukchi Sea—was transported by sea. However, ships were laid up for a significant part of the year, when the polar seas and rivers were covered with ice. During these harsh times, only the heroic polar aviation forces could supply food, equipment, and basic necessities to the polar explorers and border guards; drop off expeditions at their destinations; and conduct rescue operations. There is a reason for the saying in the polar lands "There is no life here without aviation."

Colonel Chibisov preferred to meet people and learn about the management on-site. After assuming his duties at the PAO, he left for his first trip in late July 1947.

Flying on one of the PBY-6A Catalinas that had been delivered under the Lend-Lease Program, it took Maxim 90 hours to travel a route that took him from Moscow to Dikson, Igarka, Dudinka, Khatanga, Tiksi, Kresty Kolymskiye, Providenyia Bay, Ugolnaya, and Kotelnaya and then back to Moscow. In subsequent years, he would go on to fly numerous times along this main air route on trips that could last three to four months. According to his flight log records, he flew a total of 203 hours in 1947!

From his own experience, he had fully grasped the specifics of flying at high latitudes.

The winter season, with its biting cold and fierce snowstorms, lasted for more than six months there. The summers were cold and brief. The sun that might happen to peek out had to break through a wet fog. The weather changed every hour, and this often made it necessary to urgently seek out an alternate airfield, which took dozens and sometimes hundreds of kilometers to reach.

The most valuable asset of the PAO was its heroic personnel.

Renowned pilots Vodopyanov, Malkov, Cherevichny, and others were the ones who knew the entire country. Accustomed to universal admiration, they set high standards for themselves. The polar pilots had their own informal hierarchy and adhered to long-standing traditions, some of which were remarkable, while others were not particularly beneficial for their cause. An evaluation of Mikhail Vodopyanov compiled by Maxim that has been preserved presents this polar hero in an exceptionally positive light. He deserved this, not only because of his talents as an aviator but also for his personal qualities: he was modest, disciplined, not infected with star fever, and highly respectable. Malkov was completely different: as a pilot, he was no worse than Vodopyanov, but he was an individualist and an egocentric person who was used to taking immeasurable pride in his achievements, as if oblivious to those who had worked to help achieve these feats. There was a wide range of other bright, strong personalities.

Working with such a team was interesting and challenging, but this was the cream of the Polar Aviation team.

In addition to the famous aces of the polar skies, the NSRA system also included thousands of selfless workers from the flight, technical, and support staff. Assessing the conditions of their life and work, Maxim noted in his diary,

> It wasn't an easy situation. The polar aviation basing sites were located at a great distance from one another and were scattered almost along the entire coast of the Arctic Ocean. Takeoffs and landings were made on natural strips, even in Igarka and Kresty Kolymskiye, where permanent aviation groups were located. The first thing that catches your eye is the weak technical support for the flights and the poor airfield facilities. Suffice it to say that during the polar nights, which lasted up to five months, the landing and takeoff strips were lit by weak storm lanterns under the best-case scenario. Bonfires of burning fuel oil were most common. There was a lack of housing for employees and the crews were discouraged by the absence of a normal place to rest. And this was all despite the fact that the personnel worked under extremely difficult conditions and, for the most part, temperatures ranging from -25 to -40° C. (-13 to -40° F.) ... In the small airports that had somehow been equipped, passengers lay around on the floor like bumps on a log waiting for their plane. Due to the adverse weather conditions, such waits often dragged on for several days and sometimes even a week.

In his report on flight incidents for 1946, 1947, and 1948, Maxim provided a detailed description of the unsatisfactory condition of the airfields, their poor equipment support, and the shortcomings in the work of the radio service.

For example, planes were repeatedly damaged when landing on runways with "loose snow cover," "wet soil," or "soft ground." The cause of frequent fires in aircraft was "the heating of engines with an APL-1 lamp," while numerous emergency landings were caused by water in the fuel tank that had been "pumped in together with the fuel."

He not only recorded the flaws in the work of the PAO and reported them to the authorities but also actively sought to make changes for the better.

At first, he succeeded in implementing some basic measures to establish order. Gradually, polar aviation began operating more efficiently than it had in the past. They expanded the practice of flights at night and during the polar nights. Starting from 1948, the transport plans were regularly exceeded by double-figure percentage points. Most importantly, the accident rate declined sharply. The frequent disasters involving loss of aircraft in the past now occurred only in isolated and emergency situations (for example, there wasn't a single disaster of this kind in all of 1949).

Thanks to the efforts of PAO chief Chibisov, a special government decree was adopted on the construction of seven new Arctic airfields with runways made of reinforced concrete. This same decree also defined the objectives for building housing and social infrastructure for polar aviation workers who resided permanently in the north.

As this decree was implemented, the conditions in which the thousands of people who comprised the polar aviation team worked and lived gradually improved.

Another performance evaluation signed by Afanasyev and Kuznetsov in 1947 reported the following about Colonel Chibisov's work:

> He has visited all his facilities in Arctic; he has displayed the proper efficiency in eliminating ... deficiencies and organizing things on the ground, which contributed to the successful implementation of the plan for shipping cargo and transporting people to the Arctic in navigation in 1947; he trained the polar aviation personnel particularly well in conducting ice reconnaissance and providing them with data from ships. He boldly and resolutely carries out leadership actions, demonstrating the proper level of independence and assertiveness. He skillfully organizes and plans his work ... He is demanding of himself and his subordinates. He is polite and tactful in conversation. He has a well-deserved reputation among his subordinates.

15.4 Polar dreams and feats

Despite being a native of the southern part of the Russian Empire, Comrade Stalin fell in love with the northern—polar and subpolar—territories of the Land of the Soviets under his control during the last years of his reign. What was going through his mind as he worked tirelessly to develop and populate lands that were unfavorable for human habitation with the inexhaustible labor resources of the state security services? Did he recall something pleasant from the brief period of his life in Turukhansk, when the young political exile Koba still only dreamed of assuming the role of the leader of the revolutionary masses?

Stalin's belated passion for the north was entirely platonic (he only traveled south when he left Moscow) but highly active.

Upon appointing Afanasyev head of the NSRA in 1946, Stalin read him an entire lecture:

> The polar region contains untold riches: forests and rare minerals. Only the naval fleet can solve the highly complex transport problem in order to develop the productive forces of the Far North. And we will solve it—all the conditions will be created for economic growth and cultural development of the Northern people. Look at a map: the face of our country is turned to the north. Abundant rivers—the great Ob-Irtysh basin, the mighty Yenisei, Khatanga, Anabar, Lena, Indigirka and Kolyma rivers—which are navigable, and they all flow to the north. Productive forces, industry and agriculture are rapidly developing in Siberia. It's not only timber and grain that need to be exported, but also industrial products from the Urals and Siberia. The railroads are overloaded and the only solution is to be bolder and faster in the use of Siberian rivers. Cargo should then be delivered by the fleet via the Northern Sea Route for economic needs at ports in both the west and the east. People are eager to buy Siberian timber overseas, timber exports will grow each year, and new ports need to be built and developed. The Northern Sea Route should be a normally functioning transport route. It's our route and its strategic value is

extremely high. It must securely connect the western and eastern parts of the Soviet Union.

There was one place on the map that Stalin liked in particular: the area where the mighty Ob River empties into the Arctic Ocean through a wide, deep bay. He decided that a city would be built there—to spite the American neighbors. The leader gave the command, and the courtier demiurges created the grandiose project. Even the Paradise project conceived by Peter the Great to build the city of St. Petersburg on the Baltic swamps seemed modest in comparison with Stalin's plan.

On the desolate banks, a miraculous port city was to be built with palaces, factories, and special institutions as well as a convenient harbor for oceangoing ships that had to cross the vast Arctic with a convoy of powerful icebreakers. They immediately designed and began building a railroad that was supposed to run from "sunny" Vorkuta to the future miracle city and then on to Igarka and Norilsk. There were numerous other plans concocted at that time with regard to the harsh territories of the indigenous Russian North.

Most of these magnificent ideas were unable to be implemented, in part because they were uneconomical and in part through the fault of Stalin's sluggish successors. The construction of the Vorkuta–Norilsk railroad was suspended, and the sections that had been built were simply abandoned. They never even managed to design the port city in the Lower Ob.

However, setting such goals in a practical manner created the necessary and sufficient preconditions for conducting intensive research in 1948–1950 in the Central Arctic, which until that time remained completely unexplored.[23]

Outstanding scientific discoveries were made over the course of this research, and only now has the current generation in Russia started to realize their true significance as it prepares to reap the rewards of the labor of its Soviet predecessors.

These discoveries were mainly made by people who worked in the NSRA system. A few important changes were made to the leadership of this agency on the eve of the three-year cycle of brilliant expeditions.

---

[23]   The descriptions of the polar expeditions of 1948–1950 presented in this chapter use unpublished materials from a book written by Candidate of Historical Sciences Andrei Pochtarev with his consent.

In March 1948, Afanasyev was appointed minister of the Soviet Navy. The former minister, Pyotr Shirshov, a former polar explorer who had been on several expeditions with Schmidt and Papanin, had to resign for objective reasons: he had broken down mentally following the arrest of his wife, a beautiful actress who had rejected advances by Lavrenty Beria. Afanasyev, a friend of Shirshov, was soon arrested as well—27 days after taking over as minister of the navy—and then sentenced to a long prison term in a camp. But this is another story.

Afanasyev transferred command of the NSRA to his first deputy, Alexander Kuznetsov. He had the opportunity to head the polar expeditions of 1948–1950, while PAO chief Maxim Chibisov was rightly recognized as the second leader of the expeditions in terms of actual importance.

Indeed, it was Maxim who ensured the smooth and safe delivery of the expedition members to the research sites in the remote Central Arctic as well as their safe return.

15.5 Storm at High Latitudes

The first systematic polar research carried out by the Soviet Union involved a high-latitude expedition on ANT-6 planes (HLE Sever-1 under later classifications) as well as the work of the North Pole-1 (Severny Polyus-1) drifting stations under the guidance of Ivan Papanin.

The productive work that had been initiated to study the Central Arctic was then interrupted for a long period by World War II.

The Sever-2 high-latitude air expedition was launched from Moscow in mid-March 1948 on Li-2 and Il-12 aircraft. The expedition's research personnel included 23 people.

The expedition was led by NSRA chief Alexander Kuznetsov. PAO chief Chibisov served as his deputy commander for flight operations. Mikhail Ostrekin, the director of the geophysics department of the Arctic Scientific Research Institute, was the deputy commander for research work, and Boris Vaynbaum was the deputy commander for logistics.

The chief of the NSRA
(1946-1948, 1957-1964)
A.A. Afanasyev.

The expedition was carried out on six Li-2 ski planes flown by commanders I. Cherevichny, I. Kotov, V. Maslennikov, B. Agrov, M. Kaminsky, M. Kozlov, N. Andreyev, A. Bagrov, and L. Shulzhenko as well as one Il-12 piloted by commanders M. Vodopyanov and M. Titlov and one Pe-8 flown by V. Zadkov that had been converted to transport jet fuel. The entire flight staff along with the maintenance personnel included 72 people. In addition, several aircraft from the Defense Ministry were involved in the Sever-2 expedition.

The scientific observation program had mainly been prepared by the Arctic Scientific Research Institute jointly with the main department of the Hydrometeorology Service and Leningrad State University. The program called for a wide range of scientific research on oceanography, meteorology, and geophysics.

The expedition researchers and the technical and flight personnel accompanying them arrived at the Severnaya Zemlya archipelago, where bases had been set up: a main one as close to the North Pole as possible, called Base Number 1, and an auxiliary base closer to the mainland, Base Number 2, through which regular air service was maintained with the mainland.

Flights were made from the main base to various parts of the Central Arctic, where the expedition members were dropped off on the ice. According to Maxim's memoirs, "when landing on the ice, tents were set up based on the following calculation: each tent accommodated five people, or one plane crew." After establishing temporary housing in this manner, the research envisaged by the expedition plan was then carried out.

Once they completed their work at one geographic point, the expedition members returned to the base and were then dropped off on another ice floe—and so on and so forth along the entire route specified by the expedition program over the course of several months. After this, the expedition members returned to the mainland on the aircraft.

The Sever-2 expedition performed scientific observations at eight sites located to the north and northeast of the New Siberian Islands, including an area directly over the North Pole.

At the landing sites, standard hydrological and meteorological observations were made, the components of Earth's magnetic field were identified, and the thickness of the ice cover was measured. Ice reconnaissance was conducted along the way on the flight routes.

In his diaries, Maxim wrote,

All the high-latitude air expeditions were conducted from early March until late May. The weather was more or less clear during this time, but there were always strong winds and the possibility of snowstorms or even blizzards … As summer approaches, the snow and ice begin to melt rapidly. This process kept us on our toes and caused numerous problems. Sometimes, the inhabitable ice surface that we had already equipped outside the airfield—with planes and tents for the crews to rest—would suddenly become covered with crevices. The deepest ones would spread apart, leaving wide fractures (ice leads). Therefore, at the base camp and when serving "jumping" groups, we had to intently monitor the ice on the ground after landing.

Various types of emergency situations also occurred during the landing of the jumping groups. The most serious incident took place during work in direct proximity to the North Pole on April 24 to April 27, 1948. Unfortunately, some publications have depicted important details of this incident in a contradictory and somewhat inappropriate manner. A complete picture of this event can be reconstructed by supplementing the existing sources of information with the corresponding entries from Maxim's diary.

At the time, a research group had been dropped off on the ice from three planes.

One of the planes, led by pilot I. Cherevichny with expedition chief Alexander Kuznetsov on board, immediately returned to the base after dropping off the team.

The crews of the two other planes (with commanders V. Maslennikov and I. Kotov) remained on the ice along with four researchers (geophysicists M. Ostrekin and P. Senko and hydrologists M. Somov and P. Gordienko) as well as journalist S. Morozov and cameraman V. Frolenko.

The day after the landing, the ice began to shift intensely. Maxim described this situation in a rather composed manner.

Pilot V. Maslennikov and I encountered one typical incident. While delivering barrels of fuel for the next expedition to the North Pole, we landed at a decent-looking site. We unloaded everything. We were just getting ready to take a break when we heard a crack: a crevice opened up almost directly under the plane. It began to expand right in front of our eyes and turned into a wide ice lead between two ice floes with the unloaded barrels remaining on one floe and our plane on the other. It was a good thing that we managed to catch this process as it started. The crew managed to re-steer the plane. Then we had to make an emergency takeoff altogether. We searched for a new stretch of ice that would be suitable for landing for a long time. In the Arctic Ocean, it is difficult to find a flat surface of the right size for this purpose—there are nothing but massive ice hummocks of varying height for many kilometers.

Deputy expedition chief Chibisov, as follows from his diary, was a firsthand witness of the incident—he observed it from on board the plane from which the fuel barrels had been unloaded. His entries indicate that the cracks began to appear immediately following the landing and unloading of the plane.

At the same time, the context of the memoirs of one of the firsthand witnesses to the incident, hydrobiologist P. Gordienko, implies that Kuznetsov's deputy for flight operations arrived on Cherevichny's plane along with the expedition chief. Gordienko does not indicate when Chibisov departed from the site of the incident or what kind of aircraft he flew on.

Summarizing all the extant information, we can conclude that Maxim arrived on the same plane as Kuznetsov, then took off on Maslennikov's plane, and returned to the ice floe the next day along with Maslennikov with the fuel cargo. Apparently, the PAO chief, who was always attentive to the slightest details, believed the fuel reserves initially brought for the expedition and the refueling of planes were insufficient and decided to make up for this shortfall. The second flight from the base to the ice floe in Maslennikov's plane with fuel on board proved to be much more complicated than the first flight made in the group with Kotov and Cherevichny, since they now had to land not just on any suitable ice surface but in a specific part of the Arctic wilderness. Therefore, the responsible leader and experienced pilot Chibisov flew with Maslennikov to assist him and may have even sat in the copilot's seat, as he often did during polar expeditions.

For Maxim, who was accustomed to dangerous situations and had already made several flights and landings in the Arctic, the ice compression occurring at that time did not seem like some terrible disaster. It was a normal incident and nothing more.

High Latitude Air Expedition 'Sever2', Base No. 2, 1948.]

The impressionable hydrobiologist Gordienko perceived the events much more emotionally, as reflected in his memoirs:

> Initially, thin thread-like cracks appeared in the ice and surrounded the tents like a snake. Then the cracks began to expand and passed under the planes. This happened quickly—in about 8–10 minutes. The alarm was sounded immediately and the aircraft engines began to buzz. However, the planes were unable to take off as the entire runway had become riddled with channels and crevices that were several meters wide in some spots. The pilots were only able to steer the ski planes to an uneven ice patch section. The researchers also moved their valuable devices to this area as well. An hour later, the area around the camp was hardly recognizable. While in some places the ice floes had split apart and formed ice leads and fractures that were 50–250 meters (55 – 273 yards) wide, a short distance away powerful hummocking was taking place in various place.

It was only on the third day, when the movement of the ice slowed down, that we were able to start equipping the airfield ... Our new airfield was not even enough, wide enough or long enough as required by aviation rules. We explored this section of ice on numerous occasions and consulted with one another. The conclusion was always the same: we had to take off because the Arctic elements had forced us to abandon the inhabitable ice island. And we risked it.

And yet, demonstrating their amazing skills, the pilots Kotov and Maslennikov took off from this ice in their planes on the morning of April 27, and we left the North Pole, which had been so calm at the beginning of our trip and then became so inhospitable.

This extraordinary event ended rather favorably: the expedition members were not hurt and retained their research equipment. Some of them later described the dramatic episode they had experienced in articles and memoirs.

There was nobody left to describe the details of another incident that proved to be tragic. One of the polar aviation planes went missing. As Maxim later explained, the last radio communication from the plane stated: "We are returning in about forty minutes. You can set the dinner table for the crew." That was it. We [search and rescue crews] searched intensely for this plane for several years. Different versions of the events were suggested. Since the entire expedition was shrouded in a veil of military secrecy, the top brass were worried the missing plane could have gone down (or landed) in a place where it shouldn't have: the territory of the United States or Canada.

No traces of the plane were found, and no evidence surfaced to assume it had fallen into enemy hands. The reputable polar explorers agreed that the plane had crashed for one reason or another along the route it had been traveling. This was the Arctic, after all.

In 2007, the media reported that fragments of the ill-fated plane had been found on an island in the Russian sector of the Arctic Ocean.

The research conducted during the Sever-2 expedition produced sensational results. Oceanographic work performed on April 27, 1948, confirmed a depth of 1,290 meters, which was inconsistent with the opinion of the time regarding the deepwater basin in the central part of the Arctic.

Based on the data obtained during the expedition, the researchers concluded that there was a major upheaval in the central Arctic Basin. Expedition members Y. Gakkel and V. Timofeyev reached such a conclusion independently of one another while processing the results obtained during depth sounding (after they had returned).

Further long-term research in this area led to the discovery of an underwater mountain range, which was named after Lomonosov and became part of Russia's arctic continental shelf as it was established in later years. Based on this fact as well as the right of the discoverer, Russia can now lay claim to the corresponding waters of the Arctic Ocean as part of its economic zone.

From left to right: Minister of River Fleet Z.A.Shashkov, commander of the Polar expedition for river fleet transfer along the NSRA Captain 2nd Rank F.V.Nayanov and head of Polar Aviation Authority (UPA GUSMP) Colonel M.N.Chibisov at the mission of marine fleet transfer from Arkhangelsk to the mouth of Yenisei and Ob' rivers. The summer of 1949.

This was only a small part of what the Sever-2 expedition members managed to discover, study, and record with specific figures and facts.

15.6 Celebrating Victory at the North Pole

The next high-latitude expedition was conducted in April–May 1949 and given the name Sever-4 (as the Sever-3 naval expedition on the Litke icebreaker had been conducted a little earlier).

The Sever-4 expedition was carried out under the same scenario as the previous expedition, except the area under exploration was much larger than the area explored in 1948. The number of sites where the researchers were to conduct work on the ice had tripled. Among other things, their task was to specify the boundaries of the upheaval on the bottom of the central part of the Arctic Basin.

Renowned polar pilots I.I. Cherevichny and M.V. Vodopyanov, 1948.

Similar to the Sever-2 expedition, the research program for the Sever-4 expedition was drawn up at the Arctic Scientific Research Institute. However, taking into account the experience of the previous expeditions and their members, the program was expanded considerably.

The expedition was once again led by NSRA chief Alexander Kuznetsov; his deputy commander for flight operations, Chibisov; and the deputy commander for research work, Mikhail Ostrekin.

The number of personnel of the NSRA group was approved at 221 people, including 50 researchers and 94 flight personnel members.

A total of 14 planes were used in the expedition: eight Li-2, two Il-2, one Pe-8, one C-47, and two MK-200 aircraft. Besides these planes, the expedition also employed the aviation forces of the Defense Ministry, including a C-47 plane equipped with special devices for the aeromagnetic survey of the seas in the Soviet Arctic.

Over the 27 days of the expedition, 204 landings were made on drifting ice at 32 locations in the Central Arctic, with 121 of those landings performed on skis and 83 on wheels. A wide range of scientific research of the water and air environment was conducted at 28 sites, including depth soundings in the area where the scientists presumed the upheaval discovered in 1948 would continue.

The Sever-4 expedition culminated in a parachute jump at the North Pole performed on May 9, 1949.

PAO chief Chibisov was instructed to manage the preparations and implementation of this operation. They trained for the jump without any publicity; even the ones who were selected in advance to perform the jump at the northern tip of the planet were only informed of this plan at the last possible moment.

Based on aerial reconnaissance data, the head of the operation assessed the condition of the ice and the site of the planned parachute jump and was satisfied: close to the pole, there were flat surfaces suitable for landing the plane that would pick up the parachute jumpers after they descended on the ice. They still had to wait for a window of clear weather that would be conducive for a safe jump as well as a safe return. On the eve of May 9, the clouds over the pole parted, and the bright spring sun shone over the eternal ice.

On orders from expedition chief Kuznetsov, the members of the North Pole jump team— experienced paratrooper Andrei Medvedev and medical service captain Vitaly Volovich, who also had some parachute training— were informed of the honor that had been bestowed upon them on the morning of May 9. Medvedev was urgently summoned from Base No. 2

to be informed, while Volovich was already located at the main base. The latter was called into the chief's office first.

According to Volovich's memoirs, Kuznetsov inquired about his health and then, out of the blue, asked,

"By the way, how many jumps have you made?"

"Seventy-four," I replied.

"Not bad. And what would you say, doctor, if we suggested you make your seventy-fifth jump over the North Pole?" he asked, looking me directly in the eye.

The surprise knocked the wind out of me.

"So, do you agree?" he asked.

"Of course, of course," I said quickly as if afraid that Kuznetsov might change his mind.

He began speaking again, "You will be jumping with Medvedev. Do you know our top parachute jumper? He has already left from Base No. 2 and will be here with us in about an hour and a half. You will be working with the pilot Metlitsky ... Maxim Chibisov will be in charge of the whole operation."

At exactly noon Moscow time, the Li-2 carrying the jump team took off and set course for the North Pole.

The crew was comprised of commander Nikolai Metlitsky, copilot Vladimir Shcherbina, navigator Mikhail Sherpanov, and flight engineer Konstantin Samokhvalov. Besides them, the plane also carried operation chief Chibisov and the parachute jumpers, Volovich and Medvedev.

Each member was doing his own thing. Navigator Sherpanov was plotting the course. Pilots Metlitsky and Shcherbina were flying the plane. Flight engineer Samokhvalov was making tea for the crew.

At that time, operation chief Chibisov surveyed the condition of the ice surfaces with his experienced eye and, along with the pilots, chose a site that would be suitable for implementing their plans.

The flight took about an hour. As Volovich recalls,

> While we were discussing the details of the upcoming jump, Chibisov came out of the cockpit. Tall, handsome and wearing brown leather raglan sleeves, he was a person

who was decisive, commanding and full of boundless energy.

"We're getting close to the pole," he said, leaning down to us. "The ice conditions are entirely satisfactory. There are several solid ice fields. We'll pick a good site. The weather is okay. Visibility is excellent. In three minutes, we'll begin our descent. Will six hundred meters [1,970 feet] suffice, Medvedev?"

"That's right. That will suffice," Medvedev replied.

"We've begun our descent," Chibisov said. "Wait for my command. Comrade flight engineer, you prepare the smoke canisters."

From that point, everything proceeded like a well-rehearsed play. Flight engineer Samokhvalov dropped the smoke canisters, denoting the ice field identified by Chibisov with columns of smoke, and Medvedev and Volovich jumped out of the plane and descended onto the field. A.P. Medvedev (left) and V.G. Volovich after the North Pole jump. 9th of May 1948.

A.P. Medvedev (left) and V.G. Volovich after the North Pole jump. 9th of May 1948.

Once they made it out of the snowdrifts and untangled themselves from their parachute equipment, they began taking pictures of one another and the surrounding desert of snow and ice. According to Volovich's memoirs,

We got carried away taking pictures and for a little while forgot where we were. We were quickly reminded by the ominous cracking of ice and the shifting blocks of the ice hummocks. Wasting no time, we put the parachute bags on our backs and climbed to the ridge of the ice bar. The green silhouette of the airplane loomed clearly against the backdrop of the endless, table-smooth ice field sprinkled with snow.

The plane landed close to the spot where the parachute jumpers had descended. Maxim was satisfied: the operation assigned to him had gone off without a hitch like an exercise at a training facility outside Moscow.

Prior to boarding the plane, Volovich and Medvedev managed to drink a beaker of brandy and munch on a chocolate bar that the foresighted doctor had brought along in his backpack. After all, it was a holiday: May 9, the fourth anniversary of the great victory!

However, they had to surrender their camera and film with the unique pictures. Their record-breaking jump, like everything else done during the expedition, was top secret and could not be made public—not in newspapers and not even to close family members.

The heroic parachuting Dr. Volovich, who concurrently served as a chef, recalled another typical episode from the chronicles of the high-latitude expeditions:

> One day at the airfield at Cape Chelyuskin, I was waiting for a ride to Base No. 1. The expedition facility chief asked Chibisov what to do with the doctor: he needed to fly to the base, but the plane was loaded to capacity with food. Chibisov thought for a second and then uttered a phrase that would become a "polar classic": "Ship the dumplings. The medicine can wait."

At the same time, Volovich admitted that the PAO chief had a "respectful attitude towards medicine." In this case, however, Maxim was guided by his unwavering principle: "Know how to choose the most important thing."

Good medical care is a necessity, but above all, the polar explorers needed high-quality food, without which no medicine could support the health of those working in the Arctic.

15.7 The "Ice House Odyssey

The experience of the Sever-2 and Sever-4 expeditions demonstrated that the geophysical research performed during this short spring period was clearly insufficient for the fundamental study of the natural conditions in the Central Arctic. They needed constant round-the-clock monitoring on a natural platform—drifting sea ice. Such research had been organized before, during the time of Papanin's expedition at the North Pole-1 station.

In March 1950, the next high-latitude expedition, Sever-5, was launched with the regular work of the jumping groups, who, among other things, searched for ice floes that would be suitable for the planned North Pole-2 and North Pole-3 drifting stations, where research teams led by the experienced polar explorers Mikhail Somov and Alexei Tryoshnikov were to conduct their work.

The senior personnel of this expedition remained the same. The research team included 27 people.

After completing their work program, the expedition returned home in May 1950. By this time, the North Pole-2 drifting station had been put into operation. Unfortunately, the ice floe on which Tryoshnikov's team were to be dropped off had split apart; therefore, it was decided to postpone the project to set up the North Pole-3 station.

A place for the North Pole-2 station was identified to the north of the Bering Strait, in an area where little research had been conducted and the ice drift had not been studied. The PAO was responsible for conducting landings at the station and delivering all the necessities.

Colonel M.N. Chibisov in a conversation about the equipment of the 'Sever 5' expedition with the Director of the Krasnoyarsk aircraft repair factory M.I. Shelykhin. March 24th, 1950.

In early March 1950, a squadron led by Chibisov began to transport the personnel of the drifting station to the Arctic in groups from Moscow and Leningrad. They also transported equipment, camping gear, food, and maintenance accessories. In late March, the station and the bulk of the cargo were located in Tiksi. On the night of April 1, a four-engine plane piloted by Zadkov (the first pilot) and Chibisov (the second pilot) delivered the forward group to the ice led by the station chief, well-known oceanographer and Hero of the Soviet Union Mikhail Somov.

The polar explorers got settled on the ice floe, where they would have to live for an entire year, and the North Pole-2 station was officially launched on April 2, 1950. It began drifting at the coordinates N 76°03′, W 166°36′.

From that time on, the PAO maintained constant air communication between the ice house of the Soviet polar explorers and the mainland. PAO aircraft regularly flew to the station to bring supplies and to replace the winter personnel.

During the first half of the drift prior to early November 1950, the North Pole-2 team consisted of sixteen people, including cameraman Y. Yatsun. In early November, seven people were taken from the station due to a reduction in the research program (aerological observations were stopped altogether, and geomagnetic observations were restricted). This left eleven people on the ice, including the newly arrived Dr. Volovich and geophysicist N. Milyaev.

The station was used to conduct numerous different studies: oceanographic, glaciological, astronomical, meteorological, geomagnetic, gravimetric, aerological, and more.

The polar explorers launched 291 radiosonde balloons and made 212 theodolitic observations.

The underwater soil samples taken at the station made it possible to track changes in the physical and geographic conditions of Earth for the last 50,000 years. They managed to determine there were two periods of major cooling during that time, while between those periods, the climate was warmer than it is in the current era.

In the top part of the ocean water, the oceanographers discovered and studied a layer of Pacific origin distributed between the upper desalinated Arctic water and a layer of Atlantic water.

The annual cycle of meteorological observations and the semiannual cycle of aerological observations provided the first understanding of air-mass circulation over the eastern part of the Central Arctic.

The meteorological and aerological observations transmitted from the North Pole-2 station were used by weather services and improved the quality of forecasts.

Over the period of its drift, the station accepted 71 aircraft and was visited by 58 people.

The actual drifting station initiated the study of the movement of ice in the central part of the Arctic Basin. The ice floe on which the polar explorers were based traversed a complex, winding path that covered 2,600 kilometers (1,616 miles) at an average speed of 6.90 kilometers (4.3 miles) per day, or, in terms of a straight line, 640 kilometers (398 miles) at an average speed of 1.71 kilometers (1.06 miles) per day. Starting to drift at an area where the depth was only 300 meters (984 feet), the station moved along the underwater upheaval located to the north of the Chukchi Sea.

A number of cracks occurred in the ice floe on which the camp was located during the year of the station's drifting. As a result, the size of the ice floe decreased significantly. Whereas this ice measured 3.0 by 2.4 kilometers (1.9 by 1.5 miles) when the station was opened, by the end of the expedition, it was completely destroyed, and the polar explorers had to relocate the camp to another ice floe.

However, the most dangerous incident at the station did not involve the raging polar elements. A fire occurred on July 12, 1950, during which the tent that housed the radio station burned to the ground. The following is an entry about the fire from the logbook:

> At 11:02 a.m. Moscow time, a fire broke out in camp. The tent of the radio operators caught fire. In response to the cries of radio operator Shchetinin, people came rushing over and began to put out the fire. Beside themselves, the people filled up buckets of water from a nearby lake and poured it onto the sea of flames, but the fire continued to fume and rage and engulfed everything that could or could not burn right in front of their eyes. The fuel tank in the engine exploded as a stream of flames shot up about four meters in the air with a hiss and then disintegrated. The observation materials and documents needed to be saved at any cost. The trunks filled with documents were already on fire, but were seized from the burning tent and soaked with water.

This all happened within the span of five to six minutes. The tent burned up like a torch. We had been struck at the most sensitive nerve of our camp. We were speechless, although we could hear the whole world.

M. Somov gave orders to assemble a new transmitter. K. Kurko, V. Kanaki and M. Komarov began assembling the transmitter.

For three days and three nights, with almost no sleep, these three men worked to "sculpt" a new transmitter from assorted radio parts, using a scheme they had devised. On the fourth day, it worked, and communication was restored.

On April 1, 1951, the North Pole-2 drifting station was closed at the coordinates N 81°44', W 163°48'.

But that wasn't the end for the drifting station. On April 28, 1954, while performing ice reconnaissance near the coordinates N 75°05', W 173°20', V. Masslenikov's crew discovered fragments of the ice field with remnants of the North Pole-2 station that had been left behind three years earlier. Thus, the North Pole-2 camp, which had been abandoned on April 11, 1951, at the coordinates N 81°44', W 163°48', had made a full circle in the western sector of the Arctic, moving clockwise. This means that besides the transarctic system of ice drift from east to west from the Chukchi Sea to the Greenland Sea, there is a different direction of drift in the Central Arctic along the anticyclonic ring in the eastern sector of the Arctic in Canada. The time it takes the ice in one of the branches of this system to make a complete circle is estimated at approximately four years. This was another discovery made during the series of triumphant achievements by the Soviet school of polar research.

15.8 The Ice Aircraft Carriers Project

The North Pole-2 station operated under conditions of strict secrecy. Only encrypted radio messages could be used to communicate with the mainland. Nothing was reported about this station in the Soviet media, which had provided broad coverage of the activities of the previous North Pole-1 station run by Papanin and would also do so for the following North Pole-3 and North Pole-4 stations.

One of the members of the ice drift expedition of 1950–1951, V. Volovich, later said during a television program that just before departing for the expedition, Mikhail Somov was summoned to the KGB headquarters at Lubyanka, where he was warned by a person speaking with a Caucasian accent that if the current were to carry the ice floe with the polar explorers into the territorial waters of the United States or Canada or if any American troops were to land on this ice floe, it would have to be blown up, along with all of its workers.

Why was it necessary to impose such harsh conditions on a team who were essentially engaged in ordinary scientific work (though in unusual conditions)?

Apparently, the Soviet leadership at that time did not want to disclose any details about its business in the Arctic, not the purely peaceful aspects of this work and especially not the military components of the high-latitude expeditions.

We know that Defense Ministry aircraft and personnel took part in these expeditions. The draft resolution of the USSR Council of Ministers on the results of the high-latitude air Arctic expedition of 1950 (prepared with the involvement of Maxim Chibisov and signed by Alexander Kuznetsov in late 1950) noted,

> The issue was resolved and skills were obtained in selecting and organizing aviation bases for combat aircraft, including heavy aircraft on drifting ice.

"For the first time in the history of aviation, group flights of combat aircraft (La-11, Tu-2, Tu-4 and others) were made in the harsh conditions of high latitudes, including a flight over the North Pole with landings on unprepared ice floes in the central polar basin and with limited material and technical equipment at airfields. The reliability of the combat and transport aircraft equipment in the Central Arctic has been confirmed, and methods of air navigation and the operation of various types of aircraft have been mastered and formalized.

Family photo after the return of M.N. Chibisov from the 'Sever 4' expedition. May 1949.

"Experience was acquired for the first time in group parachute jumps with full gear on the drifting ice and the organization of supplies to paratroopers with the use of aerial trains. This proves it is possible to use aircraft on a mass scale to support life and work at drifting ice airfields and feasible to use assault and small arms in the Arctic conditions.

Effectiveness was verified for general purpose and chemical aerial bombs as well as mine and demolition equipment, artillery, rifle and mortar weapons in high-latitude conditions …

Planes made a total of 388 landings on

drifting ice, including 21 landings of combat aircraft (La-11, Tu-2 and Tu-4), confirming that it was possible to establish air bases on the drifting ice of the Central Arctic for the large-scale landing of all types of aircraft.

Thus, an extensive training program was conducted for possible military action on the ice of the Central Arctic. A slight glimpse into the core purpose of this top-secret program is found in some of Maxim's latest diary entries, in which he recalled the wide range of aircraft involved in the high-latitude expeditions from the Defense Ministry and the NSRA PAO.

Such aircraft included heavy bombers, dive-bombers, and La-11 fighters, plus various transport planes, including the captured German bomber Fw-200 Condor, which had been converted into a transport aircraft.

These are generally the types of combat aircraft promptly sent to the front lines for future attacks on targets located deep in enemy territory.

In 1948–1950, the Cold War was gaining momentum and taking on the nature of global paranoia. In spring 1949, US Secretary of Defense James Forrestal had a nervous breakdown. At one point, he was rumored to have rushed out into the streets screaming, "The Russians are coming!" Shortly after being hospitalized, he committed suicide by jumping out a window on the 16th floor of the National Naval Medical Center.

Maxim must have known Forrestal (at the very least through correspondence). As US Secretary of the Navy at the time, Forrestal must have been involved in the complications that arose in 1945 with the shipment of the final consignments of Catalinas under the Lend-Lease Program.

In August 1949, the Soviet Union conducted its first test explosion of an atomic bomb. The American nuclear monopoly had been broken. But the forces of the United States and the Soviet Union remained unequal.

The US Air Force had a large fleet of outstanding long-range bombers. Starting from 1947, these aircraft also began flying over the Arctic, from airfields to Barrow Point. The Americans did not attempt to land on the ice, as they had no need to do so. Their aircraft could fly to any major Soviet city, taking off from bases in Western Europe and Japan, and also from aircraft carriers cruising close to Soviet shores. The harsh Arctic only interested the US military as a secondary theater of war.

Commander of the Polar Aviation M.N. Chibisov on many
occasions personally delivered petrol to the polar explorers
on the plane Pe-8 of the pilot V.N. Zadkov.]

At that time, the Soviet Armed Forces had no means for delivering atomic warheads to their targets on US territory. The Soviet Air Force could only respond to a US nuclear strike with retaliatory strikes on Western European and Japanese targets. In principle, this situation was acceptable for the Pentagon strategists: they were mainly concerned with fulfilling their mission to protect the territory of the United States without worrying about any of their European or Asian allies (Maxim clearly noticed this American mentality while in the United States in 1944–1945).

Guided by the ancient rule for battle "If your sword is short, take a step toward the enemy!" the Soviet military leadership decided to step into the Central Arctic. "You have aircraft carriers, but we have ice airfields. You have formidable machinery, but we have savvy and courage!"

The results of the Arctic research conducted in 1948–1950 were sent straight to Lavrenty Beria. In the late 1940s, Maxim was the one responsible for the program aimed at establishing the Soviet Union's strategic capabilities. This program included top-secret projects: nuclear projects (led by Igor Kurchatov and Boris Vannikov); rocket projects (led by Sergei Korolyov); and, as it turns out from an analysis of the high-latitude research, a special Arctic project for which Alexander Kuznetsov was the official leader and Maxim Chibisov was the responsible officer.

The successful research conducted in the Central Arctic, where the Soviet pilots made themselves at home in 1948–1950, had made it possible to create a simple yet reliable Soviet version of the retaliatory strike capability, which radically altered the entire landscape in the harsh political games between the Soviet Union and the United States.

This capability retained its importance while the US military remained unaware of it and did not take any countermeasures. The plans for deploying "ice aircraft carriers" had to be kept strictly confidential until "Day X" in order to frighten the enemy at a critical moment (for example, if the United States began threatening the Soviet Union with war) and, as a last resort, to launch a strike that would be devastating.

Anything could have happened during those years. Under certain circumstances, a leader with unique thoughts, such as Forrestal, could have easily given the fateful order, and the ultra-long-range American Boeings would have unleashed atomic bombs on Soviet cities. In this case, an armada of relatively unsophisticated planes, including even captured junk, would have taken off from the northern Soviet airfields, heading toward the North Pole and beyond, and they would have landed on the ice in order to instantly equip the staging airfields. Then the refueled bombers would have taken off from these airfields to bomb American cities, although they would no longer have had anywhere to return to.

Fortunately for humanity, things never reached that level of insanity at that time.

A few years later (around 1955–1956), Soviet experts provided the country with a truly effective weapon of strategic deterrence: intercontinental ballistic missiles. At that point, the ice aircraft carriers were no longer relevant.

15.9 The Cost of Secrecy

The jump made at the North Pole in 1949 was strictly classified. Therefore, *The Guinness Book of Records* lists the first parachute jumpers to conquer the North Pole as Americans who jumped 32 years after Volovich and Medvedev but with full and highly detailed media coverage.

An obsession with keeping everything secret, which was typical for the Soviet government machine during the last years of Stalin's reign, prevented the Soviet Union from setting precedents with respect to numerous outstanding achievements in the study of the Central Arctic.

In 1953, Marine and River Fleet Minister Zosima Shashkov appealed to the Presidium of the USSR Council of Ministers and the CPSU Central Committee Presidium with a proposal to publish the discoveries made by the expeditions of 1948–1951. He wrote,

At present, by virtue of the "top secret" label established for these expeditions, the scientific material collected is not in circulation to a large degree and is virtually not used at all for the development of Soviet science. The special scientific papers and textbooks released in the USSR are publishing outdated and erroneous information about the nature of the Arctic Ocean that is inconsistent with the actual level of our knowledge.

In recent years, the United States and United Kingdom have stepped up their scientific research in the Central Arctic and are widely publicizing this work, using this publicity to discredit the Soviet research conducted before the war. It is apparent from a number of publications that the Americans have come quite close to discovering the underwater ridges and other natural features of the Central Arctic.

The lack of information in the public media about the main results of Soviet research may result in Soviet science losing its precedence in a number of major discoveries.

Following this appeal, which was received favorably by the government and the Central Committee, Soviet research in the Arctic was conducted in a more open manner. The activities of the North Pole-3, North Pole-4, and subsequent stations were widely covered in the media. The government began to declassify information about the outstanding discoveries made by Soviet scientists in the Arctic. These discoveries became part of the universal body of knowledge about planet Earth.

However, much of the information about how the high-latitude expeditions were conducted as well as the names of the expedition participants would remain inaccessible to the media for a long time. Maxim Chibisov was among the unknown heroes of the Arctic epic.

Meanwhile, Ilya Mazuruk, the well-known polar explorer from before the war, never dropped out of the sight of the journalist fraternity. As Papanin's deputy, he ran the polar aviation operations until 1946; then he went to work for the Civil Air Fleet research institution; and in 1951, he returned to flight operations. He was a commanding officer and then deputy chief of the PAO. He flew in the Arctic and then also in Antarctica. He was always in the newspaper headlines and in front of the cameras.

Mazuruk would go on to publish numerous essays, recalling the feats he performed before, during, and after the war, and people began to perceive him as the chief hero of the Arctic.

Chibisov was unknown to journalists covering the Arctic in the 1970s and 1980s. Therefore, the belief arose in the journalism and filmmaking communities that Mazuruk had been in charge of polar aviation during the legendary expeditions of 1948–1950. Someone apparently stated this opinion, and others repeated it without actually verifying it.

Maxim Chibisov never wanted to be on the front pages of the newspapers or on television. He never even had the opportunity since all of his service took place under strict secrecy. There is a reason his performance reports always stated that he was "able to keep state secrets."

The only people who knew about his work in the Central Arctic were those who needed to know. In 1949, 1950, and 1952, he received three Orders of the Red Banner: the first two for his involvement in the high-latitude expeditions and the third "for the successful performance of a special mission in the Arctic." In 1954, the Presidium of the Supreme Soviet of the USSR published a decree awarding Maxim Chibisov a second Order of Lenin (he was awarded the first in 1945). He was given this award for the whole of his achievements during his work at the NSRA.

15.10 A Celebration inside Strong Walls

Maxim set out for these top-secret expeditions on a number of occasions, and each time, his family knew nothing about the purpose of his trip or the time of his return.

Naturally, Rosaly was anxious and worried about her husband. These concerns rubbed off on her children; after all, they could tell when their mother was in a bad mood, and they could see the tears in her eyes.

But all their anxiety and worries disappeared when the head of the family—dear husband and papa—returned to Zakharkovo airfield from his expeditions alive and well. According to Maxim's diaries,

> They always came to the airfield and looked at the cockpit where their dad sat. Once they saw me, they would get excited, start waving, smiling and looking at me with their cheerful eyes. They waited impatiently for their dad to get out of the plane. And once he was on the ground, all

three of them—Rosochka [Rosaly], Emmochka [Emma] and Lenochka [Elena]—would come rushing towards me, hugging me, hanging around my neck and kissing me all without taking a breath, not letting their beloved daddy out of their arms.

After receiving greetings from his colleagues at the Polar Aviation Office and reporting his safe return to the NSRA officials, Maxim would get in the car with his family and head home.

Along the way, Rosalia and the children would ask him all kinds of questions about the flight, how he'd felt during the flight, and whether or not he had seen any polar bears. Sometimes Maxim would ask the driver to stop, and he, Rosaly, and the kids would go to the nearest photo shop to capture the joyful mood of the entire family. Their neighbors would gather outside the building and greet him, saying, "Welcome back! You look healthy! You're so tan!" and so on.

M.V. Vodopyanov, A.A. Kuznetsov, A.P. Shtepenko, M.I. Kozlov, I.S. Kotov. 1948.

The building belonged to the Polar Aviation Office, so many of its residents had a good idea of the kinds of conditions in which their neighbor from Apartment 61 had been "tanning."

When he entered the building, Maxim felt he was inside strong walls. Things felt cozy and warm in all corners of their apartment. Rosaly and his two daughters would not let him go or out of their sight. This was the biggest celebration for the distinguished aviator's family. With the content feeling of a duty properly fulfilled, he was able to take his mind off the hard work he had performed for the benefit of the nation.

CHAPTER 16

Peacetime General

16.1 Prolonged Farewell with the Polar Aviation Office

While holding a senior position at the civilian-based Northern Sea Route Authority in 1947–1950, Colonel Chibisov continued to feel like a military man. He had never lost the desire to return to the ranks of the Armed Forces. Meanwhile, the circumstances that had prompted Maxim to leave his post as aviation division commander in 1947 had gradually lost their relevance.

Soviet-American relations deteriorated sharply in 1949–1950. NATO was established and directed against the USSR, while new conflict zones emerged in Eastern Asia due to the events taking place in China and Korea. Under these circumstances, Joseph Stalin once again changed his attitude toward the professional military. He removed Nikolai Bulagin as minister of the armed forces and replaced him with the authoritative and respected Marshal Alexander Vasilevsky, one of the coauthors of the victory in Stalingrad. Investigations that had been opened against several military commanders, including Georgy Zhukov, were dropped or at least shelved.

In February 1950, the disgraced Nikolai Kuznetsov, who had been demoted to a rear admiral and barely escaped prison in 1948, once again received a senior position. He took over the 5th Fleet, as the Pacific Fleet was called at that time. This meant the renowned admiral's associates no longer had to fear persecution.

By this time, Maxim had already done much work for the benefit of the Northern Sea Route Authority and did not feel he was under any obligation to the Polar Aviation Office. Early in the spring of 1950, just after the end of the Sever-5 expedition, he decided to return to naval aviation. An officer of such high rank as Colonel Chibisov could only do this if there was a worthy vacant position in the Naval Air Force system and with the consent of the senior leadership of the defense and polar offices. There was, however, a simpler way: by going to study at the Voroshilov Higher Military Academy, as the Academy of the General Staff was called at that time. This option was just fine for Maxim, who had long dreamed of completing the education that had been interrupted by the war.

It appears he made no attempt to conceal his decision to further his studies from his superior. Alexander Kuznetsov's reaction can be seen from the assessment he gave PAO chief Chibisov for his work from the period of January 1, 1948, to December 31, 1949. Below is the text of the document, which is dated March 26, 1950.

> Col. Chibisov has held his position since May 1, 1947. Over the evaluation period, Col. M. Chibisov distinguished himself as an assertive and energetic leader who is always interested in issues concerning the use of aviation in the Arctic. He has been to the Arctic on multiple occasions and studied its features from the standpoint of the use of aircraft. He is courageous and decisive in implementing his own decisions and orders as well as those he receives. He is self-sufficient in his work, but does not always promptly demonstrate the necessary initiative in his work. He is disciplined and demanding of himself; his insistence on high standards from his subordinates is insufficient. His organizational skills are insufficient to cover all the organizational and operational activities of the Polar Aviation Office. On a personal level, he is well trained in aviation, and he maintains up-to-date knowledge; at the same time, the combat and special training of the Polar Aviation personnel is not sufficiently organized and monitored. Divisions of the Polar Aviation

Office do not always work quickly and efficiently, as a result of which peripheral work suffers, particularly air field and air navigation services. The performance indicators of the Polar Aviation Office are as follows: the annual plans for 1947 and 1948 were met and exceeded except for a slight shortfall in the transport plan for 1948; the plan for all indicators was fulfilled by 147%.

Conclusion:

Col. M. Chibisov does not grasp the entire scope of the complex management of Polar Aviation despite his many positive personal qualities, therefore it is appropriate to send him for further studies with subsequent use in military aviation.

What immediately jumps out is the glaring discrepancy between Kuznetsov's damning conclusions and the facts demonstrating the successful work performed by Polar Aviation Office chief Chibisov, such as his exceeding the plan and achieving a sharp decline in the accident rate. The generalized wording of this evaluation report contradicts all the assessments of Maxim's skills and other features described by various leaders, including Kuznetsov himself.

In writing the assessment, the NSRA chief's hand was guided by vexation at a subordinate who had decided to leave. However, while expressing a willingness in the assessment to send Colonel Chibisov for further studies and back to naval aviation (since he supposedly "[did] not grasp the entire scope of the complex management of Polar Aviation"), General Kuznetsov then took a considerable amount of time to finally consent to Maxim's resignation as PAO chief.

Chairman of the Presidium of the Supreme Council of the USSR N.M. Shvernik awarding M.N. Chibisov with three medals. 1952.

According to Maxim's memoirs, his first two letters of resignation from the PAO were considered and rejected by the NSRA board. According to the rules of Soviet service ethics, a superior did not have the right to prevent a subordinate from pursuing further education but could delay his departure from his job for a while (not too long) due to emergency operational circumstances. Major General Kuznetsov took full advantage of this opportunity.

Apparently, he really did not want to part with Maxim, and the reasons for this are fully understandable. Kuznetsov felt comfortable in the chair of NSRA chief, while Chibisov maintained his authority with the exemplary work of the Polar Aviation Office.

Their working relationship began back in August–September 1944, when Kuznetsov was responsible for accepting the Catalinas for the Pacific Fleet. At that time, he displayed inexcusable negligence by sending a group of officers to meet seaplanes in Anadyr without giving the necessary instructions to the captain of the ship on which this group, along with the route maps for the ferry pilots, were traveling to Chukotka. The captain turned the wrong way, and the crews of the first Catalinas arriving in Anadyr found themselves in a difficult position. If the seaplanes had gotten stuck in Chukotka at that time or something else had happened on the flight to Magadan, Kuznetsov would have had to pay for it—people had been brought before a tribunal for lesser sins than that. But he got lucky, as the pilots of the special ferry group, Piskaryov and Spiridinov, overcame all the difficulties with their efforts and found the right path to Magadan using the charts they had drawn by hand on the weather maps. Chibisov, the commander of the special group, never made a fuss about this oversight.

In this incident, Alexander Kuznetsov showed his true colors. He was a talented, bright, and energetic person capable of heroic deeds. Despite such virtues, however, he sometimes committed serious blunders in his work due to a lack of attention to specific details and small things that were sometimes of great importance. This is why Kuznetsov's meteoric career was occasionally interrupted by insulting demotions.

He became famous in 1941–1942 when he commanded the aviation of the Northern Fleet, which at that time was not very powerful, and he often personally led his aviation units into combat against an enemy who had vast superiority in the air. At the turn of 1942–1943, when the Soviet breakthrough in the war occurred and it was time to establish a clear combat strategy instead of engaging in heroics, Kuznetsov was quietly transferred from the Northern Fleet to the Pacific Fleet, which was not active at war. He was appointed deputy to Pyotr Lemeshko, a strict and thorough superior who above all demanded the scrupulous performance of official duties by his subordinates. The Pacific Fleet commander and his deputy ultimately did not get along, and Kuznetsov was pushed into aviation school in March 1945 without even being given the opportunity to distinguish himself in the war with Japan.

When the Navy High Command officers were searching for a suitable candidate among their personnel for the position of deputy chief of the NSRA, they remembered Kuznetsov. In this position, Kuznetsov once again managed to make an abrupt jump up the career leader.

He was ambitious, had outstanding assertive capabilities, and knew how to take advantage of good fortune, revealing his talents and merits to the high command at just the right time. Maxim did not have a knack for all this, although he had the reputation of an exemplary worker and commander who did not allow negligence.

They seemed to complement one another in terms of their virtues, and this created a good foundation for cooperation at the NSRA. With General Kuznetsov's support, Colonel Chibisov made significant improvements to the work of the PAO. Both of them then enthusiastically took part in the work of the high-latitude expeditions.

The success of these expeditions was mainly the result of the businesslike work performed by the pilots subordinate to Colonel Chibisov, but the main glory as conqueror of the Arctic went to the expedition leader, NSRA chief Alexander Kuznetsov.

In December 1949, Kuznetsov was awarded the title Hero of the Soviet Union. The decree granting him the award stated,[24]

> A. Kuznetsov ably and courageously conducted ice reconnaissance to study areas suitable for ice airfields and the organization of research stations on them. During the most critical moment of the expedition's work at the North Pole, when the ice was broken by compression and there was a danger of losing the aircraft and scientific equipment located there, Kuznetsov personally flew to this area, landed a wheeled plane on an unequipped ice floe, and ensured the departure of the planes and the rescue of the scientific equipment with his bold leadership. Upon completion of the expedition at 32 airfields, he was the last

---

[24]   The declassified text of the decree granting Alexander Kuznetsov the title of Hero of the Soviet Union is contained in numerous publications. See "Declassified Hero of the Arctic," *Naval Collection* 2005, No. 4 (1901): 73–77.

to leave the area of work and then made a non-stop flight from the North Pole to Moscow.

Kuznetsov thus received the lofty title of leader of the heroic Polar Aviation Office pilots, many of whom also received Gold Stars. Kuznetsov's deputy for scientific work, Mikhail Ostrekin, was also awarded the title of Hero of the Soviet Union as the leader of the heroic team of scientists and polar researchers.

Maxim received two Orders of the Red Banner following the expeditions in 1948–1950 and a third in 1952 from the Defense Ministry for the successful completion of a special mission in the Arctic. But he was passed over for the title of Hero of the Soviet Union. In the process of allocating awards, PAO chief Chibisov was pushed into the second tier of Arctic conquerors along with those who performed their duties well and helped the heroes accomplish their feats. However, Chibisov flew over the polar ice and risked his life just as much as the ordinary PAO pilots who were awarded Gold Stars and just as much as Kuznetsov. But the senior officials distributing the awards apparently had somewhat different views about who deserved what.

High Latitude Expedition Members in Kremlin after state award ceremony. M.N. Chibisov is in the second row, third from right. 1952.

Maxim himself could not figure out the reasoning for why he failed to receive the title of Hero of the Soviet Union for his role in the high-latitude expeditions. Later in life, he was sometimes inclined to think (and expressed this thought to others) that he had been blamed for the airplane that went missing in 1948. But this assumption seems absurd: the reasons behind this disaster were never established, and placing the blame for it on the PAO chief would have been impossible even in the harsh Stalinist times. After all, the missing plane was flying over Arctic ice and not the Moscow suburbs!

It should be taken into account, however, that the decrees conferring titles and state awards were prepared in the office of the Presidium of the Supreme Soviet of the USSR on the basis of recommendations by the superiors of those awarded.

In late 1948, Chibisov personally signed recommendations to confer the title of Hero of the Soviet Union on PAO pilots who had particularly distinguished themselves in their missions. The NSRA chief had to recommend one of his deputies to the chairman of the Council of Ministers (most likely Lavrenty Beria). Kuznetsov prepared the corresponding recommendation for his research deputy, Mikhail Ostrekin. Perhaps Kuznetsov simply forgot (or did not want) to write a similar recommendation for his other deputy, Maxim Chibisov.

Alexander Kuznetsov flew high on the wings of polar aviation and became widely known. He gained access to the corridors of supreme power, where issues of great political importance were resolved. A sizeable hierarchical distance separated him from Maxim, who was immersed in the daily routine among pilots and engineers and among planes and engines, which, like people, did not always get enough care, affection, and grease. The problems that consumed Maxim were beyond the concern of Kuznetsov, who also gradually forgot about his long-standing promise to somehow resolve the issue of finding an apartment for the Chibisov family.

In 1950, however, Kuznetsov changed his tune. Maxim's departure threatened to cause major complications in the cumbersome management of the PAO. Therefore, General Kuznetsov kept Colonel Chibisov in the NSRA system as long as he could. After denying the two letters of resignation Maxim had submitted, his superior sent the higher authorities a petition in September 1950 requesting that Colonel Chibisov be promoted in military rank to Major General of Aviation and attached an assessment that reads as follows:

> Col. M. Chibisov is an assertive and energetic officer,
> well trained in aviation, and he maintains up-to-date
> knowledge. He has studied the Arctic theater well from

the standpoint of aviation. He took active part in the Arctic high-latitude expeditions of 1948–1950 for which he was awarded the Order of the Red Banner. He is persistent in his activities and independent in his work. He is disciplined and demanding. He has experience commanding aviation units and earned a positive assessment as commander of the 19th Separate Mine and Torpedo Aviation Division of the Navy High Command Reserve. During his command of Polar Aviation, Col. Chibisov improved its work significantly, as evidenced by the decline in the accident rate, the fact that his aviation groups regularly exceeded the plan for transport and ice reconnaissance, and the successful work of the personnel and aircraft fleet during the high-latitude air expeditions; the organization of maintenance services at the polar airfields and the air navigation service also improved considerably; the regular combat training of personnel was introduced in aviation groups with the direct involvement of Col. Chibisov. Col. M. Chibisov has excellent knowledge of the conditions under which aircraft are used in the Arctic and regularly inspects the condition of the services and their work in the Arctic. He is well-trained politically and active in party, political and social work. He enjoys well-deserved creditability. He is a member of the NSRA collegium. He is capable of keeping state secrets. He is devoted to the party of Lenin and Stalin and our socialist Motherland.

In terms of his position and personal qualities, he is fully worthy of the title Major General of Aviation.

Kuznetsov probably expected that Maxim would agree to remain at his position in the PAO if he were to receive the rank of general. But his plan failed. Despite the excellent assessment signed by the NSRA chief, the petition to award Colonel Chibisov a promotion in military rank was rejected.

Apparently, Kuznetsov had not been persistent enough in this matter, perhaps because right around the same time, his superiors were considering the issue of assigning Kuznetsov himself the rank of Lieutenant General of Aviation. Kuznetsov received this rank in early 1951 by way of exception due to his distinguished service since both Papanin (Kuznetsov's renowned predecessor as head of the NSRA) and Burkhanov (who took over Kuznetsov's position) had only been rear admirals, which corresponds to the rank of major general.

Kuznetsov's unsuccessful attempt to secure the rank of general for Maxim convinced the PAO chief once and for all of the futility of remaining in the Polar Aviation Office. In October 1950, he submitted a letter of resignation for the third time in connection with his desire to complete his studies, and this time, it was approved by the NSRA collegium.

16.2 Academic Period

After passing his entrance exams, Maxim Chibisov was enrolled as a student on January 19, 1951, in the Naval Department of the Voroshilov Higher Military Academy.

He felt comfortable there among his fellow officers, colonels and generals, who were enhancing their professional and educational level and were distinguished in terms of their age and rank.

The curriculum was extensive and substantial. After a long break, Maxim had to fill in the gaps in his knowledge at an accelerated pace in order to keep up with his peers. He would bring home books and lecture notes and study them at night, primarily in the bathroom since it was impossible to organize a separate office for studying in an area that consisted of 27 square meters (291 square feet) of living space.

In 1952, Maxim graduated from the academy with a B average and also earned a B for defending his diploma.

After graduating, he was offered a position at the academy. He agreed and was appointed a senior lecturer in the sub-department of naval warfare history within the Naval Department. What did he teach his students? One can only guess.

Even though the sub-department title contained the word *history*, it is unlikely the recent military commander was asked to hold lessons on the tactics of Ushakov and Nelson during the era of sailing fleets.

But Colonel Chibisov could easily have prepared a serious and interesting series of lectures on the combat use of naval aviation from a historical perspective and other angles. He would not have focused solely on the Soviet experience, which he knew firsthand, but would also have used examples from the rich practice of US naval aviation, about which he'd learned numerous sensitive details directly from US military officials during frank conversations "over a cup of tea" in Elizabeth City and Washington.

This was a happy time for the Chibisov family. Their beloved father and husband no longer had to take long trips and could devote lots of time to Rosochka [Rosaly] and their growing daughters.

His workday was strictly regulated. His work desk at home was not littered with mountains of documents requiring urgent reading, studying, correcting, and signing; the main materials Maxim used for his lessons at the Academy were labeled *secret* and remained at the workplace.

Maxim had managed to establish a certain order in both his work life and his family life, and he even revived some of the habits carried over from the time-worn customs of the peasant family from the village of Pushchino.

Each Friday, Rosaly baked cakes, buns, rolls with poppy seeds, and an enormous cheesecake with cream cheese on a special pan—a treat for the weekend. On Saturdays, she always made herring and potatoes for breakfast—Maxim's favorite dish from a young age.

For New Year's, Maxim always brought home a bushy tree, and the Chibisov family would decorate it with toys, candy, and tangerines.

For Easter, they baked at least two dozen cakes, not counting everything else they cooked.

Family vacation in Gurzhuf. 1953.

At parties hosted by the Chibisovs or their friends, Rosaly gladly demonstrated her singing talents and danced enthusiastically. Maxim enjoyed watching his wife waltz with other men. The girls thought their mother was behaving irresponsibly and felt bad for their father, but he was pleased that his Rosochka [Rosaly] was in a good mood, cheerful, and happy and that she enjoyed the company. He was never jealous, and she knew her husband was admiring her, which gave her even more joy.

The bonds of love and trust united husband and wife as well as parents and children. For Maxim and Rosaly, caring for their daughters was a natural and essential part of a happy family life.

Rosaly tried not to pester her husband with the children's minor problems and antics. Once her daughters grew up, they acquired a full appreciation for the pedagogical merits of their mother. In particular, the youngest Chibisov daughter, Elena, expressed the following opinion on the matter:

> Unfortunately, during my childhood and youth, I perceived my mother as she presented herself to others: a giggler, a songstress and a dancer. However, she was a very deep and wise person who understood that the life of our entire family depended on her mood. Being able to see each new day as a gift of fate, she consciously cultivated an atmosphere of joy and happiness in our home. I didn't understand it at the time and took everything for granted. It was only after several years and after my own children had grown up that I began to appreciate mother's diplomacy and the daily work she did to educate us.

Rosaly tried to make sure the girls were clean, combed, and smiling for their busy father. Maxim did not distance himself from the education of his daughters. His authority was the axis around which relations in the Chibisov family revolved.

Maxim did not tolerate sloppiness and demanded strict compliance with the reasonable rules that had been set for the girls. But endowed with the gift of a delicate attitude toward those around him, he never raised his voice. He taught his children how to think, feel, analyze, and overcome difficulties. He demonstrated how to behave in various situations with his own example.

From his life experiences as a commander, leader, and teacher, Maxim had developed an ability to delve deeply into the problems of different people. It was easy for him to put himself in other people's shoes in order to understand the reasons for their words and actions as well as to build relationships with them in certain cases. He taught his children this same ability.

Maxim displayed self-control and composure—qualities that are necessary for a military pilot—not only in his work but also in ordinary everyday situations. He knew how to hide his disappointment and irritation as well as how to nip conflicts in the bud. The rules he followed in his life were simple: "Don't stay angry for a long time." and "Be above resentment and bitterness."

He meticulously observed the old saying handed down by his father "Don't speak more than you have to." Therefore, everything he said carried weight and meaning.

As a person with a traditional peasant upbringing, Maxim maintained contact with numerous relatives and took care of his brothers and sisters as well as their children and grandchildren. Many of them sought out and found his support, receiving useful advice and real assistance. In some cases, such assistance provided salvation for people who had found themselves in difficult situations.

For their part, all of Maxim's brothers and sisters had great respect for their youngest brother and were proud of him. According to an old peasant tradition, the Chibisovs' home in the village of Pushchino was considered Maxim's hereditary property. The house had been empty since their mother's death, and for fifty years, none of their relatives had made any claims for it. Everyone expected that Simushka, the name Maxim had been called as a child, might eventually want to settle in his native home.

The last traces of this home disappeared in the late 1970s, when the city blocks began encroaching on the village of Pushchino and all the pieces of available land were bought up for gardens and summer homes by opportunistic citizens.

Maxim's family was a tiny part of a great land perceived at the time by its citizens as one big common home.

At that time, most residents of the USSR did not yet question the correctness of the Soviet system or disassociate themselves from their government, despite all its flaws. People celebrated the main Soviet holidays—May Day and the November 7 anniversary of the October Revolution—with sincere joy for the country's latest successes, which the rulers reported from the rostrum above Lenin's mausoleum.

Maxim spent the "red days on the calendar" with his family on Red Square, watching the military parade and workers' demonstrations, which were a spectacular theatrical performance in those years.

They made their way to the country's main square through meandering alleys and courtyards that only Maxim knew. After the demonstration, they would take a stroll down Vasilevsky Descent.

From there, they usually walked through Zamoskvorechye to Taganka and Abelmansky Gate, where Maxim's brothers Alexei and Ivan lived. The guests were greeted there with open arms and their favorite cakes.

Another stop on their holiday stroll was on Donskaya Street, where the family of Rosaly's brother Lev lived in a huge communal apartment. Rosalia, an expert cook, took up position at the stove alongside her sister-in-law Raya. The kids played in the one room that belonged to Uncle Lev and Aunt Raya, ran around in the vast hallway, and visited the neighbors. Their commotion did not bother the ladies as they set the table or the men as they played chess and discussed the latest political news.

Politics was a subject of interest, as major events were taking place around the world and in the Soviet Union.

The global communist movement was on the rise. The people of colonial countries were fighting for liberation from the powers of their imperialist mother countries. The first thermonuclear explosions were detonated almost simultaneously in both the United States and the USSR. The Korean War came and went.

On March 5, 1953, Comrade Stalin died. The Soviet people were overcome by deep sorrow as the departed leader's comrades divided up his posts and powers.

The Soviet Union was initially taken over by collective leadership. Georgy Malenkov became the chairman of the Council of Ministers. His first deputies were Lavrenty Beria, who was minister of the interior at the time, and Nikolai Bulganin, who was returned to the post of minister of defense, which Stalin had taken over in 1949. Management over the Communist Party apparatus was entrusted to Central Committee Secretary Nikita Khrushchev, who was not taken seriously at the time by the venerable political big shots from the Presidium of the CPSU Central Committee.

Another important event occurred in summer 1953, which inspired the following ditty: "Beria, Beria, fallen out of favor..."

The overthrow of Lavrenty Beria, the longtime leader of Stalin's repressive machine, was actively pursued by a group of senior army officials led by Georgy Zhukov. After this, military professionals, such as Marshal Zhukov and Admiral Nikolai Kuznetsov, gained unprecedented influence—for a while—in the structures of supreme power.

These changes had a direct effect on the subsequent career of Maxim Chibisov.

16.3 Flight Personnel for the Navy

Nikolai Kuznetsov, who had been rehabilitated after falling out of favor with Stalin and received the highest naval rank of "Admiral of the USSR Fleet," served as commander-in-chief of the Navy and deputy defense minister from 1953 to 1955. He called for the rapid modernization of the Soviet Navy forces and believed it was necessary to implement a broad program aimed at building new ships of all classes, including aircraft carriers.

Naval aviation had long been a subject of special concern for Admiral Kuznetsov. He saw it as the primary means for countering the growing activity of the US Navy along the Soviet coast. In the 1950s, the USSR had no money to build aircraft carriers, but naval aviation regiments and divisions started being hurriedly formed and deployed within all fleets in accordance with the directives of the Navy commander-in-chief.

A special educational institution was to be established as soon as possible in order to satisfy the growing demand for naval aviation personnel as well as mine and torpedo specialists.

Once it came time to select candidates for the director of this institution, Colonel Chibisov's name once again came up. Kuznetsov remembered him well, as did Colonel General Yevgeny Preobrazhensky, the commander of naval aviation and a Hero of the Soviet Union, who, in 1941, had commanded the aviation division that set out to bomb Berlin from the island of Saaremaa (which had been protected by the "air umbrella" of the 10th Aviation Brigade, in which Chibisov had served).

M.N. Chibisov with daughters Emilia and Elena by his house on Sadovo-Kudrinskaya Street. Moscow, 1955.

According to Maxim's memoirs, Preobrazhensky invited him in:

> for a talk and proposed that he take the position of director of the mine and torpedo aviation school in order to build it and simultaneously conduct flight training. The school was located in the city of Kamyshin. The

commander gave the following reasons for appointing Maxim to this position: "You belong to naval aviation, we met you halfway and gave you the opportunity to study at two academies. We are aware of your abilities and believe that only you are capable of completing this task. Therefore, we ask that you agree to our proposal. Your family can stay in Moscow, you will retain your living space. We won't keep you there for a long time. As soon as you get things up and running, we will transfer you to a job in Moscow." I had to agree to go command the naval aviation school.

Following the conversation with General Preobrazhensky, Maxim returned home with heavy thoughts on his mind. How would he tell his sweet Rosochka [Rosaly]?

He informed the family:

> "I've been offered a good new independent job as director of an aviation school …" And before I could even finish my speech, my dear Rosaly began asking questions:

"And where is this school located?"

"In Kamyshin near Stalingrad and not very far from Moscow," I replied.

"And where are we going to live? Are we going to have to relocate again?"

"No, Rosochka [Rosaly]. You and the kids will stay in Moscow and I'll move to Kamyshin for a short time."

"Not again! At the last place, we at least saw you every day at the garrison, but now you'll be a thousand kilometers away from us and you'll be flying again!"

"Honey, nothing can be done. I'm a military man after all. Besides, I won't be gone for long."

"Yeah, they just say it won't be long, but in reality it will be for years!"

Both of the girls started crying. "Papa, how will we live here without you? Don't go—we beg you!" they pleaded.

"My sweethearts, an order has already been prepared on my appointment."

Looking at our daughters, my sweet Rosochka [Rosaly] began to cry as well. The conversation with the family at dinner thus took place in a very trying atmosphere.

That night, the entire Chibisov family slept poorly, "and in the morning they all said they had been bothered by bad dreams about all sorts of comings and goings."

Five days later, Rosalia prepared her husband's suitcase. The whole family observed the old Russian tradition of sitting together for a little while before someone departs on a long trip, and then they all stood up at once and left the apartment. The four of them took a taxi to Kazan Train Station, where they said their goodbyes amid hugs, kisses, and tears. "Papa Max" left, and Rosalia returned home with the girls to await news from the head of the family.

The city of Kamyshin, which was founded in the seventeenth century under orders from Czar Alexei Mikhailovich, is not very big but has its own unique appearance.

Even back in pre-revolutionary times, the city stood out for its relatively high cultural standards among cities of the Lower Volga region. It has interesting ancient monuments, and the Alexandrovsky Garden, founded in 1907, a favorite spot of the locals, has been carefully preserved. The people of Kamyshin are rightly proud of their watermelons and believe they are the best in the Volga region and even prouder of pilot Alexei Maresyev, a well-known former resident of the city who became the inspiration for the main character in Boris Polevoy's well-known novel *Story of a Real Man*.

Maxim Nikolaevitch and Rosalia Borisovna on vacation in a sanatorium. Crimea, 1955.

By and large, it was a nice provincial Russian city and remained so in the 1950s, when it was designated as the site for the training of naval pilots.

When Maxim arrived, the Kamyshin Naval Mine and Torpedo Aviation School was still being erected by the military construction brigades. The cadets who had already been recruited were being temporarily housed in tents and barracks. After lessons and training flights, they often had to help the construction brigades.

The construction process and training of

the future aces had to be conducted simultaneously, and Maxim handled this objective; the school was up and running immediately under his leadership.

It took three years to build the academic and residential buildings, and the first cadet recruits succeeded in fully mastering the profession of naval pilot during this time.

The Navy command gave a worthy assessment of Maxim's work and awarded him the title of Major General of Aviation in August 1955.

When he arrived from Moscow with the general shoulder straps, he was met ceremoniously by the entire Kamyshin garrison, given that he was the chief of the garrison as the senior commander in the city. Welcome speeches were made at the airfield and, a banquet was held at the Officers' House, with an

Major General of Aviation M.N. Chibisov. 1956.

amateur concert, songs, and ditties composed specifically for the occasion.

Maxim was then congratulated on his new rank not only by friends and colleagues but also by people he did not even know on the streets. Congratulatory telegrams arrived from all corners of the country.

Such demanding military leaders as Marshal Andrei Yeremenko, Marshal Semyon Timoshenko, and Lieutenant General Stepan Prutkov came to Kamyshin on numerous occasions for inspections and to exchange experience. Maxim always had something to show the distinguished guests, and he frequently traveled to meet his colleagues for meetings and took part in field training exercises and maneuvers.

General Chibisov was one of the most respected people in all of Kamyshin. He was invited to all the city's official events. On state and military holidays, such as Aviation Day and Navy Day, he held a seat of honor on the rostrum as he inspected the parade of Kamyshin military units.

However, Maxim received the greatest satisfaction from his job. He had long enjoyed working with young people, and his teaching abilities, which had been on display even back at the dawn of his flying career, were fully revealed in Kamyshin.

Based on his long-established habit, Maxim personally and thoroughly instructed the cadets prior to their flights. He then tracked their piloting technique from the airfield tower, noting even the slightest flaws, before conducting a highly rigorous and detailed "post-flight debriefing" (Maxim loved this phrase and used it for all kinds of situations that were not always related to aviation).

The school director's door was always open, and he enjoyed when students came to him with questions on any topic. They knew Maxim would not give them the run-around—he would offer a direct reply and was never at a loss for words. Sometimes these heart-to-heart conversations lasted for hours.

Maxim often had to speak at different classrooms. He always prepared and wrote out his speech in advance, but he never looked down at his scribbled pages while speaking.

He also followed another rule: participating in sporting events almost on

M.N. Chibisov at the instructor's place in the cockpit of the training airplane Yak-18.

an equal level with his subordinates (giving preference to cross-country skiing and shooting).

All things considered, though, he knew how to be a strict boss. He did not tolerate any lack of discipline in work or everyday life. While strolling around Alexandrovsky Garden on a day off, he noticed a cadet with several vodka bottles he had just purchased protruding insidiously from his pockets. The general stopped this lover of firewater with the command "Attention!" and called over the patrol officer, who took the guilty cadet to the guardhouse.

However, such incidents were a rarity at the Kamyshin Naval Aviation School, as it became known in 1955, when "Mine and Torpedo"

At the construction of the garrison Kamyshin. 1956.

was removed from the school's name. The officers who graduated from this educational institution enjoyed a good reputation in the combat units they were sent to serve. Some of them went on to have distinguished careers in the USSR Armed Forces. Maxim had served as a good example for them.

The school director not only managed the learning process but also flew a lot himself, primarily on the Yak-18 trainer aircraft, on which pilots usually began their aviation training in the postwar period. According to the records in his flight log, he made 37 flights in the instructor zone and "under the hood" on the Yak-18 from June 29 to September 20, 1955, flying a total of 15 hours and 20 minutes. The next year, this figure increased dramatically. His total flying time was 29 hours and 39 minutes from March 7 to August 17 and 61 hours and 45 minutes from September 1 to October 12, including instructor and route flights.

Maxim felt having the opportunity to fly was one of the most appealing features of his position.

In summer 1955, Rosalia and their youngest daughter, Lena, who had just finished second grade, came to Kamyshin for the first time. Maxim immediately took them to the Lebyazhe airfield and photographed them in the cockpit of the Yak-18. In doing so, he shared with his loved ones the feelings he had while flying, and they got a chance to experience his joy. Elena later recalled, "In those moments, I felt like the happiest kid in the world."

Emilia, Maxim's eldest daughter, came to Kamyshin after her mother and sister. She had passed her final school exams that summer; entered the third year of music school; and, without giving up music, also enrolled in the philology department at Moscow State University. "My daughter is an MSU student! I never even could have dreamed of it!" her proud father told her. "You are simply prolonging my life … When you were still a baby, you couldn't understand why I was always reading something or writing in my notebook. And when I said that I was lacking knowledge, you thought I was joking. But I believe you can never have enough knowledge."

Maxim's wife and daughters missed him very much. Indeed, he, by Elena's definition, "was a festive person, and his presence created an atmosphere of joy and love."

For Maxim, each trip his dear family made to Kamyshin was a cause for celebration. He would mysteriously find a way to get onto their train as it was still approaching, and while his wife and daughters looked out the window to find him on the platform, he would make his way through the train and appear in their compartment with a bouquet of flowers.

In summer 1956, nine-year-old Elena spent her vacation in Kamyshin and had an unforgettable adventure. She had the chance to see her father in action in the role of a real leader who was accustomed to taking responsibility for those around him under extreme circumstances.

The Chibisovs spent a day at the beach with the families of two other officers. As Elena recalls,

> It was a hot and sunny day, but dad suddenly looked at the sky and said, "There's a storm approaching." He sensed this from some sign that only he knew, some barely perceptible movement of the clouds. The sky was his habitat and he was able to give a very accurate assessment of the air elements. On this occasion, he correctly predicted that it would be a strong storm and gave the command, "We're getting our things together and leaving immediately."

Cadets carefully listen to the story of flights across the continents and oceans.

We were on the left, low-lying banks of the Volga, where Kamyshin residents usually sunbathe on the nice sandy beaches. We had to return to the right, elevated banks, where a car with a driver was waiting for us near the pier. We had to cross the Volga on a four-seat motor boat, and there was only one for the three families. On father's orders, the family of Afonin, the director of the school's airfield maintenance service, crossed the river first. The motor boat returned about half an hour later and picked up the family of Turkov, the head of the garrison headquarters. Our turn came only after father's subordinates and their families had made their way to the right bank. We set off: the boat driver, dad, mom and I. The storm hit right when we were in the middle of the Volga. The downpour was so strong that we couldn't see anything around us. The waves began to rise. The motor became flooded and died. Dad tried to row, but one of the oars broke out of the oarlock and fell overboard. The motor boat was being carried by the current, which was pretty strong in the lower Volga.

Mom was sitting on the bow of the boat, trying to cover herself from the rain with an umbrella, and suddenly yelled, "Oh no, my umbrella flew away!" This was followed by, "Oh no, my sandals floated away!" Dad gave the command: "Everyone sit in the middle of the boat and hold on to the bench!" The driver had lost sight of us at this moment due to the wall of rain and was rushing around the shore with no idea what to do. We were carried down the Volga for several kilometers. It was only after the rain let up that someone noticed us and sent a motor boat to help us. It took our boat in tow to the pier. It was not a pleasant adventure, but I was never afraid because dad was there and he always knew what to do.

Another time, the whole family experienced an even more serious situation while vacationing in the Crimea in 1953. In those years, we spent each summer on the Crimean shores, particularly since Mom always wanted to visit her relatives in Simferopol—her brother Isaak and sister Marochka. One day, while at the Defense Ministry's health resort in Hurzuf, the whole family went out to sea for a trip on a small tour boat. The sea was choppy, and soon a real storm began. The waves began to flow over the sides from both the left and the right. Trying to escape the water, people began rushing about the boat, running from one side to the other. With no balance, the captain was unable to even out the boat in relation to the waves, and there was a danger that the boat might overturn. At that moment, I saw my dad standing tall on the bow of the boat, even though the waves were lashing at his back. Barely able to stay on his feet, he yelled at the top of his lungs, "Comrades! Stop panicking! Stay in your seats! You are preventing the captain from navigating the boat!" People stopped in their tracks as they listened to and obeyed his commands. Soon the boat leveled off, and we were able to moor. In this situation,

Major General M.N. Chibisov at the command tower of the airfield Kamyshin Aviation School. 1956.

Dad once again distinguished himself as a person who was able to take responsibility for other lives, soberly and calmly assess the situation, and foresee the possibility of tragic consequences. He always knew how to take command and convince people to trust him.

The vacations and holidays, with their cherished family time, flew by quickly. Maxim continued to live in separation from the ones he loved most and waited for an opportunity to return to Moscow. This moment approached as changes occurred in the USSR Armed Forces.

In February 1955, Georgy Zhukov took over as defense minister (Bulganin replaced Malenkov as chairman of the Council of Ministers at this time). The new defense minister gave the Navy only a supporting role in the strategic plans for developing Soviet defense capabilities, which were to center on ground and strategic forces armed with ballistic missiles and nuclear warheads.

USSR Navy Admiral and Deputy Defense Minister Nikolai Kuznetsov believed the Navy could and should perform independent functions in protecting the country's interests.

The disagreements in the approaches for building the Armed Forces led to a heated conflict between the two prominent military figures, which Admiral Kuznetsov was destined to lose since Marshal Zhukov had vast authority not only in military circles but also among the country's top political leaders.

In early 1956, Nikolai Kuznetsov was dismissed in disgrace, as he was held accountable for a disaster that had taken place in the Navy: the destruction of the *Novorossiysk* battleship. Many of the former commander's initiatives were eliminated and the responsibility of the Navy command was substantially curtailed.

Among other things, the decision was made to unify the system for training flight and aviation maintenance personnel, under which the Navy's aviation schools were transferred to the Air Force of the Soviet Army. In July 1956, this decision entered into force with respect to the Kamyshin school as well.

Maxim had no desire to move from naval aviation to land-based aviation. The standard program for training army pilots, which was considered exemplary, was fundamentally different from the program with which the future naval pilots were trained under the leadership of General Chibisov. In order to stay at the school, he would have had to undergo retraining himself, and the previous experience he had accumulated over his long period of service would have been rendered useless.

At the time, military aviation was switching to jet propulsion. Piloting the new high-speed planes the military was receiving involved gravitational forces that even young pilots with excellent athletic abilities had a difficult time withstanding. Meanwhile, Maxim was already over fifty.

He summed up his flying career in his autobiographical notes: "Over the years of service in the Air Force, my total flight time was 2,978 hours (a total of approximately four months in the air). I flew without any wrecks [incidents resulting in damage to aircraft]—just one engine accident—on 20 types of aircraft, starting with the U-1 and ending with the Il-28 jet."

The command of the Mine and Torpedo Aviation School before the departure of M.N. Chibisov to Moscow. 1957.]

However, he was unable to fly on par with the young, strong guys and on the new jets. He did not want to be any worse at flying than his subordinates, and he did not intend to stick around as a non-flying director of the aviation school.

He finally left this post in May 1957 after completing all the work for which he had been sent to Kamyshin. The school had been built, and the training process was running smoothly. The members of Maxim's first graduate class, who received lieutenant epaulettes, had scattered to various combat units and formations of the Navy. The objectives initially set by Colonel General Preobrazhensky had been implemented in full.

Maxim was invited to Moscow for an interesting and important job in his area of specialization.

His superiors did not want to let him go from the school. Maxim submitted a request to the Air Force commander-in-chief, Marshal Konstantin Vershinin, on three occasions and only received consent to transfer to his new position in Moscow on the third try.

Jet Frontline Bomber IL-28 was the 20th type of the airplane flown by M.N. Chibisov during the years of his military service.

16.4 In the GRU System

Major General Chibisov's next place of work was the Military Diplomatic Academy (MDA) of the USSR General Staff, the military school that specialized in training intelligence officers.[25]

This military college was established during World War II on the core of the Higher Diplomatic School, the Higher Intelligence School,

---

[25] The period of Maxim Chibisov's employment at the Military Diplomatic Academy of the GRU of the General Staff was reconstructed based on his diaries with the use of materials on the MDA and GRU that have entered the public domain, including from the website agentura.ru and *Wikipedia*.

the Institute of Oriental Culture, and several other military and civilian higher educational institutions. The MDA reported directly to the Main Intelligence Directorate of the General Staff (more commonly known as the GRU, based on the Russian acronym). According to his official status, the MDA director was also a deputy chief of the GRU.

The main contingent of MDA students were future members of diplomatic missions, attachés, and the foreign institutions of the Soviet Union as well as officers and heads of intelligence departments at major headquarters (at the level of military districts of the army and navy).

Maxim had a long and highly fruitful relationship with the military intelligence agency. Intelligence had played a significant role in his initial profession as a seaplane pilot. When he'd gone to work for the NSRA, he'd been put on a special list at the intelligence agency and officially regarded as one of its employees who had been seconded to a civilian agency.

In 1957, Maxim joined the GRU staff on a permanent basis, initially holding the position of acting senior lecturer in the Naval Discipline Department of the Military Diplomatic Academy. According to his memoirs, "my service at the Academy began with writing lectures and reading them to students. So the school year was rather stressful. I had to work regardless of the time: starting from 9 a.m. until 9–10 p.m." The main reason he had to work long days was that the rules of secrecy strictly prohibited him from removing the materials he used to prepare the lectures as well as the lecture texts themselves from the academy; thus, preparing for lessons at home was not an option.

Maxim's lectures received highly positive reviews from both the academy administrators and his students.

In the late 1950s and early 1960s, the intelligence officers, counterintelligence officers, and various special diplomats of all the major global powers had interesting jobs. The world's political map was changing rapidly. The old colonial empires were collapsing, and new states were emerging. Local conflicts were breaking out, and revolutionary and counterrevolutionary coups were taking place. The foreign policy activities of the Soviet Union had taken on a global nature. At the same time, the USSR was finding friends in some of the most remote backwoods of Africa, Asia, and Latin America.

Aid to these newfound friends was largely coordinated and sent through the GRU. Therefore, the GRU officials needed well-trained specialists to take part in operations being implemented in distant lands.

The knowledge and diverse experience of naval pilot Maxim Chibisov proved to be highly useful in the process of training these specialists. After successfully completing a one-year probationary period, he was confirmed as a senior lecturer.

In March 1959, there was a change in leadership at the MDA. Colonel General Alexander Petrushevsky retired as academy director and was replaced by Lieutenant General Vasily Khlopov, a career military intelligence officer with vast combat and diplomatic experience. Under Khlopov, the teaching of all subjects related to aviation and aviation technology was to be concentrated in the Department of the Air Force. While remaining a senior lecturer, Maxim also served concurrently as deputy chair of this department. From all appearances, he took over the teaching of a special cycle of subjects related to naval aviation.

A note then appeared in Major General Chibisov's personal file indicating that he was "at the disposal of the GRU of the General Staff" from September 1, 1960, to February 24, 1961. This means he was assigned a post outside of the MDA for almost six months—presumably to perform some sort of special task. This time, the assignment did not require him to leave Moscow. We can assume he was brought in to help develop schemes and plans for some kind of special operation involving a significant naval aviation component.

The top brass were apparently satisfied with the results of his work "at the disposal of the GRU of the General Staff." Upon completing his assignment, Maxim was invited to the personnel department of the General Staff, where he received an offer to head the Operational and Tactical Intelligence Department, one of three existing at the MDA. In his diaries, Maxim says he:

> did not express a desire [for this position], stating that I already had a firm grasp on my teaching work and requested that I be left in this position. But they argued: "You are a general and, according to your stature, you should hold the position of chair of a department or sub-department." After finally agreeing, I was appointed chair of the department by an order of the defense minister.

Arrival of Major General
M.N. Chibisov to the airfield
in Kamyshin. 1956.

Major General M.N. Chibisov at
the helm of the IL-28 bomber.

Meeting the the Commander of
the Yeysk Aviation School. 1955.

Skiing class in the School.
Kamyshin, 1956.

Inspection of the school by
Marshal S.K. Timoshenko
and Lieutenant General
S.D. Prutkov.]

Head of the intelligence officers'
meetings Major General of
Aviation M.N. Chibisov heading
the ceremonial convoy. Sokolovka
village, Moscow district, 1963.

M.N. Chibisov with the elder
daughter Emma. 1954.

M.N. Chibisov with a nephew
N.P. Chibisov - a pilot and
a frontline soldier. 1955.

The first row: the head of the school Major General Chibisov, Deputy Politics Department Colonel Podstavkin, Deputy Flight Department Menyailenko, the head of the garrison headquarters Turkov, Komsomol leader Ryndin.

On vacation in
Sochi. 1955

By the airplane Yak-
18Y with the wife and
the daughter Elena.

The handshake of
the General.

At the sanatorium
'Archangelskoe', 1957.

The daughters Elena
and Emma, 1951.

Flowers for the wife
from the airfield
in Ryazan.

CHAPTER 17

The General's Later Years

17.1 Fulfilling a Dream

Maxim's promotion aided in resolving the long-standing problem of providing the Chibisov family with its own apartment. In 1960, the administration of the Military Diplomatic Academy found a way to help the highly valued specialist and department chair by allocating a small apartment from its reserves, which was given to the Chibisovs' neighbors in exchange for their room. As a result, the Chibisovs assumed control of all 47 square meters (506 square feet) of living space in the apartment on Sadovo-Kudrinskaya Street.

Rosaly finally had the chance to fully demonstrate her domestic talents and arrange the apartment as she had long desired, although cooking remained her main focus. She tried to limit her calorie intake because she was worried about excess weight, as were most women of her age, but she took great pleasure in cooking for her husband and daughters, who did not suffer from a lack of appetite, as well as any guests who came to the Chibisov home.

Sometimes, after returning home from shopping with bags full of groceries, barely able to catch her breath, Rosaly would devour a French roll (a popular item at Soviet stores) she had just purchased at the store.

Her daughters, surprised, asked, "Mom, what are you doing? You know you're only going to torment yourself with diets later."

"I survived three famines, and there is nothing tastier than bread in life!" was her reply.

Maxim's salary allowed them to live very comfortably, but neither he nor Rosalia had a penchant for senselessly acquiring things. They bought what they needed for themselves and the children and spared no expense in this regard.

Like the other members of the high-latitude expeditions, Maxim had received large bonuses from working in the Arctic. Many Polar Aviation Office pilots had even managed to acquire personal cars.

Around that time, though, Emma entered a music school, where she started learning to play the harp. Instead of buying a car, her caring father spent all of his Arctic bonus money on this expensive musical instrument, which his daughter learned to play.

On vacation at the sanatorium 'Crimea', 1962.

Major General Chibisov acquired his first personal car a few years later, when he was already working at the Military Diplomatic Academy. The car was a Pobeda, the most popular brainchild of the postwar Soviet auto industry. In 1965, Maxim bought a Volga, a more reputable and prestigious model.

He was a good driver. While in America, he had spent many miles behind the wheel and come to appreciate the advantages of owning an "iron horse" over walking.

The loving father also instilled an appreciation for cars in his youngest daughter: he put her behind the wheel and sat in the passenger's seat. He explained how to control the levers and pedals, and she began driving with no fear. After all, her dad was right by her side. Elena was only 14 years old at the time.

Her elder sister, Emma, was already a grown woman. She had graduated from the Philology Department of Moscow State University and was taking her first independent steps in life. Elena, entering that anxious and joyful period of early adolescence, would not break away from her parents for a long time.

The family often took trips outside the city in their father's car. They would have picnics or go out picking berries and mushrooms. Maxim was not particularly into fishing or hunting (even though he had been given a hunting weapon in the Far East prior to the war). But he was an avid mushroom picker.

One day Elena and her father, along with some of his colleagues, took several cars out to an area that had an abundance of mushrooms. Her beloved father got so caught up in searching for mushrooms that he forgot about his daughter and did not come out of the forest until he had completely filled up his basket, the bags inside the basket, and even his own trousers, which he had tied into a knot and made into a crude sack. Then, after dumping all the loot into the trunk of his car, he went back to the forest. When they arrived home, Rosaly gasped when she saw the mountain of mushrooms that would have to be sorted and prepared.

Another tradition the Chibisovs established was going to the Rossiya movie theater on weekends to see all the fantastic movies that came out one after another in the 1950s and 1960s. The film *Clear Sky* made the most powerful impression on Maxim. He seemed to be imagining what it would have been like to experience the dramatic fate of the pilot and hero of the film. After all, something similar could have happened to combat officer Chibisov if, for instance, he had been unable to escape from Tallinn after it had been seized by the Germans.

Now and then, Maxim took Rosalia to the theater. She enjoyed attending the opera and operettas most of all. She remembered listening to numerous musical performances on phonograph records as a child, and now she was able to hear the luminaries of the Soviet music scene perform live.

This was how the Chibisovs lived their lives, which were filled with ordinary events that gave them the most common human joys. It was probably a happy time for both Maxim and his wife.

17.2 The Last Parade

In summer 1962, Major General Chibisov was appointed commander of a garrison for the summer training of junior officers in the village of Sokolovka outside Moscow.

He brought his wife and youngest daughter, who had just completed the ninth grade, to this summer training camp. There, fifteen-year-old Elena Chibisova first realized what exactly was hidden behind the simple words *military service*.

One day Maxim took his daughter along to training exercises held 300 kilometers (186 miles) outside the base. For the rest of her life, she would remember how, after this difficult trip, her father listened to the reports of the junior commanders on the results of the exercises and then thoroughly questioned the military doctor about the health of the personnel. The exercises had been tortuous, and there had been injuries of varying severity. After speaking with the doctor, General Chibisov called for additional special transport to take those who had been hurt to the hospital.

The training exercises of 1963 were a sort of last parade for General Chibisov.

On August 13, 1963, he was once again transferred to the disposal of the GRU of the General Staff, but this time, it was not to perform some special assignment. He was temporarily taken off staff, as if he would be given a new appointment. This all took place within the framework of events surrounding the replacement of the GRU administration.

On February 2, 1963, Army General Ivan Serov was dismissed as GRU chief. He was one of the most prominent representatives of the cohort of old special agents (during and after the war, he held important posts in state security agencies, he was the KGB chairman from 1954 to 1958, and he was considered a reliable source of support for Khrushchev). Officially, he was dismissed with disgrace following the exposure of an American spy: GRU Colonel Oleg Penkovsky, who had been protected by the GRU chief. In fact, though, Serov had a long list of previous sins: he had been involved in many crimes of the "cult of personality" era. Following the famous decisions made at the 22nd Congress of the CPSU and the removal of Stalin's body from the mausoleum, the decision was made to get rid of Stalin's hawk.

The new GRU chief was Colonel General Pyotr Ivashutin, who hailed from the First Main Directorate of the KGB and was regarded as a top-tier professional intelligence officer.[26] He strongly rebuked the activities of his predecessor. This was expected under the good-administrative-tone rules of the Khrushchev era. Moreover, Ivashutin considered Serov an amateur in matters involving operational intelligence work—and not without reason. In order to raise the work of the military intelligence agency to the proper

---

[26] Pyotr Ivashutin headed the GRU from 1963 to 1986 and is regarded as one of the most prominent intelligence officers of the twentieth century. See A. Utkin, "The Peter the Great of National Intelligence," *NVO-NG*, September 18, 2009.

level, the new chief brought with him from the First Main Department new employees who took over a number of senior positions. This resulted in a surplus of staff in the GRU system with high officer and general ranks and was followed by the standard reshuffling of personnel, which covered various GRU departments, including the Military Diplomatic Academy.

Vasily Khlopov kept his position as academy director, although he was required to radically revise the curriculum and shake up the teaching staff.

In the confusion that engulfed the MDA, Major General Chibisov found himself in a vulnerable position since, despite all his services to the intelligence agency, he did not have an education in special intelligence. Thus, he was one of the easiest people to dismiss from the academy. That was exactly what happened when the position of department chair was apparently needed to employ some general who had come over from the GRU central office.

Maxim was not fired, since there had been no complaints about his work, but he was dismissed from the staff as part of yet another reorganization (perhaps purposely contrived).

He apparently anticipated that everything would work out with a new appointment and continued to wait patiently. Eventually, he was offered the post of an attaché in London. This would have been a great place for someone younger than General Chibisov who wished to establish a career in diplomacy. For Maxim, however, the position of an attaché was unacceptable for a variety of reasons. He was not predisposed toward diplomatic work, although he had demonstrated remarkable diplomatic skills in 1944–1945 in relations with his US military counterparts. He was turned off by the prospect of going abroad, since he wanted to live in the familiar environment of Moscow; plus, he had promised Rosaly there would be no more relocations. He saw no possibility of reconciling diplomatic service with his family interests, considering he had two daughters whose futures he had to look out for.

Things moved so quickly that Maxim did not even have to prepare any "alternate airfield" for himself. By declining the offer to switch to diplomatic work, he was forced to retire from the Armed Forces "for health reasons." His honorable dismissal was registered by a decree of the Defense Ministry dated January 23, 1964, and he retained the right to wear his military uniform and other privileges granted to honored and respected defenders of the nation.

17.3 Retired but Still in the Service

Maxim wrote in his diary, "I was extremely upset about leaving military service since I was a patriot of military science and had dedicated my entire adult life to this cause. I served a total of 36 calendar years, or 44 years taking into account flight and military long service."

While retired, he did not simply want to sit at home and receive a general's pension. "After leaving the service, I thought about where I could make myself useful and began pondering my skills and training. I collected my thoughts—don't waste time, don't get used to this inactive life!—and began persistently looking for work in my field."

Within a month, he managed to find a job he really liked as a senior research associate at the Aviation Research Institute. He went back to work. He got acquainted with the administration of the institution, his direct superiors in the department, and the pilots. Maxim quickly acquired a firm grasp of the environment, the work conditions, and their objectives, which he successfully accomplished.

The institute at which Maxim found work was number-based, as they called it at the time (i.e., it was supposed to be referred to as a certain military unit number). The institute's main building, which had no sign, was located near Aeroport metro station. However, senior research associate Chibisov worked at this building only initially. He then had to travel to the institute's facilities located in Monino and Chkalovskaya. He enjoyed the work; despite becoming a civilian, he continued doing the same thing to which he had devoted the best years of his life in the military service.

M.N. Chibisov (in the first row second from the left) among the employees of the Research Institute for the Air Force. 1969.

He later wrote in his notes with some satisfaction, "I quickly gained credibility among my comrades and the command ... I actively took part in volunteer work ... I was awarded certificates of honor, a watch and the title 'Shock Worker of Communist Labor.'"

Meanwhile, life went on as usual. Maxim's daughters became adults, earned degrees, and got married. The issue of housing once again became a problem, although it was ultimately resolved through joint efforts. The families of Emilia Telyatnikova and Elena Rubina (née Chibisova) acquired their own apartments, and Maxim and Rosaly moved from noisy Sadovo-Kudrinskaya Street to a comfortable three-room apartment on Butlerova Street in a quiet, green neighborhood near Belyaevo metro station.

After working for fourteen years at the highly secret research institute, Maxim finally earned a well-deserved rest in April 1978 at the age of 72 as he recorded the main result of his career in the service with one line in his diary: "Thus, I dedicated a total of 50 calendar years (58 years including length of service) to the Air Force of our country."

After this, Major General Chibisov did not sit around idly. He remained an active community worker and often spoke at meetings of veterans. He maintained extensive correspondence with the friends and colleagues he had met over the years. He was invited to schools to meet with the younger generation, with whom he shared a lot of useful and interesting information.

Maxim spent long hours at his desk. He was always reading and preferred military history and memoirs. He made detailed studies of certain books that particularly grabbed his attention. He put his diaries in order, supplementing them with entries about events he had previously failed to record. He was aided in this by extensive correspondence with former Air Force colleagues and veterans.

Such correspondence revealed a startling fact concerning the work of his Special Operations Group [Project Zebra] in the United States in 1944–1945. An excerpt from a letter Maxim received from pilot Lev Yavoklev describes the situation eloquently:

> Both Koshchakov and I were denied identification cards as "WWII veterans." This is based on the fact that the Special Operations Group was not included in the list of units that were involved in the war. This special group didn't exist?? If it did, it should have a number. We don't know where to look for it. What should we do?

It's a shame that we did everything we could for the victory but we are not deservedly connected to this. Please help me figure this out. Advise me what to do.

My personal file does not even contain any award recommendations (it's said that in Siberia awards were granted to people who were far from the front).

It states that I simply went on a trip abroad from the 16th Reconnaissance Aviation Regiment of the Pacific Fleet Air Force (why and for what purpose is not clear to anyone). My personal file contains evaluations signed by you, but again this isn't considered proof for the title of "WWII veteran."

Waiting for your instructions. Yours, Lev. 1985.

In an effort to eliminate this injustice and attaching special value to the experience gained during the command of the special group, Maxim wrote a lengthy article and called it "Across Continents and Oceans." He wanted to publish it in the *Maritime Collection* but was denied on grounds of secrecy. This article might have attracted the attention of experts in the field of Soviet aviation history as well as the history of Soviet-American relations during World War II.

17.4 The Way Things Were

General Chibisov's daughters have numerous memories of their parents from the period when their father retired from active military service. While retired, Maxim could devote more time and attention to his loved ones, and they basked in his kind, warm aura as one would in the gentle, unobtrusive rays of the evening sun. His youngest daughter Elena Rubina recalls,

> When I think about what made our father unique, I come to the conclusion that the main secret to his charm was his ability to understand and empathize with people as well as do everything possible to help. It was only when we began raising our own children that we realized the values of his parenting system. He taught us by example how to feel, think and respect the opinions of others.

The 1960s and 1970s were generally a happy time for the Chibisovs, although Elena recalls that her

> mother began experiencing health problems in the mid-1960s. She initially suffered from angina. This was

followed by numerous fractures. It seemed like God was sending our parents all kinds of new tests in order to confirm their devotion to one another. Our mother had eight fractures in ten years! When she began learning how to master crutches once again, the entire hospital watched as dad taught mom how to walk. Our parents experienced the entire range of adversity and joys over their 53 years together. The health and mood of one of them instantly passed to the other.

Another important source of positive emotions for Maxim and Rosaly was their country house. Elena recalls,

> Living in the center of Moscow on the Garden Ring Road, our parents always felt the need for fresh air. We often went to visit our friends at their country houses, especially the Danilovs and Demyanovs. These were the families of father's colleagues from Polar Aviation. We lived with them in a single house and remained friends for many years.

At that time, even simple polar pilots received a hectare of land on which to build a country house in the prestigious communities of Mamontovka, Zhukovka and others. But dad was always opposed to any property.

It was only in 1965 that our friends and I persuaded our parents to take a small plot—the standard 600 square meters (718 square yards) that were given to anyone who wanted them. The plot was located 43 kilometers (27 miles) from the Moscow Ring Road near the city of Elektrougli close to a village that used to be called Zmeinoye Boloto. This swampy area was impassable in some areas and required huge efforts to be developed. All the stumps had to be uprooted, a well needed to be dug on the property, lights had to be installed, and they cooked their food on a kerosene stove. Eventually, a panel house was built in which they lived quite comfortably.

Dad dug up the entire plot with his own hands and planted all kinds of fruit crops. He was extremely proud of his collection of tomatoes, cucumbers and, especially, his strawberries. Mom kept herself busy with flowers, jams and pickling. They took great pleasure in doing all the chores that needed to be performed at the country house. Evidently, our dad's peasant soul was delighted about returning to the land.

In 1965, the Soviet Union triumphantly celebrated the twentieth anniversary of the victory over Nazi Germany. In previous years, celebrations had been fairly modest, but this time, the top party and government officials decided to mark the holiday with the proper pomp. The traditional spring military parade was moved from May 1 to May 9. This parade in particular had an impressive historical component with infantrymen marching in World War II–era uniforms, cargo trucks, the famous Katyusha launchers, and T-34 tanks. For the first time, the Victory Banner that had been raised over the Reichstag building in Berlin in 1945, one of the greatest national relics, was brought out for all to see.

For the first time Major General M.N. Chibisov openly demonstrates the map of the Catalinas routes of 1944-1945. Moscow, 1976.

As was his custom, Maxim went to watch the parade on Red Square and was accompanied by Elena.

As they returned home along the festive Moscow streets, they were greeted everywhere by older-looking gentlemen resembling Maxim in military uniforms with decorations and medals—veterans. At that time, there were still many veterans around who were full of enough strength and energy to lead an active life. They became the main heroes of the victory anniversary celebrations. The veterans were honored, congratulated, and given flowers.

Elena asked her father, "Dad, are you a veteran?"

He laughed and replied, "My dear, I'm a veteran of the front and three fleets!"

That was how eighteen-year-old Elena Chibisova, while on the verge of adulthood, first realized her father was a true hero. After all, he was not in the habit of talking about the deeds he had performed during the war and in peacetime.

Elena describes another memorable event from this time and her father's reaction:

In summer 1971, while on maternity leave, I spent an

entire month with my parents at the country house. It was like total immersion in childhood. Dad and I did everything together just like we used to do. We even managed to paint our little panel house.

However, on June 30 we received a huge shock when we learned that three cosmonauts had been killed on the Soyuz-11 mission: Vladislav Volkov, Viktor Patsayev and Georgy Dobrovolsky. Dad endured this event like a personal tragedy. He could not imagine a situation where the cosmonauts had "landed safely" yet were found sitting in their chairs with no signs of life. This was the first space flight with no spacesuits, and the crew capsule depressurized during preparations for reentry. Dad took all the successes and failures of Soviet space exploration very much to heart.

At his dacha with the granddaughter Ksyusha, 1974.

Maxim also took the problems and concerns of his daughters very close to heart. According to Elena,

> Dad had a knack for unexpectedly showing up at the right place at the right time (as he put it—for moral support). Such was the case, for example, on my graduation night. When all the events came to an end, including the walk to Red Square and back to the school, I saw dad waiting in the far corner of the assembly hall—at five in the morning. He had come to get me right when it was time to go home.

Dad was always there in difficult situations. He would wrap his arms around my shoulders and say, "It's okay, dear. We'll get through this too." And at critical moments he became a real lifesaver.

When I was preparing to defend my thesis in economics, my academic adviser suddenly discovered that the findings of my research work were not politically correct for that time. She panicked and demanded a radical revision of the text I had prepared, but there was no time left for this. I anticipated major problems.

Dad put on his general's uniform, went to see my adviser, and persuaded her to allow me to defend my thesis as I had originally presented it. At the time, I couldn't understand how he had managed to pull it off. Now, with my own life experience, I can imagine how dad might have spoken to her about the responsibility of teachers for the fate of their students. After all, he never let any of his cadets out of his sight during their first solo flights. Dad always gave timely corrective commands if the young pilots made any dangerous errors due to a lack of experience.

I could always rely on dad for help: not only to resolve serious problems but also for ordinary everyday difficulties. For instance, when my children were little, he often took on the duty of a babysitter so that I could go to the theater or visit friends.

At the same time, he tried not to burden anyone unnecessarily with his presence. Once my nephew Kirill was scheduled to perform at a concert at the music school, and his mother, my sister Emma, was supposed to accompany him. This was during the time when dad was very sick and he had a hard time getting around the city without any help. He didn't ask to attend his grandson's concert so as not to burden his eldest daughter with having to worry about his transportation. But once the concert began, she looked around the hall and saw her dad sitting in the last row. He had made it to the concert on his own.

The Chibisovs began experiencing their most serious health problems after Maxim retired from the research institute. Elena recalls,

> In July 1986, our parents ended up in different hospitals at almost the same time. This was actually right around the time we were planning for major celebrations: mom was turning 75 on July 29 and dad would be 80 on August 28. We had long ago decided to celebrate their birthdays on the same day and gather together all our loved ones as was customary in our family. Unfortunately, fate had other plans, and we celebrated mom's birthday in July at the 64th City Hospital and dad's birthday in August at the Burdenko Hospital.

In August, Emma and her son went on vacation, and before she returned I was literally bouncing back and forth between the two hospitals and my own children: I would go see dad one day and mom the next. The main tragedy for our parents wasn't so much their illness as it was being apart. There weren't any mobile phones at that time yet and they both repeated the same song: "My dear, we are completely separated. I would at least like to hear his (her) voice!!!"

The Marine Aviation Veterans' meeting on the Victory Day. Left to right: Filimonov, Odinoskov, Chibisov, Alekseev, Barhatov, Maslyn. 9th of May, 1984.

The Victory Day celebration. Maxim Nikolaevitch and Rosalia Borisovna Chibisov with the daughters Elena (left) and Emilia. 9th of May 1985.

The display of the ranks and positions of Major General M.N. Chibisov

When mom was released, we went to the hospital on the very first day. Mom was in such a hurry to see dad that she even refused to stop by the pharmacy for medicine. "Dad is waiting, anxious, and keeping an eye out for us." Indeed, he really was waiting for us, walking along the fence. Once she saw him, mom jumped out of the car without any assistance but found herself in the middle of the street and miraculously avoided getting run over. She saw nothing else around her except him. Their meeting was heartwarming. He couldn't take his eyes off of mom, kissed her hands, rubbed her swollen belly, and told her how beautiful she was. As was his wont, dad had prepared a treat for us: fruit, candy—everything you could buy at a small hospital store in 1986. We sat there until ten in the evening.

I took mom to my country house. Her condition became worse with each passing day. She rapidly lost her strength and couldn't eat anything. We walked around our property and even made it to the wicket fence a few times. But the next day she only got halfway there and was afraid she wouldn't have the strength to make it back. At one point, she pleaded, "Dear, take me to the doctors. I don't understand what's wrong with me!"

It was only because of my persistence that we managed to get her sent back to the hospital. In the admission room, they immediately suggested that it was pulmonary edema and I realized from the doctors' reaction that it was time to prepare for the worst.

Her body became intoxicated as the tumor decayed. After a few days on an IV, though, mom began to feel a little better. Her appetite returned, she cheered up, and once again began speaking to and singing for her neighbors in the ward. All the way up until the end of her life, she remained a woman to the core and maintained the ability to please people and attract their attention.

Dad was also unaware of his awful diagnosis and complained about his ulcers being aggravated. He was ordered to check into the hospital every three months (supposedly for a blood transfusion, but actually for chemotherapy).

I must say that, despite his high rank, dad was extremely humble and grateful. When he was released, he felt it was his duty not only to thank the doctors for their warmth and care, but also the nurses and orderlies. He knew all of them by name and found kind words for each person.

Emilia recalls,

> In the fall, mom was admitted to Burdenko Hospital. She believed that the military doctors could help her. Dad was living alone by himself at this time. On October 25, he and I went to see mom at the hospital. He walked slowly through the hospital courtyard and not as steadily as before, but he straightened his back and entered mom's room with a pep in his step so as not to upset her. They stared at each other with adoring eyes and couldn't stop talking.

Shortly before November 7, I told mom that dad missed her dearly and wanted me to take him to see her during the holidays. Mom knew that dad was to be hospitalized again in the gastroenterology unit before mid-November. To my surprise, she suddenly said, "You know, don't bring dad here during the holidays. I've lost a lot of weight and he will be upset. He will be admitted here soon anyway." Even at the very end, she was above all concerned about not causing him any distress.

Now I understand what a happy life our parents lived given that, through all the great trials of separation, war and illness, they were able to preserve their love until the last day.

Unfortunately, they would not have the chance to see each other again. Mom passed away on November 11. We went to see him the next day and he said, "It appears that a bed has become available. My hospital bag is ready. Shall we go?" I didn't know how to tell him. I could only bring myself to utter the phrase, "Mom took a turn for the worse." He looked at me intently. "She's gone?" he asked. Then he picked up the phone and gave up his place at the hospital. That evening my sister and I convinced dad to try to sleep, and we sat there all night listening to his breathing. As if delirious, he constantly twitched, sobbed, and called out for mom. For several months afterwards, he referred to both my sister and I as Rosochka (Rosaly).

Elena recalls,

> After mom died, dad stayed with me or at Emma's and sometimes at his own apartment on Butlerova Street. He didn't want to change anything in the house or his lifestyle. "I want everything here to remain the same as it was when your mom was alive," he said. He no longer went to the country house. "Everything there reminds me of her," he said.

Numerous pages in dad's diary are devoted to his "beloved Rosochka," who for more than 50 years was his "guiding star," "war bride" and "guardian angel." "She took care of the serenity in the family, preserving my health and eliminating any irritating emotions," dad wrote. "She raised the children in the same spirit. The comfort and warmth in our home gave me the strength to serve and to make the proper decisions on the ground and in the sky. Our family always maintained order and loved and cared for one another."

Towards the end, he spent more time at his home on Bulterova Street: his spirits improved, he worked on his diaries every day and wrote captions for his pictures. He hoped that one day this material would be published.

In spring 1988, we took dad for a visit to mom's grave. He had yet to see the monument and we wanted to show him that we had done everything just like he had wanted it. It was the first week of May and it was very warm out. We sat him on a bench near the fence around the grave and went to get water for the flowers. We also wanted to give dad a chance to be alone there for a little while. When we returned, we were frightened. Dad was standing there with his arms around the monument (the huge pink stone had been heated from the sun) and, despite being a person not prone to mysticism, said, "Girls, look! She's warm. Rosochka is waiting for me." He explained to us in great detail and specifics what we were supposed to do after he died and how we were to place the inscription and photo on the monument. And we listened as we choked back tears.

In January 1989, dad checked into the hospital for another round of chemotherapy. This time the treatment was unsuccessful. He refused to eat and became very weak. In addition, a quarantine was in effect due to a flu outbreak, and we weren't even allowed to see him. We were frustrated that we couldn't provide him with emotional or physical support (giving him juice, caviar and home-cooked food). I spoke with the physician in charge every day and begged him to make an exception for us and allow us to see our father, but to no avail. The instructions which the doctors were following proved to be more powerful than any reasonable arguments or requests.

When dad was released, he had lost so much weight that we hardly even recognized him. Yet, every day he got up, shaved, exercised, got dressed for breakfast, and sat down at the table just as he had in previous years—even on Sundays when he wouldn't have gone to work anyway. On February 23, he received congratulations all day in honor of Soviet Army Day. For three more weeks, he kept a stiff upper lip, fulfilling the doctor's orders and speaking on the phone with his relatives and close friends. March 12 was the first day when he did not come out for breakfast. But he still read the newspapers and listened to the news on the television.

He spent under two weeks in bed, but he was conscious the entire time, recalling his plans. When he found me or my sister by his bed in the mornings, he would immediately ask, "What happened? Why aren't you at work?" He would agree to have breakfast in bed and always tried to put us at ease: "Do what you need to do. I'll read and wait for you: one of you at lunch and the other at dinner."

Prior to departing this world, while still fully lucid, Maxim found the strength to lift the spirits of his two daughters in the same way he had once lifted the spirits of his flight crew in times of grave danger.

Elena recalls,

> Long before he died, dad asked me to go to the military commissariat with him. He introduced me to the military commissar and instructed him: "If anything ever happens to me, help my daughters lay me to rest." Dad made a list of people who should be called on his own. He understood how hard it would be for us on the day we had to bid farewell to him and tried in advance to make this day a little bit easier on us.

His post-mortem diagnosis stated: "Coronary heart disease and pulmonary edema." Not a word about cancer.

We buried him next to mom at Khovanskoye Cemetery.

Lots of people came to say goodbye to our father: members of the Aviation Research Institute, polar explorers, pilots from the ferrying groups, relatives, friends, his colleagues from Krasnaya Rechka. They all spoke many warm and kind words. Each one of them wanted to share their personal memories associated with Maxim.

The pilot and poet Pavel Filimonov read the following touching poem:

> He has not parted with his uniform even though he has taken his last sleep,
> He was our commander, like a military father.
> He spent his life within the ranks from his early youth,
> He was carried by the engine in the challenging skies.
> His whole life was tied to the navy, where he was a renowned pilot,
> And a brave warrior in battle for his conscience and not out of fear.
> He defended the honor of the homeland in military affairs hundreds of times,
> Many of us grew up in the service under his command.
> His attributes included nobility and culture,
> On the banks of the Amur, we all learned from him.
> A proud warrior is laid to rest like a living fire extinguished,
> Honored with good fame and everlasting memories.
> Strong in spirit, he burned as a bright flame,
> May you rest in peace, our esteemed general!

The signature under the text of the poem reads, "In memory of Major General of Aviation Chibisov from colleagues at Krasnaya Rechka, March 27, 1989."

The military commissar kept his promise and ensured Maxim was laid to rest with military honors: he provided an orchestra and pillows for his medals and also allocated a platoon of troops who honored the departed military commander on behalf of the USSR Armed Forces with the traditional three-volley salute.

Now Maxim and Rosalia lie side by side under a single monument with their portraits carved into the headstone. From a distance, you can see how they are smiling at us.

Twenty years later, we found in Maxim's archives a letter addressed to his beloved Rosochka (Rosaly), written on the day she died. In fact, this letter was addressed to all his descendants and can be regarded as a kind of last will and testament.

> My dear, beloved and darling Rosochka!
> I decided to write a letter while my eyes can still see, my hand can hold a pen, and my mind is still working. I want to express—perhaps for the last time—my thoughts about our life and offer some advice for the time when I will no longer be around or am even sicker should I lose the ability to speak and write.

My dear and beloved Rosochka! It is very easy to speak about and describe our life together in verse because our life was pure, honest, unselfish and immersed in mutual love for one another and our children. I have observed for the both of us how we preserved this mutual love until the end of our lives and how we preserved mutual love for the children. And they will preserve this love with dignity for us and their husbands, and their children will follow the example of their grandfather and grandmother as well as their own parents. In this regard, I bow down to you since you were the one who kept and preserved all the intensity of the warmth in our family from the very first days until the end of your life, my dear. For I, as a man, partially concealed my love inside, but it was very strong. I also very much love my sons-in-law, Andrei and Sasha, whom I consider to be my own sons, for the fact that they are good, decent and thoughtful people by nature. They lead a righteous life and love my daughters and their children as well as Rosochka and me. All that is left for me to do is give one last directive: take care of and preserve your kindred love and guard it like the apple of your eye! For one must not let love cool, especially kindred love. Chilly feelings are difficult to warm or cannot be warmed at all and turn to stone forever, which causes mutual constant pain. I repeat, be sure to hold on to your mutual love and friendship!
Meditation in Solitude, November 11, 1986.

The Victory Day celebration. Maxim Nikolaevitch and Rosalia Borisovna Chibisov with the daughters Elena (left) and Emilia. 9th of May 1985.]

With the daughters Emilia
and Elena, March 1960.

At the most cherished
general's dacha, 1970's.

Maxim Nikolaevitch with the
granddaughter Ksenia. 1974.

At the dacha with the
grandson Maxim and
the granddaughter
Ksyusha, 1978.

Maxim Nikolaevitch Chibisov with the daughter
Elena. These two photographs dating back to 1951
and 1968 respectively are made 17 years apart.

Epilogue

Our Friend Gregory Gagarin

In fall 2005, Emma Telyatnikova received a letter in the mail from Washington, DC. The letter, which contained short text and a photograph, had been sent by Gregory Gagarin.

"It has come to my attention," Gagarin wrote, "that you, Mrs. Telyatnikova, may be related to Col. Maxim Chibisov with whom I worked for 18 months at the Elizabeth City base in the United States. I am sending you a group photo of Russian and American pilots taken at this base in 1945. If you recognize your father in this picture, that's me sitting next to him."

The exact same picture was part of General Chibisov's archive, which had been handed down to his descendants.

Gagarin provided his phone numbers in Washington as well as the address and phone numbers of his cousin in St. Petersburg. This marked the start of regular correspondence between Maxim Chibisov's daughters and his American friend from the war years.

Gregory Gagarin descends from the old Russian family of Gagarin princes. His father, Grigory, defended Russia courageously on the battlefields during World War I. He was discharged in 1917 during the revolution, and after numerous harrowing adventures, he made his way to Constantinople and then to Paris, where he met his future wife, Elizaveta (née Zurabova). It wasn't their first meeting, as they had already met previously in Vladivostok, but it was in Paris that Elizaveta and Grigory decided to unite their destinies. They got married at an Orthodox church in 1921. A year later, they had a son, whom they named Gregory based on family tradition.

Gregory Gagarin with his father Grigory Andreevitch. 1934.

The younger Gregory initially studied at a regular French school before enrolling in a special Russian school since his wise mother decided that knowledge of languages was a "guaranteed piece of bread for a rainy day." Of course, his parents also wanted Gregory to know the language of his ancestors.

She proved to be right: the younger Gregory Gagarin saw favorable opportunities arise throughout his life due to the fact that he spoke multiple languages fluently: English (after coming to the United States), French, Russian, and German.

Searching for his place in the sun, the elder Gregory went to the United States, where he opened a riding school in the town of Westbury, outside New York City, with the financial support of his friend in 1929–1931. His wife and son remained in France during this time as they waited for him to get everything settled for their arrival. They moved to the United States in 1934.

The younger Grigory started going by his American name of Gregory, or Greg for short. He completed his secondary education at a private school in New York. He enrolled at the Massachusetts Institute of Technology in 1939 and graduated with a degree in electrical engineering in 1943.

Gregory was only seventeen when World War II began. The war united as allies Russia, France, and the United States—the same three countries with which he had both blood and spiritual ties (ancestry, upbringing, childhood memories, and citizenship).

Even before the United States entered the war, Gregory tried to join the US Army as a volunteer, but he was told he needed to complete

From left to right: Father Gregory A., young Gregory G., Mother Elizabeth, Garden City, NY, 1937.

his education and given the opportunity to earn a degree. Only then was he called up for active military service, although in the Navy.

"When Project Zebra was being prepared in the Washington corridors of power, I was in Boston," Gregory told the authors of this book. "I often had to read about how German submarines were actively sinking the allied ships. And we knew that we would soon be fighting directly with the Germans."

He reported for active service in the US Navy on March 29, 1943, and was commissioned as an Ensign and expected to be sent off to France, where American and British troops were already in preparation for landing. His first assignment was to study and become an expert with radar (radio detection and ranging). This training curriculum consisted of basic training at Naval Training School in Ft. Schuyler, New York, for 8 weeks; preradar school at Harvard University, Cambridge, Massachusetts, for 12 weeks; radar school at Massachusetts Institute of Technology, Cambridge; and, finally, advanced radar (airborne) school at the naval base in Corpus Christie, Texas. In January 1944, Gregory was assigned as the communications officer for a squadron of seaplanes, type PBM (Patrol Bomber Martin). In the months of March and April 1944, Gregory participated in 20 training flights using airborne radar for anti-submarine warfare out of Charleston, South Carolina, and Florida. This squadron, VPB-18, was soon to be deployed to the Pacific theater in May 1944, but at the end of April, the US Navy had other plans for a young naval officer with Russian as his native tongue, a degree in electrical engineering, and a highly qualified background in radar. One day he was summoned by his superior and asked if he still remembered any Russian.

Ensign G.G. Gagarin, USNR, 1943

Lieutenant Gagarin was perplexed by the question and remained so for a while. After receiving orders to travel to the base in Elizabeth City, he had no idea what kind of job to expect. Everything was shrouded in secrecy. Upon arriving at his destination, he saw planes with red stars and only then realized he would be playing a role in the implementation of Project Zebra.

Gregory, an American citizen descended from Russian princes, spent eighteen months working side by side with the Soviet officers. To them, he was above all a necessary mediator in their daily contacts with their American colleagues. As a professional in electronics and radio equipment, Gregory provided Russian translations of the numerous manuals and diagrams of radio electronic equipment installed on the planes being shipped to the USSR. Gregory's background in electrical engineering was crucial for establishing the correct vocabulary for technical terminology for these training, instruction, and maintenance manuals from English into Russian.

A friendly team of Russian -American military professionals developed in Elizabeth City. British pilots serving as instructors were also actively involved in this team's work. Thus, it was an international group who replicated the military alliance of the Soviet Union, United States, and United Kingdom on a much smaller scale.

The aviation group was led by Maxim Chibisov, a handsome, strong, determined, and devoted commander and a worthy representative of the country fighting desperately with Nazi Germany. Watching his former compatriots in action, the US citizen Gregory Gagarin could take pride in the fact that he had Russian blood flowing in his veins.

He also proved to be an important figure himself during this time, although he probably did not realize the full extent of his role.

For the Soviet citizens working at the Elizabeth City base, who barely spoke any English and were unaware of the peculiarities of the American way of life, the nice young man with the lieutenant's insignia was not simply a translator or a guide for the local environment. They also saw this Russian American, who performed his duties in an impeccable and responsible manner and worked selflessly alongside and together with his Russian comrades-in-arms, as a living symbol of the allied and friendly America.

Six decades later, Gregory Gagarin played a unique role in reconstructing the historical memory of one of the most remarkable stories in Soviet-American cooperation during World War II.

One of Our Own

In November 2006, Gregory Gagarin and his wife, Ann—or Annushka, as her husband sometimes calls her in the Russian style—came to St. Petersburg for a meeting of compatriots. Following the official events in Russia's northern capital, the Gagarins came to Moscow at the invitation of their "pen pals," Emilia Telyatnikova and Elena Rubina so they could finally meet in person.

The Gagarins' visit with General Chibisov's daughters took on a warm, family-like atmosphere right away. Gregory himself set the appropriate tone. When this tall gray-haired gentleman first entered Elena's home, where the guests stayed during their time in Moscow, he immediately said, "Don't worry about anything. I feel right at home."

Elena soon began to think their guest from overseas somewhat resembled her own father in terms of certain gestures and body movements he made. Perhaps Gregory developed these habits during the war years, when the young lieutenant might have,

G.G. Gagarin with his wife Ann visiting the daughters of M.N. Chibisov.

consciously or unconsciously, picked up some of the traits and mannerisms of Soviet Colonel Maxim Chibisov.

Gregory saw something dear and familiar in the faces of his hosts. He later noted in a letter, "I immediately recognized the young Maxim, Elena's son. He looks very much like his grandfather."

More than six decades had passed since Gagarin had last seen Maxim Chibisov in Paris in the fall of 1945, yet he had never forgotten what he looked like.

From conversations, the hosts learned that the Gagarins had begun their family life with a romantic tale that took place in the victorious year of 1945 and also somewhat involved Maxim.

Back in 1938–1940, Gregory spent his summer vacations helping his father hold equestrian sporting events, mainly as a judge. In late summer 1945, the senior Gregory sent a letter to his son, who was still serving in the military at the time, indicating he would be holding a dressage competition at his camp Ecole Champlain on the following weekend and asking whether Greg could come help organize the judging, as he used to do.

Gregory told his superior, Stanley Chernack, about the upcoming

---

equestrian event and suggested he be a judge, also mentioning that pretty girls would be taking part in the competition.

According to Gregory,

> Stanley replied that he was not opposed, but unfortunately he didn't have a single plane available. However, Chernack suggested a possible solution: "Go to the Russian colonel and ask for a plane. Explain to him that I take full responsibility and guarantee the plane's safety. If he agrees, I'll provide a crew."

This was a brilliant idea! I went to Maxim Chibisov and asked for permission to use one of the PBY-6A planes that were to be sent to the Soviet Union. These planes had yet to be accepted by the Procurement Commission (i.e. Chibisov and Genkin had not yet signed the acceptance statement). Therefore, the amphibious aircraft temporarily didn't really belong to anyone. After some thought, Maxim said, "Do as you see fit as long as the plane isn't damaged."

Taking one of the Catalinas that was to be ferried to the USSR, Stanley Chernack and Gregory Gagarin landed in Ecole Champlain on time and enjoyed their weekend there. During the competition, Greg met a charming girl named Ann Graves. She was a student who was also involved in equestrian sports and worked as an assistant to Grigory Gagarin.

After the war, Ann and Gregory got married, and they have lived happily together ever since for more than six decades. Gregory says he'll never forget that this fortunate meeting only took place thanks to the fact that Maxim Chibisov—a disciplined and strict officer—showed some leeway and permitted Chernack and Gagarin to use his plane.

Lieutenant Gagarin met his future wife during the final days of World War II, a fact that gives Gregory much delight.

> No incidents occurred during our return to the base the following Monday. We made the flight in three hours and upon arrival heard reports that the war with Japan had ended. At the same time, we received an order: a total ban on flights was imposed for three days (this measure was an attempt by the command to prevent any drunk pilots from taking to the skies).

We hadn't violated the order, but once we were on the ground we organized a huge party in honor of the victory along with Chibisov and the other Russian pilots, and the next day we all took a fantastic trip to the city of Williamsburg, one of the first colonial cities, which played a key role in the Revolutionary War.

It was an extraordinary day. We were treated like heroes everywhere we went and greeted with Russian shouts of "Hurrah!" The owners of the restaurants and cafes where we ate lunch with Chibisov's team refused to accept money for the food when they learned that their customers were Russian pilots, claiming that their bills had already been paid by anonymous guests. Such respect meant a lot and I am convinced after later reading Max's diary that he also felt and appreciated the attitude towards his country among ordinary people, an attitude which did not necessarily always reflect the official opinion.

While in Moscow in 2006, the Gagarins spent a week visiting the Rubins and Telyatnikovs. The hosts ensured Gregory and Ann had an interesting and busy itinerary during their stay in the Russian capital.

They visited the Moscow Council of War Veterans, where Gregory received a medal as a veteran of the Great Patriotic War and a gift book that consisted of an album with photos of prominent veterans from all the branches of service.

This was followed by a visit to the Russia Abroad Foundation Library named after Alexander Solzhenitsyn, which was established more than a decade ago through the efforts of Natalia Solzhenitsyna and Viktor Moskvin and handles the collection and analysis of various materials containing information about Russian emigration stories. The

American veteran of the Second World War G.G. Gagarin and N.D. Solzhenitsyna at the Fund's 'Russians Abroad' reception.

foundation's collection is constantly updated, including as a result of foreign private archives brought back to their historical homeland by the descendants of Russian emigrants.

Viktor Moskvin, who serves as the foundation's director, told the guests about the work being carried out by his staff and showed them the multi-volume work *The People of the Russian Diaspora*. The American descendant of Russian princes was given a volume of this major publication as a gift, and to his great surprise, in the retrospective, he found his genealogical tree from the nineteenth century to the present day, including personal data of Gregory himself and his close relatives.

The Gagarins were also introduced to the Allies and Lend-Lease Museum, where they spent several hours. In addition to touring the exhibition, they also spoke with the director of this collection of historical treasures, Nikolai Borodin; his research deputy, Alexander Nesterov; and other Lend-Lease enthusiasts. Gregory spoke to the group of war veterans who had gathered at the museum, including Igor Lebedev, who had worked at the Government Procurement Commission in Washington from 1943 to 1945. Gagarin and Lebedev had met back then, and they had much to reminisce about and discuss during their meeting in Moscow sixty years later.

During the Gagarins' visit to Moscow, they also had conversations around the table with their hosts as they recalled the events of those bygone days. The 84-year-old Gregory still had surprisingly detailed and thorough recollections of everything associated with Project Zebra. He spoke about his work with the Soviet pilots as if he were talking about events that had just recently occurred.

The hosts also found materials about which Gregory had inquired concerning the use of the amphibious planes ferried from America to the Soviet Union. These materials indicated that all the Catalinas brought to the USSR under the Lend-Lease Program were used in combat, reconnaissance, and rescue operations. They were in operational service for all the fleets of the USSR and continued to serve in Soviet naval aviation for roughly ten more years after the war.

Among other things, they discussed the manuscript of Maxim's article "Across Continents and Oceans," which had been written in the early 1980s. Gregory offered to translate the article into English, at which point General Chibisov's daughters informed their American friend of their plan to compile a book about their father.

He expressed a desire to take part in this work. The most important thing is that he was able to provide answers to the numerous questions that arose when deciphering Maxim's diary entries.

Gregory's comments shed new light on many of the documents, maps, and photos the Telyatnikovas and Rubins had preserved from their father.

A Common Cause

Gregory Gagarin's visit to Moscow provided a powerful impetus for working on the book that had been conceived by General Chibisov's daughters. One of the key aspects of Maxim's official biography began to clearly take shape following the stories told by their American guest. A general concept of the book gradually developed, and they began collecting materials for the project.

Meanwhile, Elena and Emilia continued to correspond with Gagarin. In one of his letters, he spoke in detail about his first visit to his historical homeland.

> I first came to the USSR in 1989 for the centennial of the St Petersburg Technical University [now St. Petersburg State Polytechnical University]. My grandfather was its founder and first rector. In the places we visited—Moscow, Tbilisi and Ukraine—the residents knew very little about Lend-Lease. After all, the Cold War began shortly after World War II ended.

However, Americans couldn't tell you much about cooperation between the U.S. and USSR during the war, either. It was only around 1995 that newspaper articles and books started appearing here. In 1996, someone in North Carolina suddenly remembered the military air base in Elizabeth City and that Russians had lived and worked there. The idea arose to create a thematic exhibit at the local history museum. This is how they found me and sent me to Moscow. I was given the task of searching for Soviet veterans who had worked in the U.S. as part of the Lend-Lease Program. However, I was only able to meet with Mazuruk's assistant. My request to find the contact details of Maxim Chibisov was denied. Finally, in November 2006, I came to Moscow and met his wonderful daughters and their families.

G.G. Gagarin is looking through his photo album dedicated to Project Zebra.

Thus, interest in Soviet-American cooperation during World War II, specifically the subject of

Lend-Lease, has also picked up outside of Russia over the last decade. This theme has attracted the attention of the American public thanks in no small part to the initiatives of such people as Gregory Gagarin.

In Russia, there are still very few people who know about the Lend-Lease Program and its importance during World War II, but there is considerable interest in this subject in society as people continue to discover more and more pages in the dramatic history of the twentieth century.

In recent years, American documentaries depicting the Western point of view of the war have started being released in Russia. A series of new Russian television films with similar content, under the heading *The Unknown War*, were shown around the May holidays in 2008–2009.

An attempt was made in three episodes of the film *Ferrying* to talk about the polar convoys that delivered Lend-Lease cargo to the USSR and the cooperation among the American, English, and Soviet pilots in the Arctic. This film, which has several flaws, sparked great interest among a broad audience.

The excellent documentary *Allies: With Good Faith and Fidelity* was filmed by the talented filmmaker Sergei Zaitsev, the director of the Russky Put film studio and president of the Russia Abroad international film festival. The film is based on the stories of war veterans from the Soviet Union as well as the Allied countries of England, America, and France. The vivid memories of witnesses to and participants in the military actions, supported by documentary video images, provide the viewer with a real sense of the brutal conditions in which the heroes of the film had to fight and survive. The tragedy and the pain they experienced are imprinted on the faces and in the eyes of the people who had to endure such inhuman trials and suffering.

One of the most dramatic subjects of the film is the story of American sailor William Carter, who served on a transport ship in the PQ-17 convoy, two-thirds of which was destroyed while crossing the northern Atlantic. Carter was lucky that time, as his ship made it to Murmansk as one of the few survivors of the ill-fated convoy. His main memories from the few months he spent in Russia consist of the nonstop bombing to which the polar port was subjected.

On his way back across the ocean, Carter's transport vessel was torpedoed by a German submarine. An unforgettable sight he witnessed just a few seconds before the ship was destroyed remains etched in his memory: the deadly torpedo riding along the waves of the cold sea as fluffy snowflakes fell from the sky. Some crew members were saved by a lifeboat, which made its way to shore based on the whim of the wind and the waves.

Carter had serious frostbite on his feet, which had turned black from being in the icy water for so long. This tragic black color remained with him for the rest of his life.

The national print media has released a whole series of publications on the Lend-Lease theme in recent years. However, they mainly deal with the stories of 1942–1943, when the Lend-Lease military equipment was being sent directly to the front where the decisive battles of World War II were raging. At the same time, the researchers and writers basically neglect the story of how the amphibious seaplanes were delivered to the country over a period of several months.

Lend-Lease Convoy PQ17 veteran Commander (Ret.) W.A. Carter, USNR at the Russian Embassy, Washington, D.C., 2009.

Maxim Chibisov's diaries allow us to fill in this gap in historical journalism, and this is why his daughters devoted a fair amount of attention to the ferrying of the Catalinas in their book.

Maxim Chibisov's Familiar Foreign Places

In March 2009, Gregory Gagarin sent a letter reporting that celebrations were being planned in the United States in April to mark the meeting of Soviet and American troops on the Elbe in April 1945, just before the fall of the Third Reich. He also said, "It would really be great if you, Chibisov's daughters, were to take part in these celebrations, which are being held for the first time this year."

Emilia and Elena expressed their gratitude to Gagarin and said they would be delighted to attend. Soon they received invitations not only from Gregory but also from the Museum of the Albemarle in Elizabeth City.

On April 22, 2009, the Gagarins met Emilia and Elena at the Washington, DC, airport. The warmth and hospitality they showed to Maxim's daughters were touching. Gregory had arranged for their visit with fatherly care and taken care of everything, even the smallest details.

The hosts tried to make sure their guests were able to make the most of their brief visit. Following a day of recuperation from the flight and long conversations with the Gagarins, General Chibisov's daughters began their itinerary around America, which had been carefully planned by their hospitable hosts.

On April 24, they went to Arlington National Cemetery to attend a solemn wreath-laying ceremony at the graves of World War II heroes. The day ended with a reception at the Russian Embassy—the same place Maxim had visited regularly in 1944–1945 to speak with the staff of attachés Maximovich and Khrolenko and also where he had rung in the New Year in 1945 as he dearly missed his family.

The veterans of the Second World War (left to right): I.Belousovich, F. Cohen, G. Gagarin during the wreath-laying ceremony at the Arlington National Cemetery. USA, April 24th 2009.

On April 26, Emilia and Elena visited the home of Princess Evdokia Obolenskaya, where they had been invited for tea (i.e., a charity event for a special correctional boarding school in Russia's Kaluga region).

On April 27, they took an extensive tour of Washington, DC, and the surrounding area with Gregory and Ann serving as guides.

They then traveled to North Carolina with the Gagarins in their car. Greg and Ann took turns driving and did not consider it any difficulty to drive approximately 380 kilometers (236 miles) from Washington to Elizabeth City.

Once they arrived at their destination, they spent the night at a hotel that had been booked in advance. On the morning of April 29, they went to the Museum of the Albemarle, where Gagarin introduced the guests to the director and curator and spoke about Lend-Lease, using illustrative materials the guests had brought from Russia.

In the Museum of the Albemarle in Elizabeth City E.M. Rubin (left) and E.M. Telyatnikova along with G.G. Gagarin are showing the museum's employees the flight maps of Colonel M.N. Chibisov.

The next day, the local newspaper published a kind, detailed article about the visit paid by the daughters of Russian Colonel Chibisov with a picture on the front page. [See email of photo of newspaper article.]

The Russian visitors gave the Museum of the Albemarle a stand with pictures of Maxim Chibisov and his team as well as a copy of the map from his map case.

After visiting the museum, they drove around the city, which remained virtually unchanged 65 years later. Sparing no effort, Gregory drove his guests around to all the sites their father had been to: "Here is the hotel where the ferry pilots stayed. Here is Main Street …"

He took Maxim's daughters to the small store where he recalled that the Russian pilots had liked to shop. The store, built in the mid-nineteenth century, surprisingly had not changed since the end of World War II either.

They also visited the monument to the Wright Brothers, located high up on a hill, the site where Maxim had been photographed with the Russian and American pilots back in 1944.

The tour concluded with a visit to the actual military base in Elizabeth City.

Gregory introduced Emilia and Elena to the base command and spoke in great detail—using maps—about the joint work the Russian and American pilots had carried out in 1944–1945. It turned out the American officers in charge of the base knew nothing about the ferrying operations conducted there during World War II. They expressed great interest in and appreciation for the copies of the maps and the stand with photos from the war years presented to them by the Russian guests.

Picture with the Officers of the US Coast Guard
airfield facility of Elizabeth City, 2009.

This was followed by a tour of the base territory. Gagarin showed his guests the facilities they'd used during the war: the canteen, the residential buildings, and the hangar where the soldiers had held theoretical practice and sporting events and watched films. It was clear how dear the places were to Gregory, just like the memories of the days of his distant military youth that had been carefully preserved deep in the memory of the distinguished US Navy veteran.

General Chibisov's daughters found themselves in the epicenter of the place where their father had performed the highly classified work recorded with only brief entries in his flight log: 804 hours in the air and 780 landings on different types of aircraft (Catalinas, C-47s, C-54s, and Boeings). They saw the area where five or six planes had been stationed as they were prepared for ferrying to the USSR, the place where the flying boats had been launched into the water, and the rocky spit to which the technicians had had to manually drag the planes. Finally, Gregory drove Maxim's daughters along the bay, the area where their father had trained all the ferrying crews for a year and a half as they prepared for the long flights across continents and oceans.

Following their visit to America, the creative plans of Emilia and Elena started to come to life. Their initial outline was filled in with text and enriched with new stories and details emerging from a wide range of sources.

All these years of intense work have resulted in the writing of this book, which was given the name Maxim Chibisov wanted—but was not allowed—to use to publish his article.

E.M. Rubin (author) with her father's map, showing the transportation routes of Catalinas from the USA to the USSR in the years 1941-1945.

In the Allies and Lend-Lease
Museum E.M. Telyatnikova, Major
General of aviation G.G. Zhukov,
A. Gagarina, G.G. Gagarin, Major
General of aviation I.P. Lebedev.

G.G. Gagarin, deputy head
of Allies and Lend-Lease
Museum A.R.Nesterov and
WWII veteran Major general
of aviation G.G. Zhukov.

The daughters of the Major
General of aviation M.N. Chibisov
in the Allies and Lend-Lease
Museum by the exposition
dedicated to their father.

A friendly talk in the Library-
Fund 'Russian Abroad'.

The Chairman of the Russian War
Veterans and Military Service
Committee Marshal of aviation
A.N. Efimov (right) awarding G.G.
Gagarin with a memorable medal.

General Director of the Library-
Fund 'Russians Abroad'
V.A.Moskvin (second right)
is welcoming visitors.

At the Veterans and Military
Service Committee (from left to
right): A.N.Efimov, G.Gagarin and
N.Batova visiting the memorial
to the Army General P.I.Batov.

G.Gagarin, A.Efimov and the
Head of International Relations
Department Yu.Ivanov.

At the visit to the gallery
of Military leaders of Great
Patriotic War (from left to right):
E.Rubina, N.Batova, G.Gagarin,
A.Gagarina, A.Efimov, Yu.Ivanov.

Elena Maximovna and Andrey
Borisovitch Rubin bid farewell
to Gregory and Ann Gagarin
as they depart for America.

E.M. Rubina (in the middle)
and N.P. Batova (standing) in
the USA visiting the Gagarin
family at their house.

E.M. Telyatnikova and the
Gagarin spouses on the porch of
their house in Washington D.C.

Frank Cohen with the daughters
of M.N. Chibisov - Emilia
(left) and Elena at the Russian
Federation Embassy in the USA.

A Washington D.C walk.

Charity dinner at the house
of princess E.V.Obolenskaya
(second left).

After the ceremony at the
Arlington National Cemetery.

G. Gagarin is telling the members
of the US Coast Guard of
the airfield of Elizabeth City
about the work conducted by
the American and Soviet pilots
in the years of 1944-1945.

The daughters of M.N Chibisov
visiting the Wright Brothers
monument – the same place
where their farther was
photographed in 1944.

Children, grandchildren and great-grandchildren of Maxim
Nikolaevitch and Rosalia Borisovna Chibisov. 2011.

A Background on the Gagarin Family

The Gagarins were a family of Russian nobility whose ancestral lines extend back to Rurik, the founder of Russia. The Gagarins were prominent and served in the service of the Russian Imperial government in many capacities up to 1917.

Gagarin crest.

This part of the Gagarin history begins in the late 1800s and extends through events arising from Russian revolution in 1917 and ultimately the migration of some of the family members to the United States. These events, along with the occurrence of the Second World War, formed the circumstances that contributed to the eventual successful collaboration in the Lend-Lease delivery of the PBN and PBY Catalina seaplanes from the US to Russia.

Prince Andrei Grigoryevich Gagarin (January 3, 1856 - December 22, 1920) - Russian scientist and engineer, founder and first director of the St. Petersburg Polytechnic Institute, State Councilor. Upon graduation from St. Petersburg University in science and mathematics, he served volunteers in the horse guard artillery, after which he passed the exam for officer's rank and graduated from Mikhailovskaya Artillery Academy in 1884.

From the end of 1884 he served in the St. Petersburg arsenal. In 1891 he was sent to the city of Chatellerault, France where he worked for four years as part of the commission for the delivery of 500,000 Mosin rifles, manufactured at a local weapons factory, procured by the Russian government.

Andrei Gregoryevich Gagarin

In the summer of 1885, Andrei Grigoryevich married Princess Maria Dmitrievna Obolenskaya (1864-1946).

From 1895 to 1900, A.G. Gagarin was assistant chief of the St. Petersburg gun factory, in this position he contributed to a significant increase in production at the plant.

On January 7, 1900, at the initiative and presentation of Finance

Minister S. [YU]. Witte, A. G. Gagarin was appointed the first Director of the then-established St. Petersburg Polytechnic Institute where he served until 1907.

During the First World War, A.G. Gagarin returned to military service. He served as a permanent member of the Technical Artillery Committee for the Department of Optics (1914-1917). He participated in the organization of Russia's first production facility of optical glass in St. Petersburg and the establishment of an optical glass factory in the city of Izyum in Kharkiv province. In 1916 he was appointed as a government activity inspector of the Putilov plant.

After 1917 A.G. Gagarin worked in Moscow, holding the position of senior designer at the Scientific and Experimental Institute at the People's Commissariat for Roads and Railways, and remained in this position for the rest of his life.

Andrei Grigoryevich was arrested on his way to the Gagarin country manor, "Holomki" near Porkhov in October 1918. His wife, Maria Dmitrievna, was arrested a few days later. Thanks to the assistance of the Experimental Institute, Andrei Grigoryevich was released relatively quickly. Maria Dmitrievna was imprisoned for several months, first in Porkhov and then in Butyrka prison in Moscow. She was released after M. Gorky's intercedence. Due to the difficult living conditions in Moscow in 1920, through the efforts by L.B. Kameneva, who appealed to Sovnarcom (SNK) (Soviet Narodnykh Kommissarov or The Council of People's Commissars), that A.G. Gagarin be allowed to live in Holomki, and travel to Moscow to present ready-made projects.

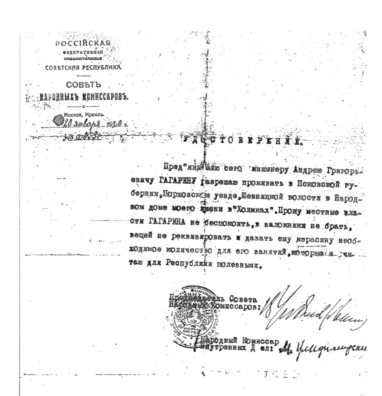

Russian

Federal

Socialist

Soviet Republic

Soviet (Committee) of

Peoples' Commissars

Moscow, Kremlin

20 August 1920

CERTIFICATE

By this decree I allow engineer Andrey Grigorievich Gagarin to live in Pskov Gubernia, Porkhovskoi Uezd, Shevnitskoi Volost, at the Peoples' House of my name at "Kholmikakh." I request local authorities not to bother Gagarin, take him into custody, nor confiscate his possessions and to provide him with kerosene in the necessary amount for his activities, which I consider useful for the Republic.

Chairman of the Peoples' Commissars'' Soviet

Signature [Vladimir Ulyanov Lenin]

Peoples' Commissar for Internal Affairs

Signature [Felix Dzerzhinsky]

Certificate permitting A. G. Gagarin to live in Holomki in 1920.

Permission by Lenin's personal signature was given (see above), and A.G. Gagarin returned to his family in Holomki. There he taught mathematics and physics at the Pskov Agricultural College and performed some design work for the local government.

Original headstone of Andrei Gregoryevich Gagarin.

A. G. Gagarin died on December 22, 1920, at the age of 65, after a appendectomy operation at the Porkhov Hospital. He was buried near the Holomki estate Village Belsoye Ustye.

After the death of her husband, Maria Dmitrievna Gagarina continued to lived in Holomky, but in 1925 the local authorities decided to evict her from the province, and in the same year she and her daughter went to Leningrad. In 1934, she emigrated to the United States, leaving only after her sons Sergei and Gregory had collected and paid the amount of $3,000 required in those years for an exit permit from the USSR. She lived in State College, Pennsylvania, with her son Grigory and wrote her memoirs.

Andrei Grigoryevich and Maria Dmitrievna had six children: sons - Andrei (1886-1937), Sergei (1887-1941), Leo (1888-1921), Gregory (1895-1963), Peter (1904-1938) – and daughter Sophia (1892-1979).

Andrew served in the Life Guard Horse Artillery Brigade beginning in 1911. In August 1914 was on the front lines in the First World War. In 1915, he served as a lieutenant of the Horse Artillery Brigade. On January 11, 1923

New monument, replacing the original headstone of Andrei Gregoryevich Gagarin, 2013.

arrested "in connection with the refusal to cooperate (with the Soviet government)", but released on July 14 [under a reprieve]. On the night of April 25-26, 1930, he was again arrested, sent to Moscow and imprisoned in Butyrskaya prison. On 21 November 1931, Andrew was sent for 3 years to work in the Kemerovo region. He worked as a rolling metal department engineer at the Kuznetsk metallurgical factory. March 18, 1933 Andrew was arrested a third time and sent to Moscow. Later, Andrew returned to work at Kuznetsktroy. On, June 28, 1937 Andrew was arrested and charged with "Preparing an armed uprising against the Soviet regime." On July 9, 1937, Peter was sentenced to VMN [Vysshaya Mera Nakazaniya (Supreme Degree of Punishment)] and shot. Later, Peter's records were rehabilitated (absolved of political / criminal charges).

Sergei was a diplomat. He served as a secretary of the Russian Embassy in Constantinople in World War I. In 1920 he served under General Wrangel in the Ministry of Foreign Affairs. In 1923, he emmigrated to the United States. He worked for the shipping company of Wurton and Lilly. He was a member of the Archdiocese of the American Archdiocese of the Russian Orthodox Church. Died on June 28, 1941 in New York at the age of 52 at Medical Center Hospital (New York). His children and descendents reside in the US. During World War II, his son, Andrew Gagarin served as a torpedo boat captain participating in guarding the convoy PQ-17 that were bringing food to Russia.

Grigory entered the law department of St. Petersburg University but later left to join the cavalry school and in 1916 appointed as Ensign in the Life Guards Hussar Regiment (Calvary). During the First World War, Grigory served in the front lines, as a commander of a machine gun crew. In September 1918, upon returning home to Holomki, Grigory was arrested as a former officer in Porkhov. He escaped while being brought out for execution and successfully reached safety in Pskov (then under German occupation). Eventually, after traveling to Vladivostok, met and married Elizabeth Nicolayevna Zouraboff and settled in Paris, France in 1921. They had one son, Grigory Grigorievich Gagarin, born in 1922. In 1925, after emmigrating to the USA, established a school for training in horseback riding. This became his main occupation,. The whole family emigrated to the United States in 1935.] In 1944, son Grigory was assigned by the US Navy to participate in the then classified mission, "Project Zebra" to deliver "Catalina" seaplanes to the USSR under Lend-Lease. Son Gregory and descendents reside in the US.

Peter worked as a senior designer in the Institute of «Hyproshacht» (coal mine shafts) in Leningrad in the 1930s. In March, 1935, arrested and sentenced to exile with his wife and new born son to Yrgiz, Aktobe

(Kazakstan) region for 5 years. Intercessions were made by Academician V. F. Mitkevich, several professors, and the submittal of a copy of the letter from Lenin on the merits of his father. As result three days later, he was released and the expulsion (to Yrgiz) was cancelled. He continued his work at the Institute. On November 21, 1937, Peter was arrested and taken from his family. He was charged with, "since 1925 he was recruited by the English consul for intelligence activities against USSR in favor of England". On January 13, 1938 – Peter was sentenced to VMN [Vysshaya Mera Nakazaniya (Supreme Degree of Punishment)] and shot in prison in Leningrad on January 18, 1938. His son, Andrei Petrovich, became a professor at St. Petersburg Polytechnic University, the institution his grandfather had helped to establish. His children, grandchildren, and descendants live in St. Petersburg, Russia today.

Leo served as a Captain assigned as an adjutant to the commander of the armed forces of the Northern Region, General V.V. Marushevsky in November 1918. In August 1919, Leo left Russia through the Crimea together with Marushevsky. Leo authored unpublished memoirs "Formation of the Northern Front". Leo settled in Constantinople and died of typhus in 1921, according to V.V. Marushevsky. No children.

Sophia received a home-schooled education and studied at the ballet school. Before the Russian revolution, Sophia the Empress's Alexandra maid of honor. With onset of the First World War (1914), she graduated from nursing school as a sister of mercy in the hospital organized at the Holomki estate. After 1918, she worked as the head of the People's House in the requisitioned estate of Holomki in Porkhov county. In 1925, she left for Leningrad with her mother, after both were expelled from Holomki manor. In early June, 1927 Sophia was arrested in Leningrad. She was released on July 6, 1927. She emigrated together with her mother Maria Dimitrijevna in 1935 and settled in the United States, after her brothers, Grigory and Sergei, paid a redemption to the Soviet government for their release. She had no children.

Leo and Sophia Gagarin

Holomki

Gagarin estate, Holomky.

A.G. Gagarin's manor house "Holomky" was built in 1913. The house is a design of the famous architect, Fomin. All engineering and communications were designed by Andrei Grigoryvich and together with his sons. In 1914 - 1915, the Prince [A.G. Gagarin] lived here, being the chairman of the parish guardianship of the families of peasants who went to war. In the First World War, the estate housed a hospital for 15 people, which was equipped and maintained by Andrei Grigoryevich Gagarin. In 1918 the estate was nationalized. In 1921, the estate became the first in Russia House of Creativity / Vacation Home for Writers and Poets.

After the war, the building until 1987 housed a sanatorium for tuberculosis patients.

In 2000, the dilapidated manor fell into the operational management of the St. Petersburg Polytechnic University. In 2004, restoration work began on the building. The exterior and existing interiors were completely restored. Now the Holomki estate has become an educational and historical reserve and also offers accommodations as a manor – hotel with beautiful interiors, terraces, ballroom, and huge halls, and 2-4 local rooms. The Museum of the Gagarin family, the Polytechnic University and the Holomky History has also been established here.

BIBLIOGRAPHY

Allies in the War in 1941–1945. Edited by V. L. Kalkov and A. S. Orlov. Moscow: Science, 1995.

Artemiev, A. M. *Russian Naval Aviation*. Moscow: Voenizdat, 1996.

Berezhnoy, S. S. *Lend-Lease Ships and Vessels*. St. Petersburg, 1994.

Ilyin, A. "Allied Planes under Lend-Lease." *International Life*, no. 7 (1995).

Kaminsky, Y. A. *In the Skies of the Polar Arctic*. Moscow: Glasnost, AS, 2006.

Kashcheyev, L. B, and V. A. Reminsky. *Lend-Lease Vehicles*. Kharkov, 1998.

Khokhlov, P. I. *Over Three Seas*. Moscow: Voenizdat, 1991.

Kornilov N. A., S. A. Kessel, V. T. Sokolov, and A. A. Merkulov. *Russian Research on the Drifting Ice of the Arctic: A Reference Guide*. State Science Center of the Russian Federation under the Arctic and Antarctic Scientific Research Institute, 2010.

Kotelnikov, V. R. "Aviation Lend-Lease." *Questions of History*, no. 10 (1991).

Kuznetsov, N. G. *The Course to Victory*. Moscow: Voenizdat, 1975.

Kuznetsova, R. V. *Naval Commander*. Moscow: Garden Ring, 2004.

Lebedev, A. A., and I. P. Mazuruk. *Over the Arctic and Antarctic*. Moscow: Mysl, 1991.

Lebedev, I. P. "Aviation Lend-Lease." *Military History Journal*, no. 2 (1991).

Lebedev, I. P. "Once Again about Lend-Lease." *United States. Economics. Politics. Ideology*, no. 1 (1990).

Lend-Lease and Russia: Collection of Articles, Collective Authorship of the Pomorsky Scientific Foundation and the US Consulate General in St. Petersburg. Edited by M. N. Suprun. Arkhangelsk: Pravda Severa, 2006.

Lurye, V. M. "In the Skies over the Atlantic." *Maritime Collection*, no. 2 (1988).

Military Chronicle of the Navy, 1941–1942. Edited by G. A. Amon. Moscow: Voenizdat, 1992.

Military Chronicle of the Navy, 1943. Edited by M. S. Monakov. Moscow: Voenizdat, 1993.

Platonov, A. V. *Tragedy in the Gulf of Finland*. Moscow, Exmo, St. Petersburg: Terra Fantastica, 2005.

Pochtaryov, A. N., and L. I. Gorbunova. *Russian Polar Aviation, 1914–1945*. Vol. 1. Moscow: Paulsen, 2011.

Russian Archive. *Great Patriotic War: Orders and Directives of the People's Commissariat for the Navy during the Great Patriotic War*. Vol. 21. Moscow: Terra, 1996.

Volovich, V. G. *On the Verge of Risk*. Moscow: Mysl, 1985.

Zabolotsky, A., and R. Larintsev. "Catalina Seaplanes in Soviet Naval Aviation during the War Years." *War, History, and Facts Almanac*, no. 9 (2009).

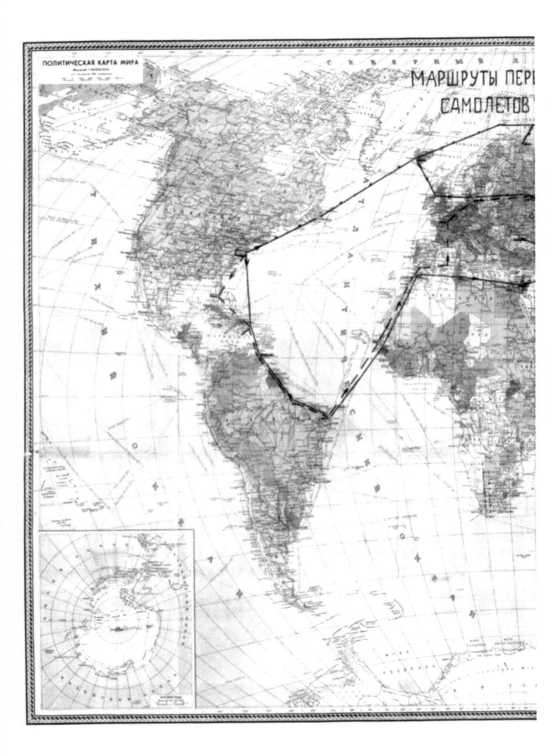

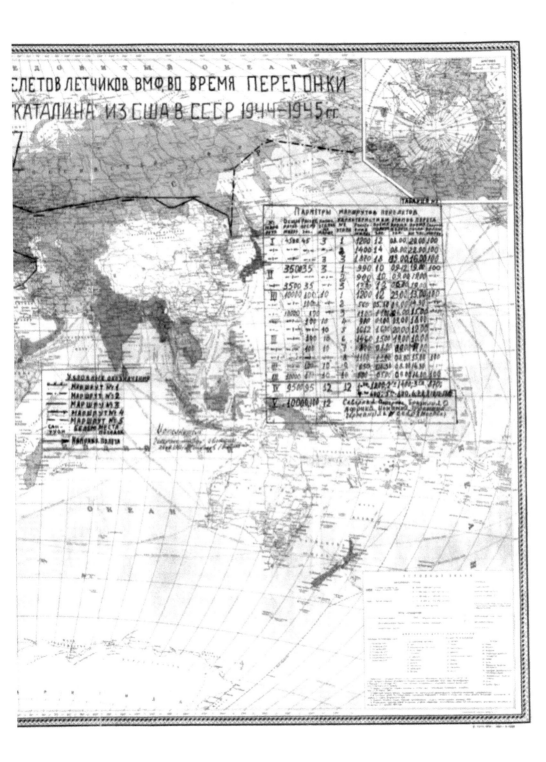

Lightning Source UK Ltd.
Milton Keynes UK
UKHW012024040821
388278UK00006B/375/J